ROUTLEDGE LIBRARY EDITIONS: 19TH CENTURY RELIGION

Volume 12

SELECTED ESSAYS OF EDWARDS A. PARK

SELECTED ESSAYS OF EDWARDS A. PARK

Edited by
BRUCE KUKLICK

LONDON AND NEW YORK

First published in 1987 by Garland Publishing, Inc.

This edition first published in 2018
by Routledge
2 Park Square, Milton Park, Abingdon, Oxon OX14 4RN

and by Routledge
711 Third Avenue, New York, NY 10017

Routledge is an imprint of the Taylor & Francis Group, an informa business

© 1987 Bruce Kuklick, Introduction

All rights reserved. No part of this book may be reprinted or reproduced or utilised in any form or by any electronic, mechanical, or other means, now known or hereafter invented, including photocopying and recording, or in any information storage or retrieval system, without permission in writing from the publishers.

Trademark notice: Product or corporate names may be trademarks or registered trademarks, and are used only for identification and explanation without intent to infringe.

British Library Cataloguing in Publication Data
A catalogue record for this book is available from the British Library

ISBN: 978-1-138-06800-1 (Set)
ISBN: 978-1-315-10089-0 (Set) (ebk)
ISBN: 978-1-138-11887-4 (Volume 12) (hbk)
ISBN: 978-1-138-12363-2 (Volume 12) (pbk)
ISBN: 978-1-315-10111-8 (Volume 12) (ebk)

Publisher's Note
The publisher has gone to great lengths to ensure the quality of this reprint but points out that some imperfections in the original copies may be apparent.

Disclaimer
The publisher has made every effort to trace copyright holders and would welcome correspondence from those they have been unable to trace.

Selected Essays of Edwards A. Park

Edited with an Introduction by
Bruce Kuklick

Garland Publishing, Inc.
New York & London
1987

For a complete list of the titles in this series,
see the final pages of this volume.

Introduction copyright © 1987 by Bruce Kuklick

The facsimiles of *Connection Between Theological Study and Pulpit Eloquence*, *The Mode of Exhibiting Theological Truth*, and *Duties of a Theologian* have been made from copies in the Yale University Library; the remaining facsimiles are from copies in the University of Michigan Library.

Library of Congress Cataloging-in-Publication Data

Park, Edwards Amasa, 1808–1900.
  Selected essays.

  (American religious thought of the 18th and 19th centuries)
  Reprint of works published 1837–1872.
  Contents: Connection between theological study and pulpit eloquence—The mode of exhibiting theological truth—Duties of a theologian—[etc.]
  1. Congregationalist churches—Doctrines.
2. Reformed Church—Doctrines. 3. Calvinism.
4. Theology, Doctrinal. I. Kuklick, Bruce, 1941–
II. Title. III. Series.
BX7231.P27 1987   230'.58   87-12836
ISBN 0-8240-6957-9 (alk. paper)

The volumes in this series are printed on
acid-free, 250-year-life paper.

Printed in the United States of America

INTRODUCTION

In 1847 on the retirement of Leonard Woods, Edwards Amasa Park (1808–1900) became professor of systematic theology at Andover Theological Seminary, arguably the most important position in nineteenth-century American divinity. Park was an able defender of Trinitarian views. He also had a concern for revivalist preaching, an interest that made him sensitive to similar priorities in Jonathan Edwards, Nathanael Emmons, and Nathaniel William Taylor. Consequently, Park also spent much of his energy preserving and proclaiming the New England theological tradition to which he believed he was the heir. Finally, as editor of *Bibliotheca Sacra*, the leading journal of Congregational orthodoxy, Park was a figure of theological power in his denomination.

Much of Park's writing was connected to elaborating his heritage—his memoirs of Samuel Hopkins and Nathanael Emmons are part of their collected works and republished as part of the Garland series in American Religious Thought. The reader, however, will also get a full idea of Park's historical interests from the material printed in this collection. Park's notions of preaching and his view of its connection to the work of the systematic theologian are also clear in this anthology of his writings. Nonetheless, most crucial in grasping Park's career is his ambitious sense of his systematic theology, and the selections in this volume concentrate on this aspect of his work.

Park thought that Edwardsean Calvinism was the one true

system of ideas. Yet he also disagreed with his predecessor Woods's exposition of this system and himself introduced into it mildly heterodox notions (mainly on the will). Unfortunately we have only a sketchy sense of what Park intended because most of his systematic work was uncompleted at his death. What he did write were more polemical pieces in his capacity as editor of *Bibliotheca Sacra.*

Park's theological method is best gauged from his justly praised "The Theology of the Intellect and That of the Feelings." In this essay he argued that the disputed issues of theology could be resolved if the puzzling language was taken symbolically or metaphorically.

The key question then became *which* were the controversial notions whose puzzlement was a function of figurative speech. Park was not wholly successful in defending his case. His methodological essay stirred up a hornet's nest of controversy. Yet in the ensuing battles, which took up most of Park's maturity, he was able to elaborate his ideas on a number of topics in Calvinist philosophy of religion.

In addition to the other writing cited above, this collection of Park's essays reprints "The Theology of the Intellect," as well as Park's responses to criticisms, mainly those made by Princeton theologian Charles Hodge. Altogether, this volume makes easily available the major writings of the leading professional Edwardsean of the nineteenth century.

Bruce Kuklick

the supreme authorities. But the matter was of too much importance to the Jews, to permit them to leave it entirely to the measures of the government. They themselves placed some of their own number at the gates, either because they knew Paul personally, or that they might see that the watch was sufficiently vigilant.*

But all their pains were fruitless. Paul was delivered by means of his friends,† who had removed him at the beginning of the conspiracy.

This second abode at Damascus must have continued some months. For that it was not very brief, is indicated by the phrase of Luke ἡμέραι ἱκαναί. Paul then returned to Jerusalem, probably about the close of A..D. 39.

ARTICLE VIII.

Connection between Theological Study and Pulpit Eloquence.

By Edwards A. Park, Bartlet Professor in Theol. Sem. Andover.

Every art is founded on some science, and every science is connected with some other science; it follows then, that every art is connected with all the sciences, and every science with all the arts. This connection is sometimes almost imperceptible; and is always more or less intimate, as the science or art is more or less extensive. Theology comprehends all other sciences as its tributaries, and with a generous reciprocity diffuses through them all a genial influence; it derives illustrations from all arts, and returns a singular and sometimes scarcely vis-

---

* So it appears on comparing Acts 9: 24 with 2 Cor. 11: 32. In the former, the Jews are represented as watching the gates; in the latter, the ethnarch alone seems to be concerned, by whose order the gates were watched.

† Acts 9: 25, λαβόντες δὲ αὐτὸν οἱ μαθηταὶ νυκτός, καθῆκαν διὰ τοῦ τείχους, χαλάσαντες ἐν σπυρίδι. 2 Cor. 11: 33, διὰ θυρίδος ἐν σαργάνῃ ἐχαλάσθην διὰ τοῦ τείχους καὶ ἐξέφυγον τὰς χεῖρας αὐτοῦ (Aretas). It appears that he escaped through the window of a house which was built close to the city wall. See a like instance Josh. 2: 15.

ible aid in the prosecution of all. The intricate and complex theory of law would be more clearly elucidated, if our lawyers were better theologians, and their pleas would be more perspicuous and cogent, if they were more fully based on the science of the God of equity. The structure of the human frame would be more thoroughly understood, if our physicians were more conversant with the analogies which may be traced between the object so fearfully made, and him who so wonderfully made it; and they would practise with more safety and skill, if their minds were more elevated, and their hearts more purified by those principles which, though but faintly traced in all the emanations, are exhibited perfectly in the universal Source. If theology render so important service to other sciences, and other arts, it must be preëminently serviceable to the science and the art of pulpit eloquence; and the preacher must feel, that his success in preaching depends not on his graces of delivery, or his beauties of style, so much as on his enlarged and familiar acquaintance with the principles of religion.

In the first place, theological study conduces to the preacher's eloquence, because it conduces to his greatest vigor of mind and heart. If the mind is strengthened by exercise, it must be strengthened by exercise on themes of theology, as much as on other themes. If it is invigorated by grappling with intricacies and abstrusities, it certainly can find no science so healthful as that which must, from its very nature, tax and task the whole soul. The mathematics will yield to theology in their tendency to discipline the intellect. A distinguished barrister of our day, who has but little faith in evangelical doctrines, recommends to his law-students the frequent perusal of the volumes which discuss those doctrines; because nowhere else can be found such invigorating argument on such elevating theories. Indeed the very allusion to the ideas, God, eternity, holiness, is sufficient to show, that whoever comes into contact with them must be intellectually quickened and expanded. If intellectually, still more so, morally. Religious affections, not less than any other, are strengthened by exercise; and these affections are exercised only upon themes directly or indirectly theological. He who communes with the truth of God, employs the means of spiritual growth. This truth has a singular and various use; it is the soul's sunshine, and aliment; its rain and dew, and also its shelter and resting place. It is not by the bare formation of his sentences, and penning of his paragraphs, that the writer of a sermon stimulates his religious purpose; it is by incorporating with himself the theological ideas, which constitute the gem of which the sermon is the casket. An excellent clergyman of New England, who when compelled by old age to abandon pulpit ministrations, continued to write his two sermons every week, simply with the intent of preserving the warmth of religious feeling by close contact with religious truth, illustrated the experience of every faithful pastor, that spiritual enlargement results from no study as it does from the study of pulpit addresses, and it results not from the rhetoric of these addresses, but from the theology of them.

The vigor of mind and heart, which is gained from doctrinal investigation, is the mainspring of effective preaching. The eloquence of the pulpit is the eloquence of thought. A feeble mind can no more wield this thought than the stripling shepherd could wield the armor of Saul. Warmth of emotion in the pulpit will not diffuse itself through the pews, unless the great object of that emotion be distinctly and vividly exhibited; and the preacher cannot exhibit what he does not fully possess. He cannot write with interest and zeal, nor can he with earnestness and energy deliver what he has written, unless he understand and feel the great bearings of his theme. He may goad up his animal susceptibilities to an intense excitement, he may saw the air, and distort his visage, and beat the pulpit cushion, and stamp his foot, and thunder with his voice, but this is not the animation which hearers wish or want. Rational, educated minds will smile at his nervous agitation and vapid remark, and will demand the excitement which is kindled by thought, and will sympathize profitably with none but intelligent emotion. When he is preaching on eternity, on the judgment, on the divine justice in eternal retributions, it will be easy to distinguish between his antic gestures, or vehement contortions of face, and that serious solemn eloquence which would be breathed into him by the deep study of those doctrines. Nothing but such deep study can impart the true sober energy, the considerate reasonable excitement, which, wherever seen, is power. The speaker may practise before his mirror, and learn to raise his hand gracefully, and explode vowels forcibly, but without intense thought on the matter of his discourses, all the rules in the world will never make him eloquent; and with this intense thought, awakening appropriate emotion, he will be eloquent without a single other rule. Other rules are useful, they make the body; this rule is essential, it makes the soul. The soul will live without the body; the body is putrefaction without the soul; both together make the man.

A distinguished fanatic, who had been tenderly nursed during a long sickness at the house of a friend, and who felt sincerely grateful for the kind attentions of that friend, was asked, on the morning of his departure, to lead in social prayer. He prayed with his wonted boisterousness, until he began to pour out his thanksgivings for the assiduous care of his host; then a subdued manner and a still small voice usurped the place of vehemence and noise. "I knew," said his friend, "that my guest felt thankful and attached to me; and it was his deep feeling that lowered his tones, and repressed the turbulence of his nerves. When therefore he was not so calm, I inferred that he had not so much feeling; and the part of his prayer which was most sincere, was that which was least impetuous." Let us not deceive ourselves. The fitfulness of nervous excitation is distinct from the sober emotion of the heart; the rodomontade in the pulpit is easily distinguished from the eloquent expounder of truth. Children, young or old, may be amused with a vociferous declaimer, as they would be with a fire eater, or wire tumbler, but even children will not be inspired by him with solemn conviction, but will turn from him with the vague feeling, that something or other is wanting, and can only say of their preacher's oratory, what was once said of a different kind of disturbance of the peace, "a tumult my lord, but I know not the meaning thereof." If Campbell's definition of eloquence be just, that it is the "art or talent by which a discourse is adapted to its end," there can be no sacred eloquence which does not more than amuse, more than interest, more than astonish, it must illuminate, and with its light which cheers must emit the heat which melts.

There is a second mode in which theological study increases the eloquence of the preacher; it gives him a proper confidence in himself and his ministrations. A minister should not be arrogant and presumptuous, neither should he be crest-fallen and craven. True self-respect is the ground of true humility, and the same knowledge which imparts the former, imparts also the latter. A man is as much entitled to respect himself, as to respect others, and a minister has as much right as any other man, to form the merited estimate of his own character. Besides, he is authorized to regard himself as a messenger from God, and in imitation of that inspired model of preachers who never disparaged his high calling, he is bound to say in word and in life, " I magnify mine office." Who among his hearers can vie in importance with the preacher of the Gospel? Physicians, jurists, statesmen must bow themselves before the pulpit, and must yield their dignified obeisance to him, who is distinguished by the appellation, " the mouth of God." He who is the *instructor* of his audience, the spiritual father perhaps of many of them, the guide and counsellor of all, should not appear before them in a crouching posture, as if it were a great favor and honor to him that they will deign to lend their ears; he should not speak as if he were about to apologize for troubling them with his words, or "beg pardon for having been born." No, he should stand up like a man, and speak like a man, and let it be known that he is a man, yea, more than a man, a preacher. Then will his words come with authority. Then will the hearers look *up* to him. But no minister will speak with that confidence which is neither too great nor too small, but just right, unless he have the mastery of his subject.

There is something in the very consciousness of understanding his doctrine, which gives him the appropriate boldness of utterance. He feels, that he can teach his hearers. However striking their superiority over him in many things, he feels that in the most important of all things he has, as he ought to have, superiority over them. He can make the wisest of them more wise. He can reprove the most learned of them for their ignorance of the one thing needful. It will be a feast for the oldest of them to hang upon his lips, even though he be on the green side of mature age. This will not make him vain; if so, he has peculiar reason to be humble, and may be sure that he has not the qualifications for an occupant of his high office. The truth properly proportioned never ministers to vanity; truth whatever it be, does good and no evil at all to him who comprehends it, and it is one great requisite of a preacher, that he be able to look at truth, just as it is, the whole truth respecting himself, and be quickened by it to cry aloud and spare not, and be emboldened to "show himself a man."

Again, theological knowledge gives the proper degree of confidence to the preacher, because it discloses the adaptedness of his themes to the moral nature of his hearers. By fully understanding a doctrine, the minister may understand how it operates on the heart, and by understanding how it operates, he feels confidence in the utility of preaching it. He is like a mechanic using sharp tools in broad day-light; if he were in the dark, he would move with faint-hearted and wavering uncertainty, but in the sunshine he knows how and where he is cutting, and strikes his chisel with confidence, that it will cleave not merely the thin air. When a preacher sees the nature and the tendency of his doctrine, he feels a mysteriously imparted expectation of success in enforcing it. He feels a rational, animating faith, that the Holy Spirit will comply with the laws of mental action, and accompany the means which are so happy in their tendencies, with the influence which is needed to develope those tendencies in saving results. He feels, when he enters the sacred desk, that he is to do something, and this assurance of success, as it increases his reliance upon the ultimate source of all success, increases also his vigor, and manliness, and life.

Still further, there is something in the very nature of theological truth, which gives confidence to the preacher. It opens, enlarges, and vivifies the mind. There is a clearness in truth; a directness and a freshness in it, which strangely disenthralls the spirit, and gives free, full scope. Truth favors freedom; freedom of thought, freedom of speech, freedom of act. Revealed by the same God, who made the soul, and all the laws of the soul, it harmonizes with these laws, moves along with them easily and happily, and jars with the mind only when the mind puts constraint upon itself, and jars with its own principles. The mind was made for truth, and of course sympathizes with it wherever found. When wounded and bruised it glides instinctively to truth, as the serpent, when self-poisoned, is said to hasten for the curative leaf. It has a kindly feeling toward all truth, and rejoices in it as a brother, and when torn from it, pines away as a dove mourning its mate. It is the heart only which is disloyal and disorganizing, and impresses the intellect into a rebellion as injurious to it as unnatural. Still the mind even when carried captive by a depraved will, looks back with yearnings to its native land; and, wherever truth points, there the mind points, unless forcibly held down; and wherever truth stays, there the mind stays, unless forcibly driven on. The words of the philosophical poet may be well applied to the secret union between the mind and evangelical doctrine, two emanations from the same source;

'T was thus, if ancient fame the truth unfold,
Two faithful needles from th' informing touch

> Of the same parent stone, together drew
> Its mystic virtue, and at first conspired
> With fatal impulse quivering to the pole;
> Then, though disjoined by kingdoms, though the main
> Rolled its broad surge betwixt, and diff'rent stars
> Beheld their wakeful motions, yet preserved
> The former friendship, and remembered still
> Th' alliance of their birth: Whate'er the line
> Which one possessed, nor pause nor quiet knew
> The sure associate, ere with trembling speed
> He found its path, and fixed unerring there."*

Point to any man, who in his preaching is fettered with doubts, trammelled with consciousness of impotency, moves with halting step, utters his doctrine in long periphrases, and explains about it and about it, and well nigh bespeaks pity for it, and never thrusts it home with energy and courage upon the conscience and the heart; and I strongly suspect that the man does not understand the gospel. "Ye shall know the truth," says Jesus, "and the truth shall make you free," and "where the Spirit of the Lord is," says Paul, "there is liberty." I love to see a preacher deeply imbued with the impression that he is a moral being, and his hearers are moral beings, and that he must aim at moral effects by moral means; that he has something to do, and his hearers have something to do; and that they must do *their* duty immediately, and he must do *his* duty fearlessly; for this impression is in harmony with actual fact, and he who makes this impression a part of his own soul "shall be free indeed." It is an old proverb, "men will praise thee when thou doest well for thyself;" and so when a minister looks and speaks and acts, as if he respected himself as a moral agent; and reverenced his official elevation; and had full faith in the efficacy of that sword which he wields, but which is nevertheless the sword of the Spirit, and when he applies doctrine with an untied hand and trustful heart, as well as with meekness and love, then will his people praise him; and the way to praise a minister is, to attend to him, and profit by him.

There is a third mode in which the minister improves his eloquence by extensive theological investigation; he acquires by it the respect and confidence of his people. A bishop, says Paul, "must have a good report of them which are without;" and an orator, says Cicero, must be confided in as a good man,

---

* Akenside's Pleasures of Imagination, B. III. p. 325—337.

or his oration will exert but diminished influence. The preacher must make objective as well as subjective preparations; for the most finished sermon will fall upon an unprepared audience, as Priam's spear upon the buckler of Neoptolemus. It is a wise remark of Hooker, " let Phidias have rude and obstinate stuff to carve, though his art do that it should, his work will lack that beauty which otherwise in fitter matter it might have had. He that striketh on an instrument with skill, may cause notwithstanding a very unpleasant sound, if the string whereon he striketh chance to be uncapable of harmony."* When an audience depreciate their minister's ability to instruct them, their very prejudice will convert his eloquence into inanity; and moreover, he will find it beyond his power to attain such eloquence before hearers who turn the cold shoulder to the pulpit, as before those who turn the eager eye and the open breast. If therefore the preacher aim at efficiency in the pulpit, he must divert the power of popular prejudice to his own favor, as the skilful pilot watches wind and tide, so as to be wafted along by the same elements, which would otherwise resist him. The preacher must appear to be pious and intelligent, and the only way of appearing to be so, is to be so. It is more than one age too late, to acquire the respect of a congregation by superficial and common-place teaching. Simple truths are on the wings of the wind. Our popular religious literature has carried them to every man's fire-side. The churches demand a higher instruction, and an ampler reasoning from the pulpit, than can be gleaned from the narratives of the nursery. They may be pleased for a time with the pleasant voice, and the pathetic tale, but like the prodigal they will soon turn away from the husks, and long for more nutritive aliment though presented in a homelier dish. Even the child who early learns to sing,

> I hate that drum's discordant sound,
> Parading round and round and round,

will soon loathe the emptiness and inflation and circumvolutions of the discourse, which rings in his ears just as monotonously as the drum, because it is filled with just the same substance. The bare belief that a preacher has no excellence but that of elocution, and no grace but that of attitude, will soon degrade his authority, while the bare belief that he is a consummate

---

* Hooker's Ecclesiastical Polity, Vol. 1. p. 207.

theologian, will invest his teachings with commanding importance. Men who are not thinkers, wish to be addressed as if they were. Unlettered men do not wish to have their minister imply by his style, that he is making great effort to become simple enough for their comprehension. The preacher who appointed a service for the lower classes, and the ignorant of his flock, had "fit audience though few." The hearer who complained, that he did not receive his "money's worth" at church, because his pastor instead of preaching in the Greek language which he had understood to be a superior one, preached only in the English which even poor men used without salaries, uttered the language of many, who demand that a sermon be elaborate, even if they be less capable than they choose to be reputed, of comprehending its instructions. But I do not wish to underrate the popular intelligence. It is a fact that all mind craves thought. Even indolent men love excitement, and even wicked men are interested in logical and eloquent exhibitions of evangelical doctrine. All the faculties, reason, judgment, imagination, memory, find congenial exercise on the truths which God has fitted to them, as he has fitted food to the stomach, and light to the eye. When Dr. Griffin was preaching his most pungent discourses in Boston, on such themes as election and free-will, the depravity of man, and sovereignty of God, his church was frequented by men who disbelieved and disliked his doctrine. As they retired from one service they would resolve not to expose themselves to the excitements of another, but the next Sabbath eve would find the opposing yet eager listeners again at Park street, not because they wished to go, but because they could not stay away; because their consciences found something vigorous to grapple with, and their whole moral nature was met exactly in its importunings. So urgently and ceaselessly does the human constitution demand the truth for which it was originally framed, that nothing but a varied and harmonious exhibition of this truth, can be permanently satisfying. If error satisfy in sickness, it will not in health; if in prosperity, not in adversity. Those old principles of mind, which rejoiced together before the fall, though they may slumber for a season after they have bidden farewell to truth, will yet rise up at last with a voice of lamentation and mourning, as Rachel rose in Rama, weeping for her children, because they were not.

The preacher who is but poorly indoctrinated, may write on a single subject without an exposure of his poverty; but when he writes on some other subject, he will be apt to show that his mind has no capacity to contain more than one thing at a time, and he will forfeit the confidence of his more discerning hearers by his self-contradictions. He does not discern the relations of truths, sees but a small distance before him, disparages to-day what he magnifies to-morrow, and preaches on one doctrine so as to nullify another. When expounding the text, "my yoke is easy," he represents the ease of religion in terms so unqualified, that repentance seems like the facile movement of the eyelid; but when expounding the text, "strive to enter in at the straight gate," he represents the agonizing of religion as surpassing even the fabled labors of Sisyphus. When preaching on the *unworthiness* of Christians, he describes them as meriting no praise for their piety, because all piety being exercised under an influence from Heaven, must be ascribed to that influence, and not at all to the active subjects of it. But when preaching on the *duty* of Christians, he will say that they are free in their holy as well as their sinful feelings, that all their acts are their own, and that their moral agency is not suspended or mutilated by the influences of the Spirit. If then they are moral and not passive Christians, if their acts are their own, if their repentance is not God's repentance, why, the hearer will ask, are they not praiseworthy. And then, this same preacher, when portraying the *guilt of sinners*, will describe them as the bond-slaves of Satan, and will declare that the influence of the fallen spirit does not in the least exculpate those who yield to him, but that sinners are moral creatures, and their guilt can never be transferred from themselves the agents, to him the tempter. But why, the hearer will again ask, does a foreign influence leave a man unworthy of praise, and yet worthy of blame? Why does not the same cause, an extraneous operation, produce in either case the same effect, the destruction of moral accountability? In almost every audience there are some, who will detect this tergiversation, and will complain of their pastor as one who sacrifices truth to popular effect, and bends all science, human and divine, to his purpose of moulding in his own way the hearts of his people. These discerning hearers will diffuse their objection through the undiscerning mass; and many will learn to look upon their religious guide, not as a vicegerent of Jehovah, standing on the sure word of revelation; but as a personal adviser and reprover, standing on his own ingenuity; they will lose their respect for him, so soon as they divest him of the divine mantle, and will parry his self-invented remonstrances as with a shield of brass.

Fourthly, theological study is important for the preacher's eloquence, because it secures to his ministrations, appropriateness and variety. Appropriateness depends upon variety; for the wants of the soul are varied, and sermons adjusted to these wants must be correspondently varied. Not only must divers characters be diversely treated, but the same individual must have different susceptibilities appealed to, different emotions excited, so that the entire soul may be edified. By various instruction he will be trained not a christian monster, but a christian man. Is it not a law of intellectual education, to exercise all the faculties? So it is the law of moral education to exercise all the graces, and they cannot all be exercised by one style of preaching, more than all the mental faculties by one subject of study. Dieteticians tell us, that we must have variety in our food or lose vigor of body, and that those tribes who confine their diet to a single article, however nutritious it be, are stunted and short-lived. What must be the state, then, of the spiritual system, which is fed from some pulpits, sabbath after sabbath, year after year, by one and the same kind of nutriment. It will be thought so, but it is not extravagant to say, that there are ministers who discourse, nearly fifty sabbaths of the year, on only two or three subjects. Whatever their text, whatever their introduction, whatever their purpose, they slide into the same hackneyed strain. Their minds have worn a channel, and flow into it naturally and of course. Not that they always use the same words, or adopt the same plan, but the whole genius of their sermons is the same, and losing the individual characteristic of every doctrine, they merge it into one tiresome generality. A late president of a college in New-England said, that he sat seventeen years under a very pious preacher, and yet heard from him only four sermons; one Thanksgiving sermon, one Fast sermon, one Funeral sermon, and one General sermon. The hyperbole of this criticism is not so great as may at first appear; for perhaps there is no department of literature, which, in proportion to the amount of mind professedly devoted to it, is so monotonous as the homiletic. Our inquisitive laymen too often complain, that their pastor brings out of his treasury things old and old. It is well, that their Athenian restlessness " to hear some new thing," be sometimes rebuked, but some ministers rebuke it by continually disappointing it. Their public prayers are but one prayer, which many in their parishes have learned by rote, and an analysis of their sermons would develop a want, greater than any one suspects, of individuality, freshness, and that fertile variety, without which the speaker cannot be appropriate, and the hearer will not keep awake.

Let us analyze three sermons, which are no caricatures, but sober specimens of a style of preaching, exhibited in more than one pulpit or even printed volume.

The subject of the first sermon is, sorrow for sin; and the divisions are three; first, the duty is commanded; secondly, the neglect of it will be punished; thirdly, the performance of it will be rewarded; and under the last division are depicted the beatific glories which will ensue from this sorrow. Every idea which the author advances is correct, but yet a minute and thorough analysis of his theme would have shown him, that he had overlooked the peculiar sympathies of it, and that his cheering portraiture of paradise must be abridged, or else be out of keeping with his good design. How can he raise tears of distress, by a bright painting of happiness as the reward of distress? For the next sermon he selects a different theme, the duty of Christian cheerfulness, and advances the three positions; first, God has commanded the duty; secondly, will reward the performance of it; thirdly, will punish the neglect of it, and he portrays the misery of despair as the result of refusing to obey the command, "rejoice in the Lord." If this be not true, what is? Doubtless it is all true; but a more radical study of the truth would have detected more of its genius and harmonies. Had the preacher penetrated into the recesses of his doctrine, and lived there, breathing its peculiar spirit, he might indeed have glanced at the woes of them who would neglect this duty, but would not have held his hearers long in an atmosphere so ill suited to diffuse the glow of cheerfulness. Every subject has its finger, and the finger points to something congenial with it; and certainly the subject of christian tranquillity does not point to the lake of gloom and the gnawing worm, as the things with which it is most congenial. Nor indeed does it point, first and foremost, to the idea, that God has commanded cheerfulness. The nature of a command, is not so homogeneous as that of some other objects, with the nature of serenity. To bring down all at once the imposing ideas of law and duty upon the delicate, spontaneous, unchained emotion of joy, is like cherishing the growth of a sensitive plant by grating on it with a file and saw. It is like calling forth the whispering music of an Æolian harp by dashing it with an iron bar. It is all right and all important, that the preacher should tell men of the law of rejoicing, and of the penalties of disobedience; but this is not the sympathetic, natural and easy development which will leave the hearers rejoicing, and thus perfect the persuasion of the preacher. His sermon may have other aims, but if its aim be to excite the commended emotion, it should be a placid, sunny sermon, the topics and the style in sweet harmony with the theme, and every sentence should be penned with the feeling, that whatever else men may be scolded into, they will perhaps be scolded into petulance as soon as into cheerfulness.

But for the third sermon, the preacher, for the sake of variety, selects a third theme as different as need be from the two preceding; but again calls in the rhetorician's charmed number of topics, "three;" God has commanded the duty; will punish the neglect, reward the performance of it. But what is the subject which is to be laid down upon this standard triangle? It is this; the duty of men to make their chief object of pursuit neither their own joy, nor their own sorrow, but the glory of God. Where now is the propriety of urging us to regard our own joy as subordinate, by a prominent reference to the eternal joy which will reward disinterestedness; and how does the instruction that we comparatively overlook our own sorrow, sympathize with the protracted threatening of everlasting sorrow as a punishment for undue self-love? It is nothing but a severe meditation on the nature of this subject, which will disclose its rhetorical, as distinct from its theological truth. The fact is, that though the third sermon should have a peculiar identity, it is in its essential spirit a repetition of the second, as the second is of the first. The three sermons are one in their main outline; the duty of obeying God, avoiding misery, obtaining happiness is the one subject; and although the subject is differently illustrated in each of the sermons as it would be in thirty more, it renders each a stiff, formal, mechanical discourse. There is not a duty in the whole moral code, but may be and often is recommended by the same stationary divisions. But why stretch every thing on one bed? Why not detect the idiosyncracy of a doctrine, its spirit, aptitude and peculiar suggestions? Nature has not given water a red color or a sweet taste, because this sameness would annoy us. Physicians say that a change even from the better to the good is often necessary, because it is a change. But we ask of a preacher, merely that he vary with his subject ; that he watch its flowings forth, and follow them ; that he wait and muse until he be borne along by the tendencies of his doctrine over all his plans and skeletons and technicalities. There is one glory of the sun, another of the moon, and one star differeth from another star in glory. There is in man an innate love of novelty, which, so far as constitutional, should be conformed to by the preacher. He need not fear ; for there is a richness and abundance in theology which will answer to every cry of the soul. No chord vibrates in our bosoms, but a chord of scriptural truth may vibrate in unison or else in fitness. It is the study of this truth, then, that is to uncover the springs of eloquence, and it is the first rule of sacred rhetoric to recommend this study. A complete theologian, one who takes in the essence and the bearings, and the inspiration, and the life of theology, is the only model of pulpit eloquence. He cannot open his mouth on his favorite science, without showing that he, rather than Plato, was the man, " upon whose lips the bees dropped honey as he lay in his cradle." Cicero says, that " if Jupiter should converse with men he would talk in the language of Plato," but we know, for the phenomenon has been observed, that when Jehovah converses with men, he speaks in the language of the theologian ; or rather, the theologian but re-echoes the eloquent words of the Divinity.

Fifthly, theological study is essential to sacred eloquence, because it discloses the precise truths which are fitted to renovate the heart. Truth is God's ; the soul is God's. One being made for the other, is adapted to it as the tenon to the mortice. A surgeon may as well overlook the distinction between a scalpel and a forceps, as a preacher overlook the distinction between doctrines, every one of which is an instrument aptly and beautifully shaped for a special purpose ; and if the surgeon should use the saw, when he ought to use the lance, he would operate less harmfully than the preacher, who applies one doctrine when he ought to apply another. If God require us to use the hammer, we should not use the fire instead thereof ; and if He require us to administer the oil of consolation, we should not in lieu thereof administer the wormwood of reproof. It is the truth, which the Spirit blesses ; the truth as it is ; not half the truth, not the whole truth with some additions ; not maimed and distorted truth, not truth which is involved in doubt and may perhaps after all be proved a lie ; but clear, plain, prominent truth. This it is which, because adapted in itself to convert men, the Spirit makes effectual in converting them. This it is which, because it harmonizes with the commanding sentiments of our moral nature, is harmonized with by the Spirit in renovating that nature ; for the Spirit is a God of harmony, and employs no instruments which are not congenial with the feelings of the operator, and the nature of the agent operated upon. It is this truth, and only this, which the minister is commissioned to unfold. If he would unfold it, he must study it, for save in an age of miracles, how knoweth any man letters having never learned ? If he do not study it, he may speak with eloquence indeed, but can never preach with sacred eloquence ; for to speak is not to preach, and it is not mere eloquence but sacred eloquence, which is adapted to secure the great effect of preaching on the heart of man.

Let the minister unfold the true doctrine of repentance, and declare that his unconverted hearers are bound to repent now, on the spot, and that they are able to do whatever they are bound to do, and let him unhesitatingly and earnestly, just as if he expected they would do it, urge them to make their election sure before they leave their seats, they will feel that if able to repent they are guilty more than unfortunate in not repenting ; and if able and pressed to repent now, they will try, and their trial will show how strong is the resistance of their voluntary selfishness, which transforms the easy into the difficult; and this discovery of their obstinate sin will be at least a salutary conviction of guilt, and perhaps the first step in their progress from sin to holiness.

On the contrary, let the preacher misunderstand the first principles of moral agency, and he will exhort his hearers to repent when they go home, or to use the means of repentance, or to form the fixed resolution of repenting at some future time; and they will feel that they are not invited to repent immediately, and will be glad to enjoy for a season the sin which they are not urged to leave ; and to enjoy the quiet which they drink in from their purpose of avoiding hereafter the end which they are now approaching. They verify the remark of Luther, that " the road to hell is paved with good resolves." Sometimes the preacher, while he exhorts his hearers to future repentance, assures them that their duty even then will transcend their ability; and thus instead of profiting them with an incentive to obedience, he only amazes them at the injustice of requiring bricks without straw.

Or perhaps in the same discourse, and without such qualification as the nature of the doctrine demands, he will perplex them with the farrago of figurative and literal statements, that they are able and unable, have at the same time power and no power to do as they should.

But even when the confounding of moral certainty with natural inability does not lead to a seeming paradox, which impairs the persuasive influence of the preacher, it leads him either to omit exhortation altogether, and abandon his hearers to be converted as and when God's sovereignty shall choose; or else to utter a lifeless and jejune appeal which has as much tendency to prostrate the walls of Jericho, or perform any other miracle on matter, as it has to effect a renovation of the heart. The appeal is "as good as dead." The worst that can be said of its rhetorical complexion is, that it is in keeping with the theology from which it emanates. The best that can be said of any exhortation which springs from error is, that it is useless. Ex nihilo, nihil fit. It is indeed a pleasant thought, that if the preacher have a peculiar liveliness of temperament, or warmth of piety he may shake off his speculations for an hour, and preach as a man, though he will have it that he is a machine. In the main, however, his necessarian faith will trammel his eloquence, and he will feel as under an incubus when he invites men to accomplish impossibilities. The difficulty is, he has substituted for the scriptural doctrine of repentance, a theory of his own; but this theory, as it will not bear inspection when in a cold thesis, is peculiarly awkward in a sermon; and as it is a poor thing in the study, so it is exactly the thing which ought not to be in the pulpit. The man is possessed with the feeling that his hearers are more than morally disabled; and he *cannot* harangue before dry bones as he would before living beings; and so he utters cold words to a cold assembly, uses sepulchral tones to grave-stones of men; and dead, dead is the whole obituary of himself and his people. His doctrine is ill-contrived for the innate susceptibilities of his hearers; and they, waiting for God's time, sleep on, till His time come, not indeed of regeneration but of sentence.

The doctrine of prayer may also be noticed, as adapted, when correctly preached, to produce the effect for which all doctrine was designed, but operating, when preached incorrectly, as a sharp sickle operates when applied as and where it should not be. A prayer is a request offered with appropriate feeling. A request, disconnected with love and humility and faith, is no more a prayer, than the mimic representations of the stage are the living realities which are only represented. A theologian will exhort sinners to *pray* not to *mock;* to pray immediately, and not defer the service until they are better fitted for it; to pray just as they are to plough and reap, eat and drink, for the glory of God and not for their selfish advantage. Unless they pray, they are in immediate and grievous peril; and if they pretend to pray while they are impenitent, they add hypocrisy to their other sins, and as if tired of modestly profaning the outer court, press forward, with a novel boldness, to profane the holy of holies. The truth makes them see on their right hand and their left, the impassable mountains; it shows them the hosts of the avenger, crowding on from the rear; it agitates them with the conviction, that to escape sidewise from duty, is to perish like sheep on the mountains; to stand still is to be cut down; straight forward is their only course, and if Jordan is before them they must swim the flood; and it is when the sinner sees himself thus shut up to one right line, which he must pursue exactly or die, that he feels his guilty impotence, and sinks down in such despair of himself, and such a fitness to depend on the aid of another, that divine grace interposes at this precise critical point, and takes to himself the glory of the passage, which the sinner should, and therefore could long since have made. Thus honoring to God, abasing and yet stimulating to man is the suasory influence of truth as applied by the Spirit.

But when a minister misunderstands this doctrine of prayer, he bewilders the impenitent by assuring them, that they cannot repent, which, in the literal sense, they can do; and yet that they can please God by praying for repentance, which in the indulgence of their selfish spirit they cannot do; that their prayers are abomination in the sight of God, and yet should be offered to Him who says, "my soul hateth them;" that they have no right to sin, yet may commit the iniquity of bending the rebellious knee at the mercy seat, and thus avert the penalty of their less sacrilegious sins committed in less solemn positions. They are told to do that for which, if they die as soon as they have done it, they will be condemned to eternal wo. They receive such advice as may encourage them to say, at the judgment,—"We are punished for following in letter and in spirit the advice of our minister." When they are exhorted to pray for their conversion, they are exhorted to pray for their *first* right feeling; and when they pray for their *first* right feeling the prayer must precede this feeling, and must of course be offered with a feeling which is not right; they pray wickedly, that their wickedness even in this very prayer may give place to the piety which they at the same time hate, and are virtually exhorted to remain in sin, until they receive some gift from on high, though it may be that their spirits will be called up, following hard after their praying breath, to the God who abhorreth the smoke of strange offerings.

To exhort sinners to pray as sinners, that they may be enabled to pray as Christians, is indeed common, and in its first impression is not so unseemly; yet is in its true implications to recommend their continuance in sin, until that future period,—a period which under such treatment is slow in coming, when a celestial influence shall render wicked prayers no longer necessary, and absolve from the anomalous requirement, that a man carry his rebellion up to the altar before he can satisfy his God. It is at his peril, that a preacher allow his necessarian philosophy to inculcate such procrastination of repentance even for an instant; he overlooks the impulses of man's moral nature; and if he produce any impression on his hearers, it will be the mischievous one, that their sin is a misfortune which Omnipotence in pity must remove; that so long as they pray against their calamity, and perform so well the condition of repentance, they do all which can be expected of them; and must leave the results to him, who will not withhold the piety which his compassion loves to bestow, and who has promised to hear even the young raven when it crieth. They lull themselves with the dream that their prayer will be effectual with a prayer-hearing God, and that, though not Christians, yet they have ceased to be obstinate like other sinners, and are raised to a distinct class, seekers, and are performing an intermediate kind of obedience, just what it should be in its exterior, just what it should not be in every thing essential. The men who abide, day after day, in this amphibious attitude are certainly beyond the jurisdiction of the Bible, which was written when there were only two classes of men in existence, one who served God, another who served him not; they are engaged in a course of obedience which their Master knows nothing of, for he never recognizes neutrals, and has given no command which can be obeyed without full and instant love; they therefore elude the humbling influence of truth, which profits the penitent and the impenitent, but passes by without touching the species of men who lie midway between something and nothing; and they often receive, as the positive recompense of their negative service, a blunt conscience, a self-complacent and self-confident heart, and an inveterate habit of waiting for God to do what he requires them to do. Thus prolific of mischief, and unsuited to the tendencies of the moral constitution, is the philosophy which describes repentance as something to be prayed for, rather than something to be performed; and teaches man to comply with the conditions of his duty, rather than do his duty. The truth of God is "quick," "cease to do evil, learn to do well;" and not hypothetical and circumambulatory, "try to pray that you may be enabled to begin the right course."

No other luminary than that which God has made, can enlighten the earth; no other doctrine than that which God has revealed, can meliorate the heart. It is then almost a truism to say, that he who would eloquently persuade men to godliness, must make his eloquence a vivid presentation of the great motives to godliness, and as these motives are all involved in divine truth, he may, without understanding that truth write elegantly and speak gracefully, but what he writes will be no sermon, and his speaking will be a declamatory profanation of the pulpit, which is not the orator's, but the "preacher's throne," and should exhibit nothing but the life and life-giving spirit of evangelical doctrine.

I remark in the last place, that sacred eloquence depends essentially on theological study, because this study discloses the essential truths which glorify God. The preacher is commanded to declare all the doctrines of the Gospel; to declare them variously, explicitly, thoroughly; and he who obeys this command, honors not only the government but also the character of Jehovah. To represent the Divine excellencies so that they shall be apprehended, is the sacred eloquence of thought; so that they shall be loved is the sacred eloquence of feeling: for if the heathen's remark be true, that to know God is to glorify him, then to make him known is to glorify him more extensively; and if to make him known be glorious to him, to make him loved is still more glorious. Whether an audience adore or despise the character of Jehovah, their very apprehension of the character will eventually honor it; and their contempt even will illustrate the boundlessness of His mercy, or the purity of His Justice. It is a thought which may always add solemnity to the preacher's emotion and energy to his eloquence, that when he portrays the Divine attributes, his words, if they be understood, shall not one of them be lost, but shall forever elicit new praise to Him who maketh even sin the occasion of new and honorable developments. If this thought be impressive, there is another still more animating to the faithful preacher, that by his vivid delineations of the Divinity, he may multiply copies of that infinite perfection, and by transfusing the Divine image may call forth the glory which comes not barely from the knowledge, but also from the love and resemblance of God.

But how can men love an object which they do not apprehend? How can souls be converted, without a notion of the Being to whom they are converted? To make Christians is the easiest thing in the world. Constantine made them by the thousands in a day. The Popes have made whole nations true to the faith, by a single decree. A single sermon may convert an audience without the aid of an interposing spirit, save perhaps the spirit of darkness. When Christians are multiplied at a protracted meeting, the great quere is, are they lovers of that excellence which constitutes Christ? Are they converted to that holiness which is the moral sum of Jehovah? From what, to what are they transformed? There is often the most lamentable ground for fear, that they are changed from the worship of one form of sin, to that of another. The Deity is not glorified by conversions, but by conversions to the truth. It is not the three letters *God*, which make the object of adoration, but a pure spirit of excellence. The indefinite preacher speaks of a something, who is nought but kindness and mercy, and he calls that something God; and then asks his hearers to love it, because it is so full of love to them. They love it, and are proclaimed as converts. But they have loved it, in another form, ever since they loved themselves. Every sinner loves it so long as he remains a sinner. They are converted only to the love of a new conformation of their own depravity. This something, it may be called God, but remains the same in essence, by whatever cognomen it be designated, and is the likeness of nothing in the heaven above, but is the image of its makers on earth, selfish, partial, and sinful. Their love to it is love to an idol. Their prayers, and praises, and songs, and obedient service to it, are all to their own creature, rather than their great Creator. The true spiritual Divinity is the discerner of the thoughts, and sees that this homage is mistaken and misapplied; was meant for another Being who wears his name indeed, but none of his attributes, and who has only a fictitious existence. Oh there are many anthems, and solemn dedications, and devout observances, which go up from nominal worshippers, but go *by* God's throne, and wander about in search of their shadowy object, which exists anywhere, rather in the regions above. Even in the true church of Christ, there is much idolatry. Intermingled with devotion to Jehovah, there is much devotion to an etherial figment of our own fancies. Secular eloquence may persuade men to love the gold of God's throne, but He does not feel praised unless we love the holiness of it. A meagre system of theology will suffice for the preacher, who inculcates the love of many things connected with religion, but God does not feel glorified unless we love religion itself. He has no corporeal ears to be pleased with the sound, God; but heareth with the Spirit, and acknowledgeth no name save his true character, inwardly appreciated and loved. With wrong views of his character we cannot actively glorify him. The first duty then of the preacher is to publish this character, so that an assimilating influence may flow forth from it upon those who hear; to hold up this living and life-imparting mystery of perfection, so that it may reflect its own likeness upon the lookers on. The more perspicuously and properly a preacher delineates the divine character in a sermon, so much the more hope may be entertained, that the Spirit will use that sermon as an instrument of good to souls and glory to God. This interposition of the Spirit is the only source of hope; this hope is the great spring of eloquence. It is needless to say, that the preacher must understand the whole system of revealed truth, if he would faithfully describe the divine perfections; for these perfections embrace the whole system. Sacred eloquence then, which is the power of speaking so as to glorify God, is the power of speaking well on all the truths of God; and peculiarly on those attributes which, in themselves, make up his essential, and in their exhibition, his declarative glory. As the sacred is the top-stone of all eloquence, so it ultimately rests on the broadest of all bases, a complete theological science.

The rule that a preacher defer writing his discourse, until he have a distinct apprehension of the topics which he means to introduce into that discourse, is elementary. With this distinct apprehension he may not always write with clearness; for he may be so deficient in his power of language, his mind may move so quickly over premises which he glances at but does not mark for remembrance, to results which he seizes at strongly and holds too nakedly for plain communication to others, or he may have formed a habit of association elevated so far above all communion with the common intellect, that he is unable to utter intelligibly what he very vividly conceives. But if a writer cannot always express with clearness the ideas which he has, he can never so express the ideas which he has not; and he may nearly as well preach in a foreign language, as in a style which does not emanate from his distinct conceptions. "Those orators," says one, "who give us much noise and many words, but little argument and less wit, and who are most loud when they are the least lucid, should take a lesson from the great volume of nature; she often gives us the lightning even without the thunder, but never the thunder without the lightning."

It is, however, by no means sufficient, that a man investigate barely those parts of his subject, which he wishes to discuss in his sermon. He must investigate all parts, before he can safely decide which to discuss and which to exclude. He must be able to take the whole subject into his hands, as a ball of ivory, and turn it over and over, and present all sides of it. Even if he deem a particular branch to be inappropriate to the pulpit, still it must be analyzed. The analysis will give impulse and acumen to his mind, suggest the most suitable and eloquent collocation of his more popular thoughts, and often initiate him into new fields of practical reflection. Every part of his doctrine has its collateral parts, its dependences, its intimations; and if he explore the circumjacent ground as well as the spot on which he intends to build, he will often discover a fruitful spot in the very darkest corners, under the most tangled shrubbery. "Even a Russian steppe has tumuli and gold ornaments; also many a scene, that looks desert and rock-bound from the distance, will unfold itself, when visited, into rare valleys." Our clergymen commit an injurious error, when they neglect and repudiate all discussion, which promises no immediate practical bearing. They should reflect, that in a great building there are rough and unsightly foundation stones, which are not to be wholly dispensed with, because they are unsuitable for a place in the parlor; on the sofa, or the piano. They should reflect, that in a finished picture there are some colorings, which will disgust if presented in bold relief, but will leave the picture yet more disgusting, if excluded from the back ground, where perhaps only a connoisseur will be able to explain their effect. A sermon is incomplete, unless its arrangement, its allusions, its whole spirit betray the author's familiarity with the fundamental and even suppressed branches of his theme. A minister need not, in these days, be afraid of study. He cannot know too much of truth. He must remember, that all sacred rhetoric is but a new arrangement of the materials of theology, and in proportion to the abundance of his materials may be the felicity of his selection. In vain will he labor to polish his discourses, unless he have given them the firm solid contexture which is derived from sacred science. Disintegrated sand-stone cannot be polished. In vain will he hope to elevate the minds of his hearers by fervent appeal, unless himself be borne aloft by his subject, his whole subject, and nothing but his subject; unless, I say, his subject raise him, and he be relieved from forcing his own progress upward, like a bird of prey dragging his subject along after him. In vain will he decorate his style with tropes, when his doctrine like a poor stray child is lost amid a forest of similes. A neat shroud is very neat, and a white fillet is very white; but a carcass is still a carcass notwithstanding the shroud, and the vacant face is still vacant, notwithstanding the fillet. In vain will he strive to impart a becoming energy to his sermons, unless he have that enthusiasm which nothing but sacred study can inspire; an enthusiasm, which is but another name for a fervent love of truth, and which is more essential for a preacher than even secular enthusiasm is for a secular orator. It is mild to say that a preacher, unskilled in the word of righteousness, will inflict upon his audience, sermons ephemeral, unimpressive, emitting their first and only light, when his administrators shall perform the duty which he should have anticipated, of consigning them to the flames; the severe fact is, that he will not only fail to teach the truth, but will teach error; error in the substance of his doctrine, error in the shading of it, error at least in the moral impressions of it; and whoever has computed the mischiefs of one error under sacerdotal sanction, may estimate the influence of one man, instructing by conjecture, warning at random, mutilating at hap-hazard the doctrines, which an angel would not dare to touch save with a delicate hand, and after a wary, circumspect survey.

feel that in offering yourselves soul and body on the altar of Christianity you are but doing a reasonable service. It is this full, unreserved, cheerful consecration, so lamentably rare among us, that is, after all, the great secret of usefulness in a Gospel minister; and where this is, it will be accepted of God, according to what a man hath, and not according to what he hath not.

ARTICLE X.

The Mode of Exhibiting Theological Truth.

By Edwards A. Park, Bartlet Professor, Theol. Sem. Andover.

Theology, it has been well remarked, may be considered in two aspects; as essential, and as modal. Essential theology is the substance of divine truth; modal theology is this substance fitly arranged. The department of christian theology is concerned with the essence of christian doctrine; the department of sacred rhetoric is concerned with the manner in which this doctrine should be presented. Theological science collects the materials; rhetorical science arranges them. The preacher's rhetoric then is a new adjustment of his theology.

The mode of exhibiting truth may be divided into two departments; the external and the intellectual. The former consists of attitudes, gestures, tones of voice or expressions of face, and is used only in oral addresses. The latter consists not merely in the words with which truth is attired, but in something more elevated and important; in the arrangement of the various parts of a doctrine; in the juxtaposition of one doctrine with another; in the order and proportion in which different doctrines are presented; in the spirit which is breathed out along with them, and in the adaptation of them to the particular state of those who are addressed. The intellectual mode of presenting truth is therefore of more general interest than the external. Its importance is felt not merely in oral but also in written addresses, and even in all doctrinal meditations.

The object of the present article is to consider, first the importance, and secondly the means of attaining the best intellectual mode of stating divine truth.

The importance of the mode in which truth is communicated is apparent, first, from the nature of mind on which truth operates; secondly, from the nature of truth itself.

1. The mind which is to be operated upon, is of such a nature that, in order to be profited by any subject, it must attend to that subject, and it will not attend unless it be pleased. To the question, "what moves the mind, in every particular instance, to determine its general power of directing to this or that particular motion or rest?" Mr. Locke replies, "the motive for continuing in the same state of action, is only the present satisfaction in it; the motive to change is always some uneasiness; nothing setting us upon a change of state, or upon any new action, but some uneasiness."*

This impulse after happiness is so various in its operations, that the mind may follow a train of ideas which in many respects is disagreeable, but the neglect of which would be still more disagreeable. Little pleasure is derived from the train itself, but the uneasiness in rejecting it would be such, that the mind chooses the less of two evils, and on the great whole finds its happiness in attention. It pursues the train, however, with irresolute and intermittent step, seizes every casual association to escape from the repulsive to some attractive objects, and by its forcible efforts to recal itself, soon becomes fatigued and in need of rest. The preacher then is to remember that, though in one sense he must be superior to the desire of pleasing men, and intent only on pleasing God, yet in another sense he must please men in order to please God. He must not neglect the great law which God has given, nor attempt to enter the heart by an avenue which God has not opened. He should honor the Creator by adapting truth to that principle, which was at the creation implanted so deeply in the soul, and which in its quick movement prompts to the acquisition of all knowledge, and may as well allure to salutary as to hurtful trains of thought. The more wisely a preacher avails himself of this ever-active and ever-leading appetency for pleasure, so much the more deeply does he arouse the interest of his hearers, and the deeper their interest so much the more impressible their hearts. It is an old rule, that an orator must first please, then instruct, then gain or conquer.

Hearers will be sometimes pleased by the congeniality of the subject with their tastes and wants, but they ordinarily demand

* Essay on the Human Understanding. Chap. 21. p. 29.

something more than a naked presentation of the subject. "If knowledge be communicated," says Augustine, "in an unpleasant manner, the advantage of it accrues only to the few who are most studious, and who desire to know all things which are to be learned, even though the things be expressed in a low and uncultivated style. When they have obtained their knowledge, they feed on it with delight; indeed it is a distinguished tendency of good minds to love, not words, but the truth contained in the words. For of what use is a golden key, if it cannot open what we desire; and what harm if the key be of wood, provided it will unlock the door of knowledge; for we desire nothing, but that the things be laid open which are now shut up. Yet since there is some resemblance between eaters and learners, on account of the fastidiousness of most men, even those articles of food which are essential to life, must be made palatable by condiments."* Though a few minds may attend to truth for truth's own sake, yet even they would attend with more constancy, and therefore with more profit, if the truth were arrayed in its appropriate garments; just as a good man would entertain his friends even if meanly apparelled, but entertain them with more cordiality if their apparel corresponded with their character. And where there is one good man, who will, for the sake of substantial excellence, overlook the repulsiveness of its first appearance, there are ten even good men, who will be deterred by the haggard envelope from penetrating to the riches which it conceals. A dull preacher may flatter himself that he has communicated the truth; but he has not communicated it, for no one has received it, and in rhetoric, communication implies not merely the giving by one man, but also the taking by another. We have perhaps heard a sermon on the shortness of life, and have almost felt, while it was "long drawn out," as if the sermon itself were almost as long as it represented life to be; but again have we heard a sermon on the same trite theme, and have been startled at the discovery of time's wonderful rapidity, seeming to have never thought of the thing before. The style of our Saviour was preëminently distinguished by wrapping the most novel beauties around the most ordinary subjects; but if any one will look into bishop Wilkins's Ecclesiastes, or into Claude's Specimens of Rhetorical Discourses, he will wonder at the great pains-taking of some men to make their discourses chiefly useful, as trials of the patience and tests of the submissive

---

* Aug. de Doctrina Christiana, Lib. IV. Cap. 11.

temper of the laity. The physician of the body and the physician of the soul have seemed to differ in one point of their practice, the former sweetening his most nauseous pills, the latter concealing the sweetest aliment beneath a distasteful exterior. Mr. Lye, a minister of the seventeenth century, in a sermon on 1 Cor. 6: 17 says, "these terms I shall endeavor $\sigma\grave{\nu}\nu$ $\theta\epsilon\tilde{\omega}$ clearly to explain." He then explains the text in thirty divisions, "for the fixing of it on the right basis," and adds, "having thus beaten up and levelled our way to the text, I shall not stand to shred the words into any unnecessary parts, but shall extract out of them such an observation as, I conceive, strikes a full eighth to the mind of the Spirit." He then subjoins fifty-six additional topics, making in the whole eighty-six divisions. Another preacher of the seventeenth century, Mr. Drake, published a sermon of one hundred and seventy divisions, to which are appended "sundry queries and solutions," and to all these is added the asseveration, that the writer "has passed sundry useful points, pitching only on that which comprehended the marrow and substance." The regular structure for the "improvement" of a discourse has been, to divide it into several heads for the use of edification, several for the use of direction, several for the use of reproof and self-examination, several for the use of exhortation, and, says Flavel in his sermon on England's duty, "it remains that I shut up all with a use of consolation." *

But of what use in stimulating the heart are all these applications, their unwieldly frame-work making them so unnatural and inexpressive. How soon will an audience who have sat sluggishly under such prolix discourses, " prick up their predestinating ears," when a subject is announced with directness and simplicity, and they see in a single sentence the nucleus of the whole sermon. An unlettered preacher, famed for dexterity in interesting an unlettered audience, took for his text the address to Noah, "thou shalt come into the ark," and proposed to draw practical instruction from the life of Noah by considering, "into what, from what, for what, with what, by what, Noah was to come;" this sudden and comprehensive, though singular announcement roused the curiosity of the rude listeners, and opened their minds to receive the truth, which when thus inserted would never drop out. How similar the division here adopted by a natural orator, to one adopted by Father Bernard, and long

---

* See Claude's Essay, Robinson's notes, Vol. I. p. 45.

celebrated in the schools, but of which the natural orator had never heard. The text was, "The Lord himself shall descend from heaven with a shout, with the voice of the archangel and the trump of God; and the dead in Christ shall rise first." The division was, "Who will descend? Whence? Whither? When? How? For what?" The freshness and liveliness of such a plan will quickly wake up the dormant inquisitiveness of an audience, engage their interest as well as attention; and the nature of the heart is such, that unless it do not merely attend but attend with interest and zeal, it will not be radically benefited. Truth is indeed the grand instrument of moral effect, and is adapted to produce all effects that are needed, but still it becomes operative, only when it has obtained full possession of the heart. It is the entrance of the divine words which giveth light; therefore they must be adjusted so that they will enter. If the city is to be razed by the besieging army, the army must first find means of getting within the walls, perhaps by a Trojan horse. If the stubborn disposition of man is to be riven by iron, the iron will not work well unless it be wedge-like in its form. Fair and smooth must the truth be, if it would glide easily into the soul's recesses; there must be no juttings out of cant phrases, rude technicalities which roughen the whole sentiment, and increase the friction of its passage. Let a preacher adopt the rule of Cotton Mather, "to crowd into his discourse as much matter as he can without producing obscurity," or let him roughcast his style by such phrases, as man's lapsed state, law-works, creature-comforts, heaven-pleasing frames, unspeakableness, worldly-mindedness, and the thousand arbitrary terms with which many Puritan sermons are crowded; he will leave his hearers as little profited as the benches which they sleep on. But let him file off unseemly excrescences, expel common-place remark and words haunted with stale associations, and let him exhibit his subject in a transparent covering, it will be seen, felt, perhaps loved. Compare the operose and awkward circumlocutions of John Owen, with the directness and pungency of Richard Baxter, and you will not wonder why the Saint's Rest is destined to live forever as a devotional classic, while the excellent treatise on Spiritual-Mindedness, even after the numerous rescissions upon it by Porter, is read from a sense of duty. Hervey's Meditations are valuable, but how many times must a sober man sigh in reading them? Cecil's Remains are written in a man's style, and the first time of reading them is an inducement and a preparative for the second. There is a sermon on "the way to be saved," preached by Dr. Edwards of Andover, and afterwards published by the American Tract Society, which will impart to a common audience a better system of religious truth, than volumes written on the same theme by some good English divines, who no sooner obtained a weighty thought, than straightway they hid it, as if for safe keeping, under a clumsy paraphrase, and whose deep instructions are now so highly prized, partly because it is so difficult to get at them through the superincumbent rubbish of words. These writers have notably reversed the advice of Usher, " to back all practical precepts and doctrines with *apt* proofs from the holy Scriptures; avoiding all exotic phrases, scholastic terms, unnecessary quotations from authors, and forced rhetorical figures; since it is not difficult to make easy things appear hard, but to render hard things easy, is the hardest part of a good orator as well as preacher."

2. The nature of truth is such that it cannot be taught without scrupulous attention to the manner of teaching. The figure of any thing is the thing itself figured, and the configuration of a doctrine is the doctrine itself in its just arrangement. To separate the mode of stating a truth from the nature of it, is to separate the contour of an image from the substance of it. The theologian flatters himself that he does the solid work at the quarry, and when he has hewn out a block of marble he throws it to the rhetorician, with the assurance that all is done except the very trifling labor of finding the statue, which lies hid somewhere in the block. It may however be asked, what is the effect of the statue, if there be abstracted from it the new manner of its existence which was given it by the sculptor's chisel? It is indeed true, that the stones, and the brick, and the wood, and the mortar, and the iron are the substantial parts of a house, and the conformation of these parts, is but a shadow; yet if this intangible conformation be taken away, there is some question what becomes of the house. "There is but one indivisible point, says Pascal, from which we should look at a picture; all others are too near, too distant, too high, too low. Perspective fixes this point precisely in the art of painting," and I may add, rhetoric fixes it in the art of preaching. The minister who disregards this doctrinal perspective, who, so be it that he really hold out the real picture, cares not in what light he holds it, nor how its lineaments are reflected to his people, will often show

them nothing but truth, and yet make them see nothing but error. He may tell more falsehoods without a single false assertion, than a false teacher would tell without a single true assertion. An audience will form a loftier apprehension of God, by hearing from some men the degrading notion that he is not a sovereign, than by hearing from others the ennobling truth that he is one. The truth is cast in the mould of error, and the error is cast in the mould of truth; as the material of Apollo's statue may be fashioned into one of Laocoon. There is a valuable class of writers, who in their exhibitions of divine sovereignty, have conjoined it so constantly and intimately with God's power and his right to be a sovereign, that the truth has seemed a hard and harsh truth, grating on the puny sensibilities of man, and leaving him motionless and awe-struck. Their representations will quadrate with the rules of an empirical logic, but are sometimes painfully discrepant with an elevated rhetoric. Their favorite doctrine, proved with so much acuteness, would appear far more amiable, and in its high meaning far more correct, if it were blended more closely with God's love, his regard to the welfare of creatures who need a sovereign. It is not an Almighty Monarch counselling for his own glory, and contriving for his own pleasure, because he has the right to do so; but it is a kind Father who sees that his own glory will be the highest happiness of the universe, and who retains his sovereignty not because it is *his* sovereignty, but because it is excellent and amiable. The matter of the doctrine is the same, yet it is more seemly, if you set it under the mild and soft shining of the Divine benevolence, than if you keep it in the light of such justice as is a consuming fire. The matter of the doctrine is the same, yet it does not appear so, when on the one hand it is folded up in a sable pall, and on the other hand is lightly shaded with a becoming gauze.

Next to the reflection upon one truth of the objects associated with it, is the proportion in which the truth is exhibited. One might suppose from reading the works of some excellent divines, that God is a being determined to make all other interests subservient to his own, and therefore causing men to act just as they do act, punishing them for sins which had been decreed as necessary for his glory, and last as well as least, a God of benevolence who has made atonement for man. These divines never say that this is the apposite representation of Jehovah, nor do they utter a word which implies that they have thus misunderstood the genius of the Gospel; but they insist on the sterner truths in such vast excess, they make election and reprobation so prominent, that grace and redemption are hidden from the view, and the lamp of mercy, instead of diffusing its radiance over and through the whole system, is like "a light that shineth in a dark place," "and the darkness comprehendeth it not." These writers by no means fail to light the candle, but they seem to think that if it be only lighted it may be put any where, under a bushel or a bed. They forget that in some matters position is every thing, and that the minutest disorder of parts is the subversion of the whole. It is indeed essential to a watch that it contain all the wheels, but yet the slightest removal of a single wheel from its proper place makes the whole machine go wrong.

Even if the tangible truth of a doctrine be not lost by infelicities of manner, the influence of it may be. The most cheering and ennobling theme may appear gloomy and dismal, by associating it with uncongenial elements, or by swelling it into a monstrous and unnatural size, or by introducing it at the wrong place or wrong time, or by some such contortions of its form as shall hide the body of the truth under some of its protruded members. So too a doctrine which is authoritative and imposing may appear like a plaything, if a single feature be made more or less prominent than justness of proportion allows. It is said that Apelles, taking the portrait of Antigonus, who had lost an eye, painted his face in profile that he might hide the blemish; and some preachers, it is feared, present an expressive doctrine in profile, and thus hide its true significancy.

There is a grandeur, sublimity, and awe in the idea of benevolence disinterested; of entire self-renunciation and self-crucifixion for the honor of the great God. Dr. Channing, in allusion to the theology of his early teacher, Dr. Hopkins, says; "His system, however fearful, was yet built on a generous foundation. He maintained that all holiness, all moral excellence consists in benevolence or disinterested devotion to the greatest good; that this is the character of God; that love is the only principle in the divine administration. He taught that sin was introduced into the creation, and is to be everlastingly punished, because evil is necessary to the highest good. To this government in which the individual is surrendered to the well-being of the whole, he required entire and cheerful submission. Other Calvinists were willing that their neighbors should be predestinated to eternal misery for the glory of God. This noble-minded man demanded a more generous and impartial virtue, and maintained that we should consent to our own perdition, should be willing ourselves to be condemned, if the greatest good of the universe, and the manifestation of the divine perfections should so require. True virtue, as he taught, was an entire surrender of personal interest to the benevolent purposes of God. Self-love he spared in none of its movements. He called us to seek our own happiness, as well as that of others, in a spirit of impartial benevolence; to do good to ourselves not from self-preference, not from the impulse of personal desires, but in obedience to that sublime law, which requires us to promote the welfare of each and all within our influence. I need not be ashamed to confess the deep impression which this system made on my youthful mind. I am grateful to this stern teacher for turning my thoughts and heart to the claims and majesty of impartial, universal benevolence."* But how completely has the idea of disinterested love, been desecrated, its dignity and moral impression lost, by a current mode of stating it. Whatever of magnificence belongs to the idea has been compressed into a short and sour phrase, "men must be willing to be damned," a phrase too laconic to express the real truth, and sometimes so uttered as to express a state of heart quite foreign from magnificent; a phrase which was once uttered by the celebrated Dr. B———y in such peculiar circumstances and with such impatience of tone, that it was understood as a provocation to personal banter, and called forth a reply too taunting and even profane to be inserted here: a phrase which, when uttered as well as it can be, would suggest the idea of severity and roughness as often perhaps as that of dignity and grandeur, and would seem sometimes to contravene the spirit of the Bible, which in its anxiety to make us willing to be saved does not, so prominently as some human systems, insist on the need of our being willing to be lost. It is nearly all a fault of mode, rather than of substance, by which disinterested submission has appeared so dissonant from rational and cheering love, and it is a signal specimen of the transforming magic of mere shape.

It is a great and grievous fault of the pulpit, that rhetorical theol-

---

* Discourse delivered at the Dedication of the Unitarian Congregational Church in Newport, R. I. July 27, 1836. By William Ellery Channing, p. 37.

ology is not appreciated. There are men who seem to regard the evangelical system, as it is exhibited in our standard doctrinal treatises, as worthy of a transfer to the pulpit, yet one of the best of these treatises devotes, and that without logical impropriety, seventy pages to the "doctrine of angels," and sixty to the fundamental theme of "the conditions of human salvation." A creed or a catechism is admired by some as embracing the vitality, because it shows the outline of the Bible; and the rugged system of question and answer, with which truant children are frightened, is thought to be the same thing with those words of pleasantness which drop as honey and distil as dew from the sacred page. But the notions, so frigidly and distortedly aggregated in our doctrinal compends, are one thing; the notions so beautifully and gracefully diffused over the sacred page are another thing. They are spirit, they are life. It is not enough when physicians send the hypochondriac to a distant watering place that he say, I have the same waters bottled up in my cellar, a chemical analysis detects the same mineral qualities, and they are so much the better for being old. There are ten thousand influences, swarming in the free air of his journey, which are essential though evanescent parts of the promised panacea. There is a spirit in theology, and though the matter of it may endure a rough handling, the spirit is ethereal, delicate, shrinking. The least roughness of temper or of tone discomposes, disfigures it. The very breath which utters a truth may taint it, as a polished surface is clouded by breath. The very gestures which enforce it sometimes mar it, as a dew drop is spoiled by a touch of the fingers. The very expression of a speaker's eye blends itself with his subject, and goes out with it, a part of it, as the fragrance of the fruit.

But it is said, we must take the constitution of theology as it is, and not strive to make infringements upon it by catering for the depraved tastes of men. Truth is truth, and so must be preached, unreservedly, as a savor of life unto life, or death unto death. Just as meat is meat and so must be administered, faithfully, to infants and giants, the consumptive, the plethoric and the asthmatic, and all simply because — meat is meat. Now the safer and the more sober way is to deny the fact; meat is not meat; in certain circumstances it is poison. Truth is not truth, often falsehood; proved by reason, demonstrated by revelation, and yet falsehood. Practically, as it will be understood, in its actual impression, in its essential bearing, it is so. It is no more truth, than music is music to one whose auricular nerves are so disordered, that the softest harmony grates harsh discord. It is no more truth, than smoothness to the man is smoothness to the insect that wonders at the mountains on the smoothest marble. Truth in its proper conformation and adjustments, in its nice adaptedness to the mind and alliance with congenial feeling; *that* is truth, that only. We have all, perhaps, heard sermons, crowded with orthodoxy condensed, and yet all that was noble and vivifying in truth, (for truth is the great and free original of which orthodoxy is but a cramped epitome), was so far from these sermons, that we could think of nothing but the dead eyes on an anatomist's table; not a humor is wanting, not a lens; each ball is perfect, but where is gone the spirit of the eyes, the power, the brightness, the expressiveness, the every thing save the cold matter and the frightful stare?—We may believe in the doctrine of human ability; but when we hear it preached in exclusion of the doctrine of human dependence, we need not believe in it, for though the earth is acted on by a centrifugal force, yet it does not move as if it were acted on by the centrifugal force alone. We may believe in baptism, and in the holy catholic church; but when these subjects are protruded into notice, as Moses used to be read, every Sabbath-day, we need no more believe in them than think that man's body is his soul. We may have faith in the Scriptures of the Old and New Testament, but when we hear them recited with scowlings of face, with barbarous and immoral tones, with fierce rheumatic gestures, we may justly doubt whether the Maker of mind ever breathed out such sentiments as these readers are scolding out.

We come now to the second branch of our subject, the means by which we may obtain the best mode of presenting truth. These means are various, but they are all modifications of the general one, a vigorous prosecution of study under the influence of pious emotion. It may not be amiss, however, to specify a few particulars.

In the first place, if we would preach in the right manner, we must faithfully consult the mental state of our hearers. To say that we must study the philosophy of mind is only to say that we must study the principles of rhetoric. We must not be content with mental science in general, for we do not adapt our discourses to mind in general. A sermon written for every body, is like a coat made for every body. There is an adaptedness in truth to every congregation, distinct from its adaptedness to all congregations, and our duty is to search out this distinctive adaptedness. "A word spoken in due season how good is it." An article of food to a man in sickness is not exactly the same thing, as that same article to the same man when in health; and a doctrine presented to an audience who are not hungering for it, is not exactly the same thing as the same doctrine presented to the same audience when they are longing for it. It seems as if the same truth became two different truths, when preached to men in different states; and as if the same man became two different men, scarcely knowing each other, when he is under the influence of different emotions. We are to preach not to the man as he was, but to the man as he is. A sermon which penetrates through the intellect to the heart, which is drank up by the heart as the thirsty earth drinketh up the rain; a sermon which is so timely that it seems to be a counterpart to the heart itself, each being imperfect without the other; which in familiar phrase goes to the very spot, and is just the thing, this is a true sermon. If it be a consolatory discourse, it comes to a family who were bereaved the week before, with a significancy in every sentence, but appears vapid and perhaps false to a family immersed in worldliness. In making our discourses not only true but *seasonable*, says Dr. Owen, "consists no small part of that wisdom which is required in the dispensation of the word." The advantage of a stated over an itinerant ministry, the advantage of preaching at home rather than on exchange is this, the pastor knows his flock, and is known of them; he can meet the exigency, can strike the very chord which will vibrate, need not preach as "one beating the air." Robert Hall in his memoir of Mr. Toller says, "It was not his practice to devote much of his time to ministerial visits. In justification of this part of his conduct, he was accustomed to quote the apostolic injunction; "Is any sick among you, let him *call* for the elders of the church."* But as God has in every thing else conjoined our interest with our duty, and made one duty facilitate another, so also in this, he has not only made it the duty of a minister to visit his people, but has made this duty the great aid of rhetorical labor. It is by coming in direct contact with mind, that the preacher learns how to address it; by hearing

---

* Hall's Works, Vol. II. p. 405.

the simple statements of his people, that he learns whether his communications are understood, whether he is giving to every one the portion which is needed. New themes for the pulpit are forced upon his mind by every conversation; new attitudes and developments of the same theme; his preaching thus becomes various, graphic, distinctive; it solves particular doubts, eases particular pains, and by thus benefiting the individuals benefits the aggregate. Says bishop Hall, "the minister must discern between his sheep and his wolves; in his sheep between the sound and the unsound; in the unsound between the weak and the tainted; in the tainted between the nature, qualities, and degrees of the disease and infection; and to all these he must know how to administer a word in season." In thus analyzing the character of his parishioners, he is performing a duty to them; yet he is also acquiring for himself a fresh and original system of mental science, more practical than any which can be learned from the books, fitting him better and therefore better for him, as David's sling was more useful to the shepherd boy than Saul's armor. I have heard of a minister who preached to a people with whom he was not acquainted, and his words, all well meant, were like firebrands to them; why he knew not, but they were incensed at his audacity, and when he afterwards learned, that the village which he thus stirred up to mutiny had long borne the opprobious epithet, Sodom, and that the villagers were peculiarly sensitive to this which they deemed a slanderous misnomer, he wisely concluded that he would thereafter always inquire into the peculiarities of his audience, before he read to it his unfortunate sermon from the text, "up, get you out of this place." This is but one instance on a small scale, of the evil which results on a large scale, from inattention to the prejudices, the capabilities, the whole state of a people on whom we are to operate.

We have read perhaps of the statue chiselled according to the rules of art, but falling and breaking to pieces, as the sculptor was in the act of fixing it on its somewhat crazy pedestal, and what a poor consolation it was to the amateur, to know that his palace contained a newly bought statue, perfect in every respect, save that it was reduced to fragments while they were putting it up. But ah! how many doctrines, wrought out with great toil, and proportioned with all skill are precious above rubies while retained in the minister's mind, but when transported to a mind of different structure and attempted to be fixed there, spoiled by the roughness of the transportation or by the weakness of the pedestal.

So essential is it for a preacher to consider not only the tendencies of the thing to be communicated, but also the peculiar fitness of the mind which is to receive the communication. Ministers, a half century since, were fond of alluding to the "jealousy" of God, but the popular associations with the word jealousy make it expressive of an attribute far from divine. They were fond of referring to the "vindictive justice" of God; and by this they meant his *vindicative* justice, that which vindicates the power of his name, and ensures the welfare of his universe; but the common associations with the word vindictive make it a most unfair appellation for the benevolent equity of Jehovah. From their own minds these preachers sent forth a pure doctrine, but into the minds of others, they put something so bruised and broken as to lose its former lineaments. We have heard of John Adams's stamp act, a very good thing in itself perhaps, but suggesting to a jealous people another stamp act, which imparted its nature to all of its name; and so when we have heard from some ministers that God is the author of sin, we know that this phrase, whether it were designed to express the truth or not, will be a conjurer to call up only dark and terrific suggestions, and to make the real meaning of these ministers invisible, amid the crowd of misshapen meanings which will fill the field of vision. If a preacher is determined at all events to be "faithful" and to declare the whole counsel of God, it were better to declare it in the Hebrew language so that it may not be understood, than declare it in such perverted terms, that it shall be ruinously misunderstood. True faithfulness does not consist in throwing out all doctrines at random, but in teaching so that men shall understand. "And it came to pass in Iconium, that they went both together into the synagogue of the Jews, and *so spake* that a great multitude, both of the Jews and also of the Greeks, believed."*

We intend no more than the truth when we say, God has decreed that men shall act as they do act; but some congregations hearing this, understand us to say, God has ordered their actions just as Augustus ordered "that all the world should be taxed," and they imagine that whatever they do is but obedience to the divine decree, like a subject's obedience to the decree of his king.

---

* Acts 14: 1.

So soon then as we discover their close association of statute or command with decree, we shall, if we be wise to win souls, introduce qualifying epithets, or else select our terms from a less obnoxious vocabulary, and show the same truth but not through the same refracting and discoloring medium. We mean to exalt the government of God when we say, he permits sin; but some men, hearing this, understand us to imply that God permits sin, just as an earthly ruler permits sabbath breaking or profaneness, that he allows and favors it. Both they and we are shocked with this idea, and when in order to justify the ways of God to man, we explain our meaning by the apology, as it appears to some, that he forbids sin in itself considered, but prefers it, all things considered; gives his revealed will against it, and keeps his secret will for it, we excite in many minds the suspicion of divine duplicity. Not that we harbor the least of such suspicion; not that we intend to insinuate the merest shadow of it, but we are using words which are two-edged swords;—suggesting philosophically one thing, and in popular prejudice another thing. Terms which are fit in scientific discussion may be fatal in popular address. We may walk about in a powder-magazine safely by day; but the torch which we carry into it to see by at night may conduce to other ends beside vision.

Secondly; in order to present a doctrine in the proper manner, the preacher must secure the moral influence of it upon his own heart. As the moral tendencies of the Bible are internal evidence of its truth, so the moral tendencies of a doctrine are a forcible argument for it, and he who, in his preaching, most clearly develops these tendencies, gives, other things being equal, the most conclusive proof of the doctrine. The old adage is not strictly true, Quod procedit e corde, redit in cor; for many a fanatic gives vent to effusions no less sincere than they are inoperative upon minds less fanatical than his own, and many a philosopher expresses his elevated emotions to men who simply gaze and wonder. When however the preacher has properly consulted the state of his hearers, then it is true that, his own heart being instinct with the spirit of his doctrine, the hearts of his hearers will answer to his, as face answereth to face in water. Then it is, that he may for a time forego attention to forms of style, and let the thought, fitly revolved and duly felt, find its own way out. Its own way will be the most natural, and of course the best way. As the beauty of a tree may be increased by trimming its branches, but still more by enriching its root, so a sermon may be made complete, not so much by adjusting its phrases, as by cultivating the emotion from which all its phrases should germinate and grow up. The intellectual influence of a doctrine upon the preacher's mind may make his sermon logical and weighty, but the moral influence of the doctrine upon his heart is all that can save the sermon from being abstract and inefficient. It is said of John the Baptist, that " he was a burning and a shining light ;" " ardere prius est," remarks an old writer, " lucere posterius, ardor mentis est, lux doctrinae." A man, under the exciting influence of a moral truth, will have thoughts and illustrations and words which seem to drop into his mind from above. It is not he that speaks, but the truth which speaks in him. He almost seems to be inspired. It was in allusion to such bright hours that Cicero said, " there never was a great man who did not at some time receive inspiration from the gods," and that so many sages of old represented poets as " losing sight of rules of art, and borne away by the divine impulse." In allusion to the same thing, it was remarked of Paul, that "he was the companion of wisdom, but the leader of eloquence ; he followed the former, but went before the latter, not rejecting her that followed," and his eloquence was perfect because, instead of being coldly sought after where he might by chance find it, it was the free emanation of his piety that burned, and of course heat came from the fire. His eloquence was representative of his subject. Any man who lets a doctrine lie on his heart until the influence of the doctrine is transfused through his heart, will shape all his words in the likeness of that doctrine; his soul being full of it, his mouth will speak it, and nothing foreign from it ; his transitions, his metaphors, his arguments, will all be tinctured with the one pervading and transforming truth which he designed to portray. The sermon is then symbolical of its theme ; a picture of it ; of course, its manner is just what it should be.

A deservedly popular preacher, in one of our cities, gave notice from the pulpit, that, on the succeeding Sabbath eve, he would discourse upon the theme of the final judgment. An immense concourse assembled to hear the sermon, thus publicly notified. An exquisitely solemn piece of music introduced the services. A short prayer, full of devout adoration, followed. The preacher announced his text, the impressive description of the last day given in Matt. 25 : 31—46. All eyes were fixed upon him. Each hearer seemed to anticipate and even to wish a pungent and thrilling appeal. But in less than ten minutes from this imposing introduction, the preacher began to vociferate, his action became vehement, his tone querulous, it was evident that something went wrong, and the fact was, he was preaching not upon his subject, but upon the common indulgence in tea and coffee; detailing the expenses of their daily use at breakfast and supper, and describing their injurious influences upon the stomach and nervous system. Is it asked, by what process of legerdemain he let himself down from the elevated theatre of an assembled world, to so small a thing as a culinary preparation? His transition was not illogical. He desired to prove, that we shall be judged not only for what we have done, but also for what we have left undone; that we shall not be able to excuse our omission of pecuniary gifts by the plea that we have nothing to give, for we may both prolong a useful life, and save money for the poor, by retrenching the superfluities of the table; and then to the condemnation of such superfluities, tea and coffee among the rest, he devoted a conspicuous part of his promised sermon on the judgment. His perceptions were clear, his heart was enlisted in the cause of benevolence, but it was not absorbed by the doctrine which should have raised it above the poor contents of a china cup; it was not assimilated to that sublime doctrine; the doctrine did not look through him, through his style, tones, and gestures; something else had interested his feelings, and an honest indignation at the money wasted in popular narcotics, led his mind from the dread tribunal which ought to have engrossed it, to a dietetic prescription, which probably did more hurt than good. Every minister should remember, that he is in some respects like the animal which is said to take its hue from the last object it touches, and when his mind has been in close contact with any theme, it catches the coloring of that theme, exhibits itself in that coloring, and of course exhibits the theme. He should be careful in preparing his discourse to touch nothing but his subject, lest he lose the tincture of it. Let him so revolve it in his mind, that meditation shall rouse up feeling, and then feeling though subsequent to thought, shall yet direct the train of it, as the rudder though at the stern of the ship directs the course of the prow.

Says Robert Hall, in his charge at the ordination of his nephew, "An excellent man was so impressed with the doctrine of the divinity of Christ, that he made it the constant topic of his ministry; every sermon he preached was crowded with proofs, or answers to objections, relating to this important topic; and the result was, that most of his hearers became Arians and Socinians! This effect was not such as he expected, or as might be thought of at the time by others; but the consequence was natural. Such discussions produced, first a dry, speculative attention to the subject, then a fiery, contentious spirit in discussion; in this state the spirit of the doctrine was lost, and the people sunk into such a frame of mind as is suited to the reception of these, or any other heresies that might be sophistically presented to them."* Now the origin of the monotonous and polemic style of this preacher was, not that he thought too much, but did not think in the right way, did not receive into his heart the feeling appropriate to his thoughts. The emotions properly excited by the doctrine of the Trinity will bear a man onward in spite of himself, to the related themes of the atonement, the death it saves from, the life it provides; of human depravity giving occasion for the atonement; of regeneration made necessary by depravity, possible by the sacrifice of the Second Person, and actual by the operation of the Third Person in the Trinity. The minister "*cannot but speak*," as opportunity will permit, of all such themes, when he is rightly and thoroughly affected by either of them; and he will speak not as an attorney, bent on carrying his argument, but as in Christ's stead beseeching men to be reconciled to God. The feeling he manifests becomes an essential part of his teaching; it is itself a proof distinct from all other proofs, and sometimes superior to all. Multitudes have been convinced by the excellence and appropriateness of the feeling, who had remained unconvinced by the solitary applications of syllogism. "There is," said bishop Wilkins, "a common relation to this purpose of divers learned men, who having a great while, with much argument and strength of reason, contended with another about persuading him to be baptized, he being learned also could well evade all their arguments. At length a grave pious man amongst them, of no note for learning, stands up and bespeaks him with some downright affectionate expressions, which wrought so effectually upon the other, that he presently submitted; yielding this reason, Donec audiebam rationes humanas, humanis rationibus repugnabam; caeterum simul atque

---

* Hall's Works, Vol. II. p. 478.

audivi Spiritum loquentem, cessi Spiritui. And 'tis storied of Junius before his conversion, that meeting once with a countryman as he was on a journey, and falling into a discourse with him about divers points of religion, he observed the plain fellow to talk so experimentally, with so much heartiness and affection, as made him first begin to think, that sure there was something more in those truths than his rational human learning had yet discovered; which occasioned his more serious inquiry into them, and afterwards his conversion. Such great power is there in these cordial expressions."*

Thirdly; another means of obtaining the right mode of religious teaching is, an imitation of the best models. There is a kind of imitation which enslaves, but another kind which elevates the mind. As the Pythian priestess, after a thorough purification in the waters of Castalis, sat on the tripod in Apollo's temple, and was there inspired by the evaporations from the subterranean cave, so he who sits with a pure heart at the feet of masters in eloquence becomes ravished with the spirit breathed out from these masters, and exhilarated as he could never be without this communion with the favored few. It is a remark of Augustine, that "if a man have an acute and fervid mind, he will acquire eloquence more readily from reading or hearing eloquent men, than from practising on the rules of eloquence." Though in theory rhetorical art is founded on rhetorical science, as every art is founded on science; yet in fact the art of rhetoric was practised before its rules were formally expressed, and these rules were suggested not a priori, but by an induction of rhetorical specimens, which were exhibited before rhetorical rules as such were ever thought of. By noticing the effect of certain modes of address, philosophers were apprized of principles on which every address should be modeled, and if the orations of Demosthenes or Cicero will suggest principles of secular eloquence, so will the sermons of Chrysostom, or Barrow, or Hall, or Whitefield suggest the principles of sacred eloquence. A critical analysis then of such discourses as have been followed by marked results, will suggest the principles on which these results have been produced; and these principles may be abstractly stated in the form of rules, or, which is far better, their excellence may be infused into our own style by a rational imitation. We do not become servile

---

* Ecclesiastes, 252, 253.

copyists of a model by seizing and retaining its spirit. When we imitate the manner which experience has proved to be most efficient, we make the manner as natural to us as it was to its authors; and any slavish mimicry, any constrained resemblance to the letter is the very thing, which makes our imitation unworthy of the name. We cannot become like an author by deviating from his ease and naturalness. We must resemble him in his independence of thought, and originality of feeling. Our imitation of his essential excellences cannot be too strict. "Such imitation," says Longinus, "is not to be looked upon as plagiarism, but as lifting our souls to the standard of the genius of others, and filling us with their lofty ideas and energy." Men may imitate foolishly to their hurt, as they may think foolishly to their ruin.

If the compositions of uninspired men are in a judicious way to be imitated, much more are those of the inspired. Holy writers, composing as they were moved by the Holy Ghost, adapted their words to the nature of mind, just as the Framer of mind, who knew what was in it, prescribed; and if we conform our words to the general principles of the scriptural model, we shall conform them to a philosophy divinely sanctioned, and of course successful. The more thoroughly we shape our discourses according to the great features of the pattern shown us in the Bible, so much the more divine will be their structure. Indeed, the imitation of the scriptural model in its essential features, is not only a rhetorical requisite, but a moral duty; so that there was more reason than one or two for the precept given to an old Swiss reformer, " si vis fieri bonus concionator, da operam ut sis bonus biblicus." It is indeed to be lamented, that the biblical manner, in distinction from the biblical matter of instruction, is not more attentively studied. It is a fruitful though too much an untravelled field. Could there be as an integrant part of theological education, a faithful inquiry into the intent and bearings, the order and relation, the primary and ultimate effect with which the sacred penmen have discussed each doctrine of the Bible, a new variety, vivacity, and power would be imparted to the teachings of the pulpit.

It is to be distinctly understood, that the most important means of acquiring the right mode of exhibiting truth is an imitation of the scriptural mode, that the scriptural mode is to be imitated in its general principles without deviation, that in its specific details it is also to be imitated, save where a cautious judgment detect valid reasons for an exception, and that there can be no such reasons, whenever these details express the same shade of meaning and produce the same moral effect, which they did when the Bible was written. It has, however, been insisted upon by some, that we must adopt the minutiae of the scriptural mode invariably, and must preach in all respects as the sacred writers wrote. This minute imitation betrays so much reverence for the Bible, that to discountenance it will appear to some imprudence at least. Yet the charge of imprudence may be hazarded in opposing any principle, which, though false, is received as true, and which, though not generally defended in form, exerts a general but tacit influence in cramping the originality, and repressing the free impulses of the pulpit. We wish a rigid virtue but a pliant eloquence; close and straight lines for the conduct, but an easy and spontaneous flow for those thoughts and emotions which persuade men to godliness. And when we search into the causes of the constrained, and unbending, and timid rhetoric which has so long been complained of in the church, we find one of these causes to be an attempt, uncommanded and unnatural, to imitate the minute details which are so excellent as to have received the sanction of Inspiration, but which, like other details of style, can be imitated only by coërcing the mind. The writer is enslaved and cannot write well, who compresses the spring and elasticity of his own spirit in copying the unessential features of any model, no matter what the model is. It may then help to throw us back upon those elements of mind, which must have their free activity in every orator, to consider the grounds for believing, that while there can be no exceptions from the rule to follow the general principles of the inspired manner, there may be frequent exceptions from the rule to follow the minute details of it.

First, it was the great principle of the sacred penmen, to accommodate themselves to the particular state of the individuals whom they addressed. They wrote for man, in the language of man, in the manner of man; yet not of man in the abstract, but men in particular; not primarily for the whole world, in all ages; but primarily for the world as it was when they wrote. Their manner in its great features was designed for, and adapted to the whole race; but in its lesser details, to the particular tastes and prejudices of particular communities. This is a fundamental principle of interpretation; and if it had been observed, metaphysicians would not have reasoned from the Bible, as if it had been written for the schoolmen ; nor visionaries as if it had been prepared for spiritualizing enthusiasts, nor would commentators have found in it so many meanings which its authors, while on earth, probably never thought of. It has too often been interpreted as if it were written in the universal language proposed by Leibnitz, whereas it *could* not have been clothed in such a costume ; and, though the peculiarities of its style are better fitted to its purpose than any other peculiarities would be, yet they make it necessary, in the nature of the case, that some sentiments should not be "conveyed in just the form which we should have chosen," and that there should be in the Bible "some things of which we cannot see the utility." *

The constitution of the race remaineth the same ; and therefore the general principles of the biblical mode, which were adapted to this constitution, have the same authority now which they ever had. The minute fashions of the world pass away ; and therefore those minute details of manner, which were adapted to obsolete or provincial fashions, have relaxed their claims for specific imitation. Those same wise men who adopted Asiatic allusions for the Asiatics, Jewish phraseology for the Jews, would not probably reject American allusions were they to write in America for Americans, and might omit some oriental hyperbole, were they to write in Scotland for Scottish logicians. A phrase needs qualification now, which did not eighteen hundred years ago; would Paul refuse to qualify? An explanation was demanded then, which is not now. Paul yielded to a demand, which then existed; would he now yield to a demand which does not exist? It is an old truth, expressed thus in a Chinese proverb, "a wise man adapts himself to circumstances, as water shapes itself to the vessel which contains it ;" now Paul was a wise man, he displayed his wisdom in shaping to the peculiarities of Philemon a very elegant epistle ; and would he now, were he to write a new epistle for a German gymnasium, shrink from adapting his style to the peculiarities of that gymnasium ? Would he deem it an irreverent innovation upon the inspired model for him to become all things to all men, that he might by all means save some ? Would he not now pursue the same plan which he did pursue originally, teaching the same truth to different classes of men, but in styles as

---

* See Lowth's Lectures on Hebrew Poetry, Stowe's Edition, Lecture II. Note A.

different as those different classes required? And if we refuse to accommodate our style to the peculiar necessities of those whom we address, do we not deviate from the first great principle of the scriptural manner? And can we conform to the essentials of that manner, without varying from it in its unessential details, as far as the condition of our people varies from that of ancient orientals?

It was the design of Him who inspired the sacred penmen, that they should suit their style to the peculiarities of the people whom they originally addressed, and therefore should not minutely imitate each other, but should each preserve a distinctiveness by introducing things new, as well as old. The style of the book of Judges is no more like that of the Pentateuch, than the taste of the Hebrews in Samuel's day, was like their taste in the time of Moses. Hosea no more squared his words by Isaiah, than Thomas Boston did by Pascal. Matthew and John varied from each other in their style, as much as they are represented to have done in their personal appearance. When the Jews were in danger of idolatry, David said, " the law of the Lord is perfect, converting the soul, making wise the simple, rejoicing the heart, enlightening the eyes, more to be desired than gold, yea than much fine gold, sweeter also than honey and the honey comb;"* and he said it without qualification. When the Jews were in danger of relying more on the law than on the Gospel, Paul said, " if they which are of the law be heirs, faith is made void, and the promise made of none effect: because the law worketh death; for where no law is, there is no transgression:" "I had not known sin, but by the law; for without the law sin was dead," the ministry of the law was the "ministration of death," " of condemnation," and " that which was made glorious had no glory in this respect by reason of the glory which excelleth."† Now there is not the shadow of a contradiction between the meaning of David and that of Paul; but there is as great diversity in their style as there was in their circumstances. The same may be said of Paul and James, who believed the same doctrine of faith and works, but yet wrote so differently that Martin Luther was for excluding the pretended epistle of James from the canon, and heaped upon it such epi-

---

* Psalm 19: 7—10.

† See Rom. 4: 14, 15. 7: 7, 8. 2 Cor. 3: 7—11. See also Calvin on 1 John 5: 3.

thets as he would now wish no one to repeat. Peter criticised the letters of one apostle as containing "some things hard to be understood," and did not seem to suppose that his own letters were, in this respect, an imitation of Paul's.

Nay the same writer differed from himself, as he addressed men in different circumstances. Paul's manner of alluding to the advent of Christ was not the same in the second epistle to the Thessalonians, with his manner in the first, and did not produce the same impression. The reasoning in the epistle to the Hebrews differs so widely from the reasoning in the epistle to the Romans, that pious and able critics have attributed the two epistles to different men; and no one will say that John's Revelation, clothed as it is in dark and terrible grandeur, was fashioned in the likeness of his bland epistle to the elect lady. Now if the sacred writers differed from themselves and even the same writer from himself, whenever the circumstances of the people required it, then certainly we may imitate them in making our style dependent somewhat upon the circumstances of an audience, even when we must differ from our models in such unessential particulars as they differed in, among themselves.

Even the quotations which the writers of the New Testament made from the writings of the old, were not always made literally; but the style of them was accommodated to the new associations of the apostolic age. A passage originally intended for one thing was often accommodated to another,* and originally expressed in one way was often expressed by the apostles in a very different way.† No one will pretend, that the criticism in Gal. 3: 16, was designed by Paul to develop the Hebrew meaning of זָרַע in distinction from its plural זְרָעִים; it was designed merely as a rhetorical comment well suited to attract the attention and the confidence of his readers.

There was often an accommodation of argument as well as phrase to the ephemeral peculiarities of the persons addressed, and an accommodation of such a kind as is not exactly after the models of occidental logic. The Jews said, that Christ cast out devils by Beëlzebub; we believe this to be a calumny, but

---

* Compare Hosea 11: 1 with Matt. 2: 15, and Jer. 31: 15 with Matt. 2: 18.

† Compare 2 Sam. 7: 14 with 2 Cor. 6: 18; also 2 Cor. 6: 17, 18, and more especially Matt. 2: 23 with the corresponding passages in the Old Testament.

we should not undertake to prove it calumnious by saying, that the ascription of Satanic influence to Christ was an equal ascription of it to the Jews themselves, who also cast out devils. Nobody now supposes that exorcism was performed by the Jews, therefore nobody would be affected by such reasoning; but when the wisest of all teachers was on earth, this reasoning was a triumphant appeal to the superstition of his accusers, and he evinced his wisdom in adopting it.* There are various trains of argument in the epistles which were admirably adapted to the minds of the early Christians, and without which the epistles would not have been good specimens of eloquence; yet we shall have no occasion to adopt those trains, until there shall be a reäppearance of the men who had never been influenced by the "Regulae Philosophandi," but had been beguiled by the peculiarities of Jewish tradition. Should the churches of New England begin to doubt, whether the priesthood of Christ be superior to the Levitical, we should not attempt to convince them by saying, that Melchisedek was a representative of Christ, and that Abraham meeting Melchisedek paid tithes to him, and received a blessing from him, and that the payment of tithes was an acknowledgment of Abraham's inferiority, and that "beyond all controversy the inferior was blessed by the superior," and that Abraham, being inferior to Melchisedek, must of course be inferior to Christ the antitype of Melchisedek, and Abraham himself being inferior, much more must his descendants be so; because, in the first place, the descendants of a man can never be exalted above their ancestor, and, in the second place, all Abraham's descendants were in him, and of course paid tithes when he paid them, "even Levi himself, who receiveth tithes, was tithed in Abraham; for he was then in the loins of his ancestor, when Melchisedek met him." This argument was once used by Paul, and very wisely used, in order to convince men, who could be convinced by no other means, that Christ's priesthood was superior to Levi's. The apostle did not design that we should introduce this argument into our logic, until we were obliged to reason with such logicians as surrounded him. Says professor Stuart, "we do not need to be addressed and reasoned with in all respects, as they (the ancient Hebrews) were. Many of their prejudices we have not, many of their doubts with respect to the superiority of Chris-

---

* See Matt. 12: 27. Luke 11: 19.

tianity, over the Mosaic religion we never entertained. Many things then, which were said with great force and propriety to them by our author, cannot be addressed to us with the *same* pertinency, nor felt with the same power." " It is hazarding nothing to say, that we now have more convincing arguments than those here used to establish the superiority of Christ's priesthood. But let it be remembered, we owe them to the New Testament which we have in our hands, and which the Hebrews had not."* While we say that such trains of reasoning as the above need not be imitated specifically, we also say that they must be imitated in their general principles. One of these principles is, that if we cannot convince men of the truth by arguments which are in themselves valid, we may resort to arguments which are in their relation valid, to the *argumentum ad hominem* for instance; we may suit our reasonings to the people, when the people cannot be benefited by reasonings suited to the general mind; and the very same principle, on which inspired men accommodated arguments to the Jewish people, allows our accommodation to a people more scientific than the Jewish; and plainly there must be some difference between an argument suited to a logical, and one suited to an illogical age. If we imitate essentially the sacred writers, we shall not argue with a deist in the technical forms which Paul used with the Jews, but shall contend for the same truth, and adopt the same principle of accommodation with Paul's; and, so far as we do this, shall deviate from those details of style, which are suited only to an ancient Jew. It were well to have it understood, that the imitation of a model is the imitation of the spirit of it, not the letter, for the letter killeth, but the spirit maketh alive. This leads to a second remark :

Second, the minute and specific imitation of the inspired model will prevent us from being faithful to that model. It is the characteristic of every valuable book, and especially of the inspired, to suggest many ideas, which it does not distinctly express; and we cannot fully develop its richness, if we venture to do nothing more than intimate where it has intimated, and imply just as tacitly as it implies. We must, if we are faithful, follow out its suggestions, and go, not merely where it goes, but also where it points. The Hebrew language had but few words, the Greek

---

* See Stuart's Com. on Ep. to Heb. Excursus 14; also his explanation of Heb. 7: 1—10.

of the New Testament, retaining the Hebrew idiom, shared also its indigence: of course the inspired men who used these languages, were obliged to pour forth their thoughts in figures of speech, and we, with our copious vocabulary, must analyze and spread out the hints which lie coiled up in these figures.

The fact is, we cannot now communicate the exact idea of Scripture, by conforming exactly to its specific modes. If we should say, without explanation, "though ye have lien among the pots, yet shall ye be as the wings of a dove covered with silver, and her feathers with yellow gold;" or, "for this cause should a woman have power on her head, because of the angels," we should say what is unintelligible. The meaning of a thousand passages depends on allusions which were once, but are not now easily understood; and if we imitate those passages exactly, we are not faithful to their meaning. A paraphrase is essential to the communication of their import, and yet a mere paraphrase is by no means an exact imitation of the Bible. That valuable work, Doddridge's Family Expositor, in attempting to exhibit the specific manner of Inspiration, has lost the essential excellence of that manner; and is about as good an image of its original, as a dead body is of a living. Indeed every mere paraphrase dilutes, benumbs, and deadens the text; and so becomes a monument of the fact, that there is no such thing in our day as a specific imitation of the Bible; the paraphrase being itself a deviation from the biblical style, and in its awkward attempt not to deviate, representing that style as vapid and spiritless. Arias Montanas, and, in less degree, Jerome, endeavored to copy the exact mode of the sacred writers, and therefore gave to their versions the character, not so much of a paraphrase as a metaphrase; but the consequence was, that "they often exhibited to their readers what had no meaning at all, and sometimes a meaning very different from, or perhaps opposite to that of the sacred penmen;" and showed that "it is impossible to do justice to an author or to his subject, by attempting to track him, and always to be found in his footsteps."* The man who should now, in speaking of his maligners, quote the language of David, would he be unfaithful to the spirit of David's imprecations? The minister who should now in reproving an audience, imitate the Saviour's reproof to the Pharisees,† or John's reproof to the "generation of vipers,"

---

* See Campbell's Four Gospels: Dissertation 10, Parts 2 and 3.
† Matthew xxiii. etc.

would be unfaithful to the whole spirit of those reproofs. The words of an inspired and an anointed man have sometimes a meaning and a power, which the same words from an uninspired and an unanointed man can never have; and though the impression which they made, "when spoken with authority," was true and good, the impression which they would make now, when spoken by frail preachers, would be false and fatal.

By imitating the Bible where it was never designed to be imitated, we are unfaithful not only to its true meaning, but also to its commands. It enjoins upon us, by precept and example, to " be wise as serpents," to be " wise master-builders," " to write according to the wisdom given unto us," "to teach men in all wisdom, to search out acceptable words," and to speak them " fitly." Now the " wisdom which is profitable to direct," is exercised in adapting means to ends; in meeting new emergencies with new appeals; and repelling objections before unheard of, with replies before unheard of. It is exercised in plying the Moslem with arguments different from those, which would convince an ancient idolater; and in reasoning with a French mathematician in a style more scientific, than the Bible has ever exhibited. It is exercised in such a consideration of the character of men, that "being crafty we may catch them with guile ;" not indeed with tricks and chicanery, but with a prudent deference to all such prejudices as, innocent in themselves, may be so managed as to become inlets of the truth. We must be faithless to all the scriptural injunctions of wisdom, unless we *invent* modes of doing good, as well as *discover* modes already invented. In vain shall we try to search out specific precedents in Revelation, for every kind of rhetorical appeal; and if we refuse to address the intellect and heart in any style, which the Bible has not specifically adopted, we must disobey its command to speak the word in season. The Bible was never designed to supersede the exercise of ingenuity, or of original thought; to discourage independent investigation into the mode of removing present difficulties, and encourage nothing but the study and adoption of former modes of removing past difficulties. It does not define man, more than reason defines him, to be *nothing but* an imitative being ; nor does it define itself to be a book for *nothing but* imitation. If we try to honor it as something to be only copied, we fail to honor it as the word of life, designed to quicken, impel, inspire. Indeed when we exalt the Bible as any thing which it does not claim to be, we do not really exalt it at all. Much as the pious man loves to pass encomiums on Revelation, he passes no sound encomium, when he extols it as a perfect system of Geology, Chemistry, Astronomy, Mental Philosophy, or Rhetoric. Some modern reformers have adopted a very plausible style of paying deference to nature, by saying, that as nature does not bolt the wheat, nor extract the alcohol, nor expose to view the gold and pearls which minister to human vanity, therefore we should not. But this is merely plausible. The same nature which, in the words of Anacreon, " has given to bulls horns, to horses hoofs, to hares fleetness, to men understanding," designed that her gift of understanding should be employed sometimes in modifying her other gifts; and nature is honored, not disparaged, by the natural but transforming processes of the mind. So too the same Being, who gave to us a written revelation, gave wisdom to apply it; and designed the difficulties in applying it to be one means of our religious trial. It is a principle of the divine administration, that man shall use his discretion and task all his powers in the application of the divine gifts. Else had the earth yielded fruit spontaneously. Else had the Bible been written, so as never to become a stone of stumbling and a rock of offence. This leads to another remark.

Third, it would be very strange if Revelation had prescribed the minute details of rhetorical mode, when it has not prescribed the minute details of moral duty. It has in morals and in sacred rhetoric, exhibited general principles, and left us to apply them specifically, as conscience and reason may judge proper. It has commanded us not to kill, and yet has given us a right to take life, whenever sound discretion shall deem it necessary for the public good. It has commanded us not to swear, and yet has given the right to take an oath, when the operations of justice require it. It has commanded us to resist not evil, but turn the left cheek to him who smites the right; and yet has left it to our own moral sense to determine, in view of this command, when we shall repel force by force, and when "appeal unto Caesar."

The examples not less than the precepts recorded in Revelation are indeterminate of moral minutiae. We have no right to do every thing which Moses, or Joshua, or Paul, or John did. The Saviour is the only man whom we are commanded to imitate in all things, yet our imitation of him must be general, and not in all cases specific. Shall they for whom an atonement has been made, act always as he did, who made the atonement; and shall there be no difference between the course of those who hope to leave earth for heaven, and the course of him who had left heaven for earth? It is a false rule that we should always conduct as the Saviour did ; not until we are in the circumstances in which he was, can we do so. Our rule is to conduct as he would, were he in our state. It has often been said that Jesus wept, but never laughed ; if this were a fact, it would only prove, that the peculiar circumstances of the man of sorrows shed a peculiar pensiveness over his character, and does not prove that he would have resisted every joyous tendency of his nature, were he a mere man, instead of being the Son of God and the Son of man. On the other hand, it is often said, that the Saviour came eating and drinking, and so was accused of being "a gluttonous man and a wine-bibber, a friend of publicans and sinners." But what if our Lord did associate with publicans and sinners, "does it follow," asks Robert Hall, "that we, who are placed at so infinite a distance beneath him, would be safe in such a contagion?"[*] And what if he did adopt a system of diet, so unlike that of John the Baptist, does it follow that it would "be safe for us to imitate this part of his conduct?" Are we able to drink of the cup of which he drank? If we say we are able, we deceive ourselves, and the truth is not in us. Because our Saviour, while yet a child, startled his mother by his disputes with aged doctors of the law, because he spent whole nights in prayer upon the mountains, because he submitted to the insults of a profligate court, when he might easily have evaded them, we are not therefore to do the same things, unless we can prove that our peculiarities are the same with his. Says bishop Taylor, "our blessed Saviour fasted forty days ; we cannot: he whipped the buyers and sellers out of the temple ; we may not, without the authority of a public person : he overthrew the tables of the merchants, but the young man in Portugal, who being transported with zeal and ignorance, beat the chalice and the sacrament out of the priest's hand, out of passion against his idolatrous service (as he understood it), had a sad event of his folly amongst men; and what reward of his zeal he found with his Maker is very uncertain."[†] Indeed we do not feel obliged in all cases to follow the specific modes of inspired men, even in regard to the ceremonials of our religion. While we deprecate all useless

---

[*] See Hall's Works, Vol. III. p. 483.

[†] Taylor's Works, Vol. XII. p. 456—7.

innovation upon these modes, while we prefer to retain them unaltered, so far as scriptural wisdom permits, we yet in many cases adopt merely their general intent and expressiveness. We are not bound to partake of the sacrament in an upper room, in a reclining posture, after a hearty meal; to eat the same kind of bread, or drink the same kind of wine with the twelve apostles. We are not bound to partake of it every Sabbath, nor every day, nor several times in a day, as they are thought to have done. If men in a warm climate, to whom cold bathing was a frequent luxury, and whose tastes in reference to personal exposures were oriental, performed the rite of baptism by immersing the body, we need not follow that specific mode, if we conjoin the same purport and significancy with a different mode, proper for us, as theirs was for them. If now we must use our discretion, as well as our memories, in performing moral and ceremonial duty, shall we not use it in reference to the manner of preaching? or is rhetoric more sacred and immutable than morals; and the means to make men good more unaccommodating, than goodness itself? While every man should adhere to every scriptural form, so far as propriety allows, he may sometimes drop the unessential, that he may retain the essential parts of that form.

"Whoever," says Dr. Paley, "expects to find in the Scriptures a specific direction for every moral doubt that arises, looks for more than he will meet with." It were indeed a great relief to the indolence of men, to have their path prescribed so exactly, that they may trace it without any effort of their own. It were far easier to *be brought* to a conclusion, how much we should disburse in charity, than to be obliged to *come* to a conclusion, by a painful contest between benevolence and covetousness. It were far easier to learn from some sign in the heavens, how far we may indulge in pleasure, intellectual or sensual, than to learn it by a slow comparison of reasons for and against indulgence. But God designs that we shall work out many of our own conclusions, so that we may be kept from idleness, the parent of vice; and he designs that we shall have a part of our probation in laboring to discover duty, as well as in our treatment of duty when discovered. Indeed a greater part of the trial of some men, as bishop Butler has well observed,[*] consists in their preparatory inquiries into the reality of virtue, than in their subsequent reception or rejection of the

---

[*] Analogy, Part II. Chap. 6.

virtue inquired into. So it were much, more pleasant, for a minister to have a model which he might copy without any tedious exercise of discretion, than to be obliged to try his reason and his piety in ascertaining where and how to copy. But the Head of the church has not singled out the sacred office for a sinecure to its occupant, nor has he designed that preachers should be exempt from the probation involved in determining how to discharge duty. They are on trial, and therefore things are not all made ready at their hands. They need the moral discipline, which they find in deciding how to rightly divide the word; in their decisions they manifest their pride or humility, reverence for God or fear of man; and for these decisions they are accountable to Him, who hath given them talents, not to be hid in a napkin, but to be used. 't is indeed true, that they may be betrayed by this latitude of manner into an improper style; so are they betrayed by the generalness of moral precepts into improper conduct. Here is the trial of spirits. A faithfully improved mind, an humble heart, will in either case lead them to the right; indolence or irreligion will lead them to the wrong. It is a deeply solemn truth, that the right mode of preaching "is set for the fall and rising again of many in Israel, and for a sign which shall be spoken against; that the thoughts of many hearts may be revealed."

Fourth, the good sense of preachers has frequently led them to sacrifice the details to the main principles of scriptural rhetoric. As they have not thought themselves required to write in the Hellenistic Greek language, because the apostles did, or to preach in the open air, or in a sitting posture, because we have reason to believe that the apostles often did; or to appear with a "bodily presence weak and speech contemptible," because Paul modestly intimates that his appearance was so regarded by the Corinthians; or to fall prostrate on the face, beat the breast, and rend the garments, because the prophets accompanied their words with such corporeal excitements; as in fine they have not often felt obliged to imitate the external mode, so they have not always felt obliged to imitate the intellectual mode of the inspired orators, in all its details. It is indeed often said and truly, that we should give to every doctrine the same prominence and proportion, which it has in the sacred volume; yet in the application of this general truth, the prudence of men has been properly exercised. No modern preacher spends so great a portion of his time as Paul spent, in proving the inefficacy of the Jewish ritual, or the impropriety of converting the Lord's supper into a sensual feast, or the folly of expecting the immediate dissolution of the world. The apostles preached in times of persecution and peril, and to new converts who needed comfort and solace. Their preaching, therefore, was more consolatory in its general strain, than the preaching of the present day ordinarily is, or should be. In the full tide of ecclesiastical prosperity, men need to be cautioned more than consoled, and so great a proportion of soothing address as was required of the apostles would be less relevant to our state, than a greater proportion of testing and trying address than was required of them. When religion is popular, there is more danger of self-deception; when religion is unpopular there is more danger of open apostasy; the apostles opposed the latter danger more prominently than the former; and, in imitation of their spirit, we oppose the former danger more prominently than the latter. As God teaches by his providences and by the pulpit-ministrations of his servants, it is but reasonable that the pulpit should administer the less comfort where the providences of God are all comforting; and should urge less to self-examination, where the trying providences of God are themselves a refiner's cupel.—The doctrine of the Trinity is taught in the Bible with great freshness and beauty, "here a little and there a little," each part of the doctrine seeming new, and the whole of it involving a variety that charms, and breathing forth a moral spirit, that is itself an argument. But we, who do not wear the loosely flowing robes of the orientals, may preach on the Trinity in a style more compact, scientific, and even scholastic. We may, do, sometimes must; and when it is objected that the word Trinity is not found in the Bible, we only reply that the Bible was not written in a scholastic age, and we are glad it was not.

Infidels have made strenuous objections to the phraseology of the Bible in its descriptions of Deity, and to the sentiment, as well as the style, of many scriptural addresses to Jehovah. We justify all that the sacred writers have said to and concerning the Deity. It is as it should have been. When we accuse uneducated Christians, now living, of irreverence in their prayers, we often do them injustice; for what would be irreverent in us, is often reverent in them. So when infidels condemn the invocations of ancient saints, they forget entirely that the poetic character, the oriental associations, the whole attitude of those saints required of them certain peculiarities, which we might imitate were we in their stead.

But because we *might* in other circumstancs, it does not follow that, in our present circumstances, we must offer prayer in the style of Ps. 69: 21—28. 109: 6—20. 137: 8,.9 ; or that we must use such metaphors, in reference to God, as are found in Ps. 44 : 23. Hosea 11 : 10, and numerous other passages, which are, in a good but peculiar sense of the term, inimitable.*

There is an infidel tract, of which it were hard to say whether sophistry or blasphemy were its chief characteristic, which contains several prayers expressed in the language of Scripture, and feigned to be offered by an occidental and an uninspired man. But this is slander against the Bible; for such prayers have a very different meaning with us, from what they had with the ancient prophets. This is slander against modern Christians; for their good sense has taught them in these cases, to deviate from the style, so far as their condition differs from the condition of inspired men.

It is not because modern preachers are irreverent, that they do not construct their sermons on the plan of the Canticles, nor introduce certain terms which the apostles introduced with perfect propriety, nor read to their congregations certain passages, which were wisely adapted by prophets to tastes very different from our own. The most strenuous advocate of minute conformity to the scriptural model, endeavors, if he be a reasonable man, to teach the truth, the whole truth, and *nothing but the truth*, and therefore avoids in *fact*, whatever he do in *theory*, certain quotations from the Bible, which were expressed in language exactly right for ancient Asia, but suggesting now something more than the whole moral truth. Reasonable men remember, that the Bible was not written in the English language. But all are not reasonable men; and I therefore remark in the last place,

Fifthly, that when preachers have attempted an undeviating conformity to the details of scriptural rhetoric, they have often done injury. I have heard a minister pray,—" if it be for thy glory sink the wicked still lower in hell," and he justified himself by saying that David offered a prayer somewhat similar; but forthwith there went abroad a suspicion that the minister was deranged, and he certainly was in this prayer. I have heard a man preach on the subject of moral reform, in such a style that he incurred very strong suspicions of being himself in need of moral reforma-

---

* See Lowth's Lectures on Heb. Poetry, Stowe's Edition, p. 62.

tion; yet he justified himself by saying, that all his expressions were used by inspired men, who wrote however before the expressions became objectionable, as well as before the English language came into use. Evil, nothing but evil is the result of such preaching. Our moral reformers must walk on sandals; and wash their feet whenever they enter a house; and cleanse their hands, if nothing else, whenever they eat; salute all their friends with kisses; must become orientals externally, before they venture to become such in their free reprimands of an almost nameless vice. By their literal quotations from the Bible, they often do injustice to its spirit, and by their original descriptions, so exuberant, transcending even the liberty of the East, they do gross injustice not only to the spirit, but also to the letter of the pure word. On the other hand, when men denounce as unscriptural all agencies established for resisting a particular vice, and say that the modern pulpit should be, like the apostolic, exclusively devoted to preaching by a Gospel minister, and not at all to lecturing by an agent, to preaching Christ and not at all to the distinct exposure of an overt evil, as licentiousness, or slavery, or Sabbath-breaking, or intemperance, then we may admit our deviation from apostolic example, without acknowledging an error either in the apostles or in ourselves; and before we abandon any system of agencies, we demand the proof that the mode pursued by twelve inspired missionaries, in the first century, is to be the specific mode for twelve thousand uninspired ministers, in the nineteenth century; and this proof can only be given by showing, that the modern system of beneficence is no more adapted to do good now, than it was eighteen hundred years ago. As soon as this is shown, and perhaps in some instances it may be, the ill-adapted system must be abandoned.

There has been and is a painful dispute in the church, concerning the scriptural authority for certain "new measures." It is sometimes said that they have no scriptural authority, just as if an apostle never countenanced protracted meetings, or early admissions into the church, or an itinerant ministry: and again it is said that they have scriptural authority, just as if any apostle ever encouraged whispering meetings, and anxious seats, and censorious, preaching prayers. Both parties are right and both wrong, in some respects; and both will continue to dispute until they unite in the imitation of the broad apostolic principle, to adopt all and only those measures which, from their relation to the human mind, and the genius of the Gospel, promise to do, not merely good, but permanent good.

It is said by some, that the apostles preached against all litigation before the national courts; if this were true, it would not follow, as some injuriously pretend, that we should preach against all appeals to our national courts; for our courts are so different from the heathen, that objections against these are not equal objections against those. It is said by some, that the apostles never preached against political slavery, and therefore the time will never come when we can properly preach against it. But may there be no reason why a few men, supported by few and feeble churches, introducing a new religion, and struggling against many peculiar obstacles, should be silent on a political theme; and yet should "change their voice," whenever the government became less despotic, freedom of speech less hazardous, and the probability of success in their labors for emancipation less decidedly negative? Might not Paul recommend to American apostles, at some future time, if not now, a course which himself, as a Roman apostle, could not pursue? Is not the question partly one of expediency; and will not a rigid adherence to apostolic example, whenever the apostle's difficulties shall be surmounted, make the pulpit less efficient than was Paul's in exterminating slavery? Is silence when we can speak, the same in significancy, as silence when we cannot speak without becoming slaves ourselves?

It is said that the apostles banished from their preaching all metaphysics and philosophy. This does not happen to be true, but even if it were, would it follow that men who have read the Novum Organum, should be addressed as the men who had not; and that we may not reason philosophically with philosophers, just as Paul reasoned judaistically with Jews? But it is further said that the apostles not merely rejected human science, but also positively condemned it; and because Paul urged upon the Colossians to "beware lest any man spoil them through philosophy and vain deceit," and upon Timothy to "avoid profane and vain babblings and oppositions of science falsely so called," therefore we should urge upon men to guard against scientific curiosity. But we forget, in our condemnation of human reasonings, that the philosophy, which Paul condemned, was mere cabalistic jargon; that the general spirit of it was developed by the frivolous judgments "in meat, or in drink, or in respect of a holy-day, or of the new moon, or of the sabbath days,"* and that modern philosophy, being itself a revelation from God, and being the handmaid of true religion, being adapted to exalt the Creator, and abase the creature, is not to be either condemned or neglected, simply because the apostle discountenanced a "philosophy falsely so called." The application of the inspired remarks on "φιλοσοφία" to the philosophy of our day, is about as wise as would be the application of the remarks against speaking in an unknown tongue to our speaking in the English language; for our language was as much unknown in Paul's time, as our philosophy was then "a vain deceit." Metaphysical and scientific disquisitions are indeed censurable, when not adapted to the character of him who reads or hears; but when we censure them merely because the apostle censured the books of Jewish wisdom, which were books of mere mummery and impertinence, we entirely mistake the purport of the apostle, and imitate the form, at sacrifice of the substance of the Bible. Indeed the condemnation of a false philosophy is an eulogium upon the true. There are many instances like these in which literal imitators are essential perverters of the Bible, and the stiff copying of the picture becomes, unintentionally, a caricature.

From time to time preachers have appeared, who hesitated not, in their pulpit addresses, to call their hearers hypocrites and liars; and when the indignant congregation have remonstrated against such incivility, their remonstrance has only provoked new assaults, and they have been aspersed for dislike of faithful preaching, and unwillingness to hear the very words of Christ. Christ did indeed in one instance apply the word ψεύστης to his hearers, and in several instances the word ὑποκριτής, but both of these words have in our language a peculiar odium of meaning, which they had not in the sacred Greek; and "for this reason" says a judicious translator, "I have in some instances considered it as no more than doing justice to the spirit of the original, to soften the expression in the common version, though otherwise unexceptionable."* And yet what if the great preacher did call his hearers not only dissemblers but hypocrites, not only false speakers but liars, do the Jewish

---

* See Rosenmueller, on Col. 2: 8, 16, and 1 Tim. 6: 20.

† Campbell's Four Gospels, Diss. 3. § 24; also Notes on Matt. 22: 18 and John 8: 55.

scribes and pharisees, whom he reproved, live in America; and if they did, could they be profited by the same words from a subaltern which might be profitable from the captain of their salvation? There have been preachers too of an opposite class, loving to prophesy smooth things, disbelieving the cardinal doctrines of the evangelical system, but yet ministering to congregations who were attached to those doctrines. If these preachers had abstained from all allusions to the principles of orthodoxy, or if they had avowed their disbelief in these principles, they would have forfeited the confidence and the pecuniary support of their people; they therefore deemed it prudent to adopt the minutiae of scriptural style, and whenever they alluded to the character of Christ, or the depravity of man, used the words of inspiration. Their hearers could not certainly object to the language of the Bible, and were for years unsuspicious of the real faith of their pastors, and would have remained unsuspicious until this day, had they not found out that every man, who believes the Bible, believes every doctrine which it teaches, and that men of every faith will subscribe to the Calvinistic, or Arminian, or any other creed, provided it be expressed in scriptural language. Who does not believe in election, total depravity, regeneration, and at the same time the opposite doctrines; in eternal punishment, and universal salvation, in the sense in which they are taught by the sacred word? and if a man, when his craft is in danger, refuses to give his creed save in the terms of the Bible, and will only say, that he believes in what the sacred writers meant by those terms, he shows a kind of reverence for the scriptural mode, which would be thought more sincere, if it were associated with more apparent reverence for the modes of honesty. Not that the language of inspiration is itself equivocal; but different sects have established such different interpretations of it, that he who would learn the meaning of a scriptural creed, must learn from other phraseology, how the creed-maker interprets his quotations. When therefore Mr. Brown of Haddington says, "God hath made me generally to preach, as if I had never read another book but the Bible; I have essayed to preach scriptural truths in scriptural language," he could not mean to recommend, that none but scriptural phrases be employed in our expositions of doctrine. He could not mean to recommend a style of preaching which would conceal heresy, and allow hearers to interpret as variously as they speculated.

The rhetorical character of the Bible must be understood, before we can decide how far to imitate its forms of style. It is composed in great part of letters, history, and poetry. Its letters are worthy of the inspired apostles; but the style of a letter to be read, must be somewhat different from the style of a sermon to be spoken. Its history is admirable; the calm unimpassioned narration has always been extolled; but how would it appear for the religious orator to describe the Saviour's sufferings, with no more emotion than was proper for the faithful historian?. The poetry of the Bible is perfect; yet discourses in prose are not to be moulded in strict conformity to it. We cannot preach in acrostics as some of the Psalms were written, nor can we adapt a sermon, as some of them were adapted, to the singing of alternate choirs; nor would the scriptural paronomasia comport with modern views of pulpit dignity. The simple truth is, the Bible is not a sermon, but a book.

When we examine the different rules, which are given for the structure of a discourse, we find that they cannot be interpreted, as requiring a rigid conformity to the scriptural mode in its details, without involving a contradiction among themselves. It is an excellent remark of Mr. Bridges, that in our sermons we are "to form alike the doctrine, the statement, and the terms upon the divine model," and also that "our Lord's pungent addresses to the scribes and pharisees exhibit the boldness of christian ministrations;" and yet this same author says, that "even the courtesies of life never restrained our Lord from his office," and he would doubtless sanction the rule, that our sermons should never violate the courtesies of life.* It is a precious remark of Witsius, "that the things of God cannot be more fitly explained than in the words of God. The man greatly mistakes, who presumes that he can explain the mysteries of Divinity more accurately, or more clearly, or more powerfully, or with greater aptitude of instruction than in the trait and phrases, which, after the example of the prophets, the apostles used, as being dictated by Him who formed the mouth and tongue of man, who "fashioneth the hearts of each," and therefore best of all knows the method of instructing and touching the heart." It is an equally precious remark of bishop Ridley, "In those matters I am so fearful, that I dare not speak

---

* See Bridges on the Christian Ministry, Vol. II. pp. 17, 76, 78. First American Edition.

further, yea, almost none otherwise than as the very text doth, as it were, lead me by the hand." In the application of this remark, Mr. Bridges says, "Inferences that appear to be strictly legitimate, must be received with the greatest caution, or rather decidedly rejected, except as they are supported by explicit Scripture declarations.'"* On the contrary, that eloquent preacher, Dr. Dwight, advocated the rule, that we should preach on various subjects, not explicitly discussed in the sacred volume. He says: "There are many duties incumbent on us, which are neither expressly commanded, nor expressly declared in the Scriptures." According to the principle that nothing is our duty, which is not thus commanded or declared in the Scriptures, "women are under no obligations to celebrate the Lord's supper, parents to pray with their children or families, or to teach them to read; nor any of mankind to celebrate the christian Sabbath; nor rulers to provide the means of defending the country which they govern, or to punish a twentieth part of those crimes which, if left unpunished, would ruin any country." "Such a code of instruction," as the Bible, "every man of thought will perceive must lay the foundation for a great multitude of inferences. Of these some will be distant and doubtful; others, variously probable; and others still, near and certain. Those which are included in the last of these classes, are ever to be received as being actually contained in the Scriptures, and as directing our faith and practice with divine authority."†

It was a well known rule of Augustine, that a "christian orator in uttering what is just, good, and sacred, must endeavor, as far as he can, first to be understood, next to please, next to secure obedience;"‡ yet he supposes that the sacred writers sometimes followed an opposite rule, to which their successors should not conform. "Although," he says, "we have quoted from the inspired authors some passages which may be understood without difficulty, yet we must not suppose that these authors are to be imitated by us in those things, which they have spoken obscurely. Their obscurity was useful. They resorted to it that they might exercise and perfect the minds of their

---

* Bridges on the Christian Ministry, p. 17.

† See Dwight's Works, Middletown ed. Vol. V. pp. 288, 289; also p. 26.

‡ De Doc. Christ., Liber IV. p. 32.

readers; might repress pride; and stimulate the diligence of those, who wished to learn; might veil the minds of the irreligious, so as to convert them to piety, or seclude them from mysteries. Indeed they spoke with this obscurity, so that their successors, who should rightly understand and expound them, might receive a different grace, unequal indeed to that of the sacred writers, yet corresponding with it and honoring it. Their expositors therefore ought not so to speak, as if they would set up themselves to be expounded with similar authority; but in all their discourses they should labor principally and chiefly to be understood." * The great principle on which Augustine would reconcile his two assertions, that the scriptural style is just what it should be, and that many deviations from it are just what they should be, is stated by himself in the following language. "As there is a kind of eloquence appropriate to youth, and another kind appropriate to old age; and as that style cannot be called eloquent, which is not appropriate to the person of the speaker, so there is a certain kind appropriate to men, who are invested with the highest authority and are plainly divine. With this latter kind the sacred writers spoke; no other kind became them; to no other men is this kind becoming; for with their character is their style strictly congruous; but for others, it appears as much too humble, as it surpasses the style of others, not in mere sound but in solidity. Where I do not understand the sacred writers, their eloquence does indeed appear to be, but probably is not in reality, less powerful than where I do understand them. Even the obscurity of their divine and profitable words was mingled with such eloquence, as is adapted to improve our intellect, not merely by finding out their meaning, but also by the mental exercise in finding it."

It is said of the epistle to the Hebrews, "argumentative throughout, connected in the train of reasoning, and logical in its deductions, each successive link is interrupted by some personal and forcible conviction, while the continuity of the chain is preserved entire to the end;" and from the general example of Paul to interweave exhortation with argument, it has been inferred that "the method of perpetual application, *where the subject will admit of it*, is perhaps best calculated for effect."† On the contrary, it is the remark of Dr. Porter, that "the con-

---

* De Doc. Christ., § 22. † Bridges, Vol. II, pp. 47, 48.

vergent method; *where the subject will admit of it*," is best adapted to ultimate success; and that in proportion as the sermon admits a running application, it is the less likely, in general, to produce any single and strong impression on the hearers." * Now there is no more essential contradiction between the rule to defer practical appeals until the close of the sermon, and the rule of the apostle to make these appeals in the body of an epistle, than there is between the whole system of our sacred rhetoric and the whole manner of the Bible.

Legh Richmond says, " keep in mind that excellent rule— Never preach a single sermon, from which an unenlightened hearer might not learn the plan of salvation, even though he never afterwards heard another discourse." But it is very certain, that there are some books in the Bible, which when read once to an unenlightened hearer, would not teach him the whole plan of salvation, and it is very certain that the rules for unity and variety of style require us so to preach, that this plan will be sometimes only implied, and unenlightened men, in order to understand it, must hear us more than once. But because the Bible was not written, in all its parts, on this rule of Mr. Richmond, we are not to infer that the rule is essentially incorrect; it is expressed, like other aphorisms, in a laconic and sententious manner, which, like the manner of the Bible, admits the specific qualifications of a sanctified judgment. Augustine says that " all those who rightly understand what the sacred writers utter, understand at the same time that they ought not to have uttered it in any other manner."† Yet the same author modestly says, that the last clause of Rom. 13: 14 "does not appear to him to flow, in the original Greek, melodiously," and that " the sacred writers, he is inclined to believe, avoided that species of beauty which results from melodious clauses."‡ But notwithstanding this commanding example, he approves of the rule, that christian preachers should not shun, but rather cultivate a musical style, and says of himself, " while in my own discourses, I do not omit attention to rhythm more than modesty compels, yet I am the more pleased that I find it very seldom in the sacred writers."§

It has been objected to views like the preceding, that the business of determining what are the general principles and

---

* See Porter's Lectures on Homiletics and Preaching, pp. 159, 166.
† Aug. De Doct. Christ. Lib. IV. § 9.   ‡ Ib. § 40, 41.   § Ib. § 41.

what the specific details of the biblical style, what parts of it must be retained, and what may be accommodated, requires more wisdom than is given to man. But the difficulty of distinguishing what is, from what is not submitted to our discretion, is a theoretical more than a practical one. Good sense, sound piety, a love of truth, and faithful thought, will be sufficient to direct any one, who is worthy of the sacred office. Such criteria as the following, however, it may not be improper to suggest. The general principles of the biblical style, are those parts of it which are essential to communicate the exact biblical meaning to all men; the particular details of it, are those parts which were useful in communicating this meaning to the men originally addressed. The former are adapted to the general principles of mental philosophy; the latter to the peculiarities of the early Jews and Christians. The former are always congruous with each other, the latter are not. Thus the general principles of dignity, sincerity, suitableness of diction to thought, tendency to interest the moral feelings, all harmonize in the style of Mark and Ezekiel; but the cool and equal flow of the Gospel would not comport with the brilliant and sublime strains of the prophecy, and the interchange of their respective costumes would be congenial with neither of the books. The general principles suggest the appropriate details, and harmonize with only those which they suggest; the details therefore may, in particular circumstances, become incongruous, not only with themselves, but also with the generic rules. Thus it is one of these rules to give to every man a portion in due season, but there are certain occasions when men are plunged into difficulties never known before, and when they cannot receive their portion in season, unless the preacher vary from all details of style, which have been known before. Details, then, which had been proper in all other cases, are now violations of the general rule. Such inappropriateness is never seen in the Bible, but is exhibited often by men "unskilful in the word of righteousness."

readers of these pages. As Evangelical Religion advances in France and Switzerland it enlists and calls forth talents of no mean order. Already there are such men as Messrs. Grand Pierre, Audebez, the Monods (Frederick, and Adolphus), Félice (correspondent to the N. Y. Observer, and Professor in the Theological Seminary at Montaubau), Merle d'Aubigne, Gaussen, Verny, Vinet, and others who would do honor to the pulpit of any country. All of those who have been just named are authors, and some of them have earned a high reputation as such, in their own country. At a future day we hope to make them better known on this side of the water, at least to those who read the pages of this Review.*

* The discourses of Mr. Audebez, enumerated at the commencement of the preceding article, are for sale at the Bookstore of Mr. John S. Taylor, in New York. We hope that not a few of those of the readers of this review who can read French, will purchase them, not only for the benefit which they may derive from a perusal of them, but also for the sake of the excellent author, who has a large family to support, on a very moderate salary, and to whose education the proceeds of these publications are devoted.

ARTICLE VI.

Duties of a Theologian.

By Rev. Edwards A. Park, Bartlett Prof. Sac. Rhet., Theol. Sem., Andover, Mass.

The whole amount of influence, which ministers of the Gospel exert upon the community, cannot be ascertained. We can not measure all the good they do, nor all the evil they prevent. Yet so great is their number, so commanding their character, and so important are the stations they occupy in the pulpit and in the academical chair, that it is not invidious to pronounce them the most useful of all public servants. Their good influence is seen in the physical, the intellectual, the social, the moral, and the religious condition of the people. The means of this influence is Christian

Truth. This truth is instinct with life and power, and penetrates into the hidden places of the soul's strength. The nature of this truth, then, its tendencies and the modes of applying it should be diligently scrutinized. The more potent the lever for the moving of the world, so much the more needful to learn what it demands for its most effective use. The duty of ministers in relation to their parochial charge has been frequently discussed; not so frequently their duty in reference to theological truth. The design of the present article is, to consider some of the duties of a theologian, *as a theologian*, as distinct from a mere pastor or preacher. The duties of a theologian are the more important, as those of a pastor and preacher result and may be inferred from them.

One of these duties is, to pay a rational regard to the opinions which have been entertained by Christians in past times. It is idle to attempt the extirpation of any sentiment, that is essential to man as a complete man. The love of novelty, when too far indulged, may form a fickle and vain character; but in its legitimate influence it favors enterprise and progress. The sentiment of veneration for antiquity may be abused so as to cause a stagnation of spirit, but it may and should be used so as to produce stability and weight of character. We should leave the two sentiments to balance each other; should keep them in a healthy state, and subservient to a higher principle than either,—the love of the true and the good.

It is natural for man to speak the truth; it is equally natural to believe what others say. The principle of veracity is met and answered by the principle of faith; and as the veracity of man is found to be imperfect, so his faith in testimony must be correspondently modified. We should give most credence to such witnesses as have the best means for knowing the truth, and the purest desire of stating it. Hence we listen with deference to the voice of the faithful in all past ages respecting the fundamental principles of Christianity. It is not to be believed that the great body of pious men, desiring to learn what these principles are, enjoying the requisite powers and opportunities for learning them, sending up frequent entreaty for the teachings of the Holy One, having such near access in earlier times to the personal instruction of inspired guides, should have united, notwithstanding their numerous and diverse peculiarities, in a false estimate of the very genius of theology. The total depravity of the heart by nature, the need and the fact of regeneration by the Holy Ghost, our dependence on the Atonement of an Almighty Saviour, doctrines set forth so prominently as these on the sacred page, and falling so directly under the cognizance of Christian feeling, can not have been radically misunderstood by the mass of believers. It is then a filial duty of the modern theologian to address himself with fresh ardor to the writings of the fathers, and to derive from them a strengthened assurance in their and our fundamental faith.

But it is also his duty to discriminate between their authority in regard to an essential doctrine, and their authority in regard to an unessential one, or to a refined speculation. In our zeal against the Catholics we would not reprobate indiscriminately the standards on which they rely; for we depend in a measure on the same: and yet we recognize no obligation, like that pretended by the Oxford divines, to submit our faith on obscure and subordinate points to the dicta of any uninspired men, however ancient, however unanimous. We have heard too much of the real presence, of baptismal regeneration, of praying for the dead, to justify an implicit adoption even of the earliest human creeds. There are theories of doctrine more recondite and less distinctly revealed than the doctrine itself; they are not to be decided by the religious feeling, the authority of which is always venerable; their proof depends on a scientific discipline, such as the fathers never had, and on a minute analysis such as they had not the ability to perform. They lived before the rational processes of induction and the fundamental laws of belief had been very distinctly explained; they lived when the world was young, we live when it has grown mature; they are the youths of the world's history, we are the hoary headed men; and for us, after the experience of centuries, to go back to the infancy of time that we may learn the refinements of philosophy, is like a parent sitting at his child's feet, and asking questions that only a man can answer. "Although," says Bacon, " the position be good, 'oportet discentem credere,' yet it must be coupled with this, ' oportet edoctum judicare.'"*

---

* On the reverence due to antiquity, see Bacon's Works, Vol. 2, pp. 45, 46, 383, 384.

The theologian must also discriminate between the authority of *the mass* of believers and the authority of a few leading minds. We only impose on ourselves when we quote the decisions of the whole church respecting this or that metaphysical subtilty. The whole church never examined it, never held an intelligent opinion concerning it. It has always been the prerogative of but few men to search for the hidden principles of things. To only three or four high-aiming intellects in as many ages has it been given of God to rise above the confiding assent of the vulgar, and to look with naked eye upon the mysteries of doctrine. The mass of men have ever followed some independent thinker; they have believed what they were told, and like gregarious animals have gone where they were led. Nor have the mass of writers, ancient or modern, been quickened with the pure desire to see every fact just as it is. Their aim has been, not to learn the eternal principle, but to gather arguments for the belief of some intellectual master. The bent of all, save an elect few, has been toward partizanship, rather than toward truth; supporting a dogma rather than inquiring for reality. It is humiliating to notice the degree in which system-makers and commentators have successively borrowed not only the thoughts, but the illustrations also and the words of three or four dominant writers. Very far then should we be from regarding the authority of the Church, as precisely coincident with the authority of a few men like Origen and Jerome. To these few belongs the authority; they did the thinking; the rest submitted. One class submitted like the marshalls of Napoleon; they intelligently justified the gigantic schemes which they could never have devised. Another class submitted like Napoleon's soldiers; they waited to hear the word; they meant to obey it, and if need be to die for it, not because they liked it, but because they liked the man, and because, like or dislike, obey they must or suffer. And another and larger class submitted barely in not opposing; and they could not oppose, because they had read nothing and heard nothing either to approve or condemn.

The theologian must also scrutinize the degree of authority that belongs to each particular speculation of these masters in doctrine. He must consider their general character as men, must watch the influence of peculiar circumstances on their mode of speculating, and must remember that when a man theorizes in view of an exigency, he is inclined to meet that exigency whether he meet the truth or not. Athanasius made a book to prove that the unpardonable sin is nothing more or less than the denial of Christ's divinity. But before we can decide how much or how little deference may be paid to his opinion, we must remember how impulsive was the controversial spirit by which he was veering, far as possible, from the belief of Arius his rival in dispute. Augustine held some peculiar notions about native depravity; and the infelicities of his early life will point out the steps by which he came to those ungracious conclusions, and will show how unsafe it is to seize at his results without examining his singular processes.

The theologian should pursue an eclectic course in regard to the opinions of his predecessors. It is a proverb, one man can do but few things well; and scarcely any man is an authority in more than one department. Such are the limitations of the mind that there must be a division of labor among intellectual as among mechanical operatives, and the dexterous worker in iron is clumsy when he acts as a joiner. For a decision on the general spirit of theology we should pay high respect to Augustine; this was his department; but for a decision on the mode of interpreting a specific scripture, we should pay higher respect to many inferior minds; for Augustine's knowledge of Greek was very inadequate, and of the Hebrew he says, " Hebraeam linguam ignoro." The way to be wise is to learn from every one what he has most diligently examined, and to sit down with him where he is at home. One man has applied the earliest and the maturest and the latest of his energies to the developement of one class of doctrines; he has been turning them over and over in his mind by morning twilight and in the forenoon, at the dinner hour and in the afternoon and evening, and clear into the night. The consequence is, he has often worked the truth out of its own shape into the shape of error; but yet this very truth he has seized so strongly, and held up so clearly, that we are indebted to him for our most lucid view of it. Another has devoted his whole activity to the elucidating of a different class of doctrines. He has studied them with an energy that must impel the mind far into their nature, and has therefore seen more of their verity and beauty than has been seen by others. But from possessing the truth he came to be possessed by it: he swelled it out into the proportions of falsehood, and combined right elements into a wrong result. The paradox of Dr. Young may be applied to each of these divines, "*Because he is in the right; he is ever in the wrong.*" Because each has turned his undivided enthusiasm to one portion of doctrine, he has presented us with a compound of good and evil; the good is very good, nothing so good: the bad is very bad, worse than if unmingled with its opposite. Now a wise man will not cast away the true because of the false, nor take the false because of the true; but will apply a candid judgment to the compound, and thereby as by a magnet will draw out the steel and leave the dross. He will remember that uninspired man has never believed the truth without some appendage of error; nor has any man believed in error as error, without some nucleus of truth; that in the words of Ullmann, "the convictions of men never stand over against each other as black and white, day and night, God and the devil; but sun-shine and shade spread themselves over all intellects in many various gradations." Nothing then can be more unwise than to adopt as a whole or discard as a whole the belief of any theologian, be he a Westminster divine, or a German Pantheist; be he a Quaker, who has pushed certain good principles into the domain of the ridiculous, or a Sandemanian, who has been so certain of some smaller truths as to overlook the spirit of both the smaller and greater. It has often been said of late, that the human mind is dyspeptic, and will not digest the pure flour of right doctrine without some triturating bran of the wrong; and yet by no means will it live on this bran alone, but must have some flour to keep itself alive. The devotee to the belief that Christ is a man, has believed a correct principle, and has often proved it more clearly than he who had the additional truth to prove, that Christ is also God. The fatalist has discovered strong and just proof of the certainty of actions, and has often been more successful on this one point than he who was burdened with both certainty and free-will. Hence it follows, that as the opposer of religion has often gleaned his arguments from the writings of sound divines, so the advocate of comprehensive truth should gain instruction from the reasoning of erroneous men. He who searches for truth as for hid treasures will go over the battle-field where lie the vanquished enemies of the cross, and will enrich himself with their jewels and diamonds, their well-wrought breast-plates and gilded swords. A sectarian zealot forgets the plainest lessons of prudence. He forgets that many of our theological systems have been written by controversialists, and that every man in the heat of dispute is prone to take partial and uncandid views, and must therefore be examined rather than trusted. He forgets that the spark of fire is not to be found imbedded in the flint alone, nor in the steel alone, but is first discerned as a third substance, distinct from either, coming from and after the concussion of both; and so the truth often shines forth in its fulness from and after the controversy rather than from either of the men who controvert; neither of these men having what each is sure that he has, the complete system, but both of them together em'tting a light that is to be searched for by the sharp-sighted observer. He is a partizan as distinguished from a theologian, who will learn nothing good from Hartley or Priestley because they were fatalists; and nothing good from Lemborch or Le Clerc, because they were defenders of a self-determining will; who reads Turretin merely to believe him, or Arminius merely to condemn him; who receives the teaching of orthodox masters, just as if their doctrine of depravity were, in their case, untrue; and who can see no scholarship and no good argument in men not favored of God with an evangelical faith. It may be reasonably feared, that one who so misunderstands the uses of human authority will want a rational regard for the authority of inspired men; that he will feel like a retainer to the Bible, a hanger on, an adherent to it as a party standard and with the narrow spirit of a party man; and will not be a *believer* in it, one who loves it with an enlarged heart, with an awe of its inward excellence, a manlike and intelligent sympathy with its life-giving doctrine. The Bible seeketh not its defenders from those who give it a blind and uncandid approval, but from those who prise it for its native worth.

Another duty of a theologian is, to cherish a liberal faith in the possibility of improving our standard theological systems. Improvement in other sciences is hailed with joy; but in theological science is often deemed both undesirable and impossible. The new is too often regarded as but a synonym with the false and untrammelled inquiry as a sign of ambition and arrogance. It is on record that Jerome, having grown old in the belief that falsehood for a good purpose is a duty, became incensed at the "daring spirit of Augustine for venturing out of the common road," and gainsaying the popular belief; and he advised the youthful reformer, "*if he burned with a strong desire of glory*, rather to seek out some champion of his own age with whom he might contend, than molest him who was a worn out veteran." With a similar complaisance were Luther, and Calvin, and Edwards, and Hopkins aspersed as innovators; and the distinctive theology of New-England has suffered less from any logical processes, than from the obloquy of the name which it has worn for more than fifty years, the name of "new divinity."

It is said that theological science differs from every other in that it came from God, and was therefore perfect at the first. It did come from God; it did come perfect from him. But is there not a wide distinction between what is perfect as given, and what is perfect as received; between the fulness of God's teaching and the completeness of man's learning? The most harmonious developements of doctrine are at first but partially comprehended by our ill-balanced minds. God reveals his truth in such a way as to try the character, and not to prevent the possibility of a distorted view; in such a way as to stimulate and guide our active search, and not to supersede our industry, that parent of the virtues. He has decreed that the perfection of doctrine shall be given as a reward to him and only him, who is earnest and piously skillful in following out the hints of nature and the Bible. And as the zeal of theological scholarship has never been what it should be, so the development of theological doctrine has not been what it should and will be. We recognize the invigorating discipline of our Creator in giving us the raw material and not the fabric ready-made; the gold in the ore, under ground, and the pearls at the bottom of the sea, and the matter of science from which we must elaborate the science for ourselves. But we recognize also the lethargy of man in eyeing the butterfly rather than digging for the silver; in neglecting to elucidate even the truths of secular science, evident as they are, subservient as they are to his temporal good. How can we suppose, then, that he has gone to the very foundations of that recondite science, which is alien from his vitiated tastes —gone past all improvement in the richest of human studies? Is it not the whole history of man, to be rising regularly, though slowly from the savage to the sage ; to enucleate by little and little the involved phenomena of life? Is it not an old proverb, that "truth is the daughter of time?" Is it not on every body's tongue that the little child standing on his father's shoulders can see further than his parent; and starting in his race where his father stopped, may go beyond his parent's goal? As every age may begin with the results of the age preceding as the tendencies of the intellect are ever upward, as the experiences of successive generations are quickening the growth of virtuous feeling and thereby of clear perception, we cannot but hope that the most extensive of all the sciences will yet be explored with new vigor and success.

We are further cheered in this hope by the relations of scientific theology to other branches of knowledge. Its main dependence is sacred hermeneutics; and when we compare the principles and modes of interpretation adopted by Calvin with those adopted by the Greek and Latin fathers, we see an advance that betokens the coming of a still riper criticism. Many important parts of the Bible are receiving new illustrations from the chronological researches of such men as Neander, and from the reports of modern travellers concerning the topography and natural history of the East. Long buried dwelling places of the old Orientals have been recently brought to light, and one of our own countrymen, though spending but three months in the Holy Land, and exploring the grounds that have been so often explored in vain, is said to have lately made new discoveries even amid the foundations of the Holy Temple. The almost magical success of Gesenius in evoking the Phenician tongue from oblivion, the freshening zeal of so many scholars in mastering the cognate languages of the Hebrew, the faithfulness of our missionaries in searching the archives of the East, the increasing facilities of communication between the old countries and the new, have made and are still making our acquaintance with the text and idoms of the Bible more minute and definite than before. The labors of such men as Walton, Mill and Kennicott, Bengel, Wetstein and Griesbach, on the various manuscripts, recensions and versions of the Bible have reflected clear light, and will reflect still clearer, on the comparative authority of our various readings, and the true meaning of many controverted passages. The Hebrew Testament can now, as all admit, be translated with more correctness than it was by the seventy-two who made the version that Christ and his Apostles used; and both the Testaments are more accurately interpreted at the present day, than they have ever been since the days of John, the last of the unerring expositors.

The nomenclature of a science frequently determines the rate of its progress. Language is too often the rudder of mind; thought preceding expression and yet expression directing the course of thought. When terms are definite and precise, speculation moves on in a sure and straight line. An improved nomenclature may be as really, though not so radically useful to the theologian, as Lavoisier's nomenclature was to the chemist. The technical phraseology of the sacred science, could not pass through the middle ages without receiving the impress of those unfortunate men, more sinned against than sinning, who were denied the privilege of free thought, and left with little to do but load their few legalized doctrines with rude and barbarous technicalities. However appropriate this phraseology may have been to the times of the schoolmen, it needs to be modified for an age of sounder wisdom and less logomachy. A reform has already begun, and without marring the purity of style may be extended. Words professionally employed to denote what they do not usually mean, are yielding place to less ambiguous phraseology, and though our guilt of Adam's sin continues as sound a doctrine as it ever was, it is expressed in language less uncouth and eccentric. There will be indeed a war against every improvement in the style of polemic divines; for a word is the last thing and the dearest thing that men give up; but truth shall conquer in that warfare though she suffer long, and like the spirit after her conflicts with the body, she shall rise from her struggling with renovated beauty.

The progress of the natural sciences also is opening the way for a progress in theology. It is enlarging the mind, and thus amplifying the view, and the view of divine truth is analytically speaking, the science of it. The theology of Robert Boyle on the benevolence of God was more expansive than that of Ambrose on the same doctrine. Astronomy has not gone up and roamed amid the stars of heaven, without bringing down her treasures of pure light for the pious student. Geology has not been feeling her way under the foundation-stones of our world, and forcing her crooked path over our hills and crags, without bringing back some useful hints about the history and value and destination of the earth. There are many doctrines of natural religion that must be settled before and without a Bible, or they will never be settled by one. And can these doctrines be illustrated no further? Shall the brightening lights of modern science shine in vain upon the very truths they were designed to illumine?

Perhaps there is no more animating prospect now open to the scholar than in the philosophy of mind. This philosophy is the last to attain completeness. Men look all about them before they look within. They go forth in the morning, and bear the burden and heat of the day, and in the cool of the evening begin to commune with themselves. And as this science comes later to perfection than others less refined, so the elementary parts of it lie hidden longer than the parts less deeply fundamental. Intellectual processes must be performed before they can be analyzed; and the elements of psychology are the last results of such analysis. The atmosphere is breathed and looked through before its oxygen and nitrogen are distinguished, and the diamond is admired before its carbon is heard of. Now it is to a clear unfolding of what are at once the first and last principles of mental science, that theology looks with her brightest anticipations, It is but a few years since the elementary laws of this science were distinctly explained by Buffier and Reid. Before that time men seemed not to know the starting point of an argument, but were running backward in search of a place whence they might begin to go forward. They were hunting for the elements of an element, and the definition of what can never be defined. They were toiling to deduce what is known only by intuition, and as they could not prove what is too evident for proof, they denied among other things their own existence. And even now some scholastic reasoners are suffering from this disregard to first principles, and as was said of the Council of Trent, "are beholden to Aristotle for many articles of their faith." They are standing out on the plain and looking up to the clouds and down to the grass, in the hope of seeing their own eyes; and because they can not discover them at the right hand or the left, they infer that they have no eyes. The truth is nigh them, even within them, in their mouth and in their heart; but laboring hard to find it, and looking a great way off, and worrying themselves out of all health and soberness, they are left to deny what is too obvious to be made more so by proof. There are men who deny that all sin consists in freely sinning; that man may be rightly punished for nothing but his own act, that power must be commensurate with duty. But such denials are soon to be unheard, as men are chastening themselves to the simplicity of intuitive belief—simplicity, that last and hardest of the virtues. Many reasoners are now training their ambitious intellects to believe what they know to be true, whether they can prove it or not; to rest contented with what they are practically unable to deny; and to wash in the Jordan of common sense, rather than do some great thing, and still retain in theory what they are compelled to discard in practice. And when the artificial deductions of the schoolmen are more fully cleared away, the foundations will be laid for a simpler, chaster, broader, stronger and more appropriate philosophy of doctrine than the pride of argument has yet allowed.

There are some improvements in theology, that depend in their own nature on the lapse of time. We may instance the interpretation of prophecies that are yet to be fulfilled; the proper estimate of certain forms of stating doctrine, certain modes of preaching, certain new and old measures of pastoral action, the comparative value of which is to be learned from their comparative influence for a series of years. There are many positions that seem to be sustained by abstract argument, and yet may be found, after a long and large experience, to harmonize too imperfectly with the deep-seated laws of the mind. It is some advance to have tried a principle, to have found it erroneous, and to return with strengthened assurance to the old truth. The Oxford divines would raise theology above any previous standard of uninspired men, if they should succeed in clearly proving that the departure of Protestants from certain notions of the ancient Church is unauthorized and injurious. A stronger faith in what was once fully believed, if that faith be the result of a more extended induction, is a new blessing; as it is likewise a blessing, and the last improvement in the wisdom of wise men, to discover that what the mind had prided itself on knowing is really unknown, yet to be learned anew, or perhaps never to be learned at all.

It is needless to add that theology has been obviously improving within the last two centuries; and the comparison between the standard systems of the present day and those of Turretin, Ridgely, or Owen, presents a rich earnest of what is to come. All these improvements have given, and all future improvements will give new power to the essential doctrines of Jesus. Some arguments for these doctrines are grown obsolete, but truer and stronger arguments are supplied. Never, never should it be forgotten, that he who would benefit the branches of theology must be piously heedful not to tear up its roots, and not to

"Prune and prune, until the quick be cut,
And the fair fruitage fall beneath the feet
Of swinish innovation."

There is danger indeed of moving too fast and too far; but is this an excuse for not moving at all? There is danger in every thing; in defect as well as in excess, in indolence and in ambition. Danger is needed for our trial as moral beings; it should modify but not prevent our activity. The mind should be cheered with the hope of rising higher and higher, or it will droop its wing and debase itself on trifles. It was made for hope, as the eye for light, and it sinks within itself when told that all is done, that there is no employment for it save in ruminating on past opinions; that all its restless strength must be swallowed up in the single power of memory. It longs to breathe a purer atmosphere than was ever inhaled before: and as the dart of Acestes kindled while it was rising toward the sun, so does the mind drink in a new vitality, when it aspires to an unattained perfection. The scholar thinks better, feels better, writes better, prays better, lives better, when he goes forth with the freeness and freshness of the sages and bards in the earliest days, willing as a modest man to see the unseen and hear the unheard, and be the first chronicler of some of the works of God.

Another duty of a theologian is, to foster a spirit of fraternal interest in the investigations of his brethren. Nothing is more seemly than the scientific co-operation of such friends as Dugald Stewart and Sir James Mackintosh, and from nothing do we turn with more sickness of heart than from the recorded animosity of a Newton and a Leibnitz. The history of theological speculation has too seldom been the history of friends, aiding each other in candid as distinguished from party research. It has too often been the history of combatants, who have striven not indeed with more noise than others, but with keener passion.

The peculiar intolerance of theological dogmatists has been owing in part to their love of power. The depravity, belonging by nature to all men, has cleaved in a measure to ministers; and while in other professions it has found an outlet in a love of gain, or of parade, or of pleasure, it has often been confined in the clerical profession to a love of authority. This is the avenue through which the concentrated sinfulness of the soul has poured itself out. It has been fostered by the apologizing name of a desire to exert a good influence. It has been favored by the ministerial station. Week after week has the consecrated man stood erect in the high pulpit, and his people have looked up while he has looked down. He has been the most learned man, perhaps the only learned man in his parish. He has been styled reverend, the ambassador of God, and has been clothed with the most sublime of all power, that over the conscience and religious sentiment. Fathers and mothers have stood in awe when he has sat down in their cottage, and children have hid themselves at the approach of a man so sacred and set apart. This reverence has been in great degree no more than is fitting; but its effect on the feelings of the recipient has too often been a proof that man in his best estate is vanity. Never contradicted in his own bishopric, he has been impatient of contradiction out of it. His own opinions he has looked upon as law, and he would fain throw mountains on the man who has had the temerity to impugn them.

There has been a second reason for the irritating style of controversial theologians. The weapons of their warfare are of refined power. When they plied the chain, the rack, the fire, they used these grosser implements as the symbols of a more subduing penalty. The symbols have gone; the relics of what they signified remain. It is yet hard for the multitude to rise above a superstitious version of the truth, that what the minister binds or looses here shall be bound or loosed hereafter. To many he yet seems to hold the keys of hell and death. He should be aware of this. It is true, he should make a vigorous opposition against essential error. He should call things by their right names. But he should beware of indulging in too hard names, and of exposing his pious brother to the unmerited jealousies of the Church. When he solemnly insinuates that a theological teacher is a heretic, when he breathes out his significant suspicions that a spiritual guide is unsound in the faith, he sends a panic through a host of confiding Christians, and they, trembling for the ark, cry earnestly to the God of Israel that the new stumbling-block may be removed out of the way. There is an inward, a still, a penetrating power in that word *heretic*, which the men who use it are too prone to forget. It is a word that rouses the fears and inflames the superstitions of praying men and women, who though the humblest are yet the most awe inspiring of all men and women, and arms thousands of the elect of God against one solitary victim, and that victim perhaps an unsuspecting enquirer after truth. It is a word that seems to take hold on eternity, and to consign the unfriended student to the companionship of the ancient apostates, who were delivered over to Satan. When uttered by a high and wary ecclesiastic, it has sounded as if the avenging omnipotence of God was wielded by the envy, or jealousy, or perhaps malice of man. No wonder that Martin Luther sighed for death, as his only hope of rescue from the odium of the Church. No wonder that even evangelical divines have lost their fraternal feeling, when they have reciprocated with each other the accusations of heresy and schism.

A third cause of the peculiar strength of theological animosities has been the encouragement they have received from conscience. Ministers have loved what they have deemed the truth. As it involves the eternal destiny of man, they have felt that they could not fight for it too valiantly, nor beat down Satan under their feet too stoutly. They have sometimes construed their obligation to rebuke and spare not, into an obligation to overbear and intimidate; and all history shows that a man is never so deeply and strongly in an evil way, as when he is there conscientiously.

The effect of this denunciating style among theologians has been various. It has sometimes disheartened the inquirer. He has started in his course like a timid hare, but he heard the sound of his pursuers, and was worried down, and he never ventured abroad again. The Alexandrian fathers, Clement, Origen, and Athanasius placed a punctuation mark after the word ἦν in the third verse of the first chapter of John's Gospel. Chrysostom was alarmed at this punctuation, and denounced it as a heresy. Epiphanius declared it blasphemous, and the sin against the Holy Ghost; and this commotion on account of a single dot contributed to delay for years the perilous work of punctuating the sacred page. The like hostility to free thought bound the energies of the schoolmen down to the most profitless inquiries. Not daring to rise up and labor in the sunshine they burrowed in darkness, and wasted on puerile conceits the power that was meant for discovery and progress. This substitution of polemic rancor for fraternal interest has driven the mind of others to an extreme of error, which they did not themselves anticipate. As the child so the man, and as every man so the theologian is apt to do right if you convince him that he is expected to do so, and is apt to do wrong if you assure his neighbors that he is past recovery. He is won to truth and repulsed into error. Arminius, if he had been kindly reasoned with instead of being rudely denounced, had never pressed his corruptions so far: and the history of many pitiable writers is this,—first, they inquired with honest intent; secondly, they were called heretics; lastly, they became heretics. This domineering spirit of ecclesiastics has incited other minds to revolution against authority. There are some spirits who will think for themselves. You might as well chain the Hellespont as them. You may stand at the portal with a pointed bayonet; they will come out and do what they list. When the bull of the pope has fallen on such a mind, and the edict of the bishop has oppressed it, and the Presbyterian book of discipline has held it down too closely, this mind has stirred under its load, and has struggled against the walls that confined it, pressing against them like lava against the sides of Etna, and at last has heaved,—and poured itself out of the rent crater, and scattered books of discipline to the four winds, and taught the aspirants for mental sway that what God has made elastic and expansive and inflammable is not to be compressed and stifled. Idle, idle this attempt to defeat the first laws of nature, that the soul of man shall go out free as the air of heaven,—go after truth, let her leadings be what they may. It is far from the brotherly spirit of the Gospel, and from the manly spirit of science, for a theologian to write a book, not for the discussion of a principle, but for undermining the influence of a man; not for establishing truth by dignified argument, but for awakening *suspicions* against a brother, such suspicions as can never be refuted, and are more mischievous than direct charges; not for convincing the high-minded student who ought to be the umpire in abstruse discussion, but for inflaming the jealousies of the uneducated people, who in some parts of our land are made the sovereigns in religion as well as politics, and who would be saved from much needless trouble, if our metaphysical disputes were conducted as formerly in Latin. The human mind is wronged and grieved, when a theologian exposes in print to the rude world's gaze the hallowed and unguarded conversations of the parlor; when he breaks open the seal of confidential letters, and feeds the vulgar appetite for scandal with the sacred privacies of brotherly intercourse; when he disturbs the sanctuary of the grave, and retails the secret opinions and personal remarks of men just gone to their reward, and brings up the bones of the peaceful dead to hurl at some envied divine, who calls for living accusers and who will sooner endure reproach than rifle in self-defence the still vestments of the tomb.* It is a pusillanimous orthodoxy and not a

---

* When a controversy is in a *progressive* state, and an individual dies before its results are developed, is it always fair to quote his opinions on a *part* of the controversy, as if they were formed after a full view of the *whole*? Is it always honorable to publish them after his death, when he cautiously abstained from publishing them during his life? Is it not probable that were he living he would choose to qualify his remarks made in conversation, and explain and correct them before they were printed? Has not a word or letter communicated in private a different *meaning* from that which is given it by its publication in a newspaper? Is it not an injury to the living, to bring against him an antagonist whom he cannot contradict without afflicting the hearts of a bereaved and beloved family? Is it not a wrong to the dead, to publish his private opinions, especially about individual character, when he has no opportunity to correct them for the press, and when they are probably the

fraternal Christianity, that prompts the devotee of a human creed to condemn philosophical research, and to confound the true revelation of nature with the philosophy "falsely so called," which and only which the Bible disapproves; to discharge the epithets proud, ambitious, skeptical, infidel, or, worse than all, and worse than any thing else, *Pelagian*, against every one who brings into theology the enterprise of a scientific discoverer, and prefers the sure word of God above all the traditions of the elders. It is humiliating to confess that the form of theological discussion has with some men ceased to be "What is truth," and has come to be "Do certain ministers in the evangelical community believe heretical doctrines." When these ministers deny that they believe what is imputed to them, a book is written to prove that they *are* heretics despite of their denial; and also to prove that modern charity is something distinct from that antiquated grace, which "beareth all things, believeth all things, hopeth all things, endureth all things." It has been given, not more quaintly than truly, as a definition of man, that he is a something which has a will of its own and longs to be a pope. Then let us remember that we are all popes, if we be thinking divines; and as we are all dignitaries so are we all brethren; and our duty is not to undermine each other's authority, but to strengthen it by aiding each other's researches; and the way to aid an investigator is, not to exclude him from our sympathies because his mind is his as distinct from ours, but to take a kindly interest in his heart's yearnings; not to avoid discussion for the sake of peace, but to labor for rational peace by brotherly discussion, and to imitate the winning voice of the infinite intellect, "Come let us reason together." Our duty is to note well the delicacy of the mind's nature; how like a field-flower it shuts itself up when no rays come

---

last opinions which he would have chosen to publish? Have not the rules of morality been sometimes violated in publishing a careless conversational remark of a departed theologian, without detailing the circumstances essentially modifying that remark, and without stating the fact that it was made in sickness, or in haste, or with some peculiar application? The manner in which controversialists should treat the memory of the dead is to be determined by the sense of honor, which has perhaps been sometimes less faithfully cultivated than the power of constructing syllogisms.

down from the sun, and it will never be forced open by the rudeness of rain and hail, but will expand itself to nothing but the light of the morning, and will drink in only the sweet influences of day. Let a minister of the Gospel never sacrifice the interest of Christian thought to the miserable politics of a school, nor give up to party what was meant for the church. Let him say sincerely what Voltaire said falsely, "I belong to no party but truth." Let him *do* something for the discovery of truth, and store up for his own and for others' use the materials for analysis and generalization. Our practitioners in physic are constantly reporting new phenomena of disease and cure in Medical Journals; our jurists record each new decision for the surer establishment of general principles; and why should not every fit practitioner in the art of saving souls describe in philosophical form such new phenomena of conversion, of revivals, of moral degeneracy, as may furnish to gifted minds matter for induction, and give more of a scientific cast to our theological systems? So shall Christian ministers, like the Jews of old, each one contribute some materials for the tabernacle; and the fellowship of so good and still a cause shall supplant the taste for personal invective and for the manoeuvres of rival partizans.

Another duty of a theologian is, to take a candid view of the causes and results of differences in religious opinion. He is said to be fortunate who can learn the causes of things. The theologian will be delivered from much needless alarm, if he know the real origin of the disputes that trouble the church. He has no right to deny the depravity of man, nor to overlook the influence of this depravity upon the speculations even of pious divines. But as he has no right to be more charitable than the truth allows, so he should not be more censorious. He has no right to ascribe *every* error in theological speculation to a *peculiar* degree of depravity in the men who embrace it. Let us not be misunderstood. On those great doctrines of faith which involve an appeal to the religious emotions, an unsanctified temper is the great source of mistake; but on the theories connected with those doctrines, on the philosophical relations of theology, men of equal piety have always differed. There are questions which piety alone can settle, and others which it can not. These last are the questions of pure intellect. A wrong solution of them is not necessarily the result of a "bad state of heart." Our "taste men" have no right to say that the "exercise scheme" must originate from a sinful disregard to the native corruption of the soul, nor have our men of no taste a right to say that the scheme they oppose must originate from a desire to conceal our own agency in our own guilt. Because a man believes that our constitution is such as will certainly lead to sin, but is not sin itself, he is sometimes significantly asked, whether he is not ignorant of his own natural depravity; and because another man asserts that our constitution is itself sin, he is sometimes accused of aiming to free himself from blame, and to cast the responsibility of his evil heart upon the Being who made it. But is there no such thing as an *honest* variance of opinion on speculative theology? Can we *never* excuse an erring brother on the ground of his early education, or innocent prejudices, or something unfortunate rather than guilty? Is it always certain that the defender of a new theory is actuated by a desire to become the founder of a sect, or to distinguish his own school or seminary? Is it always certain that the abettors of an old theory are unduly governed by a love to Scotland or Holland, or by a hatred of Germany or New England? And is it *safe* for a controversialist to throw the first stone at the moral obliquities of his brother, and insinuate that his metaphysical error must arise from a peculiar degree of spiritual blindness? Who is willing to investigate truth when he knows that every trifling deviation from the phraseology of the standards will expose him to the charge of some peculiar sinfulness? Has not the investigating spirit been already crippled, have not the churches been needlessly alarmed, have not the feelings of the pious student been too sorely lacerated by the suspicion, that an *independent* thinker is of course estranged from God? It is easier to defeat an obnoxious party by insinuations against its Christian character, than to defend the truth by abstract argument; we may sooner blight the prospects of an adversary by exciting a feverish alarm concerning his religious habits, than by a refutation of his principles. But what is effectual is not always gentlemanly or just; and what is successful for a few years is often prolific in ultimate evil.

---

* John 8: 7.

There is nothing which so deeply wounds the spirit of an inquiring scholar, as to be publicly asked the question, whether his speculations do not originate from a pride of heart.

It will soothe many agitated minds to reflect that religious disputes, instead of arising always from a want of conscientious regard to the welfare of the church, arise sometimes from so innocent a cause as the different temperaments of individuals. One divine has a phlegmatic temperament and loves to insist on human passivity; another has a sanguine temperament and loves to insist on human action and freedom; a third has a melancholic temperament and is fascinated with the inexplicable mysteries of God's moral system; a fourth has a bilious temperament and loves to combine the passive and the active, fore-knowledge and free-will. Now the phlegmatic theology in its exclusive form is erroneous; the sanguine theology is the same; and the melancholic when uncombined with others is unsound; but it is not philosophical to excommunicate men by the hundred and thousand because they have a nervous temperament or a bilious mode of reasoning. They may be all pious, equally so with their opposers, yet all imperfect, and their original prolific sin is, in this regard, a sin of the cerebrial system, rather than of the voluntary emotions.

It also relieves a suspicious community to know that some of our theological disputes arise from an honest misunderstanding of terms. Indeed the smaller the point of contention so much the more zealous are the disputers; and the church has been almost shaken to its centre, because a divine has used one word when he ought to have used another. It has seemed as if the elements would melt with fervent heat because a man has believed in "imputation" or "ability," while his opponents have all the time believed in all that he means. Earnest Christians have been so much alarmed that they could not sleep by night, because a philosophizing school have asserted that our involuntary nature is not sin; and yet the most learned opposers of this school have believed the same thing and have only refused to assert it in the same way. The jurists of England defined a navigable river to be one in which the tide ebbs and flows. This definition was good enough for England, because all her navigable rivers are also *tide-water* rivers. But in America there are a thousand streams in which the tide ebbs and flows, which, however, are so small that a boy may leap over them, and according to English law these fingers of the sea are navigable rivers. We have streams too, "into which all the waters of England might be poured without raising their level a single foot," which however are not tide-water streams, and of course according to English law are not navigable; therefore the Mississippi, the Missouri, the Ohio and Connecticut are not orthodox rivers, so long as they contravene the "venerable standards" in admitting navigation and excluding tides. Now there are many theological doctrines in which there ought to be plain sailing, but which are made unnavigable by a similar transfer to one thing of terms which were meant for another. We may lament the perversion of terms, but need not always ascribe it to a perverted heart. The man who has been contending for forty years that the phraseology of the middle ages is the only orthodox faith, is not to be therefore denounced as a sinner above his more modern brethren, but his error may often be traced to a very amiable fondness for ancient relics. And on the other hand, the man who ventures upon a vocabulary more favorable to modern navigation is not to be exscinded for a word, but is to be punished with a soft band for his preference of a sound philosophy above a bad style. One theologian accommodates himself to the circumstances of his age; his more stable brother esteemeth all circumstances alike. The former digs a dyke around his house if he lives in Holland, even though his ancestors did no such thing in Edinburgh; the latter, whose ancestors lived in the low countries and in frequent exposures to inundation, is careful to use the old precautions against being overflowed, even when he resides in the ninth story of a house on Edinburgh rock. The difference in the policy of these two men arises from a difference in the versatility of their mental character, more than from a difference in their moral feeling. It will help their mutual charity to remember this.

As a comprehensive view of the *causes* of theological dissension saves us, in some degree, from the most unanswerable and injurious of all reproaches,—reproaches for a peculiar obliquity of heart; so a like view of the *results* of these differences allays much controversial asperity. It is instructive to look over the political papers of the last twenty years, and see how many times our Union has been dissolved and ruined by the "opposite party;" and still we remain a happy and thriving people. Equally instructive is it to read the writings of divines for the last two or more centuries, and see how lamentable it is that at every period the church has been nearer dissolution than it ever was before, and error was never so threatening, and there is a "crisis" unprecedented, fearful beyond description; and still through these various periods the church has been advancing towards her millennial glory. The truth is, trouble is one part of our discipline. We must have it. We are made the stronger men and the better men by means of it. Every age has magnified its own calamities. It had been better to bear them with more fortitude. The present is said to be the age of peculiar dissension and heresy. Perhaps it is in some respects. Every age is peculiar. But the surest way to perpetuate the evils that now disturb our Zion is to exaggerate them, and to lose our temper, and cease from the discussion of principles for the sake of dismal forebodings about men. And the best way to exterminate the errors of the day is to examine them, and prove them false, and confide in the grace of God by which all things shall work together for good. Our dissensions are not without their benefit. Who would not choose to experience a gale now and then, rather than endure a tiresome and unhealthy calm? Who would not choose to enjoy the life and activity flowing from honest debate, rather than let his mind sink into the habitude of a mere appendage of an hereditary creed? We mourn over some errors of the day in reference to moral agency, and yet in consequence of the discussion resulting from these errors, this great subject is now better understood than it has been for centuries. We are sorry that some men are so extravagant in their speculations, and that others rush into equal extravagance on the other side, as if for the sake of keeping an equilibrium; that some men are too fond of innovating, and others are too fond of introducing unheard of schemes for the sake of checking innovation; that the theology of some men is going forward too far, and the theology of others timorously going backward from the correctness it had once attained; yet on the great whole the prevailing theology is more rational, scriptural and comprehensive than it has been since the age of the apostles; and it is indebted for this proficiency to the conflicts it has passed through. Few will deny that the style of preaching at the present day is more apostolical than it has been for many centuries; and its superior excellence is owing, in great measure, to the developement of truth in debate. The truth which has been already established is costly; for innumerable theories have been sacrificed to obtain it, and thousands of lives consumed in mortification and grief. It is lamentable indeed that error should prevail even for a day; but it is cheering to know that if it be an important error, it will not prevail long; it involves in itself the seeds of ruin and will soon die, so that the garden of truth may be fertilized by its remains. Good men may continue to uphold it in words, but, if left to tranquil discussion, they will renounce it in fact. The agitation then and spasmodic fear in which some have been indulging is gratuitous and unwise. A sober view of the promises of God, of the history of past dissensions, of the correlative nature of the human mind and of truth, will lead us never to despair of the church. The frail bark of old 'carried Cesar and his fortunes.'

Another duty of a theologian is to associate his doctrines more intimately with what is delicate and refined in taste, comely, humane and magnanimous in sentiment. It has been often lamented that our systems of sacred science are too frigid. They have been called bodies of divinity, and a body is always unsightly unless there be a heart within beating with warm blood. They have sometimes disdained the ornaments of refined sensibility, and have deemed it a weakness to be wedded to the graces of life. They have therefore strode on, independently and stout-heartedly, like Samson with his hand clenching a jaw-bone.

The biography of theological writers explains one reason for this fact. For the last fourteen centuries our speculations have received shape and mould from the bishop of Hippo, in whose person the continent of Africa has held a dominion over the intellect of Christians, that is almost equal to the Christian's control over the body of the African. The theological school, as well as the scientific, has had its Stagyrite, whose hand is upon us even yet, and we are glad to receive the impress of his profound wisdom and piety. We stand in filial awe of his power; but still it was a power not always adorned with the refinements of a catholic age. He lived in the day of gladiatorial shows; and though he sternly opposed them, he could not entirely escape the cauterizing influence of the public sentiment which favored them. He was led to indulge in the hardening error of persecuting his adversaries by the aid of the civil law. His youthful precocity in crime made him morbidly sick of his race, and filled him with such fear of the gentler sex that he kept too far aloof from the scenes of domestic love, and suffered not the hand of a wife or a daughter to smooth down the roughnesses and polish the hardness of his iron intellect. Discarding these genial influences from the formation of his character, he gave himself up for years to the business, not so mellowing to himself as it was useful to others, of doing battle against all the adversaries of the faith. Now as every imparted truth is a thought of him who imparts it, and as a thought is a state of the mind thinking, so the great truths which Augustine explained became part and parcel of his own nature. He infused himself into them and through them. We see his image on them, like the image of Phidias on the shield of Minerva's statue. We admire the compact jointures and firm foundations of his work. We are almost proud of it, it looks so commanding and impregnable; but still it has angles sharper than they need be, and buttresses more rough and frowning; and we can not but wish that in overpowering the intellect and taking the conscience by storm, he had also consulted the gentler and tenderer sensibilities, and given a more cheerful coloring to the messages of peace and love.

From Augustine the sceptre passed to Calvin; another mighty and devout man, who did a great work, and whose influence is yet to be more deeply felt and revered. But we do injustice to Calvin's own view of human imperfection, when we say that his trains of reasoning were not defaced by one awkward line. Looking at the portraits of the divines in his day, we see faces that speak of a firm nerve and a brawny arm; and we ask, ' Who can stand before the children of Anak?' Let us not so overrate our natures as to expect from men, called to so many rough duties for such rough times, all the grace and amenity that we find in George Herbert and William Cowper. Calvin was the Apostle of liberty; like Augustine he went beyond his age in kindliness of feeling; but if the quaint phrase of Bunyan's and Shakspeare's time may be forgiven; 'the shell of freedom was on his head.' His nicer sentiments and finer susceptibilities were somewhat blunted by the revolting scenes to which he was daily exposed. He moved about among his opponents as an honest and strong-jointed farmer moves with his flail over a threshing-floor. We should do well if we could grasp a doctrine with so strong a hand as his, if we could hold it forth with such distinctness and subduing life; but we should do better, if we could combine with this stern doctrine the mildness of Him, whose appropriate act it was to take little children into his arms and bless them.

Edwards rose up after Calvin, and it were idle to speak his praise, while many of us are so ambitious to be called by his name. The style of thinking among our divines is so far modeled after him, that his imperfections will suggest our own. And his failing was in too exclusive a regard to one portion of our sensibilities. He seemed to live apart from many of the innocent cravings and sympathies of his race. He learned early in life the great lessons of ministerial dignity. His father, the venerable patriarch of Windsor, was fond of appearing in the full dress of a clergyman, wearing even in his parochial visits a black gown and sometimes his clerical band. Pres. Edwards himself seldom visited the people of his charge, and was inclined to withdraw from promiscuous intercourse. In his singularly modest letter to the Trustees of Nassau Hall he says, "I have a constitution in many respects peculiarly unhappy, attended with flaccid solids, vapid, sizy, and scarce fluids, and a low tide of spirits; often occasioning a kind of childish weakness and contemptibleness of speech, presence and demeanor, with a disagreeable dulness and stiffness; much unfitting me for conversation, but more especially for the government of a college." He possessed a rich imagination, and might have been one of the first poets of his age, had he not chosen to be the first theologian; but he speaks disparagingly of "elegance of language and excellency of style," and says of some of his discourses, they were mostly written "at a time when the circumstances of the auditory they were preached to were enough to make a minister neglect, forget and despise such ornaments as politeness and modishness of style and method." He passed his life in a still and sequestered valley; he resigned the salutary discipline of household care to his estimable wife; when he entered his sitting room his own children, it is said, were in the habit of rising up in token of their well-merited reverence; he ate from a silver bowl, while most of his parishioners were grateful for pewter, but he ate a sparing meal and lived more like a spirit than a partaker of flesh and blood. He was indeed humble as a little child before God, but he often went forth among men, not so much like a fellow-man, as like a vice-gerent of the great law-giver. When an opponent rose up against him, he bore and pressed him down by the force of his amazing genius, and the still greater force of his honest and truth-loving temper. His reply to Dr. Taylor of Norwich is said to have contributed, in connection with other sources of mortification, to hasten the death of that eminent writer. The remarkable confessions of Major Hawley will long remain a monument of the authority which Pres. Edwards held over the conscience and the fears of the most distinguished men.[*] When he preached, it was as if one had been let down from heaven to sound one of the seven trumpets, after which seven thunders were to utter their voices. He rehearsed the threatenings of his sovereign as if he had some peculiar right, and indeed he had, to tell on whom they would fall. He stood in the pulpit with a head unmoved and a still hand, and what he had written he had written. But his hearers looked up, and the tears stole down their cheeks, and they shook like aspen-leaves, and on some occasions screamed aloud. Dr. Trumbull says, that when Mr. Edwards was preaching at Enfield, "there was such a breathing of distress and weeping, that the preacher was obliged to speak to the people and desire silence, that he might be heard." A gentleman remarked to Dr. Dwight, that when in his youth he heard Mr. Edwards describe the day of Judgment, he fully supposed that immediately at the close of the sermon, "the Judge would descend and the final separation take

---

[*] See Allen's Biog. Dict., Art. Hawley; and also Dwight's Life of Edwards, pp. 410, 411, 421—427. An interesting and very characteristic letter from Pres. Edwards to Maj. Hawley, was recently found among Maj. Hawley's papers, by that accomplished historian George Bancroft, Esq., and a copy of it was expected for insertion in this place. Through the kindness of Mr. Bancroft, it will probably be given to the public in some future number of the Repository.

place." During the delivery of one of his most overwhelming discourses in the pulpit of a minister unused to such power, this minister is said to have forgotten himself so far as to pull the preacher by the coat, and try to stay the torrent of such appalling eloquence by the question, "Mr. Edwards! Mr. Edwards! is not God a merciful being,—is he not merciful?"

We bow down before this father of our New England theology with the profoundest veneration. We read his precious volumes with awe and in tears. We are so superstitious, that we almost fear to be called profane for lisping a word against the perfect balancing of his character. And yet we can not help wishing that he had been somewhat more of a brother and somewhat less of a champion; that he had left his book on the will just as large as it is, but had made his book on the affections and sentiments more comprehensive and full; that he had been a little more like one on whose bosom we might lean our heads at a supper, and a little less like one standing in the gloom of solitude, and awing down every weakness of our poor nature. We need and crave a theology, as sacred and spiritual as his, and moreover one that we can take with us into the flower-garden, and to the top of some goodly hill, and in a sail over a tasteful lake, and into the saloons of music, and to the galleries of the painter and the sculptor, and to the repasts of social joy, and to all those humanizing scenes where virtue holds her sway not merely as that generic and abstract duty of a "love to being in general," but also as the more familiar grace of a love to some beings in particular. We do want a theology that will not frown with too great austereness on every playful sentiment, nor disdain all communion with those things which hard-nerved men call "innocent follies," but which were designed by him who remembereth our frame to make the intellect more pliant and versatile, and the manners more polished, and the whole man more human. Many of our systematic treatises on theology have been written in schools, and garrets, and cloisters, and prisons; some of them by men bearing the title of "bachelors in divinity" and the character of bachelor in humanity also; but these treatises would have been more exactly true, had they been composed amid the scenes of a more sympathizing and social life, and by men not so "intensely married" to their folios and parchments. Much of our theology has been hammered out by metaphysicians, and we all know what Burke says of these men,—" there is no heart so hard as that of a thorough bred metaphysician." Now we do not like this remark: it is, like many others of that great man, too extreme; and yet some of our best metaphysical reasoners *have* been a little too unheedful of what they have been pleased to call the "natural" or "animal virtues." We cling to their substantial doctrines with tenacious fondness, but we hope that the coming generation will study more delicacy of shading, more neatness of adjustment, and will cultivate a style more redolent of kindness and fellowship.

The great evil is, the theology of some men is wrong on principle in its divorce from morals. So many have insisted on morality alone, that some have felt bound to insist on religion alone. Religion and morality have been looked upon as not only separate but rival provinces, and the ignorant have often received an impression that they must come out from the realm of virtue into that of piety. Hence it has been said to one man, "one thing thou lackest," and to another, one thing thou possessest; and many, so they are devout worshippers, care not to be exemplary as gentlemen or comfortable as neighbors. The sins of religious men have often been the more grievous, as they were also sins against a delicate taste. The solecism has been heard in our religious phraseology, that a man is very pious and very mean; a good Christian, and for all that, none the less unamiable and disobliging and small-hearted and crooked and wilful, or ambitious or covetous or morose. It has been thought that religion covers up and atones for a multitude of sins against propriety. The honorable has been resigned to the duellist, as if there were any real honor that religion would refuse to hallow and enshrine. The beautiful in feeling and conduct has been surrendered to the gay, as if there were any true beauty that holiness would not garner into its bosom. It has sometimes been said that charities for the body, and for the mendicants who live in our streets should be left for the unconverted man to perform; while religion looks higher than all earthly good, to nothing less than the wants of the soul and the heathen. It has been implied that a preacher may as fitly blow a ram's horn as a silver trumpet, may as well appear with unwashed hands and a soiled garment as display a more pharisaical morality of divers baptisms; that the house of God may as well be left unpainted and unswept, and be used for political harrangues and for various sorts of money changers, as be preserved a symbol of the purity and dignity and sacredness of heaven. Now it belongs to a theologian to take an enlarged view of both spiritual and visible religion, of the whole nature of man, and our need of a liberal and congruous development of all inward and outward loveliness. It is his duty to invest the Christian scheme with a claim upon every sensibility, every taste, every aspiration that God has encouraged in the soul; to show that piety not only approves but requires a true self-respect, a nice sense of honor, frankness and simplicity, a generous and complaisant and candid spirit, a high esteem of talent, of learning, of courage, of patriotism, of public service, government, the arts, and of every thing that shadows forth the pristine character of our fallen race. He must let it be seen that religion is a tower of strength, and around its sides all the beauties and delicacies of natural virtue entwine themselves, and they climb up to its summit, and can not be torn away without losing their own freshness and modesty, without leaving the tower that sustained them not indeed uncomely but yet more naked and bleak than its wise founder designed, secure in an awful grandeur, standing alone in severe beauty, enrobed with the clouds of heaven and girdled with the rainbow, but laid open and bare to hail and storms; too cold, too sombre, too solitary.

Lastly, it is the duty of a theologian to attain a deep and ardent piety. The first and second and third requisite for every man who would speculate on moral subjects is involved in the command, 'thou shalt love the Lord thy God with all thy heart, and thy neighbor as thyself.' Superadded to the obligation under which he lies as a created man and a fellow man, he lies under a distinct obligation as an intellectual inquirer.—For successful study he needs an interest in his theme. We wonder at the patience of the artist, as he sits in his darkened room year after year, and adds with slowness and trembling one hair-breadth line after another to the canvass. But he could not thus protract his assiduities, unless his labor were his pleasure. And the theologian will not investigate with the needed patience, unless he love the truth which he examines. This love will be the spring of his scholarship. It will allure him onward to protracted thought, and its own gratification will be an hourly recompense for his toil. For successful study a man needs enlargement of intellect. Now it is a common remark that even a dull intellect becomes bright when kindled by religious feeling, and a change of heart is the precursor of a change in mind. Glowing with interest in a great truth the soul expands more and more to entertain that truth, and loving to stand in the sun it assimilates itself to the pure light that surrounds it.—Still further. Though it is essential to the moral agency of a man that he be able to understand many things pertaining to religion, yet there is a certain kind of truth which comes under the peculiar cognizance of rectified emotion, and so far as one is deficient in piety, so far does he want an eye for the discernment of such truth. It is only a specific form of a general proposition, that "the natural man seeth not the things of the Spirit of God, neither can he know them, because they are spiritually discerned. But he that is spiritual judgeth all things." He were a plainly incompetent critic of Homer or Milton, who had qualified himself for his task by a mere discipline in the mathematics; and we should smile at the man who set himself up as a connoisseur in music simply because he had studied the laws of sound. As an interpreter of the Bible one must have that peculiar kind of vision which seeth hidden things. As there is a language of the Greeks and Romans, the English and French, so there is a language of pious men, and it must be learned by the heart, and its very rudiments are to an unsanctified spirit like the hieroglyphics of Egypt to an unlettered Cherokee. Dr. Scott upon his knees with the Bible open before him, was in just the state of mind which philosophy would prescribe for the detection of certain features invisible to a proud inquirer. A prudent commentator will make it his first aim to be initiated into the mysteries of the sacred fraternity, and then he will understand the meaning of various badges and secret signs that are mere enigmas and perhaps follies to a scholar not elected of God. As a doctrinal theologian too, such a man as John Newton will see his way into a vital truth when such a man as David Hume would grope about like a blinded giant. Emotion as well as intellect is a part of our nature, and is often a guide where mere intellect fails. That argument which accords not with pious feeling is unwrought with the signs of truth. Not a few have reasoned themselves into false doctrine because they deemed it needful to be cold in order to be clear, and to let the lamp of feeling die out in order that the intellect may see in its own darkness. But the intellect is often the keenest in its vision when lighted up with heart-felt love; just as the physical system becomes as strong again and as brisk again when it glows with healthy excitement. "Strong argument," says John Foster, "may be worked in fire as well as in frost." As many times as one learns a new language, so many times is he said to become a man; but much more may it be said that every improvement in feeling is an improvement in manly wisdom.

Nor is it merely in the discernment of doctrine that piety is like a new sense. It suggests the proper modes of stating and defending the faith. It will rescue our divines from shaping one principle so as to flatter a Lutheran, and moulding another so as to please a Calvinist; from distorting the truth for the sake of a place in an old school or a new school; from apportioning doctrines so as to suit the schemes of a party at the hazard of losing the spirit of the Bible. For eighteen hundred years has true religion been fleeing from one field of controversy to another, and has always sighed over the incomplete and uncandid representations of her friends. Bleeding and torn she has come to the arena where modern theologians endeavor to prove the unsoundness of their brethren. She grieves over the stratagems of some, over the asperities of others, and over that fear of man that deters so many from defending an enlarged and complete doctrine. She goes over the field where our combatants are trampling down, each one some jewel of truth, and she picks up the treasures, and holds them out to the gaze of her forgetful friends. She weeps in secret places that good men choose to name each other heretics and to rive the Church asunder, rather than adopt that more honorable form of service, the speaking of revealed truth in love. She calls, and calls, "oh ye, the elect of Heaven! how long shall I be wounded in the house of my friends?—for I am the daughter of peace and my home is in the bosom of the Prince of peace. Reason ye like Christian philosophers, and not like the disputers of this world. Speak your words like courteous and highminded men, and scorn to become whisperers and busybodies. Be the noblemen of nature, and be clothed with humility as your chief adorning."

It is not too much to say that a man can never be, in all respects, a good theological writer, and suitably conform to the canons of a sound rhetoric, unless he have a heart that beats with a fervent piety, and the pulsations of which may be felt and seen in his style. Neither is it too much to say that he can not exert the influence which every minister ought to exert, unless he be known to abide in God. A large part of the people who respect religion are not theologians; they do not examine the intricate proofs of doctrine; they are bound to the truth by a confidence in their minister; and his apparent godliness is a great argument for the correctness of his teaching, But let him cease to walk in the gardens where his great and only master dwelleth; let him cease to come forth daily from that paradise with his robes exhaling the perfume of its spices, and the bond is severed by which he held together the consciences of his people. He no longer seems to be the "mouth of God ;" and to speak the words of the judge; but he utters his own words, and they fall like hail-stones upon the ice. Could I but persuade one candidate for the sacred office that his interest and his duty are linked together, and that he can never become a thorough divine unless he becomes a prayerful Christian, I should thereby convince him of one of the deepest laid truths in the philosophy of mind. And yet when I come up to these halls and groves,* I feel a renewed assurance that a meek piety is the only pledge of successful investigation. The Burton, the Wood, the Harris. the Strong, the Hyde, the Appleton, the Porter, the Moore, the Smith, the Brown, men who went forth from this classic retreat to instruct the Churches of New England, all testify that without holiness of heart no man is qualified for an independent study of sacred themes. We are the successors of an excellent ministry. Our fathers have bequeathed to

---

* This article was delivered in the form of an address before the Theological Society of Dartmouth College, on Wednesday, July 24, 1839, the day preceding commencement.

New England a theological character, not faultless indeed, but one that we love to eulogize. No where else is the mind allowed to think with so little to fetter it. No where else are the superstitions of the people so little enlisted against inquiry. No where else has doctrine been freed so thoroughly from scholastic perversions. No where else is the door for improvement, as distinct from innovation, so safely opened. But with a great sum have we obtained this freedom. Our fathers fought like true men. They were stigmatized as the enemies of established creeds, and as the lovers of metaphysics more than of the Bible. They endured reproach, and died; but they left us their New England divinity, the great principles of which shall always live. The more it is opposed as heresy and "new light," so much the more closely will we bind it to our hearts; for it is the fruit of sound sense and severe thought, and, above all, deep devotion. So please Almighty God, we will be faithful to our fathers' memories. Like them we will learn what we can. Like them we will say what we know. We will feel that of all men on earth New England men should be the last either to fear the accusation of bigotry, or to become bigots—either to be reckless in resisting authority, or slavish in compressing their speculations into the shape of a triangle or a square. We will write on our consciences the magnanimous creed of John Robinson, who told the voyagers in the May-flower that he would not foreclose his mind against the truth of God, even if it were new. Let us then give heed to ourselves and the doctrine; be first pure and always peaceable. And may our great Teacher make us cautious like Edwards, scrutinizing like Hopkins and Bellamy and Spring; honest like Emmons, who still lingers with us to rejoice in the progress of his favorite science; and above all, may we be humble as the child who asks for bread, and as God is true, shall never receive a stone.

look around and witness everywhere the beneficent results of his wise and benevolent administration, our souls with a full gush of rapturous emotion involuntarily exclaim: "The Lord reigneth, let the earth rejoice, let the multitude of isles be glad thereof."

ARTICLE III.

INTELLECTUAL AND MORAL INFLUENCE OF ROMANISM.

A Dudleian Lecture delivered before the University in Cambridge, May 14, 1845. By Prof. Edwards A. Park, of Andover Theological Seminary.

WHEREFORE BY THEIR FRUITS YE SHALL KNOW THEM.—Matt. 7: 20.

THE character of a religious system may be learned, first, from the relation of its principles to the standard of reason and scripture; secondly, from its influence on the soul of man. The influence of a system may be ascertained by an examination either of its inherent fitnesses or of its actual operations. If we confine our regard to its inward tendencies we may become visionary; our speculations not being verified by facts. If we limit our view to the consequences which have apparently flowed from it, we may become empirical and mistake the appendages of the system for the effects of it. In order to be certain that its real influence is good or evil, we must combine a philosophical inquiry into its adaptations, with an historical inquiry into its consequences; each of these different views serving to illustrate and complete the other. Our survey of Romanism, for example, may be too superficial, if we dwell on the circumstances that have occurred in its train, and pass by the commentary which they receive from the essential fitnesses of the system. Its more skilful advocates will allow that its history is stained with many dark scenes, but they affirm that although conjoined with certain evils as accidents, it has not been united with them as appropriate developments; that it has *happened* to be allied with political despotism, with the Feudal system, with the peculiar tastes of the middle ages, and has been tinctured in this manner with influences which are far from being congenial with its own spirit. We say in reply, that the evils connected with Romanism have been prominent through so many successive ages, in so many different nations, for so long a time and with such marked uniformity, as to give evidence of emanating from the very nature of the system, rather than from its ephemeral position. Certainly we may know a tree by its fruits, when we have observed these fruits for many seasons, and in various climes. Still, in all our inferences from the event to the cause we feel the more secure when we analyze the cause itself, and find *à priori* that it is intrinsically adapted to work out the same things as effects, which have been noticed as its uniform adjuncts. We may therefore be justified in attempting to show, on the present occasion, that the essential tendencies of Romanism are injurious to the mind and heart of man.

They are injurious to the mind. Our Maker intended to leave the evidences for religion such as not only to try the feelings, but also to sharpen the intellect. He designed to invigorate the reason, as well as discipline the will, by allowing arguments of real weight to exist in favor of what may be proved on the whole to be false, and in opposition to what may be proved on the whole to be true. But the Romish idea of the infallibility of the church is, in itself and its results, at variance with the nature of moral reasoning, and encourages a spirit of dogmatism incompatible with a due regard to the evidence which exists for and against the truth. Catholic[1] theologians have assumed that to their cardinal doctrines nothing can be properly objected, and have deemed it a kind of religious suicide to call in question any

---

[1] Many object to the term Catholic as applied to the church of Rome, because the term expresses a Christian virtue for which that church is not distinguished. Some refuse to employ the word, because it implies that the Romish church differs from every other in the fact of its being a visible corporation, capable of being extended over the whole world and including under one hierarchy all individuals of all nations. There is no reason, it is said, why the Romish church should monopolize the designation, Catholic, more than the Anglican Church. It is indeed true that names are things, and that a good name is precious in its influence; but when usage has so generally sanctioned the application of this term to the church of Rome, it appears hopeless to attempt a change. There is in itself no sufficient reason why those who believe in three orders of the clergy should assume the title—Episcopalians, in order to distinguish themselves from such as believe that all ordained ministers are bishops. The believers in the parity of the clergy might as well assume the title—evangelical, in order to distinguish themselves from such as exalt the diocesan bishop above the preachers of the word. If the work of giving names to sects were now to be commenced we might invent a more distinctive and expressive vocabulary than has yet been established; but we cannot, at this late day, make an innovation upon the current phraseology without more labor than profit. Still the phraseology is unfortunate. See Whateley on the Errors of Romanism, pp. 359—367.

principle which is essential to the stability of their faith.[1] They compare the evidences for their theology to those for their personal existence and identity. They fear that in canvassing the proofs for an essential dogma, they will lose their implicit faith in it, and have therefore believed without asking for a reason, or have searched for arguments rather than for the truth. Their system appears to have logical props instead of logical grounds; to have been made up first, and afterward confirmed by reasonings which had no influence in its formation. They object to untrammeled inquiry, because it results in diversities of opinion, in skepticism, in pride of intellect. These are indeed evils; but they are avoidable, are at the worst incidental to a positive good, and withal are less to be feared than the inanity and deadness and corruption which come from an unthinking reception of a human creed.

Nor is it merely by discountenancing the investigation of first principles that Romanists have injured the tone of the intellect. They have done the same by checking the instinctive longings of the soul for progress in the science of divine things. "However some men may deride new light," says Dr. Owen, "he will not serve the will of God in his generation, who sees not beyond the line of foregoing ages." The spirit of the Reformation is that of improvement, the principle of the Romanists is that of hyperconservatism. Their œcumenical councils are supposed to have established the faith of the church; the decisions of these councils are deemed infallible, and no private scholar has a right to impugn them. Now the human mind was not made to be thus stationary. It is wronged when forbidden to examine and reject the errors of past, especially of dark ages. We are but mocked, when we are told that we have powers for research, and may

---

[1] "The certainty which the church has of the truth of her tenets, is immediate; for she received her doctrines from the mouth of Christ and his apostles, and they are indelibly stamped upon her conscience, or, as Irenaeus says, upon her heart, by the power of the Divine Spirit. If she were obliged to ascertain her doctrines first by means of a learned investigation, she would fall into the most absurd contradiction with her own self, and would annihilate herself; for, as it would be the church that seeks for the ground of her doctrines, she would be presupposed to exist, inasmuch as she examines; and at the same time not to exist, inasmuch as she is obliged first to obtain an existence, that is, to learn the truth, which is her proper being, the very thing in which and by which she is. She would seek for her own self, and this can be done only by an insane man. She would resemble the man, who would first determine whether or not he had an existence by an examination of the papers written by himself!"—Moehler's Symbolik, S. 378.

exert them, and may use the multiplied helps of modern science in the pursuit of truth, still we must not cross a single boundary which the assembled bishops have prescribed; we may go onward freely, so long as we are hemmed in by the canons and anathemas of Nice and Chalcedon and Florence. It is impossible to proceed with our investigations in a proper spirit, when we feel compelled to end them at precisely the same results which had been attained before we began. The freshness and vivacity and vigor of the soul fade away when it is repressed within any other limits than those of truth; for truth is nature, and never enslaves the mind which it controls; but the restrictions of men upon the progress of thought are artificial, they keep the spirit ill at ease and thus impede its healthy action. We are indeed assured by Romish divines, that the science of theology may be advanced as a tree may increase in size and strength, the trunk and branches remaining the same, the leaves also and the fruit.[1] Nature, however, gives up the growth of the tree to its own laws, and does not cramp it with bandages of iron; but Romanism is so minute in its prescriptions as to intersect the lines of advancement in almost every point, and whatever of expansion it does not prevent it leaves sickly and ill shapen.

Equally injurious to the mental powers is the standard of thought and feeling which is held up in the Papal church. Religion ennobles the intellect by making it familiar with the eternal laws of reason and conscience, but the votaries of Rome exalt the traditions of antiquity above our own perceptions of truth, and degrade the mind by communion with triflers. The Bible, too, gives a spring and vividness to our intellectual nature. It has not laid down its instructions in the form of a condensed, methodical, inspired creed; for it would thus allay the inquisitive spirit, and repress intellectual enterprise. It has scattered its wisdom along its pages with so touching a simplicity as to quicken the mind in its search for still more of that truth which the angels desire to look into. But Romanism has done what the sacred penmen were too far sighted to attempt. She has given us creeds which claim to be inspired, and by thus compressing

---

[1] See Mochler's Symbolik, S. 363-4. "Imitetur animarum religio rationem corporum; quae licet annorum processu numeros suos evolvant et explicent, eadem tamen, quae erant, permanent. Multum interest inter pueritiae florem et senectutis maturitatem: sed iidem tamen ipsi fiunt senes, qui fuerant adolescentes; ut quamvis unius ejusdem hominis status habitusque mutetur, una tamen nihilominus eademque natura, una eademque persona sit."—Vincent of Lerins. Com. c. XXIX.

her doctrines into a narrow compass, has saved her disciples from the invigorating toil of a study like that of the Bereans. One of her greatest sins against the intellect is, her elevating the digests of her Councils into an infallible standard of truth. She has made them equal to the Bible in authority, and superior in ease of reference, in systematic arrangement, in precise definitions. Hence the New Testament loses its appropriate place in her esteem; it is neither studied by her clergymen as the highest criterion of truth, nor read by her laymen as their familiar guide. The dogmas of the church are condensed into compends which have no freshness or vitality, and the apostles who are stimulating to the intellect, are superseded by the fathers, of whose words we cannot say as of the inspired, 'they are spirit, they are life.' We are bound to speak with reverence of the early Christian authors. We owe them a large debt, chiefly for their testimony to matters of fact, not so much for their opinion on matters of doctrine. We are grateful to them for reducing theology to a system. This work might and would have been done as well perhaps or better by moderns, but it was done by the ancients and we thank them for it. They did a noble work. Not a few of them were great and good divines, and their treatises, mutilated and forged as some parts of them have been, command our admiration. Still the fathers of the church were but men, and were never fitly trained to be authorities for our faith. We suffer a great intellectual loss when we accommodate ourselves to their illogical reasonings, their fantastic speculations, their half Jewish, half heathenish conceits. To revere their Gnostic or Platonic fancies as a standard of thought, is the cause as well as the effect of a vitiated taste and of unreasonable judgments. Romanism has fostered a love for the grotesque more than for the rational, by conforming to apocryphal scriptures and to scholastic digests of the fathers, rather than to the teachings of science or of the apostles. Some of her theories are literally made up of a perverted Aristotelianism, applied to the traditionary metaphrase of a few texts of the Bible. Her divines have not consulted the Stagirite in his purity, so much as the commentaries of the schoolmen upon him; nor is it the real meaning of the earlier fathers so often as the glosses made upon them by Thomas Aquinas, Duns Scotus and Peter Lombard, to which modern discoveries of truth are to be sacrificed. It is men and not principles; it is acute rather than wise men, subtle more than profound; men whom dark ages nurtured and who kept the ages dark;

it is these before whom we are to prostrate ourselves in a homage that enervates without truly humbling the spirit.

A low standard of thought and feeling is also presented in the worship authorized by Romanists. One hour of direct intercourse with the Judge of Heaven, is more invigorating to the mind than all their supplications to the souls of the dead. Yet it is easier for them to commune with saints than with God, and therefore, instead of refining their intellect by praying to the Spirit of truth, they often waste their time in calling on St. Anthony and St. Nicholas, St. Xavier and St. Cecilia to pray for them. They cherish an indolence of mind by their circuitous method of calling on inferior saints to implore the virgin Mary that she would beseech her Son to intercede for them before the Father. Our intellectual good requires that we pray directly to Jehovah in the name of Christ. In theory, Romanists distinguish between invocation and worship, and designate the homage which they pay to departed spirits by the word $δουλεία$, and that which they pay to God by the word $λατρεία$. Some of them regard this distinction in practice as well as theory; others do not, but apply the same language to those whom they invoke, which is proper for him only whom they adore. They debilitate their higher faculties by neglecting a thoughtful converse with the Redeemer of the world, and addressing sentimental praises to her whom they call the mediatrix between the Mediator and us.[1] Revering the Queen of heaven when they ought to be adoring an infinite spirit, they lose not only a degree of mental strength, but also that distinctive power of faith which dispenses with the aid of sight. Hence they require statues and pictures as helps to devotion, and thus enfeeble the intellect by the means which they employ to assist it. He who created the soul knew well the danger of sliding from the use of statues to the adoration of them, and therefore forbad all resort to these enervating expedients for easy worship. As men now use the crucifix, so there were Jews in the time of Hezekiah who employed the brazen image as a means of facilitating their approaches to Jehovah.

---

[1] The favorite mode of representing the Saviour as a child in the arms of a beautiful virgin, is exactly fitted to make the mother, more frequently than the child, the object of invocation, and to fascinate the eye with the graces of a human form more than to expand the intellect by an exhibition of divine excellence. She is familiarly addressed as "our Lady," " the Queen of the world as well as the Queen of heaven," "the Mother of mercy," " the Mother of grace," " the Mother of God," and is practically regarded, by Romanists in common life, as more kindly intent upon our welfare than is the Almighty himself.

No device of the kind could be more innocent; for this image had been once sanctioned of heaven for a moral purpose, and around it clustered the recollections of past deliverances. But it was seized and broken in pieces by the prophet, and called Nehushtan;[1] for he saw that the people would adore the memento of him who claims supreme worship for himself alone, and they would form gross conceptions of a deity who is accommodated to them through a gross medium. It is often said that the church of Rome is free from idolatry, because she reveres not the image but the spirit which it represents. Now there are three kinds of outward idolatry. One is the worship of a mere block or stone or plant; a second is the worship of the true Jehovah emblematized by some material object; a third is the worship of a spirit which is not the true Jehovah and which is bodied forth in some visible shape. The first kind of idolatry is chargeable upon no man that ever lived; for even the victim of feticism prays to a tree, not as mere wood, but as instinct with life, and that life is the object of his homage. The second kind is idolatry in form, though not in substance. If men worship the true God through an idol, then of course they are not revering a false God. The chief evil of this practice is that it leads to the third species of idolatrous observance, that which in its formal and essential characteristics is the adoration of a being other than Jehovah. Many of the Romanists are idolaters merely in mode not in spirit. The worship offered by their Fenelon may have been, for aught we know, even purer than that offered by our Leighton. But that some of them are idolaters both formally and really, is a truth as evident as it is unwelcome. The God who is often exhibited in their popular literature, in their pictorial representations, and in the host, is a venal and a partial and a sensuous being, fascinated with glittering ornaments, with vain pageantry. The statues which represent him are sometimes the identical figures which were carved for heathen divinities. Now it is improbable, that the image of Jupiter and Hercules will be a fit expression of the excellence which is found only in heaven. The *fac-similes* of pictures designed to give an idea of the powers that ruled on Olympus, cannot be expected to purify the Christian's faith in one who inquires, "To whom then will ye liken God, or what likeness will ye compare unto him?"[2] But even if the canvass and the marble suggested no false idea of

---

[1] 2 Kings, 18: 4.   [2] Isaiah 40: 18.

Jehovah, still the use of any material representation of him deprives the intellect of a discipline, which God intended to be essential to its fullest development. There are some themes which may be illustrated by diagrams, but the divine attributes cannot be worthily studied except in spirit and in truth. The attempt to simplify them by any more visible symbol than " God is love," will bedim the mental vision as much as it gratifies the corporeal. Where men can walk by sight, they will not cultivate the principle of trust in him whom they have not seen. In order to become spiritual, they must *be shut up to the faith.*

It is not to be expected of men who allow a host of intercessors to obscure their view of the Holy One, and who use material representations even of these interceding saints, that they will place a high estimate on the preaching of the gospel. Accordingly we find that Romanism depresses the pulpit for the sake of aggrandizing the ceremony of the mass. In some ages of the church she has almost entirely discarded the sermon,[1] and sacrificed the instruction of the mind to impressions upon the sense. It is the prominence of the pulpit which gives impulse to general education, and the history of Romanism shows that where preaching is made secondary to forms, the mental character of both clergymen and laymen loses a quickening influence.

When a Protestant enters the sanctuary, he is made thoughtful by the words of prayer and the reading of the Scriptures; and we are unable to measure the degree of mental improvement which he receives from services thus adapted to his understanding. But the Romanist is not instructed by the reiteration of his stereotyped observances. He hears the Bible read in a language which imparts to him none of its meaning, and in some churches he cannot even distinguish the words of the scriptural lesson, for these are drowned in the tumult of the ringing of bells and the pealing of the organ, which are designed to honor the recital of what would be more truly honored, if it were simply made intelligible or even audible. The rational Protestant is instructed by the sacraments of Christianity. They were intended to be sermons to the mind, and thereby to the heart. But the genius of Rome has transformed them from symbolical discourses into a species of necromancy. They are described as operating not by rational appeal, but by a kind of talismanic in-

---

[1] See Father Paul Sarpi's History of the Council of Trent, p. 169, Fol. Ed. Sozomeni Hist. Eccl. Lib. VII. cap. 19.

fluence. Protestantism would sanctify men by the truth which enlightens the intellect, but Romanism depends on the mechanical working of rites that supersede our own activity. Protestantism insists, first of all, on faith by which man is to be justified, and faith involves a vigorous exercise of reason; but Romanism lays chief stress upon external ordinances which can renovate the soul without a rational contemplation of the truth addressed to it. As the supply of thought will not exceed the demand, we cannot look for mental exertion in receiving sacraments which operate independently of such exertion. In their scriptural simplicity, baptism and the Lord's supper are eloquent expounders of great truths; but a recent author commends the Romish method of administering baptism because it " envelops the originally simple act in a great abundance of significant ceremonies," and of " the most diversified symbols."[1] This imagined excellence is one of our objections to the Catholic ritual. That ritual burdens the truth, and covers it up with outward trappings. It multiplies emblems, until the principle shadowed forth by them vanishes into thin air. It appeals to the fancy, and leaves the judgment uncultivated. It is a form of ocular worship which causes the mind to linger on the surface of things, and holds it back from profound meditation. It is arbitrary and artificial, and ceremonies which are not commended by a sober judgment cannot be repeated in the church without injury to the intellect. They foster a puerile habit of thought, and a taste for meretricious display. We can see little more than an unreasonable affectation

---

[1] See Moehler's Symbolik, Sechste Auf. S. 276. " As the Lord once cured the physical deafness of a man by a mixture of spittle and dust, so is that mixture applied in baptism likewise, for the purpose of denoting the spiritual fact, that the organs of the mind are now opened to receive the mysteries of the kingdom of God. The burning candle denotes that now indeed the divine light from above has fallen into the mind, and the darkness of sin is changed into a celestial brightness. The salt designates the wise man who is freed from the foolishness of this world. The anointing with oil designates the new priest, for every Christian is a priest in the spiritual sense of the word, who has entered into the inmost sanctuary and has renewed the most living communion with God in Christ Jesus. The white garment denotes that the believer, washed pure in the blood of the Lamb, desires hereafter to retain the innocence which he lost in the first Adam and regained in the second. All these symbols are used for the sake of expressing in the most diversified methods, the one idea that a complete, permanent change should take place in man, and a new, higher, and continued existence should begin in him."—S 276, 277. But this one idea is far more perspicuously expressed when the ordinance is left in its original plainness, and not overladen with the fantastic devices of idlers.

in the attempts of the Romish priest to portray the nature of his office by the quality, figure, and coloring of his vestments. He is a ruler in the church; why does he not wear a crown upon his head? He is the enemy of sin and the defender of his people; why does he not gird on the sword as an emblem of the sword of the Spirit? Why does he not present himself at the altar arrayed in the symbols of that panoply which is described in the sixth chapter of the Epistle to the Ephesians? Why are there not twenty sacraments prescribed? There is as much reason for twenty sacraments as for seven.[1] We can see no grounds for adopting the Romish ceremonies and omitting others which the fancy may invent, save the fact that the former have been established already. But they were established for temporary or for local causes; and the same reason which at first suggested them, may now require a change. The truth is, our religious observances ought to express the reason of their institution. They ought to be chaste portraitures of such truth as can be portrayed in a manly way. They are healthful to the intellect when they are naturally appropriate to the things which they signify. The pensive brow of the preacher ought to be his mitre of gold; his look of kindness ought to be his sprinkling of the people with holy water; his elaborated discourses are more significant than his kneeling before an illuminated Bible; his earnest tones are an expressive substitute for his making the sign of the cross; and his freedom from artificial adornings should be the tasteful memento that his life is hid with Christ in God. This is a Puritan, this is a rational system of ecclesiastical forms; and as it obeys, so it improves an enlightened intellect. The antiquity of the Romish observances is indeed an argument in their favor, but their antiquity is often that of the darkest ages, and sometimes that of the letter merely, not of the spirit. There was once a reason for ceremonies which are still continued, after the excuse for them has ceased to exist. Before the invention of printing men were profited by hieroglyphical signs, more than they can be since books are become accessible to all. But the Catholic worship is a complicated system of hieroglyphics, and they are more numerous now than they were

---

[1] On the same principle that matrimony and ordination are sacraments, may the reading of the Bible, the giving of alms, prayer, the dedication of churches, civil oaths, the coronation of kings, and indeed all the more important acts of our life be considered sacramental.—See Nitzsch's Prot. Beant. der Symbolik Dr. Moehler's, S. 186, 187.

when circumstances partly justified them. There was once a propriety in using the Latin tongue in the services of the Roman Church. It was vernacular with those who heard it; therefore it was employed in prayer. At this day it is not a living language; the reason for its use has vanished; the use itself is retained in opposition to the principle which first recommended it. The original custom was to pray in the Roman tongue, but not the original custom to pray in words which had ceased to be understood; not the original and apostolic custom to use the Latin language in America; not the primitive custom to use a dead language either in America or Rome.[1] The form of the ancient practice, as now preserved, is subversive of its ancient spirit; for the principle of the early church was, that it is better to speak five words with the understanding, than ten thousand words in an unknown tongue.[2]

There is the same objection to the whole structure of the Romish theology. It is capricious and irrational, adhering to the letter of certain antique standards and rejecting the meaning of them. It encourages an arbitrary method of investigation by its tenacity of circumstances and disregard of the substance of things. It ascribes great authority to the metropolitan church at Rome. There was a time when that church deserved a peculiar deference, for it was the scene of apostolic labor; and if the very individuals who had been addressed in words of inspiration, still survived in that ancient city, they would still merit our homage. But the circumstances which gave at first a standard character to their church, have long since disappeared. What was begun with a valid reason, is continued without one; and the claims of that ecclesiastical body have become the more exorbitant, as the rightfulness of them has diminished. There was a day when tradition was the most important means of learning the truth. The Gospels were not published, and the only attainable knowledge of them was to be gleaned from those who had listened to the earliest preachers. Time enough had not then elapsed to allow confusing or corrupting changes in the traditionary accounts of

---

[1] It is not pretended that the Romanists allege no arguments for their use of the Latin language in worship beside the antiquity of the usage; but this is the real and original reason for which the custom is retained, and the other arguments in its defence seem to be devised as secondary supports of that which would be continued without them.

[2] In like manner the witholding of the Bible from the laity is often justified because it was the early custom; but the invention of printing has made the spirit of the modern practice entirely different from that of the ancient.

our Saviour. These accounts were the New Testament, written in the hearts of men. But now, what was once tradition has become Scripture; the oral instructions of the first teachers are transferred to the written page. Our appeal to the recorded Gospels is the same in substance with the primitive appeal to the remembered narratives; it is a reference to the authority of inspired men. But the Romanists adhere to tradition, as if it were as pure in the nineteenth century as it was in the first; as if the testimony of the early churches were as ancient as the record of the apostles themselves; as if that which was needful in certain circumstances were needed when the circumstances are essentially diverse. The original arguments for such antiquated dogmas having lost their force, new arguments are invented, and we know that all reasonings which are sought out and pressed into our service from afar, tend to impair the spirit of candor. The theology of Rome, symmetrical and artfully compacted as it is, yet is so constrained, and requires such fantastical explanations, as to make the mind of its students disingenuous. Even its "golden rule," as laid down by Vincent of Lerins, is one which cannot be obeyed without violence to the judgment. It sets up the standard of truth as *quod ubique, quod semper, quod ab omnibus creditum est.* It therefore obliges an inquirer for the right faith to reconcile the creed of the bishops in any one age or nation, with that of the same functionaries in every other. But this cannot be done without a tortuous and inept construction of words. The clergy of no two nations agree in every item of their belief; for they have their national peculiarities. The theologians of no two ages are precisely alike in the shading of their faith; for every age has its own spirit. Nay, if we could ascertain the exact meaning attached by independent men to the same terms, we should perceive that no two thinking divines, the world over, have adopted in all points the same views of truth. When the light shines, the rays will fall differently upon the retina of men in different positions; and the only way in which all eyes can be made to see alike is, to leave them in total darkness where they may agree in seeing nothing at all. There is a standard of truth; but the attempt to discover it among the writings of the church-fathers and schoolmen, is an attempt to coërce them into a system which they never in all particulars believed. It is an attempt to *create* in their writings what never existed there. It leads to a process of special pleading, that vitiates the sensibilities for the truth. It may exercise a subtlety like that of the doctors of the Sorbonne, but does not train the mind to an enlarged Christian philosophy. We acquire a love for the truth by seeking it in the standards which God has written for us, in the volumes of nature and grace; but we imbibe a jesuitical spirit, by endeavoring to fabricate a theological creed from materials which can be fitted into their desired position only by distorting them.

These tendencies of Romanism are illustrated by fact. A deference for truth as such, does not characterize the Romish literature. Even the writings of Moehler,[1] Klee and Wiseman are distinguished for ingenuity rather than fairness. The Tridentine fathers displayed far less of disposition or ability to decide for themselves what is truth, than of cunning in transporting from the Quirinal palace the decisions which the Pope had made for them, and in securing a majority of votes for the decrees thus clandestinely prepared, although ostensibly inspired.[2] The themes with which Catholic authors are most intimate are of inferior worth. They are the endless genealogies of bishops, the fables of the apostolical succession, the niceties of the schoolmen, themes of external interest—seldom of inward dignity. It was the di-

---

[1] It is difficult to mention any modern theological work more ingeniously fitted to produce an impression which, on the whole, is incorrect, than Moehler's Symbolik, a translation of which has been published in England, and also republished in this country. See Bib Sac. Vol. I. 554, 555. Its sophistry consists, first, in concealing the most obnoxious phases of the Catholic doctrine; secondly, in the undue prominence which it gives to such truths as have been defended by Romanists against the ill-judged attacks of Protestants; thirdly, in its appeal to the writings of individual Protestants with the same freedom as to publicly authorized Confessions of Faith, as if the works of Calvin and Melancthon were our Symbolical books; fourthly, in quoting the impassioned and extravagant remarks of Protestant controversialists, without attempting to modify those remarks by reference to the circumstances or the idiosyncracies of the men who uttered them;—a course of treatment which the writings of Martin Luther, for example, are peculiarly ill-fitted to endure; and fifthly, in tacitly assuming that the creeds and standard treatises of Protestants are as authoritative, as those of the Romanists; that the Augsburg or Helvetic Confessions are as completely and unexceptionably expressive of the private opinions of Lutherans or Calvinists, as the Tridentine Catechism or the Bull *Unigenitus* are indicative of the universal Catholic faith. Protestants, allowing as they do the right of individual judgment, are not to be bound down to their symbolical books, as Romanists are to theirs. The faith of Catholics is in their Councils; our faith is in the Bible.

[2] The disregard to truth, the sacrifice of principle to expediency, the dishonorable, not to say dishonest, methods of conducting theological discussion, which were sanctioned by the Tridentine Council, are well illustrated in Father Paul Sarpi's History of that Council, pp. 215, 346, 365, 437, 593, 621, 684, 815, et al. Fol. ed.

vine commendation of Aaron, "I know that he can *speak* well;"[1] but the Romish priest is required from the nature of his office to *chant* well, and to be a religious martinet, rather than a comprehensive reasoner. Where so little is demanded of the teachers of the people, what can be expected from the people themselves?

We have no wish to deny that many illustrious names are enrolled among the scholars of the Catholic church. The human mind will rouse itself into action in despite of all the sedatives that are applied to it. Nor would we intimate that Romanism is devoid of all tendencies to quicken the intellect; for it is not a tissue of unmingled error, and the truth which it retains is like truth everywhere, of renovating power. We yield high praise to many of the Benedictine and Augustinian monks; of the Jesuits and the Jansenists. But when we reflect on the leisure, the retirement, the wealth and the vast multitude of the Romish clergy, we ask why are there so few accomplished scholars among the hosts who ought to have been our intellectual benefactors. There must be some radical fault in the system which has reared from its millions of preachers so small a number like the French Triumvirate, and from its cloistered students so few philosophers like Malebranche, Campanella and Des Cartes; and of these few, so large a proportion who "groaned being burdened" under the faith which had been imposed upon them. We admit that Romanism encourages a spirit of inquisitiveness into the history of the past; but why has it trained no more historians like Du Pin and Jahn and Döllinger, and why has its historical curiosity been so far controlled by its sectarian interests? We commend the Romish priesthood, that they kept the records of ancient wisdom during the middle ages; but was it not characteristic of them to *keep* these records to themselves rather than disseminate them among the people? We praise them that they have fostered a taste for the fine arts; their theology is more indebted to Raphael and Michael Angelo than to all their Hugs and van Esses. But does not the taste that is nurtured by Romanism in painting, music and architecture, favor a gaudiness of ornament, an overlading of beauties? We further concede, that a rare talent for controlling the popular mind is nourished by the distinction of orders and offices in the Catholic hierarchy; by its leisure also, by its facility of transmitting principles of finesse from one generation of its priests to another, and again by the

---

[1] Ex. 4: 14.

very fact that it has an established character for sagacious diplomacy, and this character is retained from age to age, as by prescriptive right. Woolsey, Fleury, De Retz, Richelieu, Ximenes and Mendoza learned many lessons of cunning from their mother church. But the powers and inclinations for intrigue need not be fostered by a *religious* institution. The very circumstance that the Romish clergy will gain by artifice what they lose in argument, gives an intimation of the peculiar intellectual spirit of their system. But the most impressive commentary on its influence is seen in the fact that learning revived when the Reformation began; that the mother church of Rome has trained for the last three hundred years a smaller number of original thinkers than have arisen from even a half of the Protestant churches, all of which united are a minority when compared with the Papal. Why at the present day are Lucerne, Freiburg and Uri so much less enlightened than Basle and Berne and Geneva? Why is Spain so much more degraded than Holland, Portugal than Denmark, Ireland than Scotland? Why are the Austrian clergy so far inferior to the Prussian, the Bavarian to the Saxon, the French to the English? Why have the universities under the Papal system so much less of scientific enterprise, than those under the Protestant? The fundamental reason is this; the inward tendencies of Romanism are to encourage the swinging of censers more than the contemplation of truth, the adherence to authority more than principle, to systems for which there was once an apology more than to those which now vivify the intellect. Romanism is so contrived as to save men the trouble of thinking for themselves. It adopts the principle of vicarious reasoning, as well as of vicarious virtue. It does not harmonize with the natural laws of evidence; it bends them into conformity with itself and thus makes the very science of theology sectarian. It does not look outward and upward for light, but searches into its own history for justification, and seeks the living chiefly among the dead.

As feeling is elicited by thought, we must presume that a theological system which is unfavorable to the intellect will also be injurious to the heart. The doctrines of Romanism become, often, morally injurious by means of their peculiar tendency to be perverted. Many of them involve so much nicety of distinction, that they cannot be safely stated without being critically explained. But the whole system of Romanism is averse to explanation. It needs in a preëminent degree the discussions of the pulpit, but it gives little time for those instructive addresses without which its dogmas will be misunderstood. It teaches the intellect so seldom, and beguiles the fancy with such a gorgeousness of rites, that the people will often imbibe pernicious ideas of even the truths which it unfolds. Its appeals to the imagination are so striking, and to the judgment so feeble, that men will form such notions of it as are most agreeable to their vitiated tastes. When a man is bowed down under a thought of his sinfulness, and is therefore simply commanded to eat no meat for a month, he will not understand the nature of faith, and will misunderstand the nature of Christian works. There is danger, in promising a stricken penitent that, if he will give alms to the church, he may have a dispensation from rehearsing the prayers which had been required of him as a penance. He will thus regard prayer as an evil, and simony as a virtue. There must be danger, in exposing the relics of saints or of the true cross to the gaze of men, who are not cautiously guarded against the deification of that which so overawes their sensibilities. There is great danger, in employing more of religious machinery than is often and fully, in its working and its nature, explained to the people. Romanism makes shipwreck of the faith, because she has so much more sail than ballast.

There is, for example, some truth in the doctrine of satisfactions for sin, as laid down in a few standard treatises of the Catholic church.[1] The doctrine is, that certain temporal evils ensue from moral delinquency, and that these evils may be removed or at least mitigated by certain penitential acts. These acts are termed satisfactions, and may, whenever the punitive evils can be prevented without them, be dispensed with by the church. These dispensations are called indulgences; and indulgences from one form of penance, may sometimes be procured by submitting to a different form of it. But there is reason to fear, that men who have made satisfaction for the temporal penalties of the law, will consider themselves as having satisfied its eternal demands. If their sins are cancelled for this life, they will presume on the life to come. If they can obtain a dispensation from one species of suffering by the endurance of another, they will endure the loss of money as an equivalent to some physical torture; and their willingness to part with their silver will be regarded as the proof of their contrition; and their contrition, as the means of

---

[1] See Catech. ex decreto Concil. Trident. pp. 343, 347, 352; Moehler's Symbolik, 275—298; Wiseman's Lectures on the Principal Doctrines and Practices of the Catholic church, pp. 35, 68, 69.

their deliverance from punishment here below; and this their temporal deliverance, as a pledge of their never ending blessedness. Thus the whole scheme of penances and satisfactions tends to abuse. It may be explained as comparatively innocuous; but it is very seldom thus explained by the clergy, still more seldom is it thus understood by the laity; and the history of it shows, that it encourages a spiritual commerce, a barter in the things of heaven, and converts the spirit of the Gospel into a gross speculation at the shambles.[1]

Romanism becomes injurious to the moral feelings by the mystical working of its machinery. It is a discriminating remark of Schleiermacher, that "Protestantism makes the relation of an individual to the church dependent on his relation to Christ, but Catholicism makes his relation to Christ dependent on his relation to the church."[2] Irenaeus, has said, "Where the church is, there also is the Spirit of God; and where the Spirit of God is, there is the church and all grace.[3]" Now the Protestants insist on the last clause of this sentence, as true independently of the other; the Romanists insist on the first clause as true, even when they deny the second. The most accomplished Catholic Symbolist of modern times avows, Our doctrine is that "the visible church comes first, then comes the invisible; the former is the origin of the latter. The Protestants say, on the other hand,

---

[1] The expression that the doctrines of the Church of Rome are peculiarly liable to be misunderstood, is far milder than the truth will justify. Her dogmas are commonly taught in a far more objectionable form, than that in which her standards express them. The people do not generally *pervert* the instructions addressed to them, when they believe that the Virgin Mary has divine attributes, that penances in this life will supply the place of punishment in the life to come; that indulgences are a legitimate article of traffic, etc. Romanism, as taught by the Council of Trent, leads to abuses; as taught by the majority of its priests, it is abused. It may be said indeed that the system of the Tridentine fathers is not and never has been the Catholicism generally prevalent in the Papal church. Dangerous as that system is, it is far better than the theology with which the laymen of Italy, Austria, Spain and France have been contaminated. For an exposition of Romanism as it is, in distinction from Romanism as it is described by its apologists, see Letters to N. Wiseman, D. D., by William Palmer, M. A., of Worcester College, Oxford. The sophistry of Catholic theologians is often manifested in confining the attention to their system, as cautiously expressed in their most ingenious symbols, and hiding from their readers the system, as it is commonly taught and believed. It is therefore necessary to show that, in its most plausible form, their theology exerts a deleterious influence.

[2] Glaubenslehre, I. S. 24. 2. Aufl.   [3] Adv. Haer. Lib. 3.

that the visible church comes from the invisible, and the latter is the ground of the former.¹" According to the Romish doctrine, there can be no Christian goodness save that which is derived from membership of an ecclesiastical body; and the first duty of men is, not to be what they ought to be, but to connect themselves with the church; and then, nor till then, will they receive a power of doing what their conscience assures them is binding at present. Here is a collision between the ecclesiastical ethics and those of the moral faculty; and the vigor of that faculty is impaired when its demand for inward goodness is postponed to the claims of a mystical institution. The Tridentine fathers assert that man is renewed by the baptismal water,² and hence, reversing the biblical arrangement of precepts, they enjoin on men to be baptized and repent. Our feeling of moral responsibility must be weakened when we are turned away from meditation on a spiritual duty, and directed to appear before a font, where we are to receive, as by a spell, the virtue that ought to be required of us as an immediate exercise of our free will. Conscience receives its most healthy stimulus from the mandate, "Work out your own salvation," and is made inert by the proposal, that we become the passive recipients of a change wrought by the manipulations of the priest. The pressure of immediate obligation to perform our duty, is also relieved by the Romish doctrine of the Lord's Supper. That doctrine does not require us to bring our feelings now into harmony with the divine, but to make use of a sacramental charm from which will ensue a mysterious new life. It calls on us not first to live, and then to eat of the sacred emblem; but first to receive the wafer, and then to be raised from the dead by its miraculous energy. No wise method is this, however, of securing the active virtue of a Christian. We must be summoned to walk in the right way, not merely in the way to that way; summoned to do the very thing which is itself an imitation of Jehovah, not merely to perform the means of doing that thing; summoned to reduce our own wills into a state of unison with a spiritual law,

---

[1] Moehler; see Nitzsch's Protestantische Beantwortung der Symbolik Dr. Moehler's, S. 233.

[2] Per baptismum Christum induentes nova prorsus in illo efficimur creatura, plenam et integram peccatorum omnium remissionem consequentes. Concil. Trid. Sess. 14. Recte et apposite definitur, baptismum esse sacramentum regenerationis per aquam in verbo; natura enim ex Adam filii irae nascimur, per baptismum vero in Christo filii misericordiae renascimur. Catech. Rom. 2, 2, 5. See also Catech. Rom. 2, 2, 44 and 2, 2, 50.

while God worketh within us to choose that which he demandeth of us; summoned to a rational work, by rational motives, and in a rational way; not to use an amulet by which evil may be spirited from our hearts, and virtue mystically diffused through them. The great complaint of the Reformers against the Catholic system was, that it does not represent religion as resulting from profound thought so much as from sensuous impression; that it does not, like the Gospel, work from within outward, but from without inward; that it represents a sacrament as communicating, rather than presupposing, a fitness to receive it; as an *opus operatum* in itself, and dispensing with the *opus operantis* in the recipient.[1] It is true, the Council of Trent insist, that a partaker of the divine ordinances shall not interpose an obstacle to their efficient action; the forbidden obstacle, however, is not sin as such, not sin in the general, but a particular species of it,—sin against the church,—and this is the sin unto death.[2] Even Bellarmine, who demands of such as receive the sacraments a certain

---

[1] Melanchthon says, in his Apology, Art. 7, Hic damnamus totum populum scholasticorum doctorum, qui docent, quod sacramenta non ponendi obiicem conferant gratiam *ex opere operato* sine bono motu utentis. Haec simpliciter iudaica opinio est, sentire quod per ceremoniam iustificemur sine bono motu cordis, h. e. sine fide.

[2] Si quis dixerit, sacramenta novae legis non continere gratiam, quam significant: aut gratiam ipsam non ponentibus obicem non conferre, —— anathema sit. Si quis dixerit, non dari gratiam per huius modi sacramenta semper et omnibus, quantum est ex parte Dei, etiamsi rite ea suscipiant, sed aliquando et aliquibus, anathema sit. Si quis dixerit, per ipsa novae legis sacramenta ex opere operato non conferri gratiam, sed solam fidem divinae promissionis ad gratiam consequendam sufficere, anathema sit. Sess. VII. Can. 6, 7, 8. From these canons it is evident that no positive excellence, but only a negative state is required of the person receiving a sacrament. The phrase *opus operatum*, used in reference to a sacrament, denotes, according to Bellarmine, that the sacramental grace is conferred " ex vi ipsius actionis sacramentalis a Deo ad hoc institutae, non ex merito agentis vel suscipientis," and thus excludes the idea of requiring a positive Christian virtue from either the individual administering or the individual receiving a sacrament; See Guerike's Symbolik, § 54. From the administrator it is simply required, that he have intentionem saltem faciendi, quod facit ecclesia; Conc. Trid. Sess. 7. Can. 11; and from the recipient it is also barely required that he have the intention of receiving what the church imparts. In performing the rite of baptism it would appear absurd to demand of the recipient, that he exercise a Christian grace antecedently to his being made a Christian at the font; this would be a demand for the effect before the cause, the fruits of regeneration before regeneration itself. See Nitzsch's Prot. Beant. der Symbolik Dr. Moehler's, S. 159, Wiseman's Lectures on the principal Doctrines and Practices of the Catholic Church, Vol. I. pp. 63, 64.

kind of faith and of sorrow for sin, does not yet venture to require that distinctive grace which constitutes the Christian life. He simply insists on a preparative for this grace. He teaches, if we may borrow one of his illustrations, that as the wood to be burned must first be dried, and thus fitted for combustion, so that the fire may of its own energy consume the wood; in like manner must the soul be chastised into a state of recipiency for grace, before the sacrament can exert its transforming power.[1] This state of recipiency is altogether distinct from one of holiness, being a freedom from that specific obduracy which is manifested in a disrespect for the ordinances of the church, and not being a freedom from that generic sinfulness which is the ruin of the soul. Nothing but evil ensues, however, from so lightening the burden of duty as to ask for a merely negative excellence, or a merely ecclesiastical virtue. The heart will be influenced by the standard with which it is required to conform, and when our Saviour bids us to be perfect as our Father in heaven is perfect, he holds up a criterion which tends to elevate the character; and if men do not really attain perfection, they may with heaven's aid reach a higher degree of improvement than if they had aimed at a lower mark. Is it not the experience of every day, that when an outward observance is deemed the preliminary to inward goodness, and a holy motive is not insisted on as a prerequisite for the service of God, then the feelings are debased by so ignoble a standard, and religion becomes a bodily exercise that profiteth little? If baptism be regeneration, then no evidence exists that any of the apostles, except one, were ever regenerated; and even that one felt thankful that he had never performed this renovating miracle at Corinth, except upon Crispus and Gaius and the household of Stephanas.[2] If it had been useful to regard the sacrament as an indispensable channel[3] of grace, would

---

[1] Si ad ligna comburenda primum exsiccarentur ligna, deinde excuteretur ignis ex silice, tum applicaretur ignis ligno, et sic tandem fieret combustio; nemo diceret, causam immediatam combustionis esse siccitatem, aut excussionem ignis ex silice, aut applicationem ignis ad ligna, sed solum ignem, ut causam primariam, et solis calorem seu calefactionem, ut causam instrumentalem. Bellarm. de Sacramentis, Tom. III. p. 109, quoted in Moehler's Symbolik, S. 257. That the faith and penitence which Bellarmine requires are not true holiness, is further evident from his remark, that they "solum tollunt obstacula, quae impedirent, ne sacramenta suam efficaciam exercere possent, unde in pueris, ubi non requiritur dispositio, sine his rebus fit justificatio."—Ib.

[2] 1 Cor. 1: 14, 16.

[3] Quasi alveus, as the Tridentine Fathers express themselves.

the failure to administer it have been pronounced by an inspired man a fitting cause of gratitude or of submission? Would the Lord's Supper have been instituted by our Saviour in so informal a method, and left with so few rules for its observance, if he had looked upon it as a magical ceremony, or as claiming precedence of the silent graces of the heart?

The Romanists affirm that their view of the eucharist enlivens the believer, while ours is cold. There is a warmth in their doctrine, but an animal warmth. The mystery startles the natural sensibilities, more than it edifies the spirit. We, more than they, may be cheered by the Real Presence, not indeed of a material nature, but of an unseen friend who is ever with us at the breaking of the bread. We more than they may be animated by a transubstantiation, not indeed a gross and repulsive change of the fruit of the vine into literal blood; but the ennobling transference of the virtues of Jesus to our souls. It is a subjective transubstantiation, and therefore refines the spirit which is made sensuous by an objective one.

But nowhere is the mystical agency of Romanism so injurious as in its reference to the ministers of the gospel. It affects their personal qualifications. The Protestant regards them as teachers, and therefore requires them to possess and exhibit worth of character. The Romanist regards them as Priests rather than instructors, and assigns to them, as their principal duty, the offering of a vicarious sacrifice. The manœuvres which they perform at the altar demand but little of moral excellence; and what is not *demanded* of us, we seldom furnish as a gratuity. But more; the qualifications which they receive for their chief, that is, their sacramental duties, are not so much personal as official. Their whole doctrine of the priesthood abstracts the officer from the man. The grace bestowed upon the clergyman, is said by the schoolmen to be *gratis facta*, but not *gratum faciens*. It is by an electric influence from another's hands that he receives his sacerdotal virtues. Better were it for him, if they were to be obtained only by a prolonged discipline of his own heart. There is committed to him a jurisdiction over the body of Christ, but there is required of him a mere intention to fulfil the design of the church in communicating the mysterious elements. This intention is not a moral but simply an ecclesiastical one. If he do not purpose to give the real body and spirit of Jesus to the layman, then is the sacrament null.[1] Like the mesmeric performer, he may

---
[1] Conc. Trident. Sess. 7. Can. 11. Catech. Rom. 2. 1. 25.

refuse to will, and the mysterious change does not take place. If there were certain defects in the laying on of hands, then his ordination was not valid; he did not receive the imagined ecclesiastical virtue, nor did he ever become a true priest, even although he may have been inwardly consecrated by the chief Shepherd of our souls. We know that it is uncertain whether Archbishop Tillotson were ever baptized at all; whether he were ever ordained a deacon, and whether his ordination as a priest were canonical. He appears to have been an instrument of good in the church; but whether he *did* accomplish what he *seems* to have done, will depend in great measure, according to the Romanist, on the question of his receiving or not receiving the requisite grace through the sacramental avenues. If he did receive it, then all of his apparently good influence may have been really good. If he did not receive it, then of course he could never have imparted it, could never have regenerated man at the font, nor confirmed him at the altar, nor revived him by the eucharist. The same talents, the same learning, the same moral worth, the same weight of character, which appear to have been a blessing to the church, may have been, through a mere formal inadvertence, the means of deluding thousands of souls into a false and fatal security. But can it be of other than mischievous tendency, to represent the minister as indebted for his influence to the manual contact of a fellow creature, more than to his own virtues, received by communion with his bishop in the heavens? Is not his heart sluggish enough, even when the interests of a church depend upon his sanctity, and will it not become still more sensual, when he prizes his baptism with water above the baptism of the Holy Ghost and of fire? The spirit of ministerial unfaithfulness goeth not out save by prayer and fasting; and he who relies on the magic of an ordination for his official excellence, will be the less inclined to purify his soul by obeying the truth through the Spirit. If a sermon be in its nature fitted to exert a good influence, and if the preacher be in his character fitted to give emphasis to his sermon, may he or may he not anticipate success? The Romish doctrine is, that all depends upon his ecclesiastical relations; that distorted truth, from one canonically ordained, will have a better influence than well arranged truth from one whose anointing was not according to the rubric; and even a Protestant divine has recently sanctioned the idea that a substance which is little better than poison out of the true church, becomes nutritious within it; and falsehood, though deadly when uttered in unsanctified places, becomes instructive when it falls from the lips of a preacher apostolically ordained.[1] Where then is the motive for high religious culture in one who may fulfil the duties of his calling by a sacramental incantation, rather than by wrestling with his own spirit? And when the ministry, which is the heart of the ecclesiastical body, becomes enfeebled through want of moral stimulus, what shall we expect in the extremities but languor and disease?

This is another evil ensuing from the mechanical view of church officers. Such a view injures their public influence. They come to be regarded as conduits of gold or iron, through which a virtue flows, but into which it does not penetrate, and laymen become the inert receivers of a good thus mysteriously and coldly conveyed to them. Hence they look up to their pastors with awe, but feel little sympathy with them as brethren in Christ. The fact that a priest is thought to have a magnetic power, and that the people are dependent upon his will for their salvation, gives him a degree of spiritual authority that can be safely entrusted to no son of Adam. He is induced to claim and to receive a homage that is appropriate only to Jehovah. Earthly rulers bear sway over the present, but he extends his dominion over the present and future. Monarchs can afflict the body, but he has a mysterious power to destroy both soul and body in hell. Therefore does an emperor become a vassal of the confessor. The throne of the Caesars courts the favor of the Vatican. By the Pope kings reign and princes decree justice, and almost the

---

[1] The excellent Mr. Melvill, in his discourse on Heb. 8: 2, speaks of "a succession of men who derive authority in an unbroken series from the first teachers of the faith," some of whom may be "deficient and untaught, so that (their) sermons exhibit a wrong system of doctrine;" some may administer the sacraments with " hands which seem impure enough to sully their sanctity ;" and yet the ministrations of them all may be made useful by the Saviour, " superintending their appointments as the universal bishop, and evangelizing, so to speak, his vast diocese through their instrumentality." " We behold the true followers of Christ enabled to find food in pastures which seem barren, and water where the fountains are dry." "When everything seems against them, so that on a carnal calculation, you would suppose the services of the church stripped of all efficacy, then, by acting faith on the head of the ministry, they are instructed and nourished, though in the main the given lesson be falsehood, and the proffered sustenance little better than poison." Christ is represented as so taking " upon himself the office of preacher, as to constrain even the tongue of error to speak instruction to his people." These imitations of Romanism are intermingled with remarks both rational and important, and thus are made the more deleterious by the truths with which they are connected.

omnipotence of God is wielded by the vanity and selfishness of man.

Romanism exerts an unfavorable influence upon the heart by the monotony of its observances. In all lands and in all ages it seeks to preserve the same routine of forms, and thus exhibit an appearance of unity. Wherever her children wander on the earth, she aims to cheer them with the identical words, as well as gestures, that have been hallowed by their earliest associations. There is something of good in this arrangement, but more of evil. The heart of man craves a variety of appeal. It longs for a different spirit in the ceremonies observed in hours of gladness, from that which breathes through the forms for affliction. And if one man require a change for the varied circumstances of his life, much more must the wants of different men, and especially of different nations, still more of dissimilar ages, be diversified. But Romanism approaches a dying bed with the same pomp and overawing authority with which it dedicates a cathedral. The Catholic who expires with the blessing of his priest marches forward to meet the eternal One amid the illumination of sacred candles, the glitter of a crucifix and costly vases, and with a company of those who serve at the altar, all of them arrayed in white garments like angels of light, and escorting the anointed sufferer from the church militant, to that which will prepare him for the church triumphant. The same spirit of exact discipline and of etiquette, diffuses itself through the nuptial rites and those for taking the black veil. If the expression of the ceremony for one of these occasions were appropriate, that very circumstance would render it inappropriate for the other.

It is only on a superficial view that the evil of this undeviating formality can be deemed unimportant. When the rites of a church cease to be congenial with the peculiar circumstances of men, they cease to be inlets of instruction. The fact that they are inflexible, makes them ostentatious. The fact that they are ostentatious, withdraws the mind to them, and away from what they ought to signify. The fact that forms are made more attractive than meditation, converts the spirit of piety into a love of display; and when even the altar becomes a scene of parade, what must we look for in places of inferior sanctity. Some observances of the church ought to be private. It chills or shocks or degrades our sensibilities, to make known the most sacred of our feelings in methods exposed to the ribaldry of coarse men. But when these observances are stereotyped, they become public. They destroy the delicacy of emotion that shrinks away from the world's gaze, and check the spontaneous development of a religion that is healthy no longer than it is left to its own impulses. The practice, for example, of auricular confession is in itself innocent. Men ought to confess their faults one to another; but at the prompting of their own hearts, and in a manner accommodated to their peculiar susceptibilities. When that which ought to be voluntary becomes an exacted form; when the layman, who is bound to confess his sins to those who are sinned against, is required to divulge them to a priest,[1] and doomed to a penal infliction unless he succumb to this demand; when the confessor is seated in an inquisitorial chair, and the story of the penitent is whispered through a grate, in a kneeling posture, and before a crowd of strangers who are tremblingly waiting to pass through the same ordeal, then that which was a duty becomes a ceremony; attracts to itself the confidence of its performers; is regarded as a substitute for inward penitence; is transformed from a gushing out of warm feeling that cannot be repressed, into a cold and forced obedience to a law; and hence the confessional, one of the appropriate sanctuaries of piety, has been a scene of which we blush to repeat what we have heard, but of which not the half will be made known, till all the dark things which have been *whispered to the ear* in closets shall be revealed upon the housetops.[2]

The influence of Romanism appears unfavorable to the heart, in its tendency to separate religion from good morals. The essence of morality consists in such constitutional affections as are amiable, and such external deportment as is in harmony with them. The essence of religion consists in holy exercises of the will, in making all our emotions and external deeds subordinate to the universal good. Religion, therefore, is the life of morals. It can no more safely be separated from them, than the soul from the body. But Romanism undervalues morality as distinct from religion, and thus gives a false idea of religion itself. It represents our obligations to Heaven as synonymous with our duties to the church; and our duties to the church, as synonymous with certain outward observances; and those observances, as the

---

[1] The Romish "confession to the priests," is not regarded by them as a confession to their fellow men, so much as to God, who is represented by the priest.—Moehler's Symbolik, S. 234.

[2] The early Reformers denominated the confessional, *Carnificina conscientiarum*.

proofs of that love which is the fulfilling of the law. It so commends the use of the rosary, as to make a small matter of the doing of justice. The kissing of a golden crucifix is one of its most honored ceremonies in worship; and it therefore seems a comparatively humble virtue, to speak the truth. A pilgrimage to Jerusalem is esteemed of more value than the performance of one's domestic duties, and a crusader is canonized when an honest man is forgotten. There are passages in the discourses of so good men as Massillon[1] and Bossuet, which tend to divorce morality from piety, exalting the latter on the ruins of the former. Not only from the writings of Sanchez, Escobar, Molina and Lipsius, but even from the records of the infallible councils, we should be led to predict, that many Romanists would call certain frauds pious, and would therefore practise them, would keep no faith with heretics, would trust in the goodness of the end for the sanctifying of the means; that priests would ostensibly perform miracles when the people were ignorant enough to be deluded, and would cease to perform them when the laity were able to detect such imposition; that cunning men who had succeeded in their displays of miraculous power, and had made certain sacrifices for the church, would be admitted to the calendar of saints in the ages of darkness, but that promotions to this sacred class would be less frequent in the days of increasing light. All such things we should predict as the legitimate results of Romanism; but its tendencies are better developed in history than in prophecy. What is suggested as probable by the very genius of the system, is found to be actual in the narratives of freebooters who have been careful to say the apostles' creed as soon as they have secured their prey; of assassins who have made atonement for their profitable crimes by enriching their priests; of cathedrals erected, monasteries endowed, and bishops' palaces adorned at the expense of innocent men who were plundered of their treasures for the glory of religion. The spirit of mediaeval piety was in too fearful a degree the spirit of robbery and burnt-offering; of falsehood and devotedness to the church; of Ave Maria on the lips and carnage in the act. It is in the records of monks and nuns who have left their duties in the world for the observance of fasts and vigils,

---

[1] See a discourse of Massillon on giving his benediction to the standards of the regiment of Catenat, and the comments made upon one of its paragraphs by Adam Smith in his Theory of Moral Sentiments, Part III. chap. II, and by Frederic von Raumer, in his Discourse on Frederic the Great, delivered before the Berlin Academy of Sciences, p. 25.

that writers on conscience have found their most humiliating examples of the perversion of that faculty; of complacence in immoral conduct when associated with ecclesiastical observances; the immorality being the more stubborn because it was sanctioned as religious, and the religion being made the more powerful by its sympathy with the natural selfishness of the heart.

It is often claimed, that to some of our constitutional emotions, Romanism is peculiarly beneficial. It is said to have a favorable influence upon the principle of fear. It does indeed arouse this emotion, but not so as to make it harmonize with a proper self-respect, with manly courage, with firmness of resolve. It inspires an awe in view of the priest who openeth and no man shutteth, who shutteth and no man openeth; but this dread of man precludes that fear of the Lord which is the beginning of wisdom. All his life long is many a Romanist held in bondage by the thought of the enginery of punishments, that may be plied against him by the church. Thus is engendered a craven spirit, predisposing him for the endurance of ecclesiastical and political tyranny. Thus also is cherished a dread of suffering, more than of wrong; of God's punitive inflictions more than of his inward disapproval. The doctrine of purgatory too, is a heavy burden upon the mind of its believers. It presses them down with the dread of a retribution from which " the pitifulness of Christ's great mercy" may not deliver even the penitent. The dying man, although of a contrite and trustful heart, is not cheered with the hope of being this day with his Redeemer in Paradise; but a long and tedious process of purification awaits him after death, and too often must he profane his last hours with calculations on the price to be paid for his ransom from suffering. Pervading the literature of Rome there is more of an effort to intimidate men than to cheer them. The spirit of Thomas à Kempis even, and of Pascal, is not exactly that of adoption. They have an asceticism that is not found in the gospel, all the breathings of which are of peace and good will to such as receive it. Many of their imitators have less of that love which casteth out fear, than of that fear which suppresses love. They seem not to have solved the enigma of being sorrowful yet always rejoicing. Their sorrow is too much a thing by itself; and their cheerfulness too little attempered by the penitence for sins forgiven. Their practical theology is too mercantile, tinctured not enough with the scheme of grace, too much with that of penances and satisfactions. Instead of representing wisdom's ways as ways of pleasantness, it often exacts the most sacred duties as punishments for sin. It commands the *Pater Noster* to be repeated five times in the day, not because the repetition is a cordial to the soul, but because it is a fitting penalty for past misdeeds. Romanism hires men to perform holy acts by a promise of indulgences; and thus implies that such acts are in their nature distasteful to the soul of him who submits to them through fear of something worse. It says too much of the mortifying of self, and too little of the fulness and freeness of divine grace; it says too much of ecclesiastical discipline, and too little of brotherhood with the Saviour; it has imbibed too many influences from heathenism, and has incorporated with itself too many of the Jewish peculiarities, to breathe into the spirit that peace which passeth all understanding. It is a hard religion to bear, and its subjects lie under it rather than live in it.[1] It holds forth a chilling doctrine concerning sins after baptism; and no man can heartily believe that doctrine, and at the same time be truly glad in the spirit. Not but that they are often happy; but it is one thing to rejoice, and another, to rejoice in the Lord. Not but that we are bound to cherish what the apostle calls a godly fear, but we must

---

[1] Protestants are said to contradict themselves in calling the Romish system, at one time, more austere than their own; at another time, less so: see Wiseman's Lectures, Vol. 2. pp. 27, 28. But the two charges are mutually consistent; for in some relations Romanism is too onerous and severe; in other relations, too easy. First, it multiplies austerities which are not needed, which do no good; and it may with justice be denominated cruel, simply because it inflicts upon its believers unnecessary hardships, imposes burdens which are not demanded by the conscience, which do not impart spiritual peace. Its numerous physical inflictions are, in themselves, difficult to be borne; and the more so, because they do not relieve the necessities of our moral nature. Protestantism, on the contrary, requires the performance of such duties only as are rational, and conducive to the tranquillity as well as the sensitiveness of the moral powers. It is an easy system, because it imposes upon us nothing more than is requisite for our spiritual good. Secondly, Romanism is difficult in its relations to our constitution. Its pains and penalties are disagreeable to man as man. The Protestant religion is difficult in its relations to our depraved nature. Its duties are burdensome upon man not as man, but as a sinner. On the other hand, Romanism is comparatively pleasant to man as a depraved being; for it substitutes external performances for the moral submission which he dreads: and the Protestant system, though hard to our vitiated nature, is easy to our constitutional powers; for it demands only such exercises as are congenial with the principles of the soul as God originally made them. Just so, "the way of the transgressor is hard," as it ultimately affects the human constitution, but easy, as it gratifies our depraved inclinations; and the yoke of Christ is difficult to be borne by a man, viewed as one whose "heart is fully set to do evil," but is not burdensome to a man, viewed as one made for the purpose of wearing it, having a constitution fitted for it, as well as fitted by it.

avoid an excess of natural fear; for perfect love casteth out all inordinate dread; there is no ill proportioned fear in love; and that fear which exists without love, is often one of the most debasing passions of our nature.

It is cheerfully conceded to the Romanists, that their system fosters, in some respects, a spirit of reverence. Too often, however, it inspires a veneration for some ancient relic more than for the genius of a man like Luther; for the casula and holy oil more than for such piety as that of Huss or Wickliffe. An undue veneration for what is subordinate, leads to a comparative disrespect of what is of higher worth. The extravagant estimate which has been placed upon baptism, has in part occasioned the levity with which the usage of our mother tongue now treats the word Christening.[1] If it be the intimate association of contraries that produces the ludicrous, we cannot expect that even an ordinance truly noble will be regarded as such, when it is raised above its appropriate sphere, and described in phrases incompatible with its nature. Neither can we expect that the sublime mysteries of our religion will be revered as they should be, when they are brought down from the region of spirit into that of sense. We do not venerate that which costs us no effort to understand. Intellectual truths receive a deeper homage than ocular representations. But the whole tendency of Romanism is to lower the dignity of the gospel, by attempting to make its principles easy of entrance into the mind through the eye. It allows the spirit to be controlled by symbols, instead of using them as servants. The sight of a cross may fill the beholder with awe for a time, but will lose its permanent influence unless it be preceded by a devout contemplation of its meaning. Romanism, however, obtrudes this sign upon us before we have subdued our hearts to a feeling of its import, holds it out on the tower of the cathedral and at the corners of the streets, amid the tumults of business and in the moments of mirth. The cruciform church does not perpetuate a feeling of veneration for the image, part of which is daily trampled under foot. Neither does the ceremony of the Mass cause us to revere the principle involved in the crucifixion, when that ceremony is known to be in part a theatrical exhibition of the scene that oc-

---

[1] A similar remark may be made in reference to the words *priest*, *purgatory*, etc. Centuries will not banish the real irreverence, which has been occasioned by the attempt to give these words a more awful import than the truth will justify. See this subject well illustrated in Whately's Errors of Romanism, pp. 21—80.

curred on Calvary. Some of the priestly vestments are designed
to represent the garments worn by our Saviour in his last hours.
The sacristy is sometimes made to resemble his tomb. In the
darkness of that tomb we may discern an image made like unto
the Son of Man, lying a corpse with the linen napkin about his
head. Wax figures are employed in many churches to illustrate
the occurrences at Gethsemane. The darkness that covered the
earth from the sixth hour to the ninth, is rudely imitated in the
Tenebrae; so is the quaking of the earth and the rending of the
rocks. Nay, there has sometimes been a living imitation of the
Saviour's punishment on the cross, of his burial, and rising again,
and ascending toward the skies. We even see in many Catholic churches pictorial representations of God himself; one person
in the Trinity is painted as an aged man, another as a youth, a
third as a dove. But where is the limit to this infatuated symbo-
lism? We cannot define the precise limit. We must have some
symbols; we do employ them in the structure of language, in
figures of speech, in the very exercise of the imagination. We
may use any symbols which do not supersede the exercise of
faith, nor interfere with the spirituality of our devotion, nor satisfy
the mind with the show instead of the substance. There is a
religious tact, which will determine their number and character,
better than any rule can define them. And it is this Christian
sense which decides that the symbols employed by Romanists
are so multiplied, so complicated, so ostentatious, as to stifle man's
reverence for the power of godliness, and in the end for the very
form of it. The same effect is produced by some of the Romish
phraseology. What profaneness were it to speak of a Jehovah
College, or a God church-edifice; yet we hear of a Trinity College, and a Trinity house of worship, from those who believe the
name Trinity to be synonymous with Deity.[1] We hear of a Society among the brethren of Jesus, that is called " the Society of
the Holy Ghost." From this kind of familiarity with sacred things,
we should anticipate what we find, the frequent display of an irreverent spirit at the Romish altars. Not at all wonderful is it, that
even the Bishops of Trent exhibited sometimes a profane and sacrilegious temper even in their worship at the holy convocation.[2]

---

[1] In some places the street, contiguous to the Trinity church, is called Trinity street, the school-house in the neighborhood is distinguished by the same
epithet, and this " incommunicable name" is even applied to the parsonage,
the sexton, etc. etc.

[2] Sarpi's Hist. pp. 714, 727, 728.

Not at all wonderful is it, that the world has never witnessed such revolting forms of infidelity, as where the church has demanded so great reverence for her trinkets, that men at length lost their veneration for real worth. When we first think of the blasphemies of Voltaire, we are surprised at his depraved tastes; but we learn to regard him as no causeless phenomenon, by considering the tendency of the religion that was paraded before him, to provoke the scorn which a more modest ceremonial might have allayed. Men had learned in the sanctuary to combine dissimilar ideas, and it was in the extending of this combination that the wit of the French infidels in great measure consisted. It was a baleful wit; it was without excuse; but never would it have been so effective upon the people, if they had been trained by the church to revere principle and character, more than officers and their gewgaws. Never had the goddess of reason been so worshipped, if men had honored the true God more rationally; nor would "crush the wretch" have been so popular a watch-word, if Jesus had been revered in the life as much as in the host,—if his instructions had been venerated, as much as the pictures of his infancy, or some feigned relic of his garments.

There is another emotion on which the influence of Romanism is said to be favorable, but on which it is really injurious. That emotion is the love of power. A multitude of offices, one excelling another in the splendor of its insignia, tends to inflame the desire of preëminence. A domineering temper is fostered by the very nature of the Romish priesthood. When the mother brings her only child before the man of God, and feels that from his hands must issue the mysterious essence without which it had been good for that infant had it never been born;[1] when in the darkness of the night the minister with his retinue moves from the temple, from the altar, from the tomb of Jesus, to the chamber of the dying, and bears with him the body of the Lord of hosts, whereof if the dying eat he shall hunger no more; when the weeping children hang around the neck of the only one whose prayers will be availing to save their deceased father from the severities of purgatorial discipline, then is the priest clothed with a majesty and an awe which frail man was never made to associate with his own person. Seldom, seldom is it in the nature of one who has this strong hold on the sympathies of the ignorant, to resign the crown which they are so eager to place upon one's head.

---

[1] See Conc. Trid. Sess. 7. Can. 5. Cat. Rom. 2, 2, 21.

There is something too in the selection of the clergy of Rome which increases their eagerness for power. The great majority of them are from the lowest of the people. They are flattered by their elevation from such great obscurity to such singular honor. Almost at one bound they spring from a menial service to an intimacy with the papal See, and are prepared to be obsequious to the dignitaries by whom they have been made kings and priests unto God. Their numerous relations are elated with the idea, that here and there a vicegerent of heaven has been chosen from their own families. Thus are they rendered submissive to any exactions which may be made by the sacred college. Being required to live in celibacy, the priests are distracted by no household cares, they have an undivided heart, and that is given to the church. On the other hand, there is a limited number of those holding the keys of heaven, who are selected from noble families. It has always been the policy of Rome to adorn its priesthood with some of royal lineage,[1] and this band of the Lorraines and the Francis de Borgias receive as much obeisance from the plebeian clergy, as the latter receive from the mass of the people. Such a gradation of honors affords a like temptation and a like indulgence to the ambitious spirit of all, from the pope and the cardinals down to the acolyths and the ostiarii. It is this spirit that suggested the seven orders of the clergy, and the ordination of even the doorkeepers of the church. The very structure of language gives proof, that the tendencies of Romanism to foment the desire of power have been developed in fact. We have the word *bishopric*, but not the word *servantdom*. We hear much of *hierarchy*, never of *hierodoulia*. The Romish polity is thought by its friends to have been suggested by an intelligence superior to the human; and they can adduce no better argument for their belief than the exquisite fitness of this polity for holding dominion over the mind of man. Its very genius is to make the officer despotic, and the people submissive. Hence has one of its learned proselytes, Frederic Schlegel, been successful in his attempt to prove that Romanism is the natural ally of a monarchical government. It so flatters the love of power, that it will be probably sustained by kings, long after it has been abandoned by scholars and philanthropists.

Another principle to which the tendencies of Romanism are less favorable than has been claimed, is that of benevolence.

---

[1] See Paul Sarpi's History of the council of Trent, pp. 489, 490, 737.

The very effort to coërce men into a unity, prevents their desired communion. The system which encourages a love of office, must occasion feuds; and where there is a contest for preëminence, there is but little kindliness of feeling, either in him who obtains, or him who loses the mastery. The visibleness of the Catholic religion narrows the sphere of its charities. Baptism is a sign that cannot be mistaken, and whoever has received this sign is thereby both designated and made an heir of bliss. Now it is dangerous for any man to feel assured, that such a rite has made him a favorite of Heaven. He needs something more than a baptismal regeneration, to save him from an uncharitable temper toward those who have not received this decisive token of their good estate. It is dangerous for any man who obtains his Christian spirit only from the wafer, to be confident of his elevation above such as live without this discriminating sign. If a man will not bow the knee at the lifting up of the host, he pours upon religion a contempt which is odious, and which is the more profane because the neglected service is so easy. And is there not danger of losing a brother's attachment for one who is thus evidently excluded from the precincts of mercy. No easy thing is it, to harbor in the embraces of earthly fellowship those who are daily incurring the anathemas of the church that we believe to be infallible. Difficult must it be to sympathize with those who are distinguished from us as by a mark upon the forehead, the mark of such as are given over to uncovenanted mercy. Our Maker never designed that the evidences of his approval should be paraded upon our persons, so much as exhibited in our life. He never intended that we should know his true friends by any superficial tests, but by their conduct. And as the conduct of a man is not always uniform, we are taught to be slow in deeming him a reprobate, and to have a charity that hopeth all things. It lies, however, in the very nature of a system that multiplies tangible criteria of discipleship, to nourish a pharisaical temper, and to confine all the benevolence of its disciples to their own clan. Such a system draws a dividing line between the church and the world, not according to developments of moral principle, but according to distinctions of form; and whenever we judge of men by their outward badges more than their general character, we imbibe an exclusive spirit which makes a sectarian of one who ought to be a Christian. By no means, then, is it a mere concomitant of Romanism, but rather its inherent tendency, to look upon all whom it shuts out from its communion, as worthy of punishment, and to regard persecution here, as a means of saving them from greater woes hereafter. It has been in its very principle a persecuting religion, and has not only practised but *reasoned* on the ground, that if man cannot be converted save by its forms, and if the pincers and the rack can induce him to comply with these forms, then such instruments of cruelty must be used, and a benevolence seeing far into the future should suppress the impulses of kindness for the present. Wherever the ecclesiastical spirit prevails over the Christian spirit, persecution comes to be regarded as a duty, and conscience adds impetus to revenge.

It is the principle of faith, to which the Romanist claims that his theology administers peculiar strength; and he even adopts as a commendation, what Hume intended as a sarcasm, in the remark, 'our holy religion is founded on faith, not on reason.' Now faith, viewed as a moral principle, is a spirit of love to the truth wherever found, and has no sympathy with the disposition to inquire 'who is the man that speaks,' rather than, 'what is the word spoken.' The treasures of excellence that are spread out before us by Fenelon and Bossuet, we as Protestants rejoice in, if we have faith; for this principle causes goodness as such to be our delight. But when the amiable sentiments of a Zinzendorf or a Spangenberg are presented to the Romanist, are they welcomed by him? Is it not a sacrilege to receive instruction from one who is not connected with the apostles by the only chain which conveys the needed electric influence; from one who being unbaptized and unordained falls under the anathema of the church for venturing upon the sin of Korah, Dathan and Abiram? There is not another sect made so impervious by its very constitution to the influence of a candid statement, as that which calls itself no sect but the church, and a dissent from which is viewed as in its nature schismatic and heretical.—The principle of faith is also distinct from an unwarranted confidence in human merits. But the genius of Romanism is a trust in the supererogatory performances of the dead, and the genuflexions of the living. Its cardinal dogma, that we are able to do no more than God requires of us, tends to inspire a confidence in ourselves which is incompatible with true reliance on the grace of heaven. —The principle of faith is likewise a feeling of dependence on the one sacrifice upon Golgotha; but the faith of the Papist is too often a trust in the sacrifice that is offered in the daily mass. He beholds the body broken and the blood shed under a gorgeous canopy, amid clouds of incense and the melting strains of the harp and the dulcimer. He *sees* a real sacrifice, miraculous in its origin and influence. He sees one whom he believes to be a God, offered as a victim by a man, and he confides in what he sees, rather than what he has read of as done in Judea of old. Why not? Vision is more impressive than memory; an oblation made before our eyes, than one looking dim through the vista of ages. The priest who offers the beautiful and wonderful sacrifice to-day, imposes on the eye and the fancy, while the ancient man of sorrows who was meek and lowly, hath no comeliness, that men should love him or hold him in remembrance. In fact, his crucifixion is not remembered, by multitudes, who suppose themselves to be redeemed by the missal oblation. This is the profaneness of Romanism. It thrusts itself between the throne of mercy and the suppliant. It practically makes an atonement of its own; and the High Priest of our profession, who was the only Mediator between God and man, is thus shorn of his distinction, and every performer of a mass becomes, by that ceremony, a Redeemer.

I might continue this train of remark, and show that Romanism encourages a haughty temper, by teaching among other things of like kind, our competence to perform works of supererogatory merit; that it fosters a spirit of indolence and procrastination, by teaching, with many things of the same character, that our present life is not our sole opportunity of preparing for heaven, and that after we are dead we shall be subjects of prayer. But I must close. I should not have detained you so long, did I not believe that our beloved land is threatened with serious evil from the inroads of the papal church. This church is the work of ages. Thousands of minds have contributed to the perfectness of its organization, and it is so modelled that, wherever it exists, it WILL have influence. It will, at least, infuse its peculiar spirit into other religious systems. Such is its ecclesiastical police, that it will be more efficient than Protestantism, in its control over those men who act in masses. Its tendencies are so congenial with our vitiated inclinations, that argument will often give way before it. It will attract the poor by its tinsel, and the rich by its outward magnificence; the ignorant by its dispensing with the need of erudition, and the learned by the scholastic air of its literature. It allures the historian by the extent of its records, and the poet by the romance of its nunneries; the painter and the sculptor, the architect and the antiquarian, it fascinates by its masterpieces of art. It overawes the timid, and enlists the ambitious in its service. It captivates the proud by doing homage to their good works, and deceives the humble by its parade of self-mortifications. Some men will feel the power of its exclusiveness, and regard it as the safest church, if not the only true one. Others will be overborne by its dogmatism, and carried away by the mere positiveness of its claim. Some will be charmed with its ostensible oneness; many will be taken captive by the stratagems which it is so well contrived to employ; and many more will be consoled and flattered with its allowing them to be religious by proxy, with its making the priest a vicarious officer for the layman. Conservatives will admire it for its steadfastness, and radicals for its innovation upon our Puritan usages. Men of influence will often sustain it, because it gives facilities for managing the populace. Infidels will be glad of its conquests, because it makes war upon the spirituality of religion. Some of the bereaved will be drawn toward it, by its pretending to retain an influence over their departed relatives; some friends of the truth will love it, because in some things it has "kept the faith;" and all may be affected by it, because it becomes all things to all men.

As this church will have an influence, so this influence will be peculiarly injurious to a republic. Our government requires the diffusion of learning through the multitude. Romanism prefers the concentration of it among a few leading minds. Our government requires that every citizen be himself a man; forming his own judgments, acting agreeably to his independent moral principle. Romanism encourages the majority not to think for themselves, but to do what the reverend chapter may think out for them. A republic will best flourish when each of her citizens has a personal interest in her soil; but the papacy aims to monopolize for itself what is due to the State. Each of its ordained leaders is divorced from the world, and married to the church. "He hath no children," and nearly all his interests are garnered up with the Holy See.[1] He is, besides, amenable to a transatlantic government. This is said to be a spiritual government, but it is also a temporal one, and as such, is intimately allied with European despotisms. At the best, it is difficult to separate altogether our religious from our civil relations; and the court of Rome, which has been so long addicted to political manœuvres,

---

[1] See the arguments for celibacy and kindred abuses in Father Paul Sarpi's History of the Council of Trent, pp. 460, 630.

will be slow to abandon a policy which its unerring Councils have sanctioned. Its conservativeness of ancient customs is an omen of its continuing to interfere with the affairs of State.[1] It has more than one imperious motive for mingling in our political contests, and making them subservient to itself. As it has the motives, so it has the means for attempting to modify the operation of our government. Many of its friends have avowed their purpose of using these means. Many, who have formed no such purpose, are blind instruments in its execution. For the truth is, it is not congenial with the nature of a Republic, that a compact multitude of its voters should put their moral sense into the keeping of a few individuals; especially, of individuals who are accustomed to use authority instead of argument; still more, of individuals who are absorbed in their church more than in the common weal; who are ecclesiastics rather than citizens, and Jesuits more than patriots; who hold their office by tenure from a foreign power; who are accountable for their conduct to transatlantic overseers, the professed enemies of our republican system; who are banded together in an organization having all the efficiency and all the evils of secret societies, and depending for its influence, if not for its maintenance, on such a state of public feeling as is congenial with political despotism, but averse to the very constitution of a self-governing people. The danger is, that these uneducated masses of laymen will be bought and sold by their leaders to political demagogues. The very existence of such a multitude who may be disposed of in the gross, is a temptation to a species of chicanery which a free government is not fitted to endure. Our institutions were not made for embracing an eccle-

---

[1] It is one of the most discouraging characteristics of the Church of Rome, that she regards her past history with so much reverence as to make it a model for her future conduct. This veneration for herself, as she existed in times gone by, creates a repugnance to all change, even where the change would promote her interests. Her former faults will be her future character, because she incorporates herself with her history. If her past developments had been more consonant with the spirit of the gospel, her tenacity of ancient customs would be a virtue; but now her reformation is made the more improbable by the fact that she has needed, for ten centuries, to be radically reformed. This necessity of a thorough improvement has become part of her unchangeable character, and the fact that she deems herself infallible, perpetuates the most grievous of her faults. Her misfortune is, that her past history has settled down like a permanent incubus upon her spirituality; that her character is established, and that she is determined to perpetuate whatever has been already sanctioned. Hence all attempts, like those of Luther, Ronge and others, to abrogate her time-honored abuses, must end in secession from her community.

siastical empire within their elective forms; especially an empire whose history has been one of contest for sway.

I am no alarmist. I have strong confidence in the Protestant mind. It will at last prevail over Papal discipline. Our system is sustained by reason; and in the sweep of years reason will prevail over tradition. Our system is favored by conscience; and in the end conscience will triumph, though her victory be long delayed. Our sytem is founded on the Bible, and the word of the Lord endureth forever. We must imbibe, however, somewhat of the zeal of our aggressors. We must be munificent to our schools of learning. We must dedicate them, as this is dedicated, " to the truth,"[1] not to prejudice; to Christ first, as the incarnation of benevolence, and then to the church, as the company of all the good; not to the church first as an outward corporation, and to its spiritual Head as the second object of homage. We must be rational Christians, and thus oppose the spirit of Romish credulity; liberal Christians, and thus rebuke the sectarianism which excludes from the covenant of grace all who follow not us. We must be evangelical Christians, and thus condemn the formality of those who boast of fasting twice in the week; biblical Christians, and thus reform the faith of such as lose the Bible among the tomes of the fathers. We must be Christians, and thus reprove the partialities of Romanism. We must be patriots, and thus resist its tendencies to monarchical discipline. We must be men, and thus frown upon the spirit of bondage that has so long made the layman a slave of his confessor. If we have no pictures of the saints, our life must be a *fac-simile* of his who went about doing good. If we have no imposing cathedrals, we must make even our bodies the temples of the Holy Ghost. *So will he who is mighty do great things for us, and holy is his name.*

---

[1] Two of the ancient mottos of the University are, " Veritati," and " Christo et Ecclesiae."

and which contributed not more to his reputation than to the profit of the church and theological science. His earnest piety and powerful eloquence, united with a fascinating manner, now had an opportunity for full exertion. We, for the present, take leave of Beza, surrounded by his pupils and the listeners to his expositions of the word of life. His private study too is not neglected, and as we may at some subsequent time see, he is not wholly deserted by the Muses. We can easily imagine that the Catholic biographer of Calvin[1] is not at all partial when he says of his first labors at Lausanne: "The professor met with brilliant success; they flocked to attend his lectures from Berne, Fryburg and even from Germany. His language was well condensed and very correct. Those who listened to him imagined themselves hearing Melanchthon. 'He had,' they said 'the harmonious and copious style of Luther's disciple, but more warmly colored.'"

ARTICLE VI.

THE THEOLOGY OF THE INTELLECT AND THAT OF THE FEELINGS.

A Discourse delivered before the Convention of the Congregational Ministers of Massachusetts, in Brattle Street Meeting-house, Boston, May 30, 1850, by Edwards A. Park, Professor in Andover Theological Seminary.[2]

THE STRENGTH OF ISRAEL WILL NOT LIE NOR REPENT: FOR HE IS NOT A MAN THAT HE SHOULD REPENT.—1 SAM. 15: 29.

AND IT REPENTED THE LORD THAT HE HAD MADE MAN ON THE EARTH, AND IT GRIEVED HIM AT HIS HEART.—GEN. 6: 6.

I HAVE heard of a father who endeavored to teach his children a system of astronomy in precise philosophical language, and although he uttered nothing but the truth, they learned from him nothing but

---

[1] J. M. V. Audin, p. 464.

[2] When the author began to prepare the ensuing discourse, he intended to avoid all trains of remark adverse to the doctrinal views of any party or school belonging to the Convention. But, contrary to his anticipations, he was led into a course of thought which he was aware that some clergymen of Massachusetts would not adopt as their own, and for the utterance of which he was obliged to rely on their liberal and generous feeling. Although it is in bad taste for a preacher on such an occasion, to take any undue advantage of the kindness of his hearers, yet perhaps it is not dishonorable for him, confiding in their proverbial charity, to venture on the free expression of thoughts which he cannot repress without an injurious constraint upon himself.

falsehood. I have also heard of a mother who, with a woman's tact, so exhibited the general features of astronomical science that although her statements were technically erroneous, they still made upon her children a better impression, and one more nearly right than would have been made by a more accurate style. For the same reason many a punctilious divine, preaching the exact truth in its scientific method, has actually imparted to the understanding of his hearers either no idea at all or a wrong one; while many a pulpit orator, using words which tire the patience of a scholastic theologian, and which in their literal import are false, has yet lodged in the hearts of his people the main substance of truth. John Foster says, that whenever a man prays aright he forgets the philosophy of prayer; and in more guarded phrase we may say, that when men are deeply affected by any theme, they are apt to disturb some of its logical proportions, and when preachers aim to rouse the sympathies of a populace, they often give a brighter coloring or a bolder prominence to some lineaments of a doctrine than can be given to them in a well compacted science.

There are two forms of theology, of which the two passages in my text are selected as individual specimens, the one declaring that God never repents, the other that he does repent. For want of a better name these two forms may be termed, the theology of the intellect, and the theology of feeling. Sometimes, indeed, both the mind and the heart are suited by the same modes of thought, but often they require dissimilar methods, and the object of the present discourse is, to state some of the differences between the theology of the intellect and that of feeling, and also some of the influences which they exert upon each other.

What, then, are some of the differences between these two kinds of representation?

The theology of the intellect conforms to the laws, subserves the wants and secures the approval of our intuitive and deductive powers. It includes the decisions of the judgment, of the perceptive part of conscience and taste, indeed of all the faculties which are essential to the reasoning process. It is the theology of speculation, and therefore comprehends the truth just as it is, unmodified by excitements of feeling. It is received as accurate not in its spirit only, but in its letter also. Of course it demands evidence, either internal or extraneous, for all its propositions. These propositions, whether or not they be inferences from antecedent, are well fitted to be premises for subsequent trains of proof. This intellectual theology, therefore, prefers general to individual statements, the abstract to the concrete, the literal to the figurative. In the creed of a Trinitarian it affirms, that he who united in his person a human body, a human soul and a divine spirit, expired on the cross, but it does not originate the phrase that his soul expired, nor that "God the mighty Maker died." Its aim is not to be impressive, but intelligible and defensible. Hence it insists on the nice proportions of doctrine, and on preciseness both of thought and style. Its words are so exactly defined, its adjustments are so accurate, that no caviller can detect an ambiguous, mystical or incoherent sentence. It is, therefore, in entire harmony with itself, abhorring a contradiction as nature abhors a vacuum. Left to its own guidance, for example, it would never suggest the unqualified remark that Christ has fully paid the debt of sinners, for it declares that this debt may justly be claimed from them; nor that he has suffered the whole punishment which they deserve, for it teaches that this punishment may still be righteously inflicted on themselves; nor that he has entirely satisfied the law, for it insists that the demands of the law are yet in force. If it should allow those as logical premises, it would also allow the salvation of all men as a logical inference, but it rejects this inference and accordingly, being self consistent, must reject those when viewed as literal premises.[1] It is adapted to the soul in her inquisitive moods, but fails to satisfy her craving for excitement. In order to express the definite idea that we are exposed to evil in consequence of Adam's sin, it does not employ the passionate phrase, "we are guilty of his sin." It searches for the proprieties of representation, for seemliness and decorum. It gives origin to no statements which require apology or essential modification; no metaphor, for example, so bold and so liable to disfigure our idea of the divine equity, as that Heaven imputes the crime of one man to millions of his descendants, and then imputes their myriad sins to him who was harmless and undefiled. As it avoids the dashes of an imaginative style, as it qualifies and subdues the remark which the passions would make still more intense, it seems dry, tame to the mass of men. It awakens but little interest in favor of its old arrangements; its new distinctions are easily introduced, to be as speedily forgotten. As we might infer, it is suited not for eloquent appeals, but for calm controversial treatises and bodies of divinity; not so well for the hymn-book as for the catechism; not so well for the liturgy as for the creed.

In some respects, but not in all, the theology of feeling differs from that of intellect. It is the form of belief which is suggested by, and adapted to the wants of the well-trained heart. It is embraced as involving the substance of truth, although, when literally interpreted,

---

[1] See note A. at the end of the Discourse.

it may or may not be false. It studies not the exact proportions of doctrine, but gives especial prominence to those features of it which are and ought to be most grateful to the sensibilities. It insists not on dialectical argument, but receives whatever the healthy affections crave. It chooses particular rather than general statements; teaching, for example, the divine omnipotence by an individual instance of it; saying, not that God can do all things which are objects of power, but that He spake and it was done. It sacrifices abstract remarks to visible and tangible images; choosing the lovely phrase that 'the children of men put their trust under the shadow of Jehovah's wings,' rather than the logical one that his providence comprehendeth all events. It is satisfied with vague, indefinite representations. It is too buoyant, too earnest for a moral result, to compress itself into sharply-drawn angles. It is often the more forceful because of the looseness of its style, herein being the hiding of its power. It is sublime in its obscure picture of the Sovereign who maketh darkness his pavilion, dark waters and thick clouds of the sky. Instead of measuring the exact dimensions of a spirit, it says, "I could not discern the form thereof: an image was before mine eyes; there was silence and I heard a voice;" and in the haziness of this vision lies its fitness to stir up the soul. Of course, the theology of feeling aims to be impressive, whether it be or not minutely accurate. Often it bursts away from dogmatic restraints, forces its passage through or over rules of logic, and presses forward to expend itself first and foremost in affecting the sensibilities. For this end, instead of being comprehensive, it is elastic; avoiding monotony it is ever pertinent to the occasion; it brings out into bold relief now one feature of a doctrine and then a different feature, and assumes as great a variety of shapes as the wants of the heart are various. In order to hold the Jews back from the foul, cruel vices of their neighbors, the Tyrian, Moabite, Ammonite, Egyptian, Philistine, Babylonian; in order to stop their indulgence in the degrading worship of Moloch, Dagon, Baal, Tammuz, they were plied with a stern theology, well fitted by its terrible denunciations to save them from the crime which was still more terrible. They were told of the jealousy and anger of the Lord, of his breastplate, helmet, bow, arrows, spear, sword, glittering sword, and raiment stained with blood. This fearful anthropomorphism enstamped a truth upon their hearts; but when they needed a soothing influence, they were assured that "the Lord shall feed his flock like a shepherd, he shall gather the lambs with his arm and carry them in his bosom, and shall gently lead those that are with young." Thus does the theology of feeling individualize the single parts of a doctrine; and, so it can make them intense and impressive, it cares not to make them harmonious with each other. When it has one end in view, it represents Christians as united with their Lord; now, they being branches and he the vine-stock; again, they being members and he the body; still again, they being the body and he the head; and once more, they being the spouse and he the bridegroom. But it does not mean to have these endearing words metamorphosed into an intellectual theory of our oneness or identification with Christ; for with another end in view it contradicts this theory, and teaches that he is distinct from us, even as separate as the sun or morning star from those who are gladdened by its beams; the door or way from those who pass through or over it, the captain from his soldiers, the forerunner from the follower, the judge from those arrayed before him, the king from those who bow the knee to him. In order to make us feel the strength of God's aversion to sin, it declares that he has repented of having made our race, has been grieved at his heart for transgressors, weary of them, vexed with them. But it does not mean that these expressions which, as inflected by times and circumstances, impress a truth upon the soul, be stereotyped into the principle that Jehovah has ever parted with his infinite blessedness; for in order to make us confide in his stability, it denies that he ever repents, and declares that he is without even the shadow of turning. It assumes these discordant forms, so as to meet the affections in their conflicting moods. Its aim is not to facilitate the inferences of logic, but to arrest attention, to grapple with the wayward desires, to satisfy the longings of the pious heart. And in order to reach all the hiding-places of emotion, it now and then strains a word to its utmost significancy, even into a variance with some other phrase and a disproportion with the remaining parts of the system. We often hear that every great divine, like Jonathan Edwards, will contradict himself. If this be so, it is because he is a reasoner and something more; because he is not a mere mathematciian, but gives his feelings a full, an easy and a various play; because he does not exhibit his faith always in the same form, straight like a needle, sharp-pointed and one-eyed.

The free theology of the feelings is ill fitted for didactic or controversial treatises or doctrinal standards. Martin Luther, the church fathers, who used it so often, became thereby unsafe polemics. Anything, everything, can be proved from them; for they were ever inditing sentences congenial with an excited heart, but false as expressions of deliberate opinion. But this emotive theology *is* adapted to the persuasive sermon, to the pleadings of the liturgy, to the songs of Zion. By no means can it be termed *mere* poetry, in the sense of a playful fiction. It is no play, but solemn earnestness. It is no mere fiction, but an outpouring of sentiments too deep, or too mellow, or too impetuous to be suited with the stiff language of the intellect. Neither can its words be called *merely* figurative, in the sense of arbitrary or unsubstantial. They are the earliest, and if one may use a comparison, the most natural utterances of a soul instinct with religious life. They are forms of language which circumscribe a substance of doctrine, a substance which, fashioned as it may be, the intellect grasps and holds fast; a substance which arrests the more attention and prolongs the deeper interest by the figures which bound it. This form of theology, then, is far from being fitly represented by the term imaginative, still farther by the term fanciful, and farther yet by the word capricious. It goes deeper; it is the theology both of and for our sensitive nature; of and for the normal emotion, affection, passion. It may be called poetry, however, if this word be used, as it should be, to include the constitutional developments of a heart moved to its depths by the truth. And as in its essence it is poetical, with this meaning of the epithet, so it avails itself of a poetic license, and indulges in a style of remark which for sober prose would be unbecoming, or even, when associated in certain ways, irreverent. All warm affection, be it love or hatred, overleaps at times the proprieties of a didactic style. Does not the Bible make this obvious? There are words in the Canticles and in the imprecatory Psalms, which are to be justified as the utterances of a feeling too pure, too unsuspicious, too earnest to guard itself against evil surmises. There are appearances of reasoning in the Bible, which the mere dialectician has denounced as puerile sophisms. But some of them may never have been intended for logical proof; they may have been designed for passionate appeals and figured into the shape of argument, not to convince the reason but to carry the heart by a strong assault, in a day when the kingdom of heaven suffered violence and the violent took it by force. In one of his lofty flights of inspiration, the Psalmist cries, "Awake! why sleepest thou, oh Lord;" and Martin Luther, roused more than man is wont to be by this example, prayed at the Diet of Worms, in language which we fear to repeat, "Hearest thou not, my God; art thou dead?" And a favorite English minstrel sings of the "dying God," of the "sharp distress," the "sore complaints," of God, his "last groans," his "dying blood;" of his throne, also, as once a "burning throne," a "seat of dreadful wrath;" but now "sprinkled over" by "the rich drops" of blood "that calmed his frowning face." It is the very nature of a theology framed for enkindling the imagination and thereby inflaming the heart, to pour itself out, when a striking emergency calls for them, in words that burn; words that excite no congenial glow in technical students, viewing all truth in its dry light, and disdaining all figures which would offend the decorum of a philosophical or didactic style, but words which wake the deepest sympathies of quick-moving, wide-hearted, many-sided men, who look through a superficial impropriety and discern under it a truth which the nice language of prose is too frail to convey into the heart, and breaks down in the attempt.

Hence it is another criterion of this emotive theology that when once received, it is not easily discarded. The essence of it remains the same, while its forms are changed; and these forms, although varied to meet the varying exigencies of feeling, are not abandoned so as never to be restored; for the same exigencies appear and reappear from time to time, and therefore the same diversified representations are repeated again and again. Of the ancient philosophy the greater part is lost, the remnant is chiefly useful as an historical phenomenon. Not a single treatise, except the geometry of Euclid, continues to be used by the majority of students for its original purpose. But the poetry of those early days remains fresh as in the morning of its birth. It will always preserve its youthful glow, for it appeals not to any existing standard of mental acquisition, but to a broad and common nature which never becomes obsolete. So in the *theology* of reason, the progress of science has antiquated some, and will continue to modify other refinements; theory has chased theory into the shades; but the theology of the heart, letting the minor accuracies go for the sake of holding strongly upon the substance of doctrine, need not always accommodate itself to scientific changes, but may often use its old statements, even if, when literally understood, they be incorrect, and it thus abides as permanent as are the main impressions of the truth. While the lines of speculation may be easily erased, those of emotion are furrowed into the soul, and can be smoothed away only by long-continued friction. What its abettors feel, they feel and cling to, and think they know, and even when vanquished they can argue still; or rather, as their sentiments do not come of reasoning, neither do they flee before it. Hence the permanent authority of certain tones of voice which express a certain class of feelings. Hence, too, the delicacy and the peril of any endeavor to improve the style of a hymn-book or liturgy, to amend one phrase in the common version of the Bible, or to rectify any theological terms, however inconvenient, which have once found their home in the affections of good men. The heart loves its old friends, and so much the more if they be lame and blind. Hence the fervid heat of a controversy when it is provoked by an assault upon the words, not the truths but the words, which have been embosomed in the love of the church.

Hence the Pilgrim of Bunyan travels and sings from land to land, and will be, as he has been, welcome around the hearth-stone of every devout household from age to age; while Edwards on the Will and Cudworth on Immutable Morality, knock at many a good man's door, only to be turned away shaking the dust from off their feet.[1]

Having considered some of the differences between the intellectual and the emotive theology, let us now glance, as was proposed, at some of the influences which one exerts on the other.

And *first*, the theology of the intellect illustrates and vivifies itself by that of feeling. As man is compounded of soul and body, and his inward sensibilities are expressed by his outward features, so his faith combines ideas logically accurate with conceptions merely illustrative and impressive. Our tendency to unite corporeal forms with mental views, may be a premonition that we are destined to exist hereafter in a union of two natures, one of them being spirit, and the other so expressive of spirit as to be called a spiritual body. We lose the influence of literal truth upon the sensibilities, if we persevere in refusing it an appropriate image. We must add a body to the soul of a doctrine, whenever we would make it palpable and enlivening. It is brought, as it were, into our presence by its symbols, as a strong passion is exhibited to us by a gesture, as the idea of dignity is made almost visible in the Apollo Belvedere. A picture may, in itself, be superficial; but it expresses the substantial reality. What though some of the representations which feeling demands be a mere exponent of the exact truth; they are, *as it were*, that very truth. What though our conceptions be only the most expressive signs of the actual verity; they are *as if* the actual verity itself. They are substantially accurate when not literally so; moral truth, when not historical. The whole reality is at least *as* good, *as* solid as they represent it, and our most vivid idea of it is in their phases.

The whole doctrine, for example, of the spiritual world, is one that requires to be made tangible by an embodiment. We have an intellectual belief that a spirit has no shape, and occupies no space; that a human soul, so soon as it is dismissed from the earth, receives more decisive tokens than had been previously given it of its Maker's complacency or displeasure, has a clearer knowledge of him, a larger love or a sterner hostility to him, a more delightful or a more painful experience of his control, and at a period yet to come will be conjoined with a body unlike the earthly one, yet having a kind of identity with it, and furnishing inlets for new and peculiar joys or woes. It is the judgment of some that the popular tract and the sermons of such men as

---

[1] See Note B, at the end of the Discourse.

Baxter and Whitefield ought to exhibit no other than this intellectual view of our future state. But such an intellectual view is too general to be embraced by the feelings. They are balked with the notion of a spaceless, formless existence, continuing between death and the resurrection. They regard the soul as turned out of being when despoiled of shape and extension. They represent the converted islander of the Atlantic as rising, when he leaves the earth, to the place where God sitteth upon his throne, and also the renewed islander of the Pacific as ascending, at death, from the world to the same prescribed spot. When pressed with the query, how two antipodes can both rise up, in opposite directions, to one locality, they have nothing to reply. They are not careful to answer any objection, but only speak right on. They crave a reality for the soul, for its coming joys or woes, and will not be defrauded of this solid existence by any subtilized theory. So tame and cold is the common idea of an intangible, inaudible, invisible world, that few will aspire for the rewards, and many will imagine themselves able to endure the punishments which are thus rarified into the results of mere thought. Now a doctrine of the intellect need not, and should not empty itself of its substance in the view of men because it is too delicate for their gross apprehension. "God giveth" to this doctrine " a body as it hath pleased him," and it should avail itself of this corporeal manifestation for the sake of retaining its felt reality. If it let this scriptural body go, all is gone in the popular consciousness. It is not enough for the intellect to prove that at the resurrection a new nature will be incorporated with the soul, and will open avenues to new bliss or woe; it must vivify the conception of this mysterious nature and its mysterious experiences by the picture of a palm-branch, a harp, a robe, a crown, or of that visible enginery of death which, in the common view, gives a substance to the penalties of the law. Our demonstrable ideas of the judgment are so abstract, that they will seemingly evaporate unless we illustrate them by one individual day of the grand assize, by the particular questionings and answerings, the opened book, and other minute formalities of the court. The emotions of a delicate taste are, of course, not to be disregarded; but it is a canon of criticism — is it not? — that we should express all the truth which our hearers need, and express it in the words which they will most appropriately feel. The doctrine of the resurrection also seems often to vanish into thin air by an overscrupulous refinement of philosophical terminology. The intellect allows the belief that our future bodies will be identical with our present, just as really as it allows a belief that our present bodies are the same with those of our childhood, or that our bodies ever feel pleasure or pain, or that the grass is green or the sky blue, the fire warm or the ice cold, or that the sun rises or sets. The philosopher may reply, The sun does not rise nor set, the grass is not green nor the sky blue, the fire is not warm nor the ice cold, and our physical nature in itself is not sensitive. The man responds, They are so for all that concerns me. The philosopher may affirm that our present bodies are not precisely identical with those of our childhood; the man answers, They are so to all intents and purposes; and when we practically abandon our belief in our physical sameness here, then we may modify our faith in our resumed physical identity at the resurrection. But while man remains *man* upon earth, he will not give up the forms of belief which he feels to be true. He must vivify his abstractions by images which quicken his faith; and even if these images should lose their historical life, they shall have a resurrection in spiritual realities. Through our eternal existence, the biblical exhibitions of our future state will be found to have a deeper and deeper significance. They will be found to be literal truth itself, or else the best possible symbols by which that truth can be shadowed forth to men incapable of reaching either its height or its depth. In the Bible is a profound philosophy which no man has fully searched out. As this volume explains the essence of virtue by the particular commands of the law, the sinfulness of our race by incidents in the biography of Adam, the character of Jehovah by the historical examples of his love, and especially by portraying God manifest in the flesh; so, with the intent of still further adapting truth to our dull apprehension, it condescends to step over and beyond the domain of literal history, and to use the imagination in exciting the soul to spiritual research; it enrobes itself in fabrics woven from the material world, which seems as if it were formed for elucidating spiritual truth; it incarnates all doctrine, that the wayfaring man, though a fool, need not err, and that all *flesh* may see the salvation of God.[1]

But the sensitive part of our nature not only quickens the percipient, by requiring and suggesting expressive illustrations, it also furnishes principles from which the reasoning faculty deduces important inferences. I therefore remark in the *second* place,

The theology of the intellect enlarges and improves that of the feelings, and is also enlarged and improved by it. The more extensive and accurate are our views of literal truth, so much the more numerous and salutary are the forms which it may assume for enlisting the affections. A system of doctrines logically drawn out, not only makes its own appeal to the heart, but also provides materials for the imagination to clothe as to allure the otherwise dormant sensibility. The per-

---

[1] See Note C. at the end of the Discourse.

ceptive power looks right forward to the truth, (for this end was it made), from it turns to neither side for utilitarian purposes, but presses straight forward to its object; yet every doctrine which it discovers is in reality practical, calling forth some emotion, and this emotion animating the sensitive nature which is not diseased, deepening its love of knowledge, elevating and widening the religious system which is to satisfy it. Every new article of the good man's belief elicits love or hatred, and this love or hatred so modifies the train and phasis of his meditations, as to augment and improve the volume of his heart's theology.

It is a tendency of pietism to undervalue the human intellect for the sake of exalting the affections; as if sin had less to do with the feelings than with the intelligence; as if a deceived heart had never turned men aside; as if the reason had fallen deeper than the will. Rather has the will fallen *from* the intellectual powers, while they remain truer than any other to their office. It cannot be a *pious* act to underrate these powers, given as they were by him who made the soul in his image. Our speculative tendencies are original, legitimate parts of the constitution which it is irreverent to censure. We *must* speculate. We must define, distinguish, infer, arrange our inferences in a system. Our spiritual oneness, completeness, progress, require it. We lose our civilization, so far forth as we depreciate a philosophy truly so called. Our faith becomes a wild or weak sentimentalism if we despise logic. God has written upon our minds the ineffaceable law that they search after the truth, whatever, wherever it be, however arduous the toil for it, whithersoever it may lead. Let it come. Even if it should promise nothing to the utilitarian, there are yet within us the *mirabiles amores* to find it out. A sound heart is alive with this curiosity, and will not retain its health while its aspirations are rebuffed. It gives no unbroken peace to the man who thwarts his reasoning instincts; for amid all its conflicting demands, it is at times importunate for a reasonable belief. When it is famished by an idle intellect, it loses its tone, becomes bigoted rather than inquisitive, and takes up with theological fancies which reduce it still lower. When it is fed by an inquiring mind it is enlivened, and reaches out for an expanded faith. If the intellect of the church be repressed, that of the world will not be, and the schools will urge forward an unsanctified philosophy which good men will be too feeble to resist, and under the influence of which the emotions will be suited with forms of belief more and more unworthy, narrow, debasing.

But the theology of reason not only amends and amplifies that of the affections, it is also improved and enlarged by it. One tendency of rationalism is, to undervalue the heart for the sake of putting the crown upon the head. This is a good tendency when applied to those feelings which are wayward and deceptive, but an *irrational* one when applied to those which are unavoidable and therefore innocent, still more to those which are holy and therefore entitled to our reverence. Whenever a feeling is constitutional and cannot be expelled, whenever it is pious and cannot but be approved, then such of its impulses as are uniform, self-consistent and persevering are data on which the intellect may safely reason, and by means of which it may add new materials to its dogmatic system. Our instinctive feelings in favor of the truth, that all men in the future life will be judged, rewarded or punished by an all-wise lawgiver, are logical premises from which this truth is an inference regular in mood and figure. Every man, atheist even, has certain constitutional impulses to call on the name of some divinity; and these impulses give evidence that he ought to pray, just as the convolutions of a vine's tendrils and their reaching out to grasp the trellis, signify that in order to attain its full growth the vine must cling to a support. The wing or the web-foot of an animal is no more conclusive proof of its having been made with the design that it should fly or swim, than the instinctive cravings of the soul for a positive, an historical, a miraculously attested religion, with its Sabbaths and its ministry, are arguments that the soul was intended for the enjoyment of such a religion. If the Bible could be proved to be a myth, it would still be a divine myth; for a narrative so wonderfully fitted for penetrating through all the different avenues to the different sensibilities of the soul, must have a moral if not a literal truth. And so it appears to me, that the doctrines which concentre in and around a vicarious atonement are so fitted to the appetences of a sanctified heart, as to gain the favor of a logician, precisely as the coincidence of some geological or astronomical theories with the phenomena of the earth or sky, is a part of the syllogism which has these theories for its conclusion. Has man been created with irresistible instincts which impel him to believe in a falsehood? Or has the Christian been inspired with holy emotions which allure him to an essentially erroneous faith? Is God the author of confusion;—in his word revealing one doctrine and by his Spirit persuading his saints to reject it? If it be a fact, that the faithful of past ages, after having longed and sighed and wrestled and prayed for the truth as it is in Jesus, have at length found their aspirations rewarded by any one substance of belief, does not their unanimity indicate the correctness of their cherished faith, as the agreement of many witnesses presupposes the verity of the narration in which they coincide? In its minute philosophical forms, it may not be the truth for which they yearned, but in its central principles have they one and all been deceived? Then have they asked in tears for the food of the soul, and a prayer hearing Father has given them a stone for bread.

Decidedly as we resist the pretension that the church is infallible, there is one sense in which this pretension is well founded. Her metaphysicians as such are not free from error, nor her philologists, nor any of her scholars, nor her ministers, nor councils. She is not infallible in her bodies of divinity, nor her creeds, nor catechisms, nor any logical formulae; but underneath all her intellectual refinements lies a broad substance of doctrine, around which the feelings of all renewed men cling ever and everywhere, into which they penetrate and take root, and this substance must be right, for it is precisely adjusted to the soul, and the soul was made for it.

These universal feelings provide us with a test for our own faith. Whenever we find, my brethren, that the words which we proclaim do not strike a responsive chord in the hearts of the choice men and women who look up to us for consolation, when they do not stir the depths of our own souls, reach down to our hidden wants, and evoke sensibilities which otherwise had lain buried under the cares of time; or when they make an abiding impression that the divine government is harsh, pitiless, insincere, oppressive, devoid of sympathy with our most refined sentiments, reckless of even the most delicate emotion of the tenderest nature, then we may infer that we have left out of our theology some element which we should have inserted, or have brought into it some element which we should have discarded. *Somewhere it must be wrong.* If it leave the sensibilities torpid, it needs a larger infusion of those words which Christ defined by saying, they are spirit, they are life. If it merely charm the ear like a placid song, it is not the identical essence which is likened to the fire and the hammer. Our sensitive nature is sometimes a kind of instinct which anticipates many truths, incites the mind to search for them, intimates the process of the investigation, and remains unsatisfied, restive, so long as it is held back from the object toward which it gropes its way, even as a plant bends itself forward to the light and warmth of the sun.[1]

But while the theology of reason derives aid from the impulses of emotion, it maintains its ascendancy over them. In all investigations for truth, the intellect must be the authoritative power, employing the sensibilities as indices of right doctrine, but surveying and superintending them from its commanding elevation. It may be roughly compared

---

[1] See note D. at the end of the Discourse.

to the pilot of a ship, who intelligently directs and turns the rudder, although himself and the entire vessel are also turned by it. We are told that a wise man's eyes are in his head; now although they cannot say to the hand or the foot, we have no need of you, it is yet their prerogative to determine whither the hand or foot shall move. The intellectual theology will indeed reform itself by suggestions derived from the heart, for its law is to exclude every dogma which does not harmonize with the well-ordered sensibilities of the soul. It regards a want of concinnity in a system, as a token of some false principle. And as it will modify itself in order to avoid the error involved in a contradiction, so and for the same reason it has authority in the last resort to rectify the statements which are often congenial with excited emotion. I therefore remark in the *third* place,

The theology of the intellect explains that of feeling into an essential agreement with all the constitutional demands of the soul. It does this by collating the discordant representations which the heart allows, and eliciting the one self-consistent principle which underlies them. It places side by side the contradictory statements which receive, at different times, the sympathies of a spirit as it is moved by different impulses. It exposes the impossibility of believing all these statements, without qualifying some of them so as to prevent their subverting each other. In order to qualify them in the right way, it details their origin, reveals their intent, unfolds their influence, and by such means eliminates the principle in which they all agree for substance of doctrine. When this principle has been once detected and disengaged from its conflicting representations, it reacts upon them, explains, modifies, harmonizes their meaning. Thus are the mutually repellent forces set over against each other, so as to neutralize their opposition and to combine in producing one and the same movement.

Seizing strongly upon some elements of a comprehensive doctrine, the Bible paints the unrenewed heart as a stone needing to be exchanged for flesh; and again, not as a stone, but as flesh needing to be turned into spirit; and yet again, neither as a stone nor as flesh, but as a darkened spirit needing to be illumined with the light of knowledge. Taking a vigorous hold of yet other elements in the same doctrine, the Bible portrays this heart not as ignorant and needing to be enlightened, but as dead and needing to be made alive; and further, not as dead but as living and needing to die, to be crucified, and buried; and further still, not as in need of a resurrection or of a crucifixion, but of a new creation; and once more, as requiring neither to be slain, nor raised from death, nor created anew, but to be born again. For the sake of vividly describing other features of the same truth, the heart is exhibited as needing to be called or drawn to God, or to be enlarged or circumcised or purified or inscribed with a new law, or endued with new graces. And for the purpose of awakening interest in a distinct phase of this truth, all the preceding forms are inverted and man is summoned to make himself a new heart, or to give up his old one, or to become a little child, or to cleanse himself, or to unstop his deaf ears and hear, or to open his blinded eyes and see, or to awake from sleep, or rise from death. Literally understood, these expressions are dissonant from each other. Their dissonance adds to their emphasis. Their emphasis fastens our attention upon the principle in which they all agree. This principle is too vast to be vividly uttered in a single formula, and therefore branches out into various parts, and the lively exhibition of one part contravenes an equally impressive statement of a different one. The intellect educes light from the collision of these repugnant phrases, and then modifies and reconciles them into the doctrine, that *the character of our race needs an essential transformation by an interposed influence from God.* But how soon would this doctrine lose its vivacity, if it were not revealed in these dissimilar forms, all jutting up like the hills of a landscape from a common substratum.

We may instance another set of the heart's phrases, which, instead of coalescing with each other in a dull sameness, engage our curiosity by their disagreement, and exercise the analytic power in unloosing and laying bare the one principle which forms their basis. Bowed down under the experience of his evil tendencies, which long years of painful resistance have not subdued, trembling before the ever recurring fascinations which have so often enticed him into crime, the man of God longs to abase himself, and exclaims without one modifying word: "I am too frail for my responsibilities, and have no power to do what is required of me." But in a brighter moment, admiring the exuberance of divine generosity, thankful for the large gifts which his munificent Father has lavished upon him, elevated with adoring views of the equitable One who never reaps where he has not sown, the same man of God offers his unqualified thanksgiving: "I know thee, that thou art *not* an hard master, exacting of me duties which I have no power to discharge, but thou attemperest thy law to my strength, and at no time imposest upon me a heavier burden than thou at that very time makest me able to bear." In a different mood, when this same man is thinking of the future, foreseeing his temptations to an easily besetting sin, shuddering at the danger of committing it, dreading the results of a proud reliance on his own virtue, he becomes importunate for aid from above, and pours out his entreaty, with not one

abating clause: "I am nothing and less than nothing; I have no
power to refrain from the sin which tempts me: help, Lord, help;
for thou increasest strength to him who hath no might." But in still
another mood, when the same man is thinking of the past, weeping
over the fact that he has now indulged in the very crime which he
feared, resisting every inducement to apologize for it, blaming himself,
himself alone, himself deeply for so ungrateful, unreasonable, inexcusable an act, he makes the unmitigated confession, with his hand upon
his heart, he dares not qualify his acknowledgment: "I could have
avoided that sin which I preferred to commit; woe is me, for I have
not done as well as I might have done; if I had been as holy as I had
power to be, then had I been perfect; and if I say I have been perfect, that shall prove me perverse." Thus when looking backward,
the sensitive Christian insists upon his competency to perform an act,
and fears that a denial of it would banish his penitence for transgression; but when looking forward, he insists upon his incompetency to
perform the same act, and fears that a denial of this would weaken
his feeling of dependence on God. Without a syllable of abatement,
he now makes a profession, and then recalls it as thus unqualified, afterward reiterates his once recalled avowal, and again retracts what he
had once and again repeated. It is the oscillating language of the
emotions which, like the strings of an Æolian harp, vibrate in unison
with the varying winds. It is nature in her childlike simplicity,
that prompts the soul when swayed in opposing directions by dissimilar thoughts, to vent itself in these antagonistic phrases awakening the
intenser interest by their very antagonism. What if they do, when
unmodified, contradict each other? An impassioned heart recoils from
a contradiction, no more than the war-horse of Job starts back from
the battle-field.

The reason, however, being that circumspect power which looks
before and after and to either side, does not allow that of these conflicting statements, each can be true save in a qualified sense. It
therefore seeks out some principle which will combine these two extremes, as a magnet its opposite poles; some principle which will rectify one of these discrepant expressions by explaining it into an essential
agreement with the other. And the principle, I think, which restores
this harmony, is the comprehensive one, that man with no extraordinary aid from Divine grace is obstinate, undeviating, unrelenting, persevering, dogged, *fully set* in those wayward preferences which are
an abuse of his freedom. His unvaried wrong choices imply a full,
unremitted, natural power of choosing right. The emotive theology
therefore, when it affirms this power, is correct both in matter and

style; but when it denies this power, it uses the language of emphasis, of impression, of intensity; it means the certainty of wrong preference by declaring the inability of right; and in its vivid use of *cannot* for *will not* is accurate in its substance though not in its form. Yet even here, it is no more at variance with the intellectual theology than with itself, and the discordance, being one of letter rather than of spirit, is removed by an explanation which makes the eloquent style of the feelings at one with the more definite style of the reason.[1]

But I am asked, "Do you not thus explain away the language of the emotions? No. The contradictoriness, the literal absurdity is explained out of it, but the language is not explained away; for even when dissonant with the precise truth, it has a significancy more profound than can be pressed home upon the heart by any exact definitions. Do you not make it a mere flourish of rhetoric? I am asked again. It is no flourish; it is the utterance that comes welling up from the depths of our moral nature, and is too earnest to wait for the niceties of logic. It is the breathing out of an emotion which will not stop for the accurate measurement of its words, but leaves them to be qualified by the good sense of men.

If, however, this language be not exactly true, I am further asked, how can it move the heart? We are so made as to be moved by it. It is an ultimate law of our being, that a vivid conception affects us by inspiring a momentary belief in the thing which is conceived. But, the objector continues, can the soul be favorably influenced by that which it regards as hyperbolical? Hyperbolical! What is hyperbolical? Who calls this language an exaggeration of the truth? If interpreted by the letter, it does indeed transcend the proper bounds; but if interpreted as it is meant, as it is felt, it falls far short of them. To the eye of a child the moon's image in the diorama may appear larger than the real moon in the heavens, but not to the mind of a philosopher. The literal doctrines of theology are too vast for complete expression by man, and our intensest words are but a distant approximation to that language, which forms the new song that the redeemed in heaven sing; language which is unutterable in this infantile state of our being, and in comparison with which our so-called extravagances are but feeble and tame diminutives.

Astronomers have recommended, that in order to feel the grandeur of the stellary system we mentally reduce the scale on which it is made; that we imagine our earth to be only a mile in diameter, and

---

[1] See Note E, at the end of the Discourse.

the other globes to be proportionally lessened in their size and in their distances from each other; for the real greatness of the heavens discourages our very attempt to impress our hearts by them, and we are the more affected by sometimes narrowing our conceptions of what we cannot at the best comprehend. On the same principle, Christian moralists have advised us not always to dilate our minds in reaching after the extreme boundaries of a doctrine, but often to draw in our contemplations, to lower the doctrine for a time, to bring our intellect down in order to discern the practical truth more clearly, to humble our views in order that they may be at last exalted, to stoop low in order to pick up the keys of knowledge;—and is this a way of exaggerating the truth? *We do err, not knowing the Scriptures nor the power of God,* if we imagine that when for example he says, the enemies that touch his saints " touch the apple of his eye," and " he will lift up an ensign to the nations from far and will hiss unto them from the ends of the earth," he uses a mere hyperbole. No. Such anthropopathical words are the most expressive which the debilitated heart of his oriental people would appreciate, but they fail of making a full disclosure, they are only the foreshadowings of the truths which lie behind them. These refined, spiritual truths, the intellect goes round about and surveys, but is too faint for graphically delineating, and it gives up the attempt to the imagination, and this many-sided faculty multiplies symbol after symbol, bringing one image for one feature, and another image for another feature, and hovers over the feeble emotions of the heart, and strives to win them out from their dull repose, even as 'the eagle stirreth up her nest, and fluttereth over her young, and spreadeth abroad her wings, and taketh up her little ones, and beareth them on her out-stretched pinions.' Into more susceptible natures than ours the literal verities of God will penetrate far deeper than, even when shaped in their most pungent forms, they will pierce into our obdurate hearts. So lethargic are we, that we often yield no answering sensibilities to intellectual statements of doctrine; so weak are we, that such passionate appeals as are best accommodated to our phlegmatic temper are after all no more than dilutions of the truth, as " seen of angels;" and still so fond are we of harmony with ourselves, that we must explain these diluted representations into unison with the intellectual statements which, however unimpressive, are yet the most authoritative.[1]

We are now prepared for our *fourth* remark,— the theology of the intellect and that of feeling tend to keep each other within the sphere

---

[1] See Note F. at the end of the Discourse.

for which they were respectively designed, and in which they are fitted to improve the character. Both of them have precisely the same sphere with regard to many truths, but not with regard to all. When an intellectual statement is transferred to the province of emotion, it often appears chilling, lifeless; and when a passionate phrase is transferred to the dogmatic province, it often appears grotesque, unintelligible, absurd. Many expressions of sentiment are *what* they ought to be, if kept *where* they ought to be; but a narrow creed *displaces* and thus spoils them. It often becomes licentious or barbarous, by stiffening into prosaic statements the free descriptions which the Bible gives of the kindliness or the wrath of God. The very same words are allowed in one relation, but condemned in a different one, because in the former they do, but in the latter do not harmonize with the sensibilities which are at the time predominant. When we are enthusiastic in extolling the generosity of divine love, we feel no need of modifying our proclamation that God desires all men to be saved, and in these uninquisitive moods we have no patience with the query which occupies our more studious hours, "whether he desire this good all things, or only itself considered." Often, though not in every instance, the solid philosophy of doctrine, descending into an exhortation, makes it cumbrous and heavy; and as often the passionate forms of appeal, when they claim to be literal truth, embarrass the intellect until they are repelled by it into the circle distinctively allotted them.

At the time when the words were uttered, there could not be a more melting address than, "If I, your Lord and Master, have washed your feet, ye also ought to wash one another's feet;" but when this touching sentiment is interpreted as a legal exaction, an argument for a Moravian or Romish ceremony, its poetic elegance is petrified into a prosaic blunder. There are moments in the stillness of our communion service, when we feel that our Lord is with us, when the bread and the wine so enliven our conceptions of his body and blood as, according to the law of vivid conception, to bring them into our ideal presence, and to make us *demand* the saying, as more pertinent and fit than any other, 'This *is* my body, this *is* my blood.' But no sooner are these phrases transmuted from hearty utterances into intellectual judgments, than they merge their beautiful rhetoric into an absurd logic, and are at once repulsed by a sound mind into their pristine sphere. So there is a depth of significance which our superficial powers do not fathom, in the lamentation: "Behold! I was shapen in iniquity, and in sin did my mother conceive me." This will always remain the passage for the outflow of his grief, whose fountains of penitence are broken up. The channel is worn too deep into the affections to be easily changed. Let the schools reason about it just as, and as long as they please. Let them condemn it as indecorous, or false, or absurd, and the man who utters it as unreasonable, fanatical, bigoted. Let them challenge him for his meaning, and insist with the rigidness of the judge of Shylock, that he weigh out the import of every word, every syllable, no more, no less: — they do not move him one hair's breadth. He stands where he stood before, and where he will stand until disenthralled from the body. "My meaning," he says, "is exact enough for me, too exact for my repose of conscience; and I care just now for no proof clearer than this: "Behold! I *was* shapen in iniquity, and in sin *did* my mother conceive me." Here, on my heart the burden lies, and I *feel* that I am vile, a man of unclean lips, and dwell amid a people of unclean lips, and I went astray as soon as I was born, and am of a perverse, rebellious race, and there is a tide swelling within me and around me, and moving me on to actual transgression, and it is stayed by none of my unaided efforts, and all its billows roll over me, and I am so troubled that I cannot speak; and I am not content with merely saying that I am a transgressor; I long to heap infinite upon infinite, and crowd together all forms of self-reproach, for I am clad in sin as with a garment, I devour it as a sweet morsel, I breathe it, I live it, I *am* sin. My hands are stained with it, my feet are swift in it, all my bones are out of joint with it, my whole body is of tainted origin, and of death in its influence and end; and here is my definition and here is my proof, and, definition or no definition, proof or no proof, here I plant myself, and here I stay, for this is my feeling, and it comes up from the depths of an overflowing heart: "*Behold! I was shapen in iniquity, and in sin did my mother conceive me.*" — But when a theorist seizes at such living words as these, and puts them into his vice, and straightens or crooks them into the dogma, that man is blamable before he chooses to do wrong; deserving of punishment for the involuntary nature which he has never consented to gratify; really sinful before he actually sins, then the language of emotion, forced from its right place and treated as if it were a part of a nicely measured syllogism, hampers and confuses his reasonings, until it is given back to the use for which it was first intended, and from which it never ought to have been diverted.[1] When men thus lose their sensitiveness to the discriminations between the style of judgment and that of feeling, and when they force the latter into the province of the former, they become prone to undervalue the conscience, and to be afraid of philosophy, and to shudder at the axioms of common sense, and to divorce faith from reason, to rely on *church government* rather than on fraternal discussion.

---

[1] See Note G. at the end of the Discourse.

It is this crossing of one kind of theology into the province of another kind differing from the first mainly in fashion and *contour*, which mars either the eloquence or else the doctrine of the pulpit. The massive speculations of the metaphysician sink down into his expressions of feeling and make him appear cold-hearted, while the enthusiasm of the impulsive divine ascends and effervesces into his reasonings and causes him both to *appear*, and to *be*, what our Saxon idiom so reprovingly styles him, hot-headed. There are intellectual critics ready to exclude from our psalms and hymns all such stanzas as are not accurate expressions of dogmatic truth. Forgetting that the effort at precision often mars the freeness of song, they would condemn the simple-hearted bard to joint his metaphors into a syllogism, and to sing as a logician tries to sing. In the same spirit, they would expurgate the Paradise Lost of all phrases which are not in keeping with our chemical or geological discoveries. But it is against the laws of our sensitive nature to square the effusions of poesy by the scales, compasses and plumb-lines of the intellect. The imagination is not to be used as a dray horse for carrying the lumber of the schools through the gardens of the Muses. There are also poetical critics who imagine that the childlike breathings of our psalmody are the exact measures, the literal exponents of truth, and that every doctrine is false which cannot be transported with its present bodily shape into a sacred lyric. But this is as shallow an idea of theology as it is a mechanical, spiritless, vapid conception of poetry. If this be true, then my real belief is, that ' God came from Teman and the Holy One from Mount Paran; that he did ride upon his horses and chariots of salvation; the mountains saw him and they trembled; the sun and the moon stood still; at the light of his arrows they went and the shining of his glittering spear; he did march through the land in indignation, he did thresh the heathen in anger.' And if this be the language of a creed, then not only is the suggestion of Dr. Arnold[1] a right one that 'in public worship a symbol of faith should be used as a triumphal hymn of thanksgiviving, and be chanted rather than read,' but such is the original and proper use of such a symbol at all times. And if this be true, then I shall not demur at phrases in a Confession of Faith, over which, in my deliberate perusal, I stagger and am at my wit's end. Wrap me in mediaeval robes; place me under the wide-spreading arches of a cathedral; let the tide of melody from the organ float along the columns that branch out like the trees of the forest over my head; then bring to me a creed written in illuminated letters, its history

---

[1] Life, p. 102, First Am. Ed.

redolent of venerable associations, its words fragrant with the devotion of my fathers, who lived and died familiar with them; its syllables all of solemn and goodly sound, and bid me cantilate its phrases to the inspired notes of minstrelsy, my eye in a fine phrensy rolling, and I ask no questions for conscience' sake. I am ready to believe what is placed before me. I look beyond the antique words, to the spirit of some great truth that lingers somewhere around them; and in this nebulous view, I believe the creed *with my heart*. I may be even so rapt in enthusiasm as to believe it because it asserts what is impossible. Ask me not to prove it, — I am in no mood for proof. Try not to reason me out of it, — reasoning does me no good. Call not for my precise meaning, — I have not viewed it in that light. I have not taken the creed so much as the creed has taken me, and carried me away in my feelings to mingle with the piety of by-gone generations. — But can it be that this is the only, or the primitive, or the right idea of a symbol of faith? For *this* have logicians exhausted their subtleties, and martyrs yielded up the ghost, disputing and dying for a song? No. A creed, if true to its original end, should be in sober prose, should be understood as it means, and should mean what it says, should be drawn out with a discriminating, balancing judgment, so as to need no allowance for its freedom, no abatement of its force, and should not be expressed in antiquated terms lest men regard its spirit as likewise obsolete. It belongs to the province of the analyzing, comparing, reasoning intellect; and if it leave this province for the sake of intermingling the phrases of an impassioned heart, it confuses the soul, it awakens the fancy and the feelings to disturb the judgment, it sets a believer at variance with himself by perplexing his reason with metaphors and his imagination with logic; it raises feuds in the church by crossing the temperaments of men, and taxing one party to demonstrate similes, another to feel inspired by abstractions. Hence the logomachy which has always characterized the defence of such creeds. The intellect, no less than the heart, being out of its element, wanders through dry places, seeking rest and finding none. Men are thus made uneasy with themselves and therefore acrimonious against each other; the imaginative zealot does not apprehend the philosophical explanation, and the philosopher does not sympathize with the imaginative style of the symbol; and as they misunderstand each other, they feel their weakness, and "to be weak is miserable," and misery not only loves but also makes company, and thus they sink their controversy into a contention and their dispute into a quarrel; nor will they ever find peace until they confine their intellect to its rightful sphere and understand it according to what it says, and their feeling to *its* province and interpret its language according to what it means, rendering unto poetry the things that are designed for poetry, and unto prose what belongs to prose.

The last clause of our fourth proposition is, that the theology of intellect and that of feeling tend to keep each other within the sphere in which they are fitted to improve the character.[1] So far as any statement is hurtful, it parts with one sign of its truth. In itself or in its relations it must be inaccurate, whenever it is not congenial with the feelings awakened by the Divine Spirit. The practical utility, then, of any theological representations is one criterion of their propriety. Judged by this test, many fashionable forms of statement will sooner or later be condemned. Half of the truth is often a falsehood as it is impressed on the feelings; not always, however, for sometimes it has the good, the right influence, and is craved by the sensibilities which can bear no more. The heart of man is contracted, therefore loves individual views, dreads the labor of that long-continued expansion which is needed for embracing the comprehensive system. Hence its individualizing processes must be superintended by the judgment and conscience, which forbid that the attention be absorbed by any one aspect of a doctrine at the time when another aspect would be more useful. If the wrong half of a truth be applied instead of the right, or if either be mistaken for the whole, the sensibilities are mal-treated, and they endure an evil of which the musician's rude and unskilful handling of his harp, gives but a faint echo. The soul may be compared to a complicated instrument which becomes vocal in praise of its Maker when it is plied with varying powers, now with a gradual and then with a sudden contact, here with a delicate stroke and there with a hard assault; but when the rough blow comes where should have been the gentle touch, the equipoise of its parts is destroyed, and the harp of thousand strings all meant for harmony, wounds the ear with a harsh and grating sound. The dissonance of pious feeling, with the mere generalities of speculation or with any misapplied fragments of truth, tends to confine them within their appropriate, which is their useful sphere. In this light, we discern the necessity of right feeling as a guide to the right proportions of faith. Here we see our responsibility for our religious belief. Here we are impressed by the fact, that much of our probation relates to our mode of shaping and coloring the doctrines of theology. Here also we learn the value of the Bible in unfolding the suitable adaptations of truth, and in illustrating their utility, which is, on the whole, so decisive a touchstone of their correctness.

---

[1] In consequence of the length of the Discourse, this paragraph and that which follows it, were omitted in the delivery.

When our earthly hopes are too buoyant we are reminded 'that one event happeneth to all,' and "that a man hath no preëminence above a beast;" but such a repressing part of a comprehensive fact is not suited to the sensual and sluggish man who needs rather, as he is directed, to see his 'life and immortality brought to light.' When we are elated with pride we are told that "man is a worm;" but this abasing part of a great doctrine should not engross the mind of him who despises his race, and who is therefore bidden to think of man as 'crowned with glory and honor.' If tempted to make idols of our friends, we are met by the requisition to 'hate a brother, sister, father and mother;' but these are not the most fitting words for him who loves to persecute his opposers, and who requires rather to be asked, "He that loveth not his brother whom he hath seen, how can he love God whom he hath not seen?" In one state of feeling we are stimulated to "work out our salvation with fear and trembling," but in a different state we are encouraged to be neither anxious nor fearful, but to "rejoice in the Lord always." I believe in the "final perseverance" of all who have been once renewed, for not only does the generalizing intellect gather up this doctrine from an induction of various inspired words, but the heart also is comforted by it in the hour of dismal foreboding. Yet when I wrest this truth from its designed adjustments, and misuse it in quieting the fears of men who are instigated to 'count the blood of the covenant wherewith they were sanctified an unholy thing,' I am startled by the threat that 'if they shall fall away, it will be impossible to renew them *again* unto repentance.' This threat was not designed, like the promise of preserving grace, to console the disconsolate, nor was that promise designed like this threat, to alarm the presumptuous. Let not the two appeals cross each other. My judgment, and, in some lofty views in which I need to be held up by the Divine Spirit lest I fall, my feelings also are unsatisfied without the biblical announcement that "the Lord hardened Pharaoh's heart;" but at my incipient inclination to pervert these words into an excuse for sin, or a denial of my entire freedom, or of my Maker's justice or tenderness, I regard them as a "form of sound words" from which my depravity has expelled their spirit, and I flee for safety to the other words, which are a complement to the first, that "Pharaoh hardened his own heart." When even a Puritan bishop is inflated with his vain conceits, it is perilous for him to concentrate his feelings upon the keys with which he is to open or shut the door of heaven. Such a man should oftener tremble lest having been a servant of servants here, he be cast away hereafter. But with a melancholic though faithful pastor, this application of Scriptures may be reversed. We delight in the thought, that he who hath made everything beautiful in its season, who sendeth dew upon the earth when it has been heated by the sun,—and again, when it has been parched by drought, sendeth rain; who draweth the curtains of darkness around us when the eye is tired of the bright heavens, and irradiates the vision when the night has become wearisome; who intermingleth calm with tempest and parteth the clouds of an April day for the passage of the sun's rays,—hath also adopted a free, exuberant, refreshing method of imparting truth to the soul; giving us a series of revelations flexile and pliant, flitting across the mental vision with changeful hues, ever new, ever appropriate, not one of its words retaining its entire usefulness when removed from its fit junctions, not one of them being susceptible of a change for the better in the exigency when it was uttered, but each being "a word spoken in due season, how good is it."

There is a kind of conjectural doctrine, which in the Swedenborgian and Millenarian fancies is carried to a ruinous excess, but which within, not beyond the limit of its practical utility may be either justified or excused. Our feelings, for example, impel us to believe that we are compassed about with some kind of superior and ever wakeful intelligence. To meet this demand of the heart, Paganism has filled the air with divinities, but a wiser forecast has revealed to us the omnipresence of an all-comprehending mind. Still our restless desires would be sometimes gratified by a livelier representation of the spiritual existence around us, and accordingly in the more than paternal compassion of Jehovah, he maketh his angels ministering spirits, sent forth to attend upon the heirs of salvation, and to animate our spiritual atmosphere with a quick movement. But even yet, there are times when the heart of man would be glad of something more than even these cheering revelations. We are comforted with the thought that our deceased companions still mingle with us, and aid us in our struggles to gain their purity, and that, after we have left the world to which thus far we have been so unprofitable, we shall be qualified by our hard discipline here, for more effective ministries to those who will remain in this scene of toil. Such a belief however is not one which the reason, left to itself, would fortify by other than the slightest hints. It is a belief prompted by the affections, and the indulgence in it is allowed by the intellectual powers no farther than it consoles and enlivens the spirit which is wearied with its earthly strifes. If we begin to think more of friends who visit us from heaven than of Him who always abideth faithful around and over and within us, if we begin to search out witty inventions and to invoke the aid of patronizing saints, if we imagine that she who once kept all her child's sayings in her heart will now lay up in her motherly remembrance the *Ave Marias* of all who bless her image, then we push an innocent conjecture into the sphere of a harmful falsehood. The intellectual theology recognizes our felt need of a tenderness in the supervision which is exercised over us, but instead of meeting this necessity by picturing forth the love of one who after all may forget her very infant, it proves that we are ever enveloped in the sympathies of Him who will not give away to his saints the glory of answering our feeble prayers. The intellectual theology does indeed recognize our felt want of a Mediator, through whose friendly offices we may gain access to the pure, invisible, sovereign, strict lawgiver. But instead of an unearthly being canonized for his austere virtues, it gives us him who ate with sinners, who called around him fishermen rather than princes, and lodged with a tax-gatherer instead of the Roman governor, so as to remind us that he is not ashamed to call us brethren. Where men looked for a taper, it gives a light shining as the day, and hides the stars by the effulgence of the sun; where they looked for a friend it gives a Redeemer, where for a helper, a Saviour, where for hope, faith. It takes away in order to add more, thwarts a desire so as to give a fruition. It not so much unclothes as clothes upon, and swallows up our wish for patron saints in the brotherly sympathies of him who ever liveth to make intercession for us.

In conclusion allow me to observe, that in some aspects our theme suggests a melancholy, in others a cheering train of thought. It grieves us by disclosing the ease with which we may slide into grave errors. Such errors have arisen from so simple a cause as that of confounding poetry with prose. Men whose reasoning instinct has absorbed their delicacy of taste, have treated the language of a sensitive heart as if it were the guarded and wary style of the intellect. Intent on the sign more than on the thing signified, they have transubstantiated the living, spiritual truth into the very emblems which were designed to portray it. In the Bible there are pleasing hints of many things which were never designed to be doctrines, such as the literal and proper necessity of the will, passive and physical sin, baptismal regeneration, clerical absolution, the literal imputation of guilt to the innocent, transubstantiation, eternal generation and procession. In that graceful volume, these metaphors bloom as the flowers of the field; *there* they toil not neither do they spin. But the schoolman has transplanted them to the rude exposure of logic; here they are frozen up, their fragrance is gone, their juices evaporated, and their withered leaves are preserved as specimens of that which in its rightful place surpassed the glory of the wisest sage. Or, if I may change the illustration, I would say that these ideas, as presented in the Bible, are like oriental kings and nobles, moving about in their free, flowing robes, but in many a scholastic system they are like the embalmed bodies of those ancient lords, their spirits fled, their eyes, which once had speculation in them, now lack lustre; they are dry bones, exceeding dry. Not a few technical terms in theology are rhetorical beauties stiffened into logical perplexities; the exquisite growths of the imagination pressed and dried into the matter of a syllogism in Barbara. Many who discard their literal meaning retain the words out of reverence to antique fashions, out of an amiable fondness for keeping the nomenclature of science unbroken, just as the modern astronomer continues to classify the sweet stars of Heaven under the constellations of the Dragon and the Great Bear.[1]

In this and in still other aspects our theme opens into more cheering views. It reveals the identity in the essence of many systems which are run in scientific or aesthetic moulds unlike each other. The full influence of it would do more than any World's Convention, in appeasing the jealousies of those good men who build their faith on Jesus Christ as the chief corner-stone, and yet are induced, by unequal measures of genius and culture, to give different shapes to structures of the same material. There are indeed kinds of theology which cannot be reconciled with each other. There is a life, a soul, a vitalizing spirit of truth, which must never be relinquished for the sake of peace even with an angel. There is (I know that you will allow me to express my opinion,) a line of separation which cannot be crossed between those systems which insert, and those which omit the doctrine of justification by faith in the sacrifice of Jesus. This is the doctrine which blends in itself the theology of intellect and that of feeling, and which can no more be struck out from the moral, than the sun from the planetary system. Here the mind and the heart, like justice and mercy, meet and embrace each other; and here is found the specific and ineffaceable difference between the Gospel and every other system. But among those who admit the atoning death of Christ as the organific principle of their faith, there are differences, some of them more important, but many far less important, than they seem to be. One man prefers a theology of the judgment; a second, that of the imagination; a third, that of the heart; one adjusts his faith to a lymphatic, another to a sanguine, and still another to a choleric temperament. Yet the subject matter of these heterogeneous configurations may often be one and the same, having for its nucleus the same cross, with the formative influence of which all is safe.

---

[1] See Note H. at the end of the Discourse.

Sometimes the intellectual divine has been denounced as unfeeling by the rude and coarse preacher, who in his turn has been condemned as vulgar or perhaps irreverent by the intellectual divine; while the one has meant to insinuate into the select few who listened to him, the very substance of the doctrine which the other has stoutly and almost literally *inculcated* into the multitudes by which he was thronged. The hard polemic has shown us only his visor and his coat of mail, while beneath his iron armor has been often cherished a theology of the gentle and humane affections. Dogmas of the most revolting shape have no sooner been cast into the alembic of a regenerated heart, than their more jagged angles have been melted away. We are cheered with a belief, that in the darkest ages hundreds and thousands of unlettered men felt an influence which they could not explain, the influence of love attracting to itself the particles of truth that lay scattered along the symbols and scholastic forms of the church. The great mass of believers have never embraced the metaphysical refinements of creeds, useful as these refinements are; but have singled out and fastened upon and held firm those cardinal truths, which the Bible has lifted up and turned over in so many different lights, as to make them the more conspicuous by their very alternations of figure and hue. The true history of doctrine is to be studied not in the technics, but in the spirit of the church. In unnumbered cases, the real faith of Christians has been purer than their written statements of it. Men, women, and children have often decided aright when doctors have disagreed, and doctors themselves have often felt aright when they have reasoned amiss. "In my heart," said a tearful German, "I am a Christian, while in my head I am a philosopher." Many who now dispute for an erroneous creed have, we trust, a richer belief imbedded in their inmost love. There are discrepant systems of philosophy pervading the sermons of different evangelical ministers, but often the rays of light which escape from these systems are so reflected and refracted, while passing through the atmosphere between the pulpit and the pews, as to end in producing about the same image upon the retina of every eye. Not seldom are the leaders of sects in a real variance when the people, who fill up the sects, know not why they are cut off from their brethren, and the people may strive in words while they agree in the thing, and their judgments may differ in the thing while their hearts are at one.

Thus divided against itself, thus introverting itself, thus multiform in its conceptions, so quick to seize at a truth as held up in one way, and spurn at it as held up in another, so marvellous in its tact for decomposing its honest belief, disowning with the intellect what it embraces with the affections, so much more versatile in regulating its merely inward processes than in directing the motions of an equilibrist, thus endued with an elastic energy more than Protean,— thus great is the soul, for the immense capabilities of which *Christ died*. Large-minded, then, and large-hearted must be the minister, having all the sensibility of a woman without becoming womanish, and all the perspicacity of a logician without being merely logical, having that philosophy which detects the substantial import of the heart's phrases, and having that emotion which invests philosophy with its proper life,— so wise and so good must the minister be, who applies to a soul of these variegated sensibilities the truth, which may wind itself into them all, as through a thousand pores; that truth, which God himself has matched to our nicest and most delicate springs of action, and which, so highly does he honor our nature, he has interposed by miracles for the sake of revealing in his written word; that word, which by its interchange of styles all unfolding the same idea, by its liberal construction of forms all enclosing the same spirit, prompts us to argue more for the broad central principles, and to wrangle less for the side, the party aspects of truth; that word, which ever pleases in order to instruct, and instructs in such divers ways in order to impress divers minds, and by all means to save some. Through the influence of such a Bible upon such a soul, and under the guidance of Him who gave the one and made the other, we do hope and believe, that the intellect will yet be enlarged so as to gather up all the discordant representations of the heart and employ them as the complements, or embellishments, or emphases of the whole truth; that the heart will be so expanded and refined as to sympathize with the most subtile abstractions of the intellect; that many various forms of faith will yet be blended into a consistent knowledge, like the colors in a single ray.; and thus will be ushered in the reign of the Prince of peace, when the lion shall lie down with the lamb, when the body shall no more hang as a weight upon the soul, and the soul no longer wear upon its material frame-work, when the fancy shall wait upon rather than trifle with the judgment, and the judgment shall not be called as now to restrain the fancy, when the passions shall clarify rather than darken the reasoning powers, and the conscience shall not be summoned as now to curb the passions, when the intellect shall believe, not without the heart, nor against the heart, but *with the heart unto salvation;* and the soul, being one with itself, shall also be one with all the saints, in adoring one Lord, cherishing one faith, and being buried in one baptism; and when we who are united unto Christ on earth, he dwelling in us and we in him, shall, in answer to his last prayer for us, be made perfect with him in God.

Note A. Page 535.

This reasoning is valid only on the supposition that our Saviour died for all men. —One of Mr. Symington's arguments for the doctrine that Christ made his atonement for a part only, not the whole of the race, is derived, singular as it may appear, from the "rectitude of the divine character." He says in his Treatise on the Atonement, Part I. Sect. XI. § II. 2: "The supreme Being gives to every one his due. This principle cannot be violated in a single instance. He cannot, according to this, either remit sin without satisfaction, or punish sin where satisfaction for it has been received. The one is as inconsistent with perfect equity as the other. If the punishment for sin has been borne, the remission of the offence follows of course. The principles of rectitude suppose this, nay peremptorily demand it; justice could not be satisfied without it. Agreeably to this reasoning it follows, that the death of Christ being a legal satisfaction for sin, all for whom he died must enjoy the remission of their offences. It is as much at variance with strict justice or equity, that any for whom Christ has given satisfaction should continue under condemnation, as that they should have been delivered from guilt without a satisfaction being given for them at all. But it is admitted, that all are not delivered from the punishment of sin, that there are many who perish in final condemnation. We are therefore compelled to infer, that for such no satisfaction has been given to the claims of infinite justice — no atonement has been made. If this is denied, the monstrous impossibility must be maintained, that the infallible judge refuses to remit the punishment of some for whose offences he has received a full compensation; that he finally condemns some the price of whose deliverance from condemnation has been paid to him; that, with regard to the sins of some of mankind, he seeks satisfaction in their personal punishment after having obtained satisfaction for them in the sufferings of Christ; that is to say, that an infinitely righteous God takes double payment for the same debt, double satisfaction for the same offence, first from the surety, and then from those for whom the surety stood bound. It is needless to add that these conclusions are revolting to every right feeling of equity, and must be totally inapplicable to the procedure of Him who '*loveth righteousness and hateth wickedness*.'

Mr. Symington's inferences in this paragraph are correct, if his premises are to be understood as intellectual statements of the truth. But Dr. Jonathan Edwards (in his Works, Vol. II. p. 26) teaches us that " Christ has not in the *literal* and *proper* sense paid the debt for us;" that this expression and others similar to it are "metaphorical expressions, and therefore not literally and exactly true." He says further (Works, Vol. II. p. 48) concerning *distributive* justice, that it "is not at all satisfied by the death of Christ. But *general* justice to the Deity and to the universe is satisfied." A similar remark he appends with regard to the satisfaction of the law. See also Andrew Fuller's Works, Vol. IV. pp. 92—100. 1st Am. Ed.

A true representation seems to be, that although Christ has not literally paid the debt of sinners, nor literally borne their punishment, nor satisfied the legislative or the remunerative justice of God in any such sense or degree as itself to make it *obligatory* on him to save any sinners; yet the atonement has such a relation to the whole moral government of God, as to make it *consistent* with the honor of his legislative and retributive justice to save all men, and to make it essential to the highest honor of his benevolence or general justice to renew and save some. Therefore it satisfies the law and justice of God *so far and in such a sense*, as to render it proper for him not only to give many temporal favors, but also to offer salvation to all men, bestow it upon all who will accept it, and cause those to accept it, for whom the interests of the universe allow him to interpose his regenerating grace.

NOTE B. Page 540.

It has already been explained, that *the* theology of the intellect, is the system which recommends itself to a dispassionate and unprejudiced mind as true, and the present discourse has no direct and prominent reference to the various forms of intellectual theology which, in the view of such a mind, are false. It has also been explained, that *the* theology of the heart is the collection of statements which recommend themselves to the healthy moral feelings as right, and the present discourse has no direct and prominent reference to the various forms of representation which are suggested by and suited to the diseased, the perverted moral feelings. One of the most graphic descriptions of a theology which is neither of a sound intellect nor sound heart, but is alike impervious to argument, reckless of consequences, and dependent on an ill-balanced state of the sensibilities, may be found in the following Letter to Dr. Henry Ware, Jr. That calm reasoner had published a sermon in opposition to some injurious sentiments which had been recently propounded at Cambridge, and in acknowledging the receipt of the sermon, the advocate of those sentiments replied :— If your discourse " assails any doctrines of mine,— perhaps I am not so quick to see it as writers generally,— certainly I did not feel any disposition to depart from my habitual contentment, that you should say your thought, whilst I say mine.

"I believe I must tell you what I think of my new position. It strikes me very oddly, that good and wise men at Cambridge and Boston should think of raising me into an object of criticism. I have always been,—from my very incapacity of methodical writing. — 'a chartered libertine,' free to worship and free to rail, — lucky when I could make make myself understood, but never esteemed near enough to the institutions and mind of society to deserve the notice of the masters of literature and religion. I have appreciated fully the advantages of my position; for I well know, that there is no scholar less willing or less able to be a polemic. I could not give account of myself if challenged. I could not possibly give you one of the 'arguments' you cruelly hint at, on which any doctrine of mine stands. For I do not know what arguments mean, in reference to any expression of a thought. I delight in telling what I think ; but if you ask me how I dare say so, or, why it is so, I am the most helpless of mortal men. I do not even see, that either of these questions admits of an answer. So that, in the present droll posture of my affairs, when I see myself suddenly raised into the importance of a heretic, I am very uneasy when I advert to the supposed duties of such a personage, who is to make good his thesis against all comers.

" I certainly shall do no such thing. I shall read what you and other good men write, as I have always done,— glad when you speak my thoughts, and skipping the page that has nothing for me. I shall go on, just as before, seeing whatever I can, and telling what I see ; and, I suppose, with the same fortune that has hitherto attended me; the joy of finding, that my abler and better brothers, who work with the sympathy of society, loving and beloved, do now and then unexpectedly confirm my perceptions, and find my nonsense is only their own thought in motley. And so I am your affectionate servant, R. W. EMERSON."

One of the amazing mal-adjustments in human life, is that in which a pious man has such idiosyncracies, or has been so mis-educated as to believe in a false intellectual system, and to feel an impulsive attachment to it. He is of all men the most incorrigible. Argument is wasted upon him, and his prejudices are the more unyielding because fortified by conscience. He is also an unhappy man, for his erroneous views do not harmonize entirely or easily with his pious feelings. Hence he often becomes a schismatic, a disorganizer, a crossed and uncomfortable member of society, a public phenomenon.

Note C. Page 542.

The censure frequently pronounced upon the style in which writers like Baxter, Bunyan, and Davies describe the punishment of the lost, is no further merited, than this style can be shown to be unfaithful to the truth, or to the imperative necessities of the minds to which it was addressed. If the publications of the American Tract Society, which are designed not for philosophical criticism but for practical impression, should, as some would have them, describe the future state of the lost as it is described by a merely scientific theologian, they would forfeit their popular influence, and perhaps would convey error instead of truth to the mass of their readers. That all uninspired volumes are imperfect in delineating "the terrors of the Lord," is doubtless true. Their imperfection, however, does not consist in their using the Biblical forms of statement, but in their deviating from or else misapplying these forms. Our Saviour adopted a different phraseology from that of the prophets before him, and that of the apostles after him; and a wise preacher would not exhort a Newton and a Leibnitz in the same terms, although he would use the same great ideas, which he would employ in addressing little children, or in expostulating with the rudest and coarsest of malefactors. The Biblical impression of the particular incidents in the eternal punishment of some and the eternal blessedness of others, is of course the best impression which can be made upon the heart; but the mental eye hath not seen, nor ear heard of the exact, precise instruments which God hath prepared for the retribution of those who hate, or of those who love him.

Note D. Page 545.

It is on the principles indicated in the preceding topic, that the aphorism of Pascal (Thoughts, ch. III.) may be explained: God "has chosen that" divine truths "should enter from the heart into the mind, and not from the mind into the heart, in order to humble that proud power of reasoning, which pretends it should be the judge of things which the will chooses, and to reform that infirm will which is wholly corrupt through its unworthy inclinations. And hence, instead of saying, as men do when speaking of human things, that we must know them before we can love them, which has passed into a proverb, the saints, when speaking of divine things, say, that we must love them in order to know them, and that we receive the truth only by love; — which is one of their most useful maxims." These words mean, not that the heart ever perceives, for the intellect only is percipient, but that holy feelings prompt the intellect to new discoveries, furnish it with new materials for examination and inference, and regulate it in its mode of combining and expressing what it has discerned. An affection of the heart toward a truth develops a new relation of that truth, and the intellect perceives the relation thus suggested by the feeling. On the same principles may we interpret the celebrated paradox of Anselm, of Canterbury: "I do not seek to understand a truth in order that I may believe it, but I believe it in order that I may understand it." This remark may be made to appear rational by the paraphrase: I first have some idea of a doctrine; I then cordially believe all that I have an idea of; next, by the love involved in this hearty faith I am inspirited to form still more definite ideas of that which I had before perceived clearly enough to believe it affectionately; and at last, by the relation which is thus developed between the doctrine and my feelings, I obtain yet more distinct and extended ideas of it, so that I may be said to understand it.

Note E. Page 549.

The preceding illustration suggests *some*, not all, of the causes why the doctrine that men are unable to be more virtuous than they really are, becomes less injurious as it is taught by pious divines than as it is taught by infidel philosophers.

One generic cause is, that the earnest preacher often contradicts in his exhortation what he has seemed to advocate in his discussion; but the intellectual deist has not the *heart* to modify his denial of human freedom; he retains in all exigencies the unbending theory, that man has no power to be better than he is.

A *second* subordinate cause, really included in the first, is, that the Christian points this doctrine chiefly to the present or the future, but the infidel extends it equally to the past. The pious necessarian has a good moral purpose in declaring that the *present* and *future* obligations of men, do and will exceed their power; he designs to foster thus a spirit of dependence on God; but, for another good moral purpose, he shrinks from informing men that their *past* obligations exceeded their power. The reckless fatalist, however, is as willing to assert that men *have* obeyed the law heretofore to the extent of their ability, as that men *will have* no ability, without supernatural aid, to obey the law hereafter. He is ready to stifle remorse by assuring the convicts of a penitentiary, that they have possessed no more power than they have exercised to choose aright; that is, their choices have been as benevolent as they could have been. It is doubtless true, that in precisely the same sense in which a man *is* or *will be* unable to perform his duty, in that sense he *has* performed his duty as well as he was able to perform it, has done all the good which was possible for him to do. But the best feelings of a Christian forbid his use of such language in regard to the past, favor his use of the opposite, and thus induce him to mitigate the evils of asserting without qualification that man's power is less than his duty.

A *third* reason, why the necessarianism of Christian divines becomes less injurious than the fatalism of infidel philosophers is, that the most trust-worthy of these divines acknowledge their necessarian doctrine to be expressed in the language of the emotions, while the fatalist contends for the intellectual exactness of his phraseology. The wise preacher believes in only a moral, the fatalist in a natural impotence. In Andrew Fuller's Apparent Contradictions Reconciled (Works, Vol. VIII. pp. 51—55, First Am. Ed.), his fourth proposition is, "The depravity of human nature is such that no man, of his own accord, will come to Christ for life;" and his fifth proposition is, "The degree of this depravity is such, as that, figuratively speaking, men cannot come to Christ for life." The younger Pres. Edwards says (Works, Vol. I. p 307), "Dr. Clarke, in his Remarks on Collins (p. 16). gives a true account of moral necessity: 'By *moral necessity* consistent writers never mean any more than to express in a figurative manner the *certainty* of such an event.'" Dr. Day (on the Will. p. 107) remarks, "We are not justified in pronouncing this *figurative* use to be wholly improper" (inadmissible). The elder Pres. Edwards, although he may not have applied the epithet *figurative* to the necessarian terminology which he employs, yet often applies to it the epithet *improper*, which means in this connection not inadmissible but figurative. "No inability whatsoever," he says (on the Will, Part III. Sect. IV.), " which is merely moral, is properly called by the name of *inability*." Natural inability "alone is properly called inability." "I have largely declared," he says in his Letter against the literal necessarianism of Lord Kames (Works, Vol. II. pp. 293–4, Ed. 1829), " that the connection between antecedent things and consequent ones which takes place with regard to the acts of men's wills, which is called moral necessity, is called by the name of *necessity* improperly; and that all such terms as *must, cannot, impossible, unable, irresistible. unavoidable, invincible,* etc., when applied here, are not applied in their proper signification, and are either used nonsensically and with perfect insignificance, or in a sense quite diverse from their original and proper meaning, and their use in common speech ; and that such a necessity as attends the acts of men's will is more properly called *certainty* than *necessity*; it being no other than the certain connection between the subject and predicate of the proposition which affirms their existence."

So sure is it that man with his unrenewed nature will sin, and only sin in his moral acts, and so important is it that this infallible certainty be *felt* to be true, that our hearts often incline us to designate it by the most forcible epithets. These epithets often make the truth appear obvious to those whom pride has removed to a distance from it, just as the colossal proportions of a statue raised above the capital of a pillar, make the statue appear like the exact image of a man to those who look up to it from the remote valley. But if we infer from the literal meaning of necessity, that our so-called necessary choices are in fact inevitable, we commit the same mistake as if we should infer from the colossal dimensions of the statue, that the individual represented by it is a giant. It is easy to see, that the language of feeling in which divines may and do occasionally express the certainty of wrong choice, must be different in its influence from the language of the intellect in which fatalists invariably express their doctrine of the necessity of all choice. The demands of a soul which loves to invoke aid from Heaven, are met by a faithful description of that certainty which, in the words of Pres. Day (Examination of Edwards, p. 167), is a " necessity falsely so called." The truth is mournful, humbling, well fitted to awaken a spirit of prayer, that man left to himself will *invariably, surely* sin. but it gives no sanction to the demoralizing falsehood that, in the literal and proper sense, he *must inevitably* sin.

That the terms of feeling and of common life should have been adopted as the scientific nomenclature on the subject of the will, has been submissively regretted by our best theologians. He must be a strong man who can bear up under this cumbrous nomenclature without lapsing sometimes into its literal, which is not its technical meaning ; and many a Samson having been overpowered by its heaviness, has been compelled to " grind in the prison-house" of Gaza. In one of his most eloquent passages, Pres. Edwards thus laments the deceptive influence of these " terms of art :" " Nothing that I maintain supposes that men are at all hindered by any fatal necessity, from doing and even willing and choosing as they please, with full freedom ; yea, with the highest degree of liberty that ever was thought of, or that ever could possibly enter into the heart of any man to conceive. I know it is in vain to endeavor to make some persons believe this, or at least fully and steadily to believe it ; for if it be demonstrated to them, still the old prejudice remains, which has been long fixed by the use of the terms *necessary, must, cannot, impossible*, etc.; the association with these terms of certain ideas inconsistent with liberty, is not broken ; and the judgment is powerfully warped by it ; as a thing that has been long bent and grown stiff, if it be straightened, will return to its former curvity again and again." (Works, Vol. II. pp. 293, 294. Ed. 1829.)

The epithets *figurative, improper*, when applied by the Edwardses, Fuller, Day, and others, to the necessarian phraseology of the will, are to be understood according to the principles laid down in the preceding Discourse, pp. 537, 538.

Note F. Page 550.

We have a safeguard against the dreams of visionaries in the two principles already stated, that reason has an ultimate, rightful authority over the sensibilities, and that it will sanction not only all *pious* feelings, but likewise all those which are *essential* developments of our original constitution. As the head is placed above the heart in the body, so the faith which is sustained by good argument, should control rather than be controlled by those emotions which receive no approval from the judgment. The perfection of our faith is, that it combine in its favor the logic of the understanding with the rhetoric of the feelings, and that it exclude all those puerilities and extravagances, which have nothing to recommend them but the pretended inspirations of the fanatic. Whenever a discrepancy exists between a creed and an expression of devotional feeling, as for example between the "Thirty-nine Articles" and the "Book of Common Prayer," the symbol of faith ought to be in a style so prosaic and definite as to form the decisive standard of appeal, and to explain, rather than be explained by the liturgical, which are apt to be fervid utterances.

Note G. Page 552.

The fallen, evil nature, which precedes and certainly occasions a man's first actual sin, is, like all other evil, odious, loathsome. So prolific is it in results which are so melancholy, that while we are trembling at its power, we are roused up to stigmatize it as "sinful." We may thus earnestly reprobate it, if we do not insist that the word "sinful" shall be interpreted, in scientific language, to mean that quality which is itself worthy of punishment. In our abhorrence of this disordered state of our sensibilities, we may call it "blamable," if we do not insist that a man is to be blamed for being involuntarily in this calamitous state; we may call it "guilty," if we mean by this word "intimately connected with guilt," or "exposing us to suffering," for this diseased nature leads to sin, and thereby to its most painful consequences. We may in fact apply any epithet whatever to our inborn, involuntary corruption, provided that this epithet express our dread or hatred of it, and do not require the belief that a passive condition, previous to all active disobedience, is itself deserving of punishment. As there was much that was amiable in the young man who possessed nothing holy, so there is much that is unamiable, and still not properly sinful, in every man. But although in our fervid diaries we may often pour these unmeasured reproaches upon our corrupt nature, yet in a scientific treatise we embarrass ourselves by using the emotional, as if it were didactic language; by applying the loose terms of the heart to themes where the sharpest discrimination is needed; by speaking, as many do, of a kind of sin for which the man who is charged with it does not, in the view of conscience, deserve to be punished; by reasoning about a state for which the child involuntarily subjected to it is "guilty," but not himself properly blamable. The well-schooled divine *may*, although he seldom *does* escape the confusing influence of this ambiguous nomenclature; but men who are conversant with only the "English undefiled" of our literature, are led by such a peculiar, when used as a dogmatic phraseology, into serious, perhaps fatal prejudices against the truth. When these terms, often allowable for the heart, are used for the intellect, they change their character, and although meant for "the lights of science," they fall of their artificial purpose, and become "in many instances the shades of religion."

Is it said, however, that a passive nature, existing antecedently to all free action, is itself, strictly, literally sinful? Then we must have a new language, and speak, in prose, of moral *patients* as well as moral agents, of men *besinned* as well as sinners, (for *ex vi termini* sinners as well as runners must be active); we must have a new conscience which can decide on the moral character of dormant conditions, as well as of elective preferences; a new law, prescribing the very *make* of the soul, as well as the way in which this soul, when made, shall act; and a law which we transgress (for sin is "a transgression of the law") in being before birth passively misshapen; we must also have a new Bible, delineating a judgment scene in which some will be condemned, not only on account of the deeds which they have done in the body, but also for having been born with an involuntary proclivity to sin, and others will be rewarded not only for their conscientious love to Christ, but also for a blind nature inducing that love; we must, in fine, have an entirely different class of moral sentiments, and have them disciplined by Inspiration in an entirely different manner from the present; for now the feelings of all true men revolt from the assertion, that a poor infant dying, if we may suppose it to die, before its first wrong preference, *merits* for its unavoidable nature, that eternal punishment, which is threatened, and justly, against even the smallest real sin. Although it may seem paradoxical to affirm that "a man may believe a proposition which he knows to be false," it is yet charitable to say that whatever any man may suppose himself to believe, he has in fact an inward conviction, that "all sin consists in sinning." There is comparatively little dispute on the nature of moral evil, when the words relating to it are fully understood.

Note II. Page 559.

It is a noted remark of John Foster, that many technical terms of theology, instead of being the signs, are the monuments of the ideas which they were first intended to signify. Now it is natural for men to garnish the sepulchre of one whom, when living, they would condemn.

When it is said in palliation for certain technics of theology, that they are no more uncouth or equivocal than are the technics of some physical sciences, we may reply, that the sacred science above all others should, where it fairly can, be so presented as to allure rather than repel men of classical taste, and not superadd factitious offences to the natural "offence of the cross." True, we may be deceived by the figurative terms of mineralogy or botany, but we are less liable to mistake the meaning of words which refer to material phenomena, than the meaning of those which refer to spiritual, and then an error in physics is far less baneful than one in religion. If chemical substances were denoted by words borrowed from moral science, if one acid were figuratively called "sanctification," and one alkali were termed "depravity," and one solution were denominated "eternal punishment," we should weep over the sad results of such a profane style, even if it were well intended. And on a similar principle, when we read of "the vindictive justice of God," although we revere the authors who use the term in its technical sense, we mourn over the ruinous impression that will be made by such a piously meant phrase. Doubtless it may be needful for us to refer occasionally to the obnoxious technics which were once in such authoritative use, but if we make them *prominent*, or if, in employing them, we neglect to explain their peculiar meaning, we unwittingly convey false and pernicious ideas to men who are wont to call things by their right names.

It is against some first principles of rhetoric to say, that we may safely regulate our scientific nomenclature by the figurative expressions of the Bible. These expressions are easily understood in the spirit which prompted them, but are less easily understood in the spirit of the schools. If all the Biblical figures were arranged into a system, and if, when thus classified, they were reasoned upon as literal and dogmatic truths, we should have, on an extended scale, the same allegorical logic, which we now have on a scale so limited as to conceal many of its injurious effects. Perhaps we should then begin to shape the Copernican and Newtonian philosophy in the mould of the passage, "The Lord maketh the earth empty, and maketh it waste, and turneth it upside down." Some errors are most easily refuted by carrying them out to their entire length with all possible consistency. An extreme view of them develops their essential nature. What is a large part of Quakerism, and even Swedenborgianism, but a collection of fancies, interesting as such, but now flattened into theories?

ARTICLE VII.

TICKNOR'S SPANISH LITERATURE.

History of Spanish Literature. By George Ticknor. In three volumes. New York: Harper & Brothers, 1849.

By Prof. C. C. Felton, Cambridge.

THE appearance of a work like the present is an important event in our literary history. For completeness of plan, depth of learning, and thoroughness of execution, nothing superior has been produced in the English language, in our day. It will take at least an equal rank with either of the works of Hallam, and with the best historical productions of the continent. Mr. Ticknor has had ample time, abundant means, and every opportunity which travel and residence in Europe, and extensive acquaintance with the most eminent men in literature could give him. He has surveyed his subject in all its bearings with unwearied industry and the most conscientious determination to understand it thoroughly. Possessing a comprehensive knowledge of ancient and modern literature, he has been able to illustrate the literature of Spain by just comparisons, and to assign to it its true position in the history of the achievements of the human mind. The breadth of his culture and the catholic spirit with which all his judgments seem to have been formed, have saved him from giving an undue importance or prominence to the literature for which he evidently has a strong predilection, and which he understands better than any scholar ever understood before. If we compare this work with

finite reality as well as the infinite reality? This, too, exists in the mind clearly and distinctly, and it is not to be supposed, argues Descartes, forgetting utterly his inductive or psychological method, that God would deceive us in such a matter, he concludes that the external world has a real and not merely apparent or phenomenal existence.[1] Our mental faculties prove the existence of God, and the existence of God proves the validity of our mental faculties, is the vicious circle which throws inextricable confusion into the Cartesian philosophy.[2]

[To be continued.]

ARTICLE IX.

REMARKS ON THE BIBLICAL REPERTORY AND PRINCETON REVIEW. VOL. XXII. NO. IV. ART. VII.

By Edwards A. Park, Abbot Professor in Andover Theol. Seminary.

In the Biblical Repertory for October, 1850, has been published a Review of the last Convention Sermon delivered before the Congregational Ministers of Massachusetts. Some admirers of this Review have published the remark, that no one can mistake "the hand" that is in it, and have fitly characterized its author as "one of the most accomplished Reviewers in the country." As it is said to have emanated from a well-known theological instructor; as it suggests some grave questions of rhetoric; and as it illustrates various evils incident to anonymous criticism, it seems entitled to a dispassionate regard. There is no need, however, of canvassing all the principles, right and wrong, which are advanced in the Review, nor of commenting on *all* the wrong impressions which it makes, with regard to the sermon. We shall content ourselves with noticing a few, as specimens of the many mis-statements into which the critic has inadvertently lapsed.

It is a familiar fact, and one of great practical importance, that there are two generic modes of representing the same system of religious truth; the one mode suited to the scientific treatise, the other to the popular discourse, hymn book, liturgy. They differ not in language *alone*, but in several, and especially the following particulars: first, in the images and illustrations with which the same truth

---

[1] Meditation Quatrieme, p. 93.
[2] Meditation Cinquieme — particularly the close, pp. 107, 108.

is connected; Reinhard's Dogmatic System, for instance, not admitting the fervid imagery which glows in his eloquent discourses; secondly, in the proportions which the same truths bear to each other: Van Mastricht's scientific treatise, for example, giving less prominence to some, and more to other doctrines, than would be given to them in the earnest sermons of Krummacher; thirdly, in the arrangement of the same truths; Turretin's arrangement not being adapted to the ever varying wants of men, women, and children; fourthly, in the mode of commending the same truth to popular favor; a treatise of Ralph Cudworth, depending on nice distinctions and scholastic proofs, but a practical sermon of John Bunyan, depending on a bold outline and the selection of a few prominent features which win the heart at once; fifthly, in the words, and collocations of words used for expressing the same class of ideas; the truths in Ridgeley's Body of Divinity not being clothed in the language proper for an impassioned exhortation, or for popular psalmody. The design of the sermon under review is, to develop some practical lessons suggested by this plain distinction between these two modes of exhibiting one and the same doctrine.

One of these lessons is, the necessity of the preacher's enlivening a single abstract doctrine by concrete exhibitions of it; as, for example, the doctrine of eternal punishment, or of the general judgment, or of the resurrection, by images of the fire, darkness, worm, gnashing teeth, throne, open books, palm branch, white robe, etc. etc.[1] Another of these lessons is, the importance of inferring certain great doctrines from their congeniality with constitutional or pious feeling, and of ennobling the manifestation of this feeling by the clear statement of those doctrines.[2] The expressions of feeling are premises from which the intellect must deduce important corollaries; while it must not force upon these expressions the meaning which might be derived from a rigid analysis of them, but, making allowance for their unguarded terms, must penetrate into their substantial import. So far from its being a design of the sermon to deny that "truth is in order to holiness," as a reader of the Review would infer, a design of the sermon is rather to show that "every doctrine which [the intellect discovers in the Bible or in nature] is in reality practical, calling forth some emotion, and this emotion animating the sensitive nature which is not diseased, deepening its love of knowledge,

---

[1] Bib. Sac. pp. 540–542. Throughout this article reference is made to the edition of the sermon in the Bibliotheca Sacra for July, 1850.
[2] Bib. Sac. pp. 542–546.

elevating and widening the religious system which is to satisfy it. Every new article of the good man's belief elicits love or hatred, and this love or hatred so modifies the train and phasis of his meditations as to augment and improve the volume of his heart's theology."[1]

Instead of its being a tendency of the sermon to discountenance logical studies, one object of it is to show that "we lose our civilization so far forth as we depreciate a philosophy truly so called;" and "our faith becomes a wild or weak sentimentalism, if we despise logic," p. 543. Instead of the sermon's being adapted, as the Review implies, p. 660, to represent 'diversities of doctrinal propositions as matters of small moment, and make light of all differences which do not affect the fundamentals of the Gospel,' it reiterates the idea in various forms, that the "metaphysical refinements of creeds are useful," that "our spiritual oneness, completeness, progress, require" us to "define, distinguish, infer, arrange our inferences in a system," and that although "there is an identity in the *essence* of many systems which are run in scientific or aesthetic *moulds* unlike each other," yet even some of these unessential differences are more important, others less so, than they seem. Hence is inferred the duty "to argue more for the broad central *principles*, and to wrangle less for the side, the party *aspects* of truth," and to guard against what Dr. Hodge calls "a denunciatory or censorious spirit," which "blinds the mind to moral distinctions, and prevents the discernment between matters unessential and those vitally important."[2]

Many pious men are distressed by the apparent contradictions in our best religious literature, and for their sake another practical lesson developed in the discourse is, the importance of exhibiting the mutual consistency between all the expressions of right feeling. The discrepancies so often lamented are not fundamental but superficial, and are easily harmonized by exposing the one self-consistent principle which lies at their basis.[3] The assertions, for example, that God repents of having made our race and that he never repents, although contradictory in themselves, are not so in their fit connections; for they refer not to the same specific truth, but to different truths, both of which, however, may be reduced to the same ultimate principle,

---

[1] Bib. Sac. p. 543.
[2] See Hodge on Rom. 14: 1-23, also Bib. Sac. pp. 543, 559-561. It may be stated here, once for all, that whenever quotations are made in this article from the Review, or from the sermon, the writer has introduced his own italics, for the purpose of making this article the more definite.
[3] Bib. Sac. pp. 546—550.

that the changeless God is disposed to punish sin. So the assertions God is a rock and God is a Spirit, are contradictory if interpreted as divines often interpret language, by its letter, but they are not contradictory if interpreted as divines ought to interpret language, by its intent; for they relate not to the same specific idea, but to different ideas, both of which, however, may be reduced to the same ultimate principle, that the immaterial Divinity is a strong and sure support of his people.

Numerous and serious errors arise from understanding figurative expressions as if they were literal, and from transferring prosaic, vapid formulas, into sacred songs, fervent prayers, pathetic appeals. For this cause another practical lesson developed in the sermon is, the importance of keeping in their appropriate sphere the two modes of expressing truth, and the importance of appreciating the evil which results from unduly intermingling them.[1] Much of this evil finds its way into the religious character of men. Every controversial essay exposes it. Every day we see that the careless intermixture of the two forms of truth "confuses the soul," raises feuds in the "church," encourages "*logomachy*," "makes men uneasy with themselves and therefore acrimonious against each other," causes them to "sink their controversy into a contention and their dispute into a quarrel," etc. Often "the massive speculations of the metaphysician sink down into his expressions of feeling and make him appear cold hearted, while the enthusiasm of the impulsive divine ascends and effervesces into his reasonings, and causes him both to *appear* and to *be*, what our Saxon idiom so reprovingly styles him, hot-headed." Sermon, p. 553. We have no right to press our dogmas so far as to check the natural tendency of men to use language which, if interpreted according to the letter, is not correct. We must allow them to say that the sun rises and the fire is hot. An eminent and excellent divine once commenced an epistle to a friend with the exhortation not to pray for power to do right, because all men have this power but are merely disinclined to use it; and he closed the letter with an affectionate petition that his friend might be *enabled* to discharge his duty in this respect. The feelings *will* express themselves in words which the intellect left to itself would never have devised. We must do justice to these feelings. Let them have free play. This, however, is no excuse for inferring from the language of emotion, that the idea denoted by the literal interpretation of that language is the truth. If

---

[1] Bib. Sac. pp. 550—553.

so, the Romanists have gained their controversy and Galileo was rightly proscribed. We must not build a fortress of polemic theology on a mere flower of rhetoric; if so, we do not consolidate the fortress, and we crush the juices out of the flower. How much of theological mysticism has resulted from regarding the stanza of Cowley, that with God

> "Nothing is there to come, and nothing past,
> But an eternal *now* does always last,"———

as if it were a scientific formula, not less exact than poetical? How much of ethical error has arisen from interpreting the fervid exhortation, that impenitent sinners should pray for grace to put forth their first holy choice, as if this exhortation were designed to imply that they may pray without holiness for aid in performing their first right act. Rigidly explained, the phrase must have this meaning, but was it intended for a logical or a popular phrase? And is it not often understood, in the sense which *is* not indeed, but which nevertheless *ought* always to be designed, as a stimulus to immediate repentance, a stimulus applied so vehemently that the solecism of the words is overlooked.

Other practical lessons suggested in the discourse are, the importance of making our sermons less dull and stiff, by making them less abstract; the importance of rendering our theological treatises less ambiguous by writing them in a style less in need of qualification; the importance of a larger charity toward good men, and of a deeper reverence for the one system of inspired truth which unites in its maintenance so many classes of devotees.

But the Reviewer seems not to have noticed the true practical aims of the sermon. He was led, perhaps, into his misapprehensions of it by its title. This title is distinctly affirmed to have been chosen "for want of a better,"[1] not because it is all that could be wished. Let us then state some of the reasons which may justify it.

First, it is less cumbrous than any other which would be equally expressive of the author's meaning. The title might have been, The form of theology suggested by and best suited to the calm processes of the intellect, and the form of theology suggested by and best fitted to awaken and then to gratify the right feelings. Or it might have been, Theology in the form prompted by the reasoning powers and best adapted to speculation, and theology in the form prompted by the sensibilities and suited to excite and then satisfy emotion.

---
[1] Bib. Sac. p. 534.

But the title actually selected is, The Theology of the Intellect and that of the Feelings. This need not be misunderstood, for it is expressly defined as not denoting two *kinds* of truth essentially unlike, but as denoting two dissimilar *modes* of representing one and the same truth. A brief Proposition, when definitely explained, is allowed as a convenience to all preachers.

Secondly, the title was selected as a deferential and a charitable one. It was designed to mitigate prejudices, by conceding somewhat to them. The representations which are classified under the theology of feeling are often sanctioned as "the true theology," by the men who delight most in employing them. What the sermon would characterize as images, illustrations and intense expressions, these men call *doctrines*. It is a *doctrine*, for instance, that the bread is Christ's body; that men are regenerated in baptism; that the sins of a man are forgiven by God if a minister forgive them; that moral inability is not a mere desperate unwillingness, but a literal powerlessness; that guilt is as literally imputed to the innocent as innocence is imputed to them, and that innocence is as literally imputed to the sinful as sin is imputed to them. In like manner the conceptions most obviously denoted by such terms as eternal generation and procession, are often said by the men who are most fond of using these terms, to be necessary parts of "the correct theology." In deference to this frequent usage, these conceptions may be named "the theology of the heart." We call one system of theology "rational" or "liberal," simply because it is called so by its advocates; much more then may we designate by the phrase "emotive theology," those representations which are so tenaciously defended by multitudes as the truth fitted both for the feeling and the judgment. It appears less invidious to designate them by some such phrase, than to stigmatize them as merely figurative or poetical modes of statement. The sermon repeatedly declares, that there is a depth of significancy in some of these representations, which cannot be adequately expressed by the words figurative, imaginative and poetical, for these words have often an import too superficial; that the language of the emotions, even when dis-*sonant* from the accurate statements of truth, has yet a meaning which is perfectly correct, but is "more profound than can be pressed home upon the heart by any exact definitions." It affirms, that even when Dr. Jonathan Edwards, and Andrew Fuller, and Dr. Day call our "moral inability" a figurative term, they use the word figurative in a sense which needs to be explained, or it will be misunderstood.[1]

---

[1] Bib. Sac. pp. 537, 538, 549, 567. See also note B. to the second pamphlet edition of the sermon.

Therefore, one design of the discourse is to show the dignity and importance of those subjective conceptions which, although not conformed to the literal verity, are yet, like all vivid conceptions, attended with a momentary belief in their conformity to it, and which enliven our more accurate ideas of it, and which, being supposed by many to be logically correct, may be honored with a more respectful name than *mere* fancies or metaphorical representations.[1]

A third reason for the title is, that it is conformed to the analogy of language. As a substance, though distinguishable, is yet inseparable from its form, the name of the substance is often applied to the form. We speak of a syllogistic and of a popular argument, when we mean merely two different ways of expressing the very same argument. We speak of the language of eloquence and of logic, of the imagination and the passions, when we refer to the same identical language in different arrangements. We allude to the Jehovah of the Old Testament and the Jehovah of the New, without implying that there are two different Gods, but implying only that there are two different manifestations of God. The Sabellians, in order to avoid Tritheism, speak of God the Father, *and* God the Son, *and* God the Spirit, as one God in three modes of development; but, according to the Reviewer's way of interpreting the title of this sermon, the Sabellians may be fairly charged with being Tritheists, and believing in three different Supreme Beings. Diverse names are often applied to dissimilar forms or states of the same essence; as to one material substance when it is exhibited in dissimilar shapes; to the soul itself in different modes of its activity. The same ideas and even words, as they are presented in differing combinations, are denominated eloquence, poetry, or prose. Men distinguish between a doctrinal and a practical sermon, a didactic and a controversial theology, between the theology of one master and that of another,[2] between the theology of Paul and that of John, when they fully admit and intend only to declare by these phrases, that exactly the same truths are presented in diverse styles for different ends. Why then may we not distinguish between an intellectual and an emotive theology, when we expressly affirm that each differs from the other in form rather than in

---

[1] Bib. Sac. pp. 540, 549.

[2] Prof. Tholuck has said that the theology of Pres. Edwards *and* the theology of Hegel, on the subject of the will, *are* the same; of course he could not mean the same in form. Dr. Channing has said that the theology of Dr. Hopkins *and* the theology of Fenelon, on the subject of disinterested benevolence, *are* the same; of course he could not mean the same in style and *contour*.

essence? If we may speak of a belief or conviction of the head as distinct from a belief or conviction of, i. e. prompted by the heart, when we mean essentially one and the same mental belief or conviction, why may we not speak of a theology of the head as distinct from a theology of, i. e. prompted by the heart, when we mean the same theology in essence? This appellation is by no means unusual, even in familiar converse. And for the Biblical Repertory to distort the title of the sermon into an affirmation of "two theologies" (a phrase never used in the discourse) substantially opposite to each other, is as marked a violation of the rules of speech, as it would be to represent the eloquence of the outward manner, of the reasoning process, of the passionate address, of the direct exhortation, as four radically different "eloquences." But this remark anticipates one class of the misapprehensions developed in the Review.

1. The Repertory mis-states the very object of the discourse. It describes the sermon as advocating not two different forms but two essentially antagonistic "*kinds* of theology," two opposing sets of "*doctrine*," both equally correct. It recognizes no difference between an image or symbol, and a truth. As many of its reasonings are directed against the wrong subject, they spend themselves like arrows aimed at the wrong target. It is needless to refute them, after they have been shown to result from a misunderstanding of the theme.

The Review mis-states the object of the discourse, first, by omitting the formal *definition* of its title. In introducing the subject, after having stated that "when preachers aim to rouse the *sympathies of a populace*, they often give a brighter coloring or a bolder prominence to *some lineaments* of a doctrine than can be given to them in a *well compacted science*," the discourse proceeds, "There are two *forms* of theology of which the two passages in my text are selected as individual specimens, the one declaring that God never repents, the other that he does repent. *For want of a better name* these two *forms* may be termed the theology of the intellect and the theology of feeling. Sometimes, indeed, both the mind and the heart are suited by the *same modes of thought*, but often they require dissimilar *methods*."[1] And immediately afterwards, lest this should be misunderstood, the subject is thus reännounced: " What then are some of the differences between these two kinds of REPRESENTATION?" Now, against the canons of fair criticism, the entire paragraphs containing this formal definition are omitted by the Reviewer. The true intent of the discourse is thus in a degree hidden from his readers. This definition

---

[1] Bib. Sac. p. 534.

given in form at the outset, adds an emphasis to many subsequent phrases which our critic has either kept entirely out of view, or the *meaning* of which he has in some degree concealed by his one capital omission. No reader of the sermon needs to doubt, that the theology of feeling is "*the form of belief* which is suggested by and adapted to the wants of the well trained heart;"[1] contains the '*literal truth* presented in appropriate *images;*' allows '*discordant representations* of the one self-consistent *principle;*' sanctions "an interchange of *styles* all unfolding the same *idea;*" includes "*forms* of language which circumscribe a *substance of doctrine*, a *substance* which *fashioned* as it may be, the intellect grasps and holds fast; a *substance* which arrests the more attention and prolongs the deeper interest by the *figures* which bound it." With the preceding definition the whole tenor of the discourse shows its object to be, the delineation of "*our mode of shaping and coloring* the doctrines of theology," and these doctrines are "those *cardinal truths* which the Bible has lifted up and turned over in so many different lights as to make them [the truths] the more conspicuous by their very alternations of *figure and hue.*"[2] Accordingly, the discourse delineates the *one doctrine* of Future Punishment and the "*symbols*" by which it is illustrated; the *one doctrine* of the Resurrection, and the "*pictures*" by which it is enlivened; the *one doctrine* of the General Judgment and the *poetical conceptions* which vivify it;[3] the *one doctrine* of Regeneration "revealed in dissimilar *forms;*" the *one doctrine* of man's unwillingness to repent, expressed in '*phrases* which disagree with each other;'[4] all these "symbols," "pictures," "poetical conceptions" and illustrative images not being distinct doctrines but only distinct modes of representing the same doctrine, not belonging to theology as used for speculation but belonging to theology as employed for impression.

Throughout the sermon the distinction is between the "*intellectual statements* of doctrine," and the more "*impressive representations of it,*" i. e. of the same doctrine; and it is declared in apology for even the anthropopathical style, that "into more susceptible natures than ours the *literal verities* of God will penetrate far deeper than even when shaped in their most pungent *forms*, they [i. e. the literal verities] will penetrate into our obdurate hearts." But notwithstanding all these various and wearisome repetitions of the same idea, the Reviewer makes the impression that the sermon really advocates "two conflicting theologies," which are unlike in *substance* as well as in *style;* two

---

[1] Bib. Sac. p. 535.
[2] Ibid. pp. 555, 560.
[3] Ibid. pp. 540–542.
[4] Ibid. p. 547.

antagonistic "*doctrines*" pertaining to the sinful nature, the atonement, etc. He has made this impression, partly by omitting the author's essential definition of his theme. Is it not a rule of controversy, that a writer's formal definitions shall be formally quoted by his antagonist? Does not the sermon state that its title is selected "for want of a better," and does not this imply that the title may be perverted, unless it be defined? Why, then, does the critic fail to apprize his readers that the title has been defined, and why does he thus make it easy to misrepresent the entire scope of the sermon? We wish to be distinctly understood. The "accomplished Reviewer," of whom his admirers say that no one can mistake "*his hand*" in these criticisms, is by no means accused or suspected by us of *dexterity* in keeping important explanations out of sight; but is merely reminded of his inadvertence in not bringing them clearly and prominently into view; an inadvertence which is none the less hurtful because it is accidental. His fault, however, is not one of omission merely; for,

Secondly, he mis-states the very object of the sermon by explaining the theme in words and with illustrations which the discourse neither uses nor justifies, but clearly opposes.[1] He has not only *left out* the phrases which *interpret* the Proposition, but has also *put in* phrases which *misinterpret* it. The fact is a curious one, that whenever he seems to gainsay the main distinction between the two forms of religious truth, he departs from the phraseology of the discourse, and substitutes a phraseology of his own. His objections would seem inapposite, if he did not prepare the way for them by defining the object of the discourse in words which he himself has introduced, not with the design we presume, but with the result of caricaturing that object. Thus he repeatedly conveys the idea that the sermon directly authorizes such unqualified terms as "two theologies," "two kinds of theology," one of which is conformed to the "logical consciousness," the

---

[1] It is singular that not only the Reviewer's literal language does injustice to the literal language of the sermon, but his figures of speech do injustice to the figures of the sermon. Thus he says, p. 660: "The temple of God which temple is the church, is not to be built up by *rubbish*," but the sermon speaks of the "jealousies of those good men who build their faith upon Jesus Christ as the chief corner stone, and yet are induced by unequal measures of genius and culture to give different *shapes* to structures of the same *material*;" and again "the *subject matter* of these heterogeneous *configurations* may often be one and the same, having for its nucleus the same cross, with the formative influence of which all is safe." p. 559.

other to the "intuitional consciousness,"[1] the one "true to the feelings and false to the reason, the other "true to the reason and false to the feelings;" whereas none of these unmodified phrases have been employed, and some of them have been designedly rejected as inaccurate, by the author of the discourse.[2] But the Reviewer may say that the sermon must be considered as advocating two essentially different theologies, because it speaks of a theology of the intellect *and* a theology of the heart. In the same method of reasoning, it may be inferred, that because the author of the sermon believes in the divine Creator, and in the divine Preserver, and in the divine Governor, and in the divine Lawgiver, therefore he believes in four first persons of the Trinity; and because he believes in the divine Redeemer, and in the divine Mediator, and in the divine Judge, and in the divine Intercessor, therefore he believes in four second persons of the Trinity; and because he believes in the divine Renewer, and in the divine Sanctifier, and in the divine Comforter, and in the divine Inspirer of truth, therefore he believes in four third persons of the Trinity. The simple fact is, that our critic, without intending to abuse, has distorted language.

Having thus described the sermon as advocating two radically opposite kinds of theology, the Reviewer has (innocently, we presume) prepared his readers for a new dualistic invention, and he therefore represents the discourse (without specifying wherein) as proceeding on the supposition "that the feelings perceive in one way and the in-

---

[1] In unfolding (or rather obscuring) the design of the sermon, the Reviewer says (p. 646) of its author, " he proposes the distinction between the theology of feeling and that of the intellect. There are two modes of apprehending and presenting truth. The one by the logical consciousness (to use the convenient nomenclature of the day) that it may be understood; the other by the intuitional consciousness, that it may be felt. These modes do not necessarily agree; they may often conflict, so that what is true (?) in the one, may be false (?) in the other." These terms, "logical and intuitional consciousness," are the well known terms of Mr. Morell; and a reader of this Review, who had not read the sermon, would infer that the sermon advocated Morell's philosophy. For the honor of this Reviewer, we trust that he did not intend to excite a suspicion at once so false and so hurtful; but by using these suspicious terms, which he must have known were not in the sermon, he has prepared the way, as really as if he had designed it, for several of his subsequent charges.

[2] The sermon alludes once to " different *kinds* of theology which cannot be reconciled with each other," and alludes to them as *contradistinguished* from the different *forms* of theology which are the theme of the sermon. It characterizes them as two antagonistic systems of *intellectual* belief; and specifies, for an example, the theology which inserts and that which omits "the *doctrine* of justification by faith in the sacrifice of Jesus," p. 569.

tellect in another," that "the perceptions themselves vary, so that what appears true to the feelings, is apprehended as false to the intellect," that there are "different percipient agencies in the soul," two conflicting intelligences in man; the one seeing a thing to be true, and the other seeing it to be false, and yet both (each?) seeing correctly from its own position and for its own object."[1]

Now, we presume that in the history of theological criticism, there have been more singular caricatures than this; and accordingly this may be endured with patience. Let us then calmly consider the foundation of this oft repeated charge, that the sermon represents the soul as not "a unit," but as having "a dualism" in it. The only foundation for it is, that the discourse contains a prolonged account of the feelings as distinct from, and often as opposed to the reason. But what shall we say of those metaphysical systems in which one volume is devoted to the intellect, and a separate volume to the sensibilities? What shall we say of the common language of men, in which we hear every day that the judgment governs the fancy, or the imagination controls the judgment, the passions mislead the conscience, and contend with each other; the "old man" and the "new man" struggle together in the same man, we have "a divided soul," "a divided heart," are "double minded," etc. etc.[2] Does any one pretend to find in this ordinary speech an implication that the soul is dichotomized and subdichotomized into ten or twenty "conflicting agents?" One might as well make this pretension, as profess to discover an implied "dualism" in the sermon which is thus bisected. What shall we say of this very Review, speaking, as it does so often, of an expression "*false* to the taste and to the feelings."[3] Does the taste perceive *falsehood?* Do the feelings *perceive* it? What shall we say of its peculiar remark, that the phrase "God the mighty Maker died," has to be *defended* by the *intellect* at the bar of the *feelings?*[4] What shall we say of the "dualism" which is found between this Reviewer *and* Dr. Hodge; for Dr. Hodge says in his Commentary on Romans 7: 15–23, that "there is a conflict between the natural authoritative sense of right and wrong and [the] corrupt inclinations," that "*indwelling sin wars* against the *renewed principle*, and brings the soul into *captivity* to itself," and he deliberately affirms that the

---

[1] Bib. Rep. pp. 663, 669, 666.

[2] When a man says, I have a soul and body, does he mean that the "I" is separate from the soul and body? What does he mean by *my soul, myself?*

[3] Bib. Rep. p. 632.   [4] Ibid p. 666.

word "I, in the language of the apostle, includes, as it were, *two persons*, the new and the old man."[1]

Now, can a fair critic infer from this language, that the Reviewer *and* Dr. Hodge, (if we may continue so long in our dualism,) and all men are ready to reason on the principle that one person is two persons, and has two souls? Why, then, does the Reviewer draw such an inference from the sermon? *Every body knows* that such language is necessary in this imperfect state of being. Just in proportion to the clearness with which we aim to distinguish between the dissimilar processes of the soul, must we employ terms which, if pressed to the letter, would imply not a "dualism," but an indefinite multiplication. Two things which cannot be separated, may yet be distinguished throughout a prolonged description. We may reason for hours on the distinction between the substance and the attributes of matter, without implying that there is a separation between them. The Reviewer's charge of dualism rests on his own oversight of the difference between *distinct* and *separate*. We can no more easily converse without alluding to an apparent division in the soul, than without saying that the sun sets, or ice is cold. Usage justifies such representations. It requires them. We should be mere pedants without them. All philosophers admit them. But such expressions, as they are generally understood, are reconcilable with the truth that the soul is simple and indivisible. For this undivided agent has different states or modes of activity, and in relation to these different states or modes of activity, it assumes different names. The conscience is the soul viewed as capable of acting in one manner; the will is the same spirit viewed as capable of acting in a different manner; the intellect is the same soul viewed as capable of perceiving; and the heart is the same spirit viewed as capable of loving what is perceived. And here is suggested another reason why the modes of presenting truth which are adapted to the soul in one method of its action, may receive a different name from that applied to the modes

---

[1] One of the sweeping assertions made by the Reviewer is, that "the Bible *never* recognizes that broad distinction between the intellect and the feelings which is so often made by metaphysicians," Bib. Rep. p. 671. But does it not often represent a pure spirit as having a percipient eye and ear, and a feeling heart, bowels of mercies, etc.? Dr. Hodge says, (Com. on Rom. 14: 1-23) that "conscience or a sense of duty is not the *only* and perhaps not the most important *principle* to be appealed to in support of benevolent enterprises;" "but we find the sacred writers appealing *most frequently* to the pious and benevolent *feelings;*" and yet the Reviewer says that the Bible "*never* predicates depravity or holiness of the feelings as distinct from the intelligence."

of presenting the same truth which are adapted to the soul in another method of its action. And this illustrates the persistive error of the Review, which detects in these two modes of presenting truth, two radically antagonistic "kinds of theology," because the word theology is applied to each; and which also detects in the two different modes of the spiritual activity which the sermon describes, two intelligences, or "*such a dualism in the soul.*" Why did not the Review push its consistency still farther, and because the sermon describes two different modes of teaching astronomy and natural philosophy, charge it with advocating two radically opposite astronomies and philosophies? The sermon specifies two diverse methods of representing our personal identity; therefore, there are two opposite identities in each individual, as our critic might infer, if he should persevere in the course which he has begun. We will not borrow his own decorous language, and say of his reasoning on this subject, that it "indicates a most extraordinary confusion of mind;" we only say that it makes a confusion of mode with essence, the forms of a thing with the thing itself.

It is indeed possible, (for what is not possible?) that from some rhetorical phrases in the sermon, if they be interpreted as if they were found in a mathematical treatise, and if also they be severed from their relations, an inconsiderate or else a resolute critic might force out an inference in favor of "two percipient principles in the soul;" as with the same ease he might infer a similar dualism from the language of every man, not excepting the author of the seventh of Romans, and especially from the most carefully written treatises of this Reviewer. But the argument of the discourse is independent of that rhetorical and convenient phraseology; it might be conducted with the more cumbrous phrases of "the soul in the state of reasoning," "the soul developing itself in the mode of emotion or volition," etc. Indeed, the direct aim of a note to the sermon,[1] is to show that "the heart (*never*) perceives, for the intellect *only* is percipient, but holy feelings prompt the intellect to new discoveries, furnish *it* with new materials for examination and inference, and regulate it in its mode of combining and expressing what *it* has *discerned*. An affection of the heart towards a truth develops a new relation of that truth, and the *intellect* perceives the relation thus suggested by the feeling," etc. If there are any principles underlying and pervading the whole dis-

---

[1] Bib. Sac. pp. 564, 565. This note is not even referred to by the Reviewer, and still seems to have drawn from him the concession, that the author would "deny that he held to any such dualism in the soul." Bib. Rep. 660.

course, they are that "the theology of the intellect is the one *system* which recommends itself to a dispassionate and unprejudiced *mind* as *true*," (perceived to be true by the intellect); and that "the theology of the heart is the *collection of statements* which recommend themselves to the healthy moral feelings as *right*," (not *perceived* to be *true* by the heart);[1] that while the intellect is the only faculty which apprehends truth, and while it forms various conceptions of it, the feelings are more gratified with some of its conceptions than with others, and those conceptions of doctrine, which are peculiarly congenial with the excited heart, belong to its favorite cast of theology; that the Bible teaches one and only one definite system of doctrines; these doctrines contemplated by the mind arouse the sympathies of the heart, and these sympathies prompt to varied forms of expressing the same doctrine. As the Reviewer has well said, p. 657, "it is because such doctrines are didactically taught in the Bible, and presented as articles of faith, that they work themselves into the heart, and find expression in its most passionate language," language, however, which the critic must and does repeatedly affirm to be different from the style fitted for speculation.

What does the Reviewer mean, then, when he represents[2] the sermon as teaching, that "conflicting apprehensions are equally true," and as ascribing "to the sacred writers conflicting and irreconcilable representations?" Over and over it is asserted in the discourse, that while the intellectual theology is "accurate not in its spirit only but in its letter also," the emotive theology involves "the substance of truth, although when *literally* interpreted it may or may not be false."[3] The purpose of one entire head in the sermon[4] is to prove, that the one theology is precisely the same with the other in its real meaning, though not always in its form; that the expressions of right feeling, if they do contradict each other "*when unmodified*," can and *must* be so explained as to harmonize both with each other and with the decisions of the judgment; that "literally understood these expressions are dissonant from each other; their dissonance adds to their emphasis; their emphasis fastens our attention upon the principle in which they all agree; this principle is too vast to be vividly uttered in a single formula, and therefore branches out into various parts, and the lively exhibition of one part contravenes an equally impressive statement of a different one; the intellect educes light from the collision of these repugnant phrases and then modifies and reconciles them into" the

---
[1] Bib. Sac. p. 563.　　　　　　[2] Bib. Rep. p. 664.
[3] Bib. Sac. pp. 534, 535.　　　　[4] Bib. Sac. pp. 545–550.

harmonious and harmonizing truth. The sermon repeats, again and again, that it is *impossible* to believe contradictory statements " without qualifying some of them so as to prevent their subverting each other;" that the reason " being that circumspect power which looks before and after, does not allow that of these conflicting statements each can be true save in a qualified sense;" and that such statements *must* be qualified by disclosing the fundamental " principle in which they all agree for substance of doctrine," " the principle which will rectify one of the discrepant expressions by explaining it into an *essential* agreement with the other."[1]

But there is a third way in which the Reviewer makes a wrong impression with regard to the very object of the sermon. He implies and assumes, that the representations fitted for the excited sensibility are supposed in the sermon to be always different from the representations fitted for the calm intelligence. He feels satisfied that he has annihilated the distinction between the style of the intellect and that of the feelings, when he has cited passages which belong to both! He hurries on to the inference, that if the theology of the intellect " aims to be intelligible rather than impressive," then of course the theology of the heart must *always* not only aim to be, but absolutely *be* unintelligible! And he gives plausibility to this (his undesigned) caricature of the sermon, by omitting its oft-repeated explanations. One of these explanations is stated in the most prominent paragraph of the discourse, thus: " *Sometimes*, indeed, both the mind and the heart are suited by the *same* modes of appeal."[2] A second of these explanations is stated as an introduction to the analysis of the style suited to the heart, thus: " In some respects, *but not in all*, the theology of feeling *differs* from that of intellect."[3] A third of these explanations is stated in another prominent passage, thus: " Both of [these forms of theology] have *precisely the same* sphere with regard to *many* truths, but not with regard to all."[4] Yet not a single one of these explanations has the Reviewer so much as even noticed. He has quoted passages immediately *before* and immediately *after* them, but has not quoted *them*. In despite of numerous other repetitions of the same modifying thought, as where the sermon so often says that the representations prompted by feeling are often minutely and literally accurate, this critic has persisted in reasoning as if the sermon had affirmed precisely what it has denied, that the two generic forms of theology differ at all times, in all respects, and

---

[1] Bib. Sac. pp. 546, 548.
[2] Ibid. p. 534.
[3] Ibid. p. 535.
[4] Ibid. p. 551.

in regard to all doctrines. One object of the sermon is, to state the differences between the two generic forms, where any differences exist, and it is repeatedly announced that they do exist at some but not all times, in some but not all respects, in regard to some but not all truths. The Reviewer might as well say, that when we speak of prose as distinct from poetry, we must mean that no passages are suitable both for an essay and a poem; he might as well say that when we speak of "doctrinal" as distinct from "experimental" preaching, we must mean that they are unlike in all particulars, as he can say that when we speak of the intellectual theology as distinct from the emotive, we must mean that all parts of the one are unfitted for the other. Turretin's Theology is called scientific, because in its primary intent and as a whole it is fitted to aid our speculations; still, in some particulars, it is practical in its tendencies. Baxter's Saints' Rest is called practical, because in its primary intent and as a whole it is fitted to move our affections; still, in some particulars, it is scientific. So the theology of and for the intellect is represented in the sermon as likewise suited in a degree to the heart, and *vice versa;* but the primary and general scope of the one is easily distinguished from the primary and general scope of the other. The style of the pulpit would be as much improved as the style of our doctrinal treatises, if this distinction were more faithfully observed.

Without staying to comment on the many similar instances in which our critic has begun his quotations directly *after*, or has broken them off directly *before* the remarks in the sermon which qualify them, let us proceed to another class of his undesigned mis-statements.

2. He gives an erroneous view of the main theory of the discourse, with regard to the peculiar language of the emotions. We have just seen, that the expressions of the heart are not described in the sermon as uniformly differing from those of the judgment. Here is one error of the Reviewer. He has committed another in supposing, that the sermon "does not discriminate between mere figurative language, and the language of emotion."[1] Now, the sermon not only repeats the idea that the theology of feeling differs from that of intellect in other particulars than in its use of figures, for it differs in "proportions of doctrine," in "the especial prominence given to" certain features of it, etc. etc.; but the sermon also reiterates the idea, that the language appropriate to the sensibilities is not *uni-*

---

[1] Bib. Rep. p. 674.

formly figurative, but "may or may not be false when *literally* interpreted," and "aims to be impressive, *whether it be* or be not minutely accurate;"[1] that it often consists of those earnest, intense expressions which, not being hyperbolical, are not ordinarily termed figures of speech; that *merely* figurative expressions do not constitute the language of emotion, for this language is often characterized by the *abundance* and *boldness* of its metaphors; that it is not merely figurative or poetical in the sense of arbitrary or unsubstantial,[2] and still mere poetry often admits the most literal expressions. From the saying that the heart "sacrifices abstract remarks to visible and tangible images," must an expert critic infer that the heart is *never* satisfied with a plain expression? Must he rush on from "often" to "always," from "frequently" to "universally," from a qualified sentence to a rash one?

The Reviewer[3] makes the following criticism: "Our author represents the feelings as expressing themselves in figures, and demanding 'visible and tangible images.' We question the correctness of this statement. The highest language of emotion is generally simple." — And suppose we concede to the Reviewer, that the *highest* language of feeling is *generally* simple, must we therefore retract the remark that "sometimes both the mind and the heart are suited by the same modes of thought, but often they require dissimilar methods"? (Sermon, p. 534.) The Reviewer proceeds to say that "nothing satisfies the mind when under great excitement, but literal or perfectly intelligible expressions. *Then is not the time for rhetorical phrases.*" And after these remarks, which he ought to have qualified, he quotes some impassioned phrases of the Bible, as specimens of "the simplest form of utterance." And suppose that these phrases were every one apposite, must we therefore recant the remark that, "in some respects, *but not in all*, the theology of feeling differs from that of intellect"? (Sermon p. 535.) Has not our critic, however, made some unexpected mistakes in his citations of simple as opposed to figurative phrases? Has he not quoted some passages which Gerhard would not record as literally accurate statements? He has, for instance, actually cited as unrhetorical, the well known words, "Against thee, thee only have I sinned." Now, it so happens that John Milton has specified these very words as an example of a highly figurative style. "Yet some would persuade us," says the poet, "that this absurd opinion was king David's, because in the fifty

---

[1] Bib. Sac. pp. 535, 536. [2] Ibid p. 538. [3] Bib. Rep. p. 650.

first Psalm he cries out to God, 'Against thee only have I sinned;' as if David had imagined that to murder Uriah and adulterate his wife, had been no sin against his neighbor; whenas that law of Moses was to the king expressly, Deut. xvii. not to think so highly of himself above his brethren. David, therefore, by those words could mean no other, than either that the depth of his guiltiness was known to God only, or to so few as had not the will or power to question him, or that the sin against God was greater beyond compare than against Uriah. Whatever his meaning were, any wise man will see that the pathetical words of a Psalm can be no certain decision to a point that hath abundantly more certain rules to go by."[1] We have heard of a respectable clergyman in our land, who from the passage, "Against thee, thee *only* have I sinned," attempted to prove that "all sin is against God only," that David committed no offence against Uriah, who must soon have died, even if he had not been slain in battle; nor against Bathsheba, who was elevated in consequence of the sin to great renown; nor against the Jewish people, etc. etc. Now, if the expression of David be not rhetorical, not figurative, not distinguishable, and our Reviewer cites it as not distinguishable from the simple language of the judgment, this preacher's inferences were correct. Another divine of no mean name has inferred from the phrase in the same penitential prayer, "Create in me a clean heart," that the Psalmist had not been regenerated before the sin which he here laments; for, in praying that a clean heart may be *created,* he implies that it did not antecedently exist. Now, it is very obvious that the sermon under review was aimed against such a use of such phrases, a use which is far too frequent and too lamentable to be sanctioned by the precipitate assertions of even so eminent a Reviewer.

There is one more particular in which our critic mis-states the theory of the discourse with regard to the peculiar language of emotion. He implies that the discourse represents this language as not at all under the supervision of the intellect, as entirely independent of logical rule. Assuming that the style for the feelings is identified with the figurative, and is described as uniformly different from the intellectual style, he criticizes the sermon as not only giving two intelligences to one man and making two radically opposite theologies, but also as justifying figures of speech which are intended to express a doctrinal error. He says that the author of the sermon "evidently

---

[1] English Prose Works of Milton, Vol. II. pp. 164, 165.

confounds two things which are as distinct as day and night; viz. a metaphor and a falsehood; a figurative expression and a doctrinal untruth. Because the one is allowable, he pleads for the other also."[1] But is it not sufficiently easy for the Reviewer to perceive, that one design of the sermon is to justify the emotional, or, as the Reviewer will have it, the figurative theology, because when explained aright it never opposes but contains the substantial truth? Does not the sermon repeat over and over that the fit language of emotion never really *means* what is logically incorrect; that it is "substantially accurate when not literally so," and that whatever diversity there may be in the modes of faith which the mind or heart adopts, yet "the central principles of it" are always one and the same truth?[2] Does the Reviewer really suppose, that because "the theology of feeling when literally understood may or may not be false," therefore, according to the sermon, it is to be literally interpreted and believed although false? "It is a canon of criticism," says the sermon (p. 541), "that we should express all the *truth* which our hearers need, and express *it* in the *words* which they will most appropriately feel."

But the Reviewer goes farther still. He has read in the discourse that the Bible, when "it represents Christians as united to their Lord," "*does not mean* to have these endearing words metamorphosed into an intellectual theory of our oneness or identification with Christ," and when "it declares that God has repented," etc., "it *does not mean* that these expressions, which as inflected by times and circumstances impress a truth upon the soul, be stereotyped into the principle that Jehovah has ever parted with his infinite blessedness," and when the Psalmist cried, "Awake! why sleepest thou, O Lord," and Martin Luther exclaimed, "Hearest thou not, my God; art thou dead?" they used "words that excite no congenial glow in technical students, viewing all truth in its dry light, and disdaining all figures which would offend the decorum of a philosophical or didactic style, but words which wake the deepest sympathies of quick-moving, wide-hearted, many-sided men, who look *through* a *superficial* impropriety and discern *under* it a *truth* which the nice language of prose is too frail to convey into the heart, and breaks down in the attempt."[3] But although the Reviewer has seen this idea repeated more times than there are pages in the sermon, he yet without a blush represents this very sermon as teaching that the feelings do not need to be nourished by the truth, and that in devotional exercises we may express

---

[1] Bib. Rep. p. 665.   [2] Bib. Sac. pp. 535, 537, 540, 545, 555, 561, etc.
[3] Bib. Sac. pp. 538, 539.

doctrines which we do not believe. He says, "In *opposition* to this view, *we* maintain that the feelings demand truth, i. e. truth which satisfies the intellect in the approbation and expression of their object;" the soul "cannot believe what it knows to be a lie;" "the hymn book or liturgy of no church contains doctrines contrary to the creed of that church."[1] What the sermon calls the "poetic license" of hymn books, the "style of remark which for sober prose would be unbecoming, or even, when associated in certain ways, irreverent;" what it calls "the words, not the truths, but the *words* which have been embosomed in the love of the church," all this the Reviewer confounds with a meant doctrinal falsehood. When the sermon says that some poetic stanzas "are not accurate expressions of dogmatic *truth,*" the critic flies to the conclusion that they are intended to teach dogmatic error! He thus complains of the sermon as recommending a style of worship "profane to the feelings and a mockery of God." He makes the impression that he is impugning the discourse when he asserts, that "to use in worship expressions which the intellect pronounces to be doctrinally untrue is repudiated by the whole Christian church as profane."[2]— We are willing to forgive the Reviewer seven times and seventy times seven; but we beg leave to ask, how many times he really needs to be told, that the sermon never justifies expressions which are untrue in the *doctrines* designed to be taught by them, and that it only justifies some expressions which overpass "*at times* the proprieties of the didactic style," and which are untrue in their *literal meaning?* It insists as plainly as it can insist, that men must understand the language of the intellect "according to what it *says,*" for it is definite and precise; and must understand the language of the heart "according to what it *means,*" for the words "God came from Teman," do not mean that he moves from place to place, etc. It insists that the hyperbolical language, so called, is to be interpreted "as it is meant," and when so interpreted it "never transcends" but rather "falls short of" the real verity; that all the emotional language, indeed, is the "most natural utterance" of "a heart moved to its depths by the *truth.*"

One cause of the Reviewer's mistakes on this subject is, that he does not seem to recognize the power or even the existence of those conceptions which the mind forms for the sake of illustrating and vivifying its ideas of the substantial truth, as such conceptions are distinct from the mind's ideas of the substantial truth itself; and therefore he

---

[1] Bib. Rep. p. 665.   [2] Ibid. p. 667.

does not properly estimate the force or design of figurative language. We were not prepared to expect from so learned a man such a sentence as the following, (Bib. Rep. p. 652): "Figurative language when interpreted literally will of course express what is false to the intellect, *but it will in that case be no less false to the taste and to the feelings.*" Now, of what use is the figure? What is the power of its primary, as distinct from its secondary meaning? The obvious principle is, that figurative language causes the mind to form certain conceptions which, although not according to the exact truth, yet often illustrate it. These conceptions are, often at least, combined with a momentary belief in the presence of the objects conceived, and thereby they often so interest the mind as to give it a more vivid idea of the truth to be illustrated; further, the comparison between the conception proximately, literally suggested, and the idea remotely, figuratively suggested, often interests the mind in its examination of the exact truth; and thus the taste is pleased, the intellect aided, and the feeling awakened by the conception, which the mind would not form, were it not for the figurative language, and which would have no influence were it not for the understood literal meaning of that language.

But all figures are not equally adapted to illustrate, to please, and to excite. Some are used merely for convenience, as many figures of syntax and etymology. Others are used chiefly for illustration, as what rhetoricians call the "explaining comparisons." Others are used mainly for ornament, as what rhetoricians call the "embellishing comparisons." Others still are used for the excitement of feeling, as what rhetoricians call, the "figures of passion," which are distinct from "figures of the imagination." The figures of passion belong to the peculiar language of feeling; the other figures are appropriate, under proper restraint, to the language of the intellect, although many of them are more frequently used in that of the heart. If the literal terminology were of itself copious and versatile enough, it would be, as it is not now, uniformly employed in our reasoning processes. As the argumentative style *abounds* with plain, so the emotive style *abounds* with figurative diction. Because the sermon under review asserts that the intellectual theology prefers "the literal to the figurative" we must not leap to the conclusion that the sermon would exclude the figurative altogether from this theology. Because a man prefers gold to silver, we must not infer that he would trample silver in the dust. Still there are some figures, those of passion, which the well known rule is to exclude from the didactic theology.

They are too bold for calm discussion; they need to be modified too laboriously; they suggest conceptions so vivid, as to be mistaken for the premises of an argument, rather than to be regarded, as they should be, the illustrations of the truth.

Of these passionate figures, so often found in the theology of feeling, some are used by impulse more than by design. "When the mind," says Dr. Campbell,[1] "is in confusion and perplexity, arising from the sudden conflict of violent passions, the language will of necessity partake of this perturbation. Incoherent hints, precipitate sallies, vehement exclamations, interrupted perhaps by frequent checks from religion or philosophy, in short, everything imperfect, abrupt, and desultory, are the natural expressions of a soul overwhelmed in such a tumult." The words which are uttered in such a state, though obscure in themselves, are perspicuous as expressive of the feelings, they work upon our sympathies and prompt us to form more vivid ideas of the object which thus excites the soul than we could form, if the words uttered had been in themselves more precise. Let these words, however, be transferred from their fit connections into a didactic treatise, and they *may* be absolutely unintelligible. There are other figures of passion which are designed to give us vivid ideas of an object in one of its particular aspects, when the mind has no power to form a definite, precise idea of that object as a whole. These figures, also, are often obscure in themselves, and their very obscurity rouses the imagination and heart, and under the stimulus of this excited sensibility the mind forms a more impressive notion of the entire object than it would form were it not thus stimulated. Thus, says Dr. Blair,[2] obscurity "is not unfavorable to the sublime. Though it render an object indistinct, the impression, however, may be great; for, as an ingenious author has well observed, it is one thing to make an idea clear, [precise], and another to make it affecting to the imagination; and the imagination may be strongly affected, and in fact often is so, by objects of which we have no clear [precise] conception. Thus we see that almost all the descriptions given us of the appearances of supernatural beings, carry some sublimity, though the conceptions which they afford us be confused and indistinct. Their sublimity arises from the ideas which they always convey, of superior power and might joined with an awful obscurity." And Mr. Burke[3] says, "I think there are reasons

---

[1] Philosophy of Rhetoric. Book II. Ch. VIII.
[2] Rhetoric. Lecture III.   [3] On the Sublime and Beautiful. Sect. IV.

in nature, why the obscure idea, when properly conveyed, should be more affecting than the clear." "The mind is hurried out of itself by a crowd of great and confused images, which affect because they are crowded and confused." "In nature, dark, confused, uncertain images have a greater power on the fancy to form the grander passions, than those have which are more clear and determinate." On some subjects, he adds, "a clear idea is therefore another name for a little idea." So in his celebrated parallel between Dante and Milton, Mr. Macaulay says,[1] that the former "gives us the shape, the odor, the sound, the smell, the taste, he counts the numbers, he measures the size" of all which he describes. "His similes are the illustrations of a traveller" "introduced in a plain, business-like manner," "in order to make the meaning of the writer as clear to the reader as it is to himself." "Now, let us compare," proceeds Mr. Macaulay, "with the exact details of Dante, the dim intimations of Milton.— The English poet has never thought of taking the measure of Satan. He gives us merely a vague idea of vast bulk. In one passage the fiend lies stretched out huge in length, floating many a rood, equal in size to the earthborn enemies of Jove, or to the sea-monster which the mariner mistakes for an island. When he addresses himself to battle against the guardian angels, he stands like Teneriffe or Atlas; his stature reaches the sky. Contrast with these descriptions, the lines in which Dante has described the gigantic spectre of Nimrod. 'His face seemed to me as long and as broad as the ball of St. Peter's at Rome; and his other limbs were in proportion; so that the bank which concealed him from the waist downwards, nevertheless showed so much of him, that three tall Germans would in vain have attempted to reach his hair.'"

In accordance with these very simple principles, not dug out of the depths of German metaphysics, but taken from the surface of Blair's Rhetoric, the sermon under review describes the theology of feeling as introducing "obscure images," "vague and indefinite representations," all of which, however, so affect the heart as eventually to aid the mind in forming more vivid ideas of the truth than it would have otherwise formed. These very obscurities are intelligible as exhibitions of excited feeling, but often would not be intelligible if used as didactic statements. The emotive theology is also described as introducing other figures 'the most expressive which the debilitated heart will appreciate, but which yet fail of making a full disclosure,

---

[1] Miscellanies, Vol. I. p. 32.

and are only the foreshadowings of the truths which lie behind them."[1] But the Reviewer, opposing the theory of the sermon with regard to figurative language, says,[2] that this language "is just as definite in its meaning, and just as intelligible as the most literal." He ought to have qualified his remark, and said, first, that *some* figurative language is thus perspicuous; and secondly, that some is in itself designedly indefinite, and its indefiniteness is more expressive than its precision would be; thirdly, that some is easily intelligible if properly used in its fit connections, and yet may not be intelligible out of those connections; and fourthly, that there are some kinds of writing, the prophetical for instance, of which the minute signification was not intended to be obvious to all readers. But, according to the Reviewer's unmodified statement, the prophetical style would be as perspicuous to us as the style of the Gospel narratives; the highly wrought figures of Hebrew poets would present no more difficulty to commentators than do the simplest phrases in John's epistles, and figurative language would be as common as plain language now is in works of science. The Reviewer sweeps on too fast and too far. He fails to discriminate between a vivid idea of one feature of an object, and a definite idea of the whole object; and also between clearness and preciseness. Figures of speech may be clear, when they express not only the notion intended, but also something more; in expressing more they are not precise. He also fails to discriminate between the intelligibleness of figures when they are used in their proper place, and their intelligibleness when they are used out of their proper place;[3] just as if the figure, "a man ought to hate his father and mother, brother and sister," which is perfectly clear in one connection, would be equally clear if transferred without a qualifying phrase to a dogmatic treatise; just as if "The Way of Life," might fitly contain an unmodified exhortation to "The duty of hatred towards parents and benefactors." The Reviewer himself, where he has no theory to controvert, has hit the truth far more nearly than in these controversial criticisms; *id.* in commenting on the seventh of Romans, he represents Paul as exclaiming: "It is not I therefore, my real and lasting self, but this intrusive tyrant [sin] dwelling within me that disobeys the law;" and then the commentator adds: "This *strong* and *expressive* language, though susceptible of a literal interpretation which would make it teach not only error but nonsense, is still perfectly perspicuous and correct because accurately *descriptive of the common*

---

[1] Bib Sac. pp. 550, 566, etc.   [2] Bib. Rep. p. 651.   [3] Bib. Sac. pp. 551, 555, 556.

feelings of men." In different words,— this vehement language *in other connections* might be nonsensical, but in its present connection it is clear in its import, because it is perfectly expressive of agitated feeling. Again, the very gentleman, of whom it has been said without any sinister intent, that no one can mistake "his hand" in this Review, explains the celebrated passage, Rom. 9: 3, "I could wish that myself were accursed," etc., with the remark, "The difficulty arises from pressing the words too far, making them express *definite ideas*, instead of *strong and indistinct emotions.*" Similar criticisms are frequent in this commentator, who is in an ungraceful *dualism* with the Reviewer. If we should retort upon him his own courteous accusations we should say, "It is to be remembered that it is not the language of excited, fanatical, fallible men that our [critic] undertakes thus to eviscerate," by representing it as having been uttered *without definite ideas,* etc. But are these the fitting accusations for a Christian and a *divine?*

In what way can we account for it, now, that when the learned commentator comes to criticise a New England sermon, he should have forgotten the rhetorical principles with which he was once familiar? He does not discriminate between the truth that often "obscurity favors the sublime," and the error that obscurity is proper for science. Because the sermon says that "*often*" when a passionate phrase is wrested from its fitting adjustments and transferred to a dogmatic treatise, it appears unintelligible or absurd, the Reviewer represents the sermon as teaching that all passionate phrases are absurd or unintelligible. We shall soon see that, according to him, the theology of feeling is characterized in the discourse, as a collection of statements which are false and incapable of being understood. He reasons on the principle that because a mathematician could not, without an absurdity, attempt to prove that something is less than nothing, therefore when men confess in prayer that they are less than nothing, they have no meaning. He might as fairly say, that because a natural philosopher would be unintelligible in advancing the proposition that there can be a point in space which is underneath the very lowest point, therefore there is no idea conveyed in the poetic hyperbole:

> "Which way I fly is hell, myself am hell;
> And in the lowest depth, a lower deep
> Still threatening to devour me, opens wide
> To which the hell I suffer seems a heaven."

In regard to the nature of such figurative language as is peculiarly appropriate to the theology of the heart, there is indeed an obvious difference between the sermon and the Review, but there is a difference equally obvious between this Review and some other productions of its reputed author. The following is a notable illustration. The sermon says,[1] in a style which might appear to be sufficiently guarded: "*Left to its own guidance,*" (the intellect) "would never *suggest* the *unqualified* remark[2] that Christ has fully paid the debt of sinners, for it declares that this debt may justly be claimed from them; nor that he has suffered the *whole* punishment which they deserve, for it teaches that this punishment may still be righteously inflicted on themselves; not that he has *entirely* satisfied the law, for it insists that the demands of the law are yet in force. If it should allow those as logical premises, it would also allow the salvation of all men as a logical inference, but it rejects this inference and accordingly, being self-consistent, must reject those when viewed as literal premises. It is adapted to the soul in her inquisitive moods, but fails to satisfy her craving for excitement. In order to express the definite idea that we are exposed to evil in consequence of Adam's sin, it does not employ the passionate phrase, 'we are guilty of his sin.' It searches for the proprieties of representation, for seemliness and decorum. *It gives origin* to no statements which require apology or essential modification; no metaphor, for example, so bold and so liable to disfigure our idea of the divine equity, as that Heaven imputes the crime of one man to millions of his descendants, and then imputes their myriad sins to him who was harmless and undefiled." Now, the Reviewer confronts this passage with remarkable decision,[3] and avers, not that some, but that "*all* the illustrations" [and among them is the phrase, "God the mighty Maker died"] "which our author gives of modes of expression which the theology of the intellect would not *adopt*" [give origin to, suggest] "are the products of that theology. They are the language of speculation, of theory, of the intellect, as distinguished from the feelings." What, then, are

---

[1] Bib. Sac. p. 535.

[2] The sermon admits, p. 568, that the intellect may make an occasional use of such remarks, *when* they are qualified, and *after* they have been suggested by the feelings, but says that, "*left to its own guidance* it would never suggest" them. But the Reviewer, while he fairly quotes the *rest* of the sentence, drops from it the important qualifying words, "left to its own guidance," and he thus fails to give its full meaning. Afterwards, also, he confounds the words "suggest," "give origin to," which the sermon uses, with the word *adopt*, which he seems to use as their synonym.

[3] Bib. Rep. p. 648.

those illustrations? One is the "*unqualified* remark that Christ has *fully* paid the debt of sinners." Does not the Reviewer himself qualify this phrase, in his common explanations of it? Why does he so often teach that Christ has not paid the debt of sinners *in any such sense* (which would be the ordinary sense of the phrase) as to make it unjust for God to demand the sinner's own payment of it? Why does he teach, that although the debt of sinners is paid, *in a very peculiar sense*, yet it is not so paid but that they may be justly "cast into prison until they themselves have paid the uttermost farthing?" Another illustration is, the "*unqualified remark* that Christ suffered the *whole* punishment which sinners deserve." And does not the Reviewer elsewhere thrust in various modifications of this phrase, saying that Christ did not suffer *any* punishment in such a sense as renders it unjust for the entire punishment of the law to be still inflicted on transgressors; that he did not suffer the whole, the precise eternal punishment which sinners deserve,[1] that in fact he did not suffer any punishment at all in its *common* acceptation of ' pain inflicted on a transgressor of law on account of his transgression, and for the purpose of testifying the lawgiver's hatred of him as a transgressor?' Why, then, does the Reviewer here represent this "unqualified remark" as identical with the ambiguous phrase, "Christ bore our punishment," and as a "summation of the manifold and diversified representations of Scripture?" Another of these illustrations is, the equally unmodified statement that "Christ has entirely satisfied the law." How many times has the Reviewer elsewhere asserted that Christ has not satisfied the law *as a rule of duty*, but that it still continues and will always continue its demand for perfect obedience? Of course he does not believe, without a qualification, that "Christ has *entirely* satisfied the law." Why, then, does he here treat this "unqualified remark" as identical with the loose phrase "Christ has satisfied the law," and as a "*precise* representation" of the truth. The statements that "Adam's sin is imputed to us, and our sin is imputed to Christ," are likewise characterized by the Reviewer as not less "purely addressed to the intellect," not less

---

[1] Dr. Joseph Huntington, believing that Christ literally endured the precise punishment threatened in the law, reasons thus: Sinners "in their surety, vicar or substitute, i. e. in Christ, the head of every man, go away into everlasting punishment, in a truly gospel sense. In him, they suffer infinite punishment; i. e. he suffers (it) for them, in their room and stead;" and therefore as they have once suffered the whole curse of the law, they cannot be justly exposed to it the second time; hence Universalism.

"purely abstract and didactic formulæ," than any others. It is a matter of literary history, that to impute sin to a man is, in the common primary use of the terms, the same as to accuse him of having committed it; and that when these terms are employed in the sense of merely treating a man in certain respects as if he had committed the sin, they are used with a secondary meaning, stronger and more nervous than the unimpassioned intellect would have prompted for itself. So the phrase, "guilty of Adam's sin," is a figure of speech; i. e. "a mode of speaking or writing in which words are deflected from their ordinary signification, or a mode more beautiful and *emphatical* than the ordinary way of expressing the sense." As all of these phrases have originally a like figurative character, (in the best meaning of the term, figurative,) so they retain this character after they have been transferred to the technical dialect. They retain it just so long as their scientific is different from their primitive and ordinary signification. They were originally prompted by a desire to enstamp deeply upon the heart, certain doctrines in certain individual relations. They were not *originally* intellectual statements, but have been *transferred* from their pristine to the dogmatic sphere. They still continue, however, to be impressive rather than transparent, to be vehement rather than explicit. And therefore it is notorious, that long after they have been explained and re-explained so as to abate their primitive force, and give them a technical diverse from their obvious meaning, the common usage will yet reässert its claims, and these very terms are to be again qualified, and once more softened down, limited, restricted, hedged in with adjuncts, defined as often as employed, and after all, they are misunderstood by multitudes who contend for them, who *will have* it that doctrinal terms are used in their plain sense, and who thus make it needful for these giant-like and long-suffering divines, whose business is the taking care of these evasive words, "to pace forever to and fro on the same wearisome path, after the same recoiling stone." Such is the character of these emphatic utterances, even when transmuted into what are called "intellectual propositions." Their history has made them useful for reference. Their own nature makes them often eloquent in use. They are natural modes of developing the heart's deepest affections in certain pensive moods; but '*left to its own guidance*, the intellect would never have *suggested* them as *unqualified*.' Being figurative in the scientific sense of the term, they are exciting; some of them being often obscure when used in prosaic connections, irritate their already excited devotees, and induce them to upbraid where they ought to reason. John Foster says of such devotees to the technical style, that "if a man has discarded or has never learned the accustomed theological diction, and speaks in the general language of good sense, as he would on any other subject, they do not like his sentiments, even though according with their own; his language and his thoughts are all Pagan; he offers sacrifice with strange fire." And a celebrated political writer has said of such men, "They will themselves die or make others die for a simile."

8. This topic, however, introduces another class of the Reviewer's unintended mis-statements. He gives a wrong idea of the doctrinal illustrations in the discourse.

It is a melancholy truth, distinctly asserted by the writer of the sermon, that man has a "fallen," "evil," "loathsome," "corrupt," "odious" "nature, which precedes and certainly occasions (his) first actual sin." This is the doctrine in its prosaic, but it may be stated in an intensive form; and one aim of the sermon is to justify the occasional use of such words, as that this "diseased" and "disordered" state of the sensibilities is "sinful," "blamable," "guilty;" provided that such words be used, not for implying that there can be a literal sin which is uncondemned by conscience, i. e. the power of deciding on the moral character of acts; not for implying that our "inborn, involuntary corruption" can be the sole ground why a subject of it, *if he can be supposed to be* innocent of all actual disobedience, should be condemned to a punishment which supposes that the punished one is personally and literally ill-deserving on account of his "transgression of the law;" not as implying that a soul merits a legal penalty merely for the passive condition in which it was created; but the words "sinful, blamable, guilty nature" are to be sometimes justified, provided that they are used for historical reference, or for vehemently expressing "our dread or hatred of this" evil nature, which is so intimately connected with our actual sins, and so surely as well as justly exposes us to punishment on account of them.[1] But the Reviewer, without any fair attempt to explain the principles on which the use of these words is allowed or disallowed, satisfies himself with reiterating the charge, that the doctrine of our sinful nature is affirmed in the discourse to be true to the feelings and false to the intellect.[2] We think that the Reviewer would have done more justice to himself, if he had acknowledged that when *he* uses the term "sinful nature" as denoting a nature antecedent to all sinful exercise of it, he

---

[1] Bib. Sac. pp. 567, 568.　　　　　[2] Bib. Rep. pp. 664, 673.

does not mean by "sinful" what men generally mean by the word, a quality which is condemned by our "power of discerning the moral character of acts;" he does not mean by sinful a quality for which the being who has never harbored it is personally ill-deserving; but he means a peculiar kind of sin, and uses the term with a very peculiar signification; and he differs from the sermon, therefore, not so much with regard to the doctrine, as with regard to the propriety of often designating that doctrine by a common word used in a sense which men in common life do not give it, a sense which they frequently and fatally misunderstand. What does a man gain by calmly denominating that passive condition a sin, for which alone the subject of it cannot be personally reproved by conscience, nor be condemned as himself deserving of a real and proper punishment.

It is another sad truth, plainly declared by the author of the sermon, "that man with his unrenewed nature will sin and only sin in his moral acts;" that "man, with no extraordinary aid from divine grace, is obstinate, undeviating, unrelenting, persevering, dogged, *fully set* in those wayward preferences which are an abuse of his freedom;" and "so important is it that this infallible certainty be felt to be true, that our hearts often incline us to designate it by the most forcible epithets," to express an accurate *dogma* in a more impressive *form*. It was, therefore, one design of the sermon to justify the occasional use of such phrases as, "man is unable to repent," "sin is necessary," provided that such terms be used to express strongly and impressively the certain, fixed unwillingness of unrenewed man to do right.[1] But the Reviewer, although he must know full well that this doctrine of the sermon has the sanction of President Edwards, yet with apparent coolness represents the sermon as denying the doctrine of inability and affirming this doctrine to be "false to the intellect."[2] He goes farther still[3] and declares that the theory of the discourse represents feeling and knowledge "in *perpetual* (?) conflict," "the one teaching the doctrine of inability, the other that of plenary power," and he implies that the discourse represents the same man as having "the *consciousness* of inability to change his own heart, and yet the *conviction* that he has the requisite power." The critic means well, but it would be interesting to learn how he became unable to see that man is not once represented in the sermon as having a consciousness opposed to his conviction, but is uniformly represented as having both a *consciousness* and a *conviction* of his *unwil-*

---

[1] Bib. Sac. pp. 548, 566, 567.   [2] Bib. Rep. pp. 664, etc.
[3] Bib. Rep. pp. 673. 661.

lingness to repent, and as often expressing this unwillingness by the forcible word inability. Will the Reviewer never distinguish between "two doctrines," and the same doctrine expressed in two forms? He has not done honor to himself as a fair-minded critic, in so strangely perverting or *ignoring* the following passage of the sermon: "The emotive theology, therefore, when it affirms this [i. e. the natural] power is correct both in matter and style; but when it denies this power, it uses the language of emphasis, of impression, of intensity; it means the *certainty* of wrong preference by declaring the *inability* of right; and in its vivid use of *cannot* for *will not* is accurate in its *substance* though not in its form;" and this "discordance being one of letter rather than of spirit is removed by an explanation which makes the eloquent *style* of the feelings at one with the more definite *style* of the reason."[1]

Besides often affirming that there is an infallible certainty of man's continued impenitence until he be regenerated by the Divine Spirit, the sermon introduces the statements, that man's "*unvaried* wrong choices imply a full, unremitted *natural* power of doing right," and that "the character of our race needs an essential transformation by an interposed influence from God."[2] The Reviewer now springs to the charge that the first of these statements is "a vapid formula of Pelagianism," and the second is "a very genteel way of expressing the matter which need offend no one, Jew or Gentile, Augustin or Pelagius."[3] Does the Reviewer mean to say, that Pelagius would have sanctioned either of the above cited statements when fairly presented in its connections? Did Pelagius recognize our "disordered nature," our "unvaried, undeviating wrong choices," our "natural" as *opposed* to our "moral power?" Did he suppose that the character of the *race*, as well as of particular individuals, needs not only an improvement but also an *essential transformation*, and that this radical change must be effected not only by moral suasion, but by the *interposed* influence of the Holy Spirit? Will not the Reviewer acknowledge then, that the two statements so offensive to him are wrested from their adjuncts and merely caricatured, when they are held up as involving the substantial error of Pelagianism?

The author of the sermon has never doubted but firmly believes, that in consequence of the first man's sin all men have at birth a corrupt nature, which exposes them to suffering, but not punishment, even

---

[1] Bib. Sac. p. 548. See also 547, 565–567.
[2] Bib. Sac. pp. 547, 548.
[3] Bib. Rep. pp. 655, 656.

without their actual transgression; which, unless divine mercy interpose, secures the certainty of their actual transgression, as soon as they can put forth a moral preference, and of their eternal punishment as the merited result of this transgression; a corrupt nature, which must be changed by the supernatural influence of the Holy Ghost before they will ever obey or morally please him; and therefore the author believes that men are by nature, i. e. in consequence, on account of it, sinners, and worthy of punishment "for all have sinned." But the Reviewer is bold enough to say, that the two passages "a sentence of condemnation passed on all men for the sin of one man," and "men are by nature the children of wrath," are represented by the author of the sermon as "impressive but not intelligible," "true to the feelings but false to the reason."[1] We do not believe that the Reviewer intended to make a false as well as injurious impression by these words; he probably leaped to the inference, as untrue in itself as it is illogically drawn, that if some figures of speech do *sometimes appear* false and unintelligible when they are transferred from their proper to an improper place, then *the two above cited passages* not only *appear* but *are* both false and unintelligible *in this place* and as they are ordinarily used. This inference, however, is rejected as a mere paralogism by the writer of the discourse.

The author of the sermon has never doubted but fully believes, that all converted men will be, on the ground of Christ's death, not only saved from punishment but raised to happiness, will be not only pardoned but justified, not only treated in important respects as if they had never sinned, but treated in important respects as if they had been positively and perfectly holy. Still, the Reviewer, both without and against evidence, has preferred the charge that the author represents the passage "men are not merely pardoned but justified," as "not intelligible," and as "false to the reason."[1] Now here is a definite and an unfair accusation, to which we reply by asking a definite and a fair question. When and where has the author denied that the doctrine of justification as distinct from that of pardon, is intelligible or true? If the Reviewer has not borne "false witness against" the author, let him prove his witness to be correct. If he has been thoughtlessly betrayed into an accusation not more injurious than it is groundless, let him have the kindness to remember the words of Mr. Pitt: "Whoever brings here a charge without proof, defames." It is of no use for him to say that because the sermon represents *some*

---

[1] Bib. Rep. p. 674.　　　　　[2] Ibid p. 674.

figures of speech as absurd when in their wrong connections, therefore the sermon represents the phrase "men are not merely pardoned but justified" as absurd in the particular connections in which it is generally used. The primary meaning of the word justify, is altogether less conspicuous and embarrassing than the primary meaning of the word impute, and *if* the sermon *had* affirmed the word impute to be ordinarily "*unintelligible*," the Reviewer had no right to draw the false inference that the word justify would be characterized in the same manner. Because some pictures appear to be mere daubs, unless viewed at *one* specified angle, the Reviewer must not dash on to the conclusion that the Sistine Madonna is a mere daub, when it is viewed at all the angles which are commonly taken.

It is a solemn truth, distinctly avowed in the discourse,[1] that "There is a life, a soul, a vitalizing spirit of truth, which must never be relinquished for the sake of peace even with an angel. There is (I know that you will allow me to express my opinion)[2] a line of separation which cannot be crossed between those systems which insert, and those which omit the doctrine of justification by faith in the sacrifice of Jesus. This is the doctrine which blends in itself the theology of intellect and that of feeling, and which can no more be struck out from the moral, than the sun from the planetary system. Here the mind and the heart, like justice and mercy, meet and embrace each other; and here is found the specific and ineffaceable difference between the Gospel and every other system. But among those who admit the atoning death of Christ as the organific principle of their faith, there are differences, some of them more important, but many far less important than they seem to be." And, again, the author of the discourse avers,[3] in the most prosaic language, that "the atonement has such a relation to the whole moral government of God, as to make it *consistent* with the honor of his legislative and retributive justice to save all men, and to make it essential to the highest honor of his benevolence or general justice to renew and save some. Therefore it satisfies the law and justice of God *so far and in such a sense*, as to render it proper for him not only to give many temporal favors, but also to offer salvation to all men, bestow it upon all who will accept it, and cause those to accept it, for whom the interests of the universe allow him to interpose his regenerating grace." But

---

[1] Bib. Sac. p. 559.

[2] As the discourse was delivered before a Convention of Trinitarian and Unitarian clergymen, such a parenthetic clause seemed to the author to be decorous.

[3] Bib. Sac. pp. 562, 563.

our critic represents the sermon as denying that Christ satisfied the law and justice of God, as "explaining away the scriptural representations of the satisfaction of divine justice by the sacrifice of Christ," and as intimating that "because I may express the truth that Christ was a sacrifice by calling him the Lamb of God who bears the sin of the world, I may in solemn acts of worship so address him without believing in his sacrificial death at all."[1] It is a noticeable fact, that while the sermon *deduces* the intellectual truth of a vicarious atonement from the demands of holy feeling, and definitely affirms, p. 544, that "the doctrines which concentre in and around a vicarious atonement are so fitted to the appetences of a sanctified heart as to gain the favor of a *logician*, precisely as the coincidence of some geological or astronomical theories with the phenomena of the earth or sky, is a part of the syllogism which has those theories for its conclusion;" yet the Reviewer inverts this whole process, and, p. 673, unblushingly represents the sermon as teaching that feeling and knowledge are in "perpetual (?) conflict," "the one craving a real vicarious punishment of sin, the other teaching that a symbolical atonement is all that is needed." Anxious to find some excuse for this charge of the Reviewer, we have searched for one in vain. He will not attempt, we imagine, to extenuate his fault by pleading that the author speaks of a "vicarious *atonement*," while the Reviewer speaks of a "vicarious *punishment*;" for the Reviewer himself will acknowledge that "in the most strict and rigid" meaning of the term, "punishment has reference to personal guilt."[2]

The author of the sermon believes, and has never implied the contrary, that Christ's death being vicarious, his sufferings being substituted for our punishment, we are literally unable, after having once sinned, to be saved without him; that we are not only redeemed from eternal punishment by his propitiatory sacrifice, but, even after we have been regenerated by his Spirit, we are entirely dependent on his grace in sending the same Spirit to secure our continuance in holiness; and, moreover, that we are every instant preserved in being by his Almighty power, so that without him we literally *cannot* even exist; and still it is boldly declared in the Review, that the sermon represents the passages, "without Christ we can do nothing" and "he hath redeemed us from the curse of the law by being made a curse for us," as "not intelligible" and as "false to the reason!"[3] But the accom-

---

[1] Bib. Rep. pp. 653, 664, 665, 674. [2] Princeton Theol. Essays, Vol. I. p. 141.
[3] Bib. Rep. p. 674.

plished critic, not satisfied with inflicting this injury, has actually made the following cool statement: "The phrase that 'God came from Teman' or 'he made the clouds his chariot,' *when interpreted according to the laws of language,* expresses a truth. The phrases, 'Christ took upon him our guilt,' 'he satisfied divine justice,' *when interpreted by the same laws,* express, as our author thinks, what is false."[1] If the Reviewer is able to say all this, what will he not say next? He has not only concealed some of the most important *declarations* of the sermon, but has published the non-existent thoughts of its author. "*As our author thinks!*" Is it not a rule of comity in letters, never to report that a man believes what he emphatically denies that he believes? The phrases "Christ took upon him our guilt, and satisfied divine justice" are false, "as our author thinks," "when they are interpreted according to the use of language!" Really, unless we had learned long ago not to be surprised at anything which can be said by anonymous critics, even when in the main they are good men, we should be astonished at this apparently sober charge. Might not the Reviewer have easily seen it to be one aim of the discourse to prove, that all such phrases, when interpreted according to the laws of language, express what is intellectually and morally true? to prove that they must be explained according to what they *mean,* and that they always mean what the intellect can reconcile with other truths? The eager critic has here committed two faults. The first is a fault of logic; for he has taken the premise, that passionate phrases when explained literally and without qualification, and so not according to the laws of language, are *often* untrue, and has hence inferred that these phrases when explained with the proper qualification, and according to the laws of language are untrue. His reasonings may be reduced to this enthymem: The sermon states, pp. 522, 563, that Christ has satisfied the law and justice of God, so far and in such a sense as to render it not a matter of legal obligation, but a matter of propriety and consistency for him to regenerate some men, offer salvation to all men, and bestow numerous favors on the elect and non-elect; therefore, it follows that the phrase Christ "satisfied divine justice," *when interpreted according to the rules of language, expresses, as our author thinks, what is false.*

As the first error of the Reviewer in this charge is one of logic, so the second is one of controversial ethics. He has asserted that his own inference from the sermon is the actual opinion of the author of

---

[1] Bib. Rep. p. 665.

that sermon. And here his ethical fault is the more unseemly, because the Reviewer's inference is illogical, and the author's premise is a simple one, laid down in many of our elementary works. We should advise our critic to review Dr. Hey's Canons of Controversy, if we could suppose him ignorant of the rule, that one should never impute his own inferences, especially his unwarrantable inferences, to another man who is innocent of them. He should not impute them literally, by affirming outright that the innocent has committed these errors; nor should he impute them figuratively, by treating the innocent as if he had been guilty of these wrong conclusions.

If the Reviewer had pursued to its full length the principle which he seems to have adopted in some of his criticisms, he would have said, that the sermon denies the doctrine of Eternal Punishment, because it implies that this doctrine would be true, even if there were to be no literal fire or worm; that the sermon denies the doctrine of the General Judgment, because it implies that this doctrine would be true, even if there were to be no opened books; that the sermon denies the doctrine of the Resurrection, because it implies that this doctrine would be true, even if the same particles of matter composing our earthly bodies should not compose our spiritual bodies. For the Reviewer seems to have reasoned on the strange principle, that if the same doctrine be presented in two forms, one prosaic and one poetical, then the doctrine is denied, or is described as false to the intellect. Obviously, the sermon never intimates that any truth is false to the intellect. This language, and the idea suggested by it, are merely of the Reviewer's imputation. He has, apparently, reasoned thus: the sermon affirms that certain doctrines are, at certain times, associated with certain images, and expressed in certain words, which the intellect would never have suggested for the purposes of speculation; and therefore the sermon affirms that those doctrines are false to the reason. Just as if the sermon would have denied the truth of John 21: 25, provided that it had declared the possibility of the world's containing more books than can be ever written.

But the Reviewer is not satisfied even with these imputations. Although the sermon was designed to be homiletical rather than doctrinal, yet it incidentally teaches the dogmatic truths of Eternal Punishment, the Resurrection, the General Judgment, man's Entire Sinfulness, his Native Corruption, his need of Regeneration by the interposed influence of God, the Vicarious Atonement, and "the doctrines which concentre in and around" it; and it repeatedly represents all Christian truth as that "which God himself has matched to our nicest and most delicate springs of action, and which, so highly does he honor our nature, he has interposed by miracles for the sake of revealing in his written word."[1] Still, the Reviewer often characterizes the sermon as "inimical to the proper authority of the Bible," "subversive," "destructive" of it, as exhibiting sad affinities to Rationalism; and as fit to be associated in some of its doctrinal tendencies, with the writings of Schleiermacher, Röhr, Morell, etc.[2] In his Eleventh Letter on Clerical Manners and Habits, Dr. Miller says: "Let all your conduct in judicatories be *marked* with the *most perfect* candor and uprightness:" "Men in the main upright and pious, do sometimes indulge in a species of indirect management, which minds delicately honorable and strictly desirous of shunning the very appearance of evil, would by no means have adopted. Such are the little arts of concealment," etc.: "Never employ language toward any fellow member (of a judicatory) which you would not be willing to have directed toward yourself."[3]

Suppose, now, that in criticising this Review, we should use his own *argumentum ad captandum vulgus*. There are fundamental heresies, that of the Theopaschites that of denying the Trinity to be eternal, the Godhead to be perfect, etc., of which he might be convicted, as easily and as honorably as he has convicted the sermon of a neological spirit. Take a single illustration. It is an established principle, that the properties and attributes of either nature by itself, may be applied and ascribed to the whole person who combines two natures, but that the properties and attributes of the whole person cannot be ascribed, without qualification, to either nature by itself. Thus we may affirm that man, compounded of soul and body, eats and thinks, but not that the soul eats, nor that the body thinks; the complex being is perhaps corpulent and sentimental, but the body is not sen-

---

[1] Bib. Sac. pp. 561, 544.

[2] We will do justice to the charitable spirit of the Reviewer, and say, that in one passage on p. 646, he makes the following concession: "We are far from supposing that the author regards his theory as subversive of the authority of the Bible. He has obviously (?) adopted it as a convenient way of getting rid of certain doctrines (?) which stand out far too prominently in Scripture, and are too deeply impressed on the hearts of God's people, to allow of their being denied."— The charm of this passage lies in the fact that it purports to be apologetic. It begins to be a serious question with us, whether we have any acquaintance with the author whose designs are thus charitably explained; whether we have ever read a paragraph of his discourse. Either we are lamentably ignorant of the sermon, or else the gentleman who has assailed, has radically misapprehended it.

[3] Miller's Letters, pp. 320, 328.

timental, nor the soul corpulent. On the same principle we may affirm, that Christ, compounded of God and man, is immutable, and died, but not that the man is immutable, or the God died. If we say that God has died, we speak poetically or erroneously. But the Review defends the phrase, "God the mighty Maker died," as "a dogmatic truth," for "its strict doctrinal propriety," its "doctrinal fidelity," and even goes so far as to state that this phrase belongs to "the language of speculation, of theory, of the intellect, as *distinguished from the feelings*."[1] But, if it be true that God the mighty Maker died, then it is true on the principle that all which Christ did and suffered, God did and suffered; and all which was done by Jehovah, was done also by the man Christ Jesus. And this profane principle the Reviewer adopts; and so accordingly he believes, not only that the worlds were made by a man, the eternal decrees formed by the son of a carpenter, but also that, as Christ, so the eternal Deity was born, was educated, was ignorant, was lost by his parents, was carried about from place to place, was fatigued; God the Spirit was refreshed by food and sleep; God the Mighty was unable to bear his cross, was weak and not mighty; God the Maker was (contrary to one of the Reviewer's creeds) both begotten and also made; God the immutable grew in stature, was subject to daily, hourly change; God who is ever blessed, was at one period the greatest sufferer on earth, was nailed to the cross; the everlasting God was dead, not living; and therefore unchangeable power, wisdom, blessedness, and even life cannot be ascribed to him, "as our Reviewer thinks." Now, we will do this Reviewer the *justice* to say, that if we should imitate him in imputing to him as his own belief, the inferences which he has never avowed, but which might be drawn from his words, as fairly as he has drawn inferences from the sermon, we should do what our self-respect forbids us to do.

Pitiable indeed is the logomachy of polemic divines. We have somewhere read, that the Berkeleians who denied the existence of matter, differed more in terms than in opinion from their opponents who affirmed the existence of matter; for the former uttered with emphasis, "We cannot prove that there is an outward world," and then whispered, "We are yet compelled to believe that there is one;" whereas the latter uttered with emphasis, "We are compelled to believe in the outward world," and then whispered, "Yet we cannot prove that there is one." This is not precisely accurate, still it

---

[1] Bib. Rep. pp. 666, 648.

illustrates the amount of difference which exists between the Reviewer and the author of the humble Convention sermon. Let us listen to them in an imagined colloquy. The Reviewer exclaims aloud, "I believe in a sinful nature preceding all sinful exercise of it," and then whispers, "This passive nature is not sinful in the sense of being condemned by the conscience of one who never acted amiss; men are not personally blamable for being born with it; they do not deserve the fatal sentence at the judgment merely for the way in which they were made." The author exclaims aloud, "I believe that man's nature preceding all exercise of it contains no such sin as itself deserves to be tried, blamed, condemned at the judgment, and punished forever," and then he whispers, "Still this nature, as it certainly occasions sin, may be sometimes called sinful in a peculiar sense, for the sake of intensity." The Reviewer cries on a high key, "I believe that the sin of the guilty is imputed to the innocent under a just administration," and then adds in a lower tone, "The word impute, however, is not here used in its more obvious meaning, and does not imply that the imputation affects the character of the innocent or makes them actually displeasing to God." The author cries with a loud voice, "I believe that the sin of the guilty is not imputed to the innocent," and then adds on a lower key, "The innocent, however, are made to suffer in consequence of the guilty, and being thus treated in certain respects as if they had done wrong, sin may be sometimes said, for the sake of a deep impression, to be imputed to them." The Reviewer exclaims in a loud tone, "I believe that the innocent are justly punished for sin which they have never committed," and then adds in a milder accent, "They are not punished however in the most strict and rigid meaning of the term, but are only made to suffer on account of the sin of those with whom they are connected, and for the purpose of sustaining the law as inviolable." The author exclaims in a bold tone, "I believe that the innocent are not justly punished for sin which they have never committed, for, in the words of Andrew Fuller,[1] "*real* and *proper* punishment is not only the infliction of natural evil for the commission of moral evil, but the infliction of the one upon the person who committed the other, and in displeasure against him; it not only supposes criminality, but that the party punished was literally the criminal:" still in a milder accent the author adds, "The suffering of the innocent for the guilty may be sometimes called punishment with a peculiar meaning, for the

---

[1] Fuller's Works, Vol. IV. p. 34.

sake of unusual force." The Reviewer exclaims with earnestness, "All men sinned in Adam," but he explains with deliberation; "They did not literally exist in him, and his voluntary acts cannot be reckoned theirs strictly and properly." The author is earnest in saying, "All men did not literally exist in Adam, and could not have strictly and literally sinned before they existed;" but he is careful to add, "Adam's fall was so infallibly connected with the total depravity of his descendants, as to give a true and deep meaning to the phrase, which may be sometimes used as an intense one, that they sinned in him." The Reviewer proclaims aloud, "I believe in a limited but not general atonement," and then whispers, "It is sufficient, however, for the non-elect as well as the elect." The author proclaims aloud, "I believe in a general but not limited atonement," and then repeats with diminished emphasis, "It was never decreed, however, that this atonement should result in the regeneration of the non-elect." Says the Reviewer, "I will use terms in their technical, although it is not their most obvious meaning;" says the author, "I will generally use terms in their more obvious, although it is not their technical meaning." Whereupon the Reviewer speaks out: "You are inimical to the proper authority of the Bible;" to which the author responds, "You found this charge upon a mere difference about words, about the emphasis to be given them; about the modifications of voice with which the words are to be uttered; and it is notorious that a dispute about words leads to more and still more words, and ends, if it end at all, in hard and sharp words; it is what our polemic divines ought by this time to be tired of, logomachy."

4. But we have already anticipated a distinct class of the Reviewer's unintentional mis-statements. He represents the sermon as unguarded in its tendencies. He says that "it enables a man to profess his faith in doctrines which he does not believe,"[1] and thus to advocate opposing creeds. Is such an objection worthy of such a critic? Does not he himself cling to the creed that the children of Adam are punished for the sin of their father, and also to the Biblical creed "that the son shall not bear the iniquity of the father;" "neither shall the children be put to death for their fathers; every man shall be put to death for his own sin?" But the critic will respond, these apparent discrepancies can be reconciled; and we rejoin, one aim of the sermon is to show that all creeds which are allowable can be reconciled with each other; for, as far as allowable, they contain underneath their diversified forms the substance of the truth and of nothing but the truth.

Dr. Blair remarks[1] what every body knows, that "all passions, without exception, love, terror, amazement, indignation, anger and even grief throw the mind into confusion, aggravate their objects, and of course prompt to a hyperbolical style." In accordance with this trite saying, the sermon makes an hypothetical assertion,[2] that if a creed be wrongly viewed as "a triumphal song of thanksgiving," and if agreeably to this view it be written in the style of a highly poetical effusion, and if when written in this style it be chanted under the influence of thrilling music and amid the pomp of a gorgeous ceremonial, then, in such a false position, the cantilator of such a creed may be so rapt in enthusiasm as to sing the ecstatic words without inquiring for their "precise" import. Who could imagine that the following inference would be drawn from the foregoing truism:— If a man with *false* views of the nature of a creed, may be so overcome by the minstrelsy of a cathedral as to cry out, "credo quia impossibile," while he cantilates an imaginative Confession, which is obscure in its sublimity, and confusing by its crowd of images; then it follows that a student acting, as a student ought to act, deliberately and circumspectly, may with set purpose subscribe a plain and precise creed when he knows it to be false both in its language and in its meaning. The man who can reason thus will soon conclude that if Peter spoke on the mountain without knowing what he said, then he wrote his epistles under the same kind of afflatus. We cannot imagine what a person means by extorting such inferences, but whatever he means, we forgive him.

That the Reviewer arrives at any of his accusations by reasoning in this way, we do not affirm. We cannot divine the process by which he comes to some of his charges. Sometimes he appears to adopt the premise, that the language of the Bible or of a creed must not be qualified at all, and if it be qualified then it is, (to use a word of his own) "eviscerated" of its meaning. But he "explains away" the literal import of many technical terms, just as really as they are explained away in the sermon. And as for qualifying the language of the Bible, does the Reviewer infer the "real presence" from the plain phrase "this is my body;" or the necessity of the pedilavium from the still plainer phrase, "ye ought to wash one another's feet." It were just as fair for us to affirm that he "explains away" the Bible when he denies that God manifests frowardness, Ps. 18: 26, as it is for the Reviewer to affirm that the sermon "explains it away." He has used, *totidem verbis*, the same argument of "rationalistic tenden-

---
[1] Rhet. Lect. XVI.   [2] Bib. Sac. pp. 553, 554.

cies," which the Romanist brings against the Protestant. It is the notorious *argumentum ad invidiam.*

But he is more definite in one of his charges. He says that the sermon proposes "no adequate criteria for discriminating between the language of feeling and that of the intellect," leaves "every one to his own discretion in making the distinction, and the use of this discretion, regulated by no fixed rules of language, is of course determined by *caprice* or taste;" that the sermon is "*perfectly* arbitrary" in explaining figurative language, etc., and its operation "must be to subject [the teachings of the Bible] to the opinion and prejudices of the reader," etc.[1]

All the principles of Morus and Ernesti on Interpretation, cannot, of course, be collected into one Convention Sermon. But this sermon does propound some criteria for discriminating between the true and the false.

One of these criteria is, the agreement of a doctrine with right or Christian feeling. Whatever *words* this feeling sanctions are thereby signified to be correct in form; whatever *meaning* it sanctions, is thereby signified to be *true* in fact. Every statement is to be disapproved "which does not harmonize with the well ordered sensibilities of the soul." "In this light we discern the necessity of right feeling, as a guide to the right proportions of faith," pp. 546, 555.

A second of these criteria involved in the first, is the agreement of a doctrine with the *necessary* impulses of the soul. Reason "will sanction not only all pious feelings, but likewise all those which are *essential* developments of our original constitution," p. 567. "Whenever a feeling is constitutional, and *cannot* be expelled—whenever it is pious and cannot but be approved, then such of its impulses as are uniform, self-consistent and persevering, are data on which the intellect may safely reason, and by means of which it may add new materials to its dogmatic system." "Has man been created with *irresistible* instincts which *impel* him to believe in a falsehood? Or has the Christian been inspired with holy emotions, which allure him to an essentially erroneous faith? Is God the author of confusion, in his Word revealing one doctrine, and by his Spirit persuading his saints to reject it?" p. 544. Whatever the Reviewer may say of these necessary impulses, Dr. Hodge cannot disparage them, for he says in his Commentary on Rom. 3: 1–8, "What God forces us, from the very constitution of our natures, to believe, as for example, the existence of the external world, our own personal identity, the differ-

---

[1] Bib. Rep. pp. 652, 653, 673, 674.

once between good and evil, it is at once a violation of his will and of the dictates of reason to deny or to question."

A third of these criteria involved in the two preceding is, the moral tendency of a doctrine. Whatever belief is on the whole useful, the same is thereby signified to be true; whatever mode of expressing this belief is useful, the same is thereby signified to be right. "So far as any statement is hurtful, it parts with one sign of its truth. In itself, or in its relations, it must be inaccurate whenever it is not congenial with the feelings awakened by the Divine Spirit. The practical utility, then, of any theological representations, is one criterion of their propriety." "Here also we learn the value of the Bible in unfolding the suitable adaptations of truth, and in illustrating their utility, *which is on the whole so decisive a touch-stone of their correctness*," p. 555. The Reviewer may say, perhaps, that this tendency of a doctrine is "no adequate criterion" of its truth; but Dr. Hodge says in his Commentary on Rom. 8: 1–8, "There is no better evidence against the truth of any doctrine, than that its tendency is immoral." Now, the preceding extracts from the sermon are not desultory passages, but are parts of lengthened paragraphs, the *main object* of which is to show that a standard of truth is to be found in the congeniality of a statement with pious or constitutional feeling, and in its moral tendencies; see pp. 544, 545, 555–558. *So far forth* as, and *in whatever sense* it is agreeable and healthful to our moral feelings, to say that God exacts of men more than he gives them power to perform, to say that he imputes to them a crime which they never committed, just so far forth, and in just that sense, may we be entitled to believe those sayings as substantially true.

But a fourth criterion propounded in the sermon is, the agreement of a doctrine with the feelings of good men in general. "These *universal* feelings provide us with a test for our own faith." Pious men differ in the minute philosophical forms of truth, but their unanimity in the substance of it, indicates "the correctness of their cherished faith, as the agreement of many witnesses presupposes the verity of the narration in which they coincide." "The broad substance of doctrine around which the feelings of all *renewed* men" (the point of the argument lies in the word "*renewed*," which the Reviewer changes into "reverent")[1] cling ever and everywhere, "*must* be right," for it

---

[1] The sentence of the Reviewer is the following: "The church is not infallible in her bodies of divinity, nor her creeds, nor catechisms, nor any logical formula; but underneath all, there lies a grand substance of doctrine, around which the feelings of all reverent men cling," etc., Bib. Rep. p. 654.

is precisely adjusted to the soul, and the soul was made for it," pp. 544, 545. In whatever sense the feelings of all good men welcome the Reviewer's "dogma," that the Maker of the world has once died, *in that sense* is the dogma indicated to be correct.

A fifth criterion is the agreement of a doctrine with other well known truths. Correct figures of speech disagree with each other; correct literal statements, never. The intellectual theology "regards a want of concinnity in a system, as a token of some false principle. And as it will modify itself in order to avoid the error involved in a contradiction, so, and for the same reason, it has authority in the last resort to rectify the statements which are often congenial with excited emotion," p. 546.

A sixth criterion mentioned in the sermon is, the agreement of a doctrine with the inferences of reason enlightened by revelation. The chief aim of pp. 546–550 is, to show that "as the head is placed above the heart in the body, so the faith which is sustained by good argument, should control rather than be controlled by those emotions which receive no approval from the judgment." "In all investigations for truth, the intellect must be the authoritative power," it "explains, modifies, harmonizes the meaning" of all conflicting statements; must bring them all "into unison with the intellectual statements which, however unimpressive, are yet the most authoritative." And the reason draws its inferences from the works of God, but chiefly from his "miraculously attested" word. So far forth and in whatever sense it can be *proved* that the innocent are punished for the guilty, just so far forth and in that sense, is the statement true. It is now a noticeable fact, that at the very time when the Reviewer condemned the sermon, as leaving every one to his "*caprice or taste*" in distinguishing between literal and figurative language, he had upon his table the edition of the sermon containing these words:[1]

"No one hesitates to say that the poetic view of astronomy, in which the sun is described as masculine, the moon as feminine, the stars as children of the moon, should be reduced into a consistency with the philosophical view, and that the demonstrable science should not be distorted so as to harmonize with the graceful fable. Neither does any one shrink from interpreting the assertion, God is a rock, into an accordance with the assertion, God is a spirit; for both statements cannot be literally true, and the one which commends itself to the intellect, is the rightful standard by which to modify the one suggested by the heart. Else the *fancies* and *caprices* of man will be, what his reason and conscience ought to be, his guide."

If, then, an interpretation be intuitively perceived to be correct, or be proved so by valid argument from the word or works of God, if it substantially agree with other interpretations known to be right, if it have been generally received as true by *"renewed"* men, if it have a healthful moral influence, if it accord with our constitutional or pious feeling, then it has so many signs of its correctness. All these criteria, and others also, are stated by the author, who is *"perfectly arbitrary in the application of his theory,"* and according to the Reviewer "adopts or rejects the representations of the Bible *at pleasure*, or as they *happen* to coincide with or contradict his own preconceived opinions."[1]

The author does, indeed, recognize (Sermon, p. 555) the solemn truth that "here," in his theme, "we see our responsibility for our religious belief. Here are we impressed by the fact that much of our probation relates to our mode of shaping and coloring the doctrines of theology." We cannot escape from this probation. Our Almighty Sovereign designs to try our hearts in our detection of the principles which are communicated to us in symbols. It were, indeed, congenial with our love of ease, to have our duties for every day written out with exactness on the palms of our hands, that we may simply look and read. It were pleasant if God had arranged the stars of heaven into letters and sentences all unfolding our precise relations to him, and modifying themselves into new testaments of truth whenever we needed new light. But instead of thus accommodating our listless spirit, he has required us to *dig* for our knowledge, to *work* out our salvation with fear and trembling; and has made the probation of all men, and the chief probation of some men to consist in their mode of regulating their judgments, imagination and feelings in the pursuit of wholesome doctrine. Let us not attempt to flee from our appointed trial, but let us endure it as men with humility and prayer. Let us not arraign our Maker because he has sown the path of investigation with perils; but let us meet the perils with a manly trust in his guidance. All study is dangerous; but the neglect of it is more so. Candor may be abused to our hurt; bigotry will be used to our sorer mischief. If we aim to be fair inquirers for truth, we may err; if we strive to be pugnacious defenders of a party we shall lapse into sad mistakes. Let us ever bear in mind that we are to give account at the great day, not only for every idle, injurious, defamatory word, but also for the narrow, clannish, sectarian spirit with which we may have discussed the truth. Who is sufficient, without God's help, for *preaching* or even for *thinking* of that Gospel which "is set for the fall and rising again of many in Israel."

---

[1] Bip. Rep. p. 684.

ARTICLE VII.

UNITY AMID DIVERSITIES OF BELIEF, EVEN ON IMPUTED AND INVOLUNTARY SIN;

WITH COMMENTS ON A SECOND ARTICLE IN THE PRINCETON REVIEW RELATING TO A CONVENTION SERMON.

By Edwards A. Park, Abbot Professor in Andover Theol. Seminary.

It is a grateful anticipation of all believers, that the leopard will one day lie down with the kid. It is also a consoling idea, that even now many wranglers in the church are disputing less on theology than on lexicography. The inward union of good men will soon be, and indeed already is more extensive than we imagine. In our bellicose propensities, we magnify the rumors of war. "Among those who admit the atoning death of Christ as the organific principle of their faith, there are differences, some of them more important, but many far less important, than they seem to be."[1] There are differences. It were idle to attempt an entire fusion of our evangelical creeds into one. These differences are important. All truth is important. The more exact our ideas of the Gospel, so much the more worthy will be our imaginative illustrations of it. Just in proportion as the theology of the head is the more complete, may the theology of the heart be the more copious and impressive, and the whole religious life may be the more in unison with heaven. Every new truth may call out some new grace, and if we have no idea of law, we can have no motive of obedience.[2] But let us not plunge into extremes. Let us not infer that pious men, believing "the doctrines which concentre in and around a vicarious atonement,"[3] must either become latitudinarian and care nothing for their differences, or else denounce each other as Pelagian, and magnify their minor disagree-

---

[1] Convention Sermon, Bib. Sac. Vol. VII. p. 559.

[2] See Convention Sermon, pp. 542—546. Notwithstanding all that is here said on the necessity of religious knowledge for the culture of religious feeling, our critic devotes several pages of his last Review (Biblical Repertory and Princeton Review, Vol. XXIII. pp. 333—345) to prove, that this sermon is founded on a theory which rests on the principle that religion is a "blind feeling"! Is not the Reviewer in haste? He contradicts himself by elsewhere condemning the sermon for its theory that all moral character consists in a choice to obey or disobey a known law!

[3] Convention Sermon, p. 544.

ments. At the present day, when Christians long for a more obvious unity in the faith, it is cheering to reflect on the particulars and on the methods in which they do harmonize, notwithstanding their frequent discords.

And, first, it is a delightful idea that the great majority of good Christians have received their faith immediately from the Bible, and have therefore agreed in adopting its essential truths. The men who trouble Israel are not the fair-minded theologians, but the polemic divines. It is these who go around beating the drum, brandishing the sword, crying "To arms," and already have their quarrels filled the world with spiritual orphans; but the women and children who pray in the vales and in the mountain fastnesses, have not understood the meaning of the war-cry; they have been called Lutherans, or Calvinists, or Zuinglians, or Baptists, or Methodists, or Presbyterians, and have scarcely known wherefore, but one thing they have known, and this has been their chief joy — that "Blessed is the Lamb of God who taketh away the sin of the world." "The great mass of believers have never embraced the metaphysical refinements of creeds, useful as these refinements are; but have singled out and fastened upon and held firm those cardinal truths which the Bible has lifted up and turned over in so many different lights as to make them the more conspicuous by their very alternations of figure and hue."[1] We insist on the usefulness of these metaphysical refinements, and being so understood we shall not be accused of undervaluing any truth when we say with our worthy Reviewer, that "the mass of true Christians, in all denominations, get their religion directly from the Bible, and are but little affected by the peculiarities of their creeds."[2]

As yet, then, being in some measure harmonious with our critic, let us proceed to a second remark: pious men often adopt systems which agree with each other in their essential principles, but are irreconcilable in subordinate particulars. Augustinism is essentially right, notwithstanding its theory of baptismal regeneration; and Pelagianism is essentially wrong, notwithstanding its acknowledgment of Christ's divinity. The doctrinal system of Pictet, is different from that of Bellamy, but the difference is superficial, not fundamental. The great truths involved in the atonement of our blessed Lord, overpower various errors in philosophy, which may be fabricated around it; and every system which includes and is formed mainly

---

[1] Convention Sermon, p. 560.
[2] Bib. Repertory, Vol. XVII. p. 85. This article is generally imputed to our Reviewer.

upon those truths, has the right substance, even although it may have some unsightly protuberances. Those doctrines are the requisites for a faith which saves. They are welcomed by various sects. In a late Convention sermon, it was therefore said, that there is an "identity in the essence of many truths which are run in scientific or aesthetic moulds, unlike each other."[1] This *ought* not to have been understood as meaning, that the moulds, i. e. *the scientific theories*, are the same, but that the substance of the *religious truth* cast into them, is the same. The truth that Christ was a vicarious sacrifice in suffering the most expressive pain for sinners, is not *philosophically* identical with the notion that he suffered the exact punishment of sinners; yet, the general system of Dr. Edwards, which includes the vicarious sacrifice in one of its philosophical forms, is *essentially* like the general system of Abraham Booth, which includes the same doctrine in another of its philosophical forms. It was not said in the above named sermon, that *all* systems were alike, but that *many* are. Our earnest Reviewer perseveres in confounding "many" with "all." He says of the author: "When he stood up — to foretell the blending of *all* creeds into one colorless ray;" but the author said for himself: "*Many* various forms of faith will yet be blended into a consistent knowledge, like the colors in a single ray."[2]

Thirdly, we are also pleased to observe, that good men often contend about modes of presenting truth, when they agree in the truth presented. The same doctrines presented in certain forms constitute the theology of the intellect, and presented in other forms constitute the theology of the heart.[3] This latter theology often "indulges in

---

[1] Convention Sermon, p. 559.

[2] Compare Bib. Rep., XXIII. p. 341, with Bib. Sac.. VII. p. 561.

[3] A form of a truth involves *that* truth in *that* form. Modes of theological exhibition are theological doctrines exhibited in certain modes. A style of theology is theology in a particular style. It is immaterial whether we say that the theology of the intellect is a kind of theological representation, or that it is theology represented in a certain method. "The theology of the intellect and feelings" is one system of truths exhibited in two modes. This is the single theory of the sermon under review. The attempt of the Reviewer, in Bib. Repert. Vol. XXIII. pp. 333—339, to prove that there is another and a "German" theory, can serve no other purpose than to link the sermon with the (to many persons) "*hard name*" of Schleiermacher. It is an unworthy attempt. Had he given a fair exhibition of either the German theory or the sermon, he could not have failed to show their antagonism. He pretends that the sermon grows out of the indirect idea that "right moral feeling may express itself in wrong *intellectual* forms," by which he means, *false statements literally understood*. No such thing. The contrary is asserted throughout the discourse. If the Reviewer will take the trouble

a style of remark which for sober prose would be unbecoming, or even when associated in certain ways, irreverent;" "in language which we fear to repeat."[1] The Princeton Reviewer, for example, makes the following remark: "Paul says that Christ, though he knew no sin, was made sin; i. e. a sinner."[2] If Paul *had* said that Christ was made a sinner, we would reverently repeat the words, even as we say with awe, "Then the Lord awaked as out of sleep, and like a mighty man that shouteth by reason of wine."[3] But inspired men never venture upon the declaration that our blessed Lord was made a sinner; and if uninspired authors wish to invent such phrases, they should do it with caution, and should step on this perilous ground with their shoes from off their feet. We hope, indeed, that our Reviewer means to express a *truth* by such a bold declaration, and that he here deviates from New England theology in respect of taste rather than doctrine. We believe also that other divines have, in certain states of mind, a right idea concealed under their dangerous, intense phraseology, when they say, as does the excellent Dr. Crisp, "Christ himself becomes the transgressor in the room and stead of the person that had transgressed; so that in respect of the reality of being a transgressor, Christ is as really the transgressor as the man that did commit it was, before he took it upon him."[4] Interpreted as bold metaphors, such expressions may sometimes, but always with extreme peril, be borne for a moment in the theology of excited feeling; but when literally interpreted, they belong neither to the theology of a sound head nor to that of a good heart, but are the occasions of infidelity and sin.

Fourthly, it is also a pleasant reflection, that good men often believe in a false doctrine as logically deduced from certain premises, and reject it in their pious meditations. They disagree as logicians with the advocate of truth, but as devotional Christians, they agree

---

to examine the discourse, he will see that the word "intellectual" is one of his own interpolations, and is an unwarrantable gloss.

[1] Conv. Sermon, Bib. Sac. VII. p. 538.   [2] Bib. Rep. VII. p. 426.
[3] Psalm 78: 65.
[4] See Crisp's Sermons, edited by Dr. Gill, Vol. I. pp. 429, 431, 437, 440, 261 —264, 301, etc. We *must* believe that this good man does, in certain moods of feeling, use these terms in a figurative sense, although he denies that he so uses them here. "To affirm," he says, p. 438, "that the Lord laid upon Christ the *guilt* of sin and not the *sin* itself, is directly contrary to Scripture; for you have many testimonies affirming that the Lord lays *sin* upon him; what presumption then is it for a man to say, he lays on Christ the *guilt*, and not the *sin itself*." "See how careful the Spirit of God is to take away all suspicion of a figure in the text," (he bare the *sins* of many). p. 430.

with him. "Dogmas of the most revolting shape, have no sooner been cast into the alembic of a regenerated heart, than their more jagged angles have been melted away."[1] Lest our Reviewer suspect this remark of Germanism, let him have the goodness to reperuse his own saying: "this is a doctrine which can only be held as a *theory*. It is in conflict with the most intimate moral convictions of men;" and further, "it is a product of the *mere* understanding, and does violence to the instinctive moral judgment of men;"[2] and further still: "even among those who make theology a study there is often one form of doctrine for speculation, and another simpler and truer for the closet. [!] Metaphysical distinctions are forgotten in prayer, or under the pressure of real conviction of sin, and need of pardon, and of divine assistance. Hence it is that the devotional writings of Christians agree far more than their creeds."[3] Our critic here agrees very happily with the *Schleiermacherian* sermon, which declares that "in unnumbered cases, the real faith of Christians has been purer than their written statements of it."[4]

Sometimes, however, the erroneous formulas of the metaphysician are not "*forgotten*" in his prayers, but are merged into a merely intense expression of practical truth. In his study he regards them as literal statements; in his closet he uses the same words as bold metaphors. While his heart is cold, he adopts them as *a* theology of the intellect; but when his heart is warm, he changes them into *the* theology of feeling.[5] The ice mountain in which he is frozen up as a scholar, melts into pure and refreshing water around him when he is in the glow of devotion. Imagine, if you can, that an exemplary divine should exclaim in his address to God: "I have 'done as well as I could do;' 'I have had no more power to change my disposition than to annihilate myself,' therefore 'I have lived up to the very extent of my ability,' but 'my debt has been fully paid,' and now 'it

---

[1] Conv. Sermon, p. 560.

[2] Bib. Rep. XVII. pp. 91, 87. Here, and throughout this Article, the *italics* are made by the author of the Article.

[3] Bib. Rep. Vol. XVII. p. 85.   [4] Conv. Serm. p. 560.

[5] Our earnest Reviewer not only confounds "*many*" with "*all*," but also "*a*" with "*the*." *The* theology of the intellect is not, as he seems to think, Pelagianism, but it is the theology of a *sound* mind, i. e. it is the truth. *The* theology of feeling is not a class of doctrines adapted to a *wrong* heart, but to a *right* one; i. e. it is the truth, the same in substance but not in form with the preceding. On the other hand, *a* theology of intellect may be any form of religious error, and *a* theology of feeling may be any kind of injurious theological statement. See Conv. Serm., Note B. Not all the expressions of our Reviewer belong to *the* theology of feeling.

would be unjust to punish me;' 'I claim heaven as my right'"—could there be any doubt that he used this language in a metaphorical sense, and that he meant something entirely different from the proper import of his words? Will a broken-hearted sinner use such phrases at the throne of grace, otherwise than as eloquent exhibitions of a truth which they do not *literally* express? Will not the false theories with which these phrases are allied, vanish into poetical illustrations of sacred doctrine, when the man, as right-*hearted*, becomes stronger than the man, as wrong-*headed*?

Fifthly, it is also cheering to know that when divines act as *men*, instead of theorists, they often relinquish their erroneous notions, and agree with the advocates of right doctrine. Not only as good Christians, but also as unsophisticated human beings, they accept the truth. Thus there is an habitual unity while there is a scholastic difference among many theologians. Human nature is too strong for bad logic. As children gaze at the sun until their eyes are darkened, so metaphysicians often reflect on a theme until their minds are *bewildered*. They see it in a blur. They have disordered, by straining, their vision. They are confident, pugnacious, but in their practical moods they think like other folks; Berkeley and Hume made but little use of their scepticism when out of doors. The absurdities of divines often fall off from them around the domestic hearth or in the circle of social prayer. So far as the theology of New England is a distinctive system, differing from that which has been so nobly opposed by Edwards and Dwight of Connecticut, it is the theology of the Bible explained by common sense. It is theology conformed to the fundamental laws of human belief. It is the theology which all good men adopt when they act in the capacity of men, in distinction from mere scholars or polemics. This is its glory. The church has ever been for it in its substance, even when against it in its forms. It is in fact nothing new, save in the precision and consistency of its statements. It is "the great granitic formation," if we may venture to use the strong words of our Reviewer, in which the fathers before and after Augustine, and even that imperial divine himself loved to build their practical religion. It has been, we are glad that it has been, grown over with rich mosses, and beautiful wild flowers, and fragrant briers and medicinal herbs. But we are sorry that distant observers fasten their gaze upon the surface, and mistake the beautiful drapery for the very rock itself, and think to build their triangular turrets upon the flowers, which were never meant to be crushed and bruised under the artificial masonry.

Let us give one illustration of the fact that men *must* often, whether they will or not, obey those principles of common sense by which He who inspired the Bible meant that we should explain it, and by which the New England divinity has been shaped into its distinctive form. Andrew Fuller says: "I have proved that *natural strength* is the *measure* of men's *obligation* to love God," and he often repeats, "we are only *required* to love God with all our strength."[1] But our worthy Reviewer regards this as one radical principle of Pelagianism, and remarks: "If there is anything of which the sinner has an intimate conviction, it is that the heart, the affections, his inherent moral dispositions are beyond his reach; that he can no more change his nature than he can annihilate it."[2] Does this gentleman, then, who will, we trust, admit the sinner's obligation to be holy, agree with the advocates of "ability commensurate with obligation?" No, not always, not in some of his theorizings, not at the moment of his controverting that truth. But what will he say as a *man*? Can a child be under obligation to lift up a mountain with his unaided hand, or to see through the globe with his unaided eye, or to hear the conversation of the antipodes with his unaided ear? 'By no means,' our critic will respond, 'for the maxim that ability is commensurate with obligation *does* apply to external acts.'[3] Very well. The first step is gained. Can a child be under obligation, then, to learn all the languages of the world in one day, or to understand all the sciences in one hour? 'By no means,' our Reviewer will answer, 'that old maxim *does* apply to intellectual operations.' Very well. Then a second step is gained. Now for the third. You say that "the maxim has no more to do with the obligations of moral agents in reference to moral acts than the axioms of geometry have;"[4] nothing at all, then, to do with moral acts! This is sweeping enough. But let us see. Can a man be under moral obligation to love God this moment with a love *infinitely* more ardent than that of the highest angel? Can he be under moral obligation to love the universe with a benevolence equal to that of God himself? Can the infant of a day be under moral obligation to exercise as much of holy feeling as is exercised by Him who is omnipotent? Are not these *moral acts*? You have wisely conceded that a creature cannot "be required to create a world, nor an idiot to reason correctly."[5] Why not? Because *in these things* power must be equal to duty. But can a creature be under obligation to *annihilate* the world, or to *annihilate* his own nature?

---

[1] Fuller's Works, Vol. II. pp. 538, 656, and frequently elsewhere.
[2] Bib. Rep. XVII. pp. 329, 330. [3] Ib. p. 329. [4] Ib. [5] Ib.

Is he able to annihilate himself? No. And yet he is equally unable to make himself a new heart! Is he then required to perform this impossibility? And if not required to repent, does he disobey any requisition in not repenting? Does he sin? Now we *know* that we shall get the right answer at last. We know that there is in every man a *vis medicatrix*, curing the soul as well as the body of its disorders, and working itself through all sorts of metaphysics, and now it forces from the Biblical Repertory the following words, which " end the strife :" "*Man cannot be under obligation to do what requires powers which do not belong to his nature and constitution.*"[1] Still again it affirms, in language more unguarded than we have ever employed: "The unfortunate and *improper* use of the word 'necessity' by Edwards and his followers, has done more to prejudice the minds of *sensible* men against his system than all other causes. According to the *proper* usage of language, liberty and necessity are diametrically opposite; and to say a thing is necessary and at the same time free, is a *contradiction in terms*. Certainty and necessity are not the same; for although everything necessary is certain, everything certain is not necessary. Volitions, in certain given circumstances, may be as certain as any physical effects, but volitions are free in their very nature. A *necessary* volition is an absurdity, a thing *inconceivable*. To call this certainty a 'moral necessity,' a 'philosophical necessity,' will forever mislead, and produce confusion of ideas in the most *exact* thinkers."[2] These words are indeed rather extravagant, but their main import is satisfactory, and they show that divines writing as *men* and not as partizans, are *compelled* to admit the whole theory of natural power which our Reviewer has condemned as Pelagian, when found in a "practical" sermon. And yet will he abide by these principles? Will he not sometimes violate the fundamental laws of human belief? On pp. 329, 330, of his Reply to our Remarks, he asserts the doctrine of necessity with as much force as it was ever asserted by Hobbes or Belsham. And does he mean what the Repertory elsewhere affirms, that this necessity is a certainty *rather* than necessity?[3] If so, why does he condemn a New England sermon for uttering the same truth? That sermon represents a sinner to be as unable to repent as he is to annihilate both himself and the universe — in the figurative sense which Jonathan Edwards and Andrew Fuller attach to the word *unable*. But the fact is, our Reviewer is misled by his strong language. Instead of using

---

[1] Bib. Rep. VII. p. 372.   [2] Ib. XVII. p. 638.
[3] Ib. XV. pp. 46, 47, and in many other passages.

it, he allows himself to be used by it, and in criticising a New England sermon he does really think that a just God requires men under penalty of eternal death, to accomplish literal impossibilities! But his mind is too elastic to be always overpowered by this metaphysics; and just so truly as he is a man, not merely a good or great man, but a *man*, he does and must often pay allegiance to the fundamental law of human belief, that a being will never feel remorse or suffer a moral punishment for doing what he was literally and invincibly necessitated to do, or for not doing what was as strictly impossible as to annihilate himself.

Sixthly, not merely in their pious meditations, nor in their capacity as men in distinction from theorists, do certain advocates of error come over upon the side of truth; they do so in some of their speculative moods. In the devious paths of false doctrine, they must now and then double their track. For the sake of maintaining one theory, they will gainsay what they had advanced in maintaining another. Our critic has given several interesting examples of an occasional harmony even in speculation with the men whom he opposes.

It is often said by Dr. Crisp, that it would not be just, or even "honest," for the Deity to exact of us a payment of the debt which Christ has already paid for us; "that the Lord hath no more to lay to the charge of an elect person, yet in the height of iniquity, and in the excess of riot, and committing all the abominations that can be committed; I say, even then, when an elect person runs such a course, the Lord hath no more to lay to his charge, than he hath to lay to the charge of a believer; nay, he hath no more to lay to the charge of such a person, than he hath to lay to the charge of a saint triumphant in glory."[1] In an attempt to explain such statements, it was said in a late Convention Sermon, that the intellect, *left to its own guidance*, "would never suggest the *unqualified* remark, that Christ has fully paid the debt of sinners, for it declares that this debt may justly be claimed from them; nor that he has suffered the whole punishment which they deserve — for it teaches that this punishment may still be righteously inflicted on themselves."[2] But our Reviewer answers, that each of the above named "unqualified" remarks is true, and here he was outright in collision with the sermon.[3] We

---

[1] Crisp's Sermons, edited by Dr. Gill, Vol. I., p. 570. See the same idea advanced in equally or more perilous language, on pp. 261, 263, 264, 463, 487, 557, 573, etc.

[2] Bib. Sac., Vol. VII. p. 535.   [3] Bib. Rep., Vol. XXII., pp. 648, 649.

then commented on his answer;[1] and in his Reply, he has taken pains to qualify the original statements, and he now says: "Christ has paid the debt of sinners *in such a sense* that it would be unjust to exact its payment from *those who believe;*" "Christ has suffered the punishment of sin, *in such a sense* that it would be unjust to exact that punishment of those *who accept his righteousness.*"[2] He thus gives up the word *sinners*, and substitutes *believers!* This is *one* interesting qualification. How, then, does the matter stand? Justice and merit are correlative terms. Where one is, the other must be; where one is not, the other cannot be. If it be unjust to punish a man, that man deserves no punishment. If he deserve no punishment, he is not sinful. But every man has been sinful and ill-deserving. What has become of his sin and demerit? Are they annihilated? If they do not belong to him, they must belong to another. Hence, we have been told, they are "transferred," "communicated," "imputed" to Christ. Therefore, the adorable Saviour is a sinner. This has been said a thousand times. But is he *morally* a sinner? No! our critic will answer. Is he, then, morally undeserving? No. Are our sins *morally* imputed to him? No, "not morally but juridically." Then, do they not morally belong to us? Yes. Then, are we not morally undeserving? Yes. Then, would it not be morally just to punish us? Yes. And to exact our debt of us? Yes. Then that "unqualified" phrase is qualified the second time, and it now stands: The punishment of sinners cannot be justly inflicted on them, provided that the sinners are believers, and the justice spoken of, is not a *moral* justice, but external and legal. In his Reply, our critic expresses his second qualification thus: "In *themselves*, they [believers] are hell-deserving; to *them*, their acceptance is a matter of grace, because it is not their own righteousness, but the righteousness of another, that is the ground of their justification."[3] We are happy to see, then, that he agrees with us in acknowledging, not only in his confessions at the throne of grace, but also in some of his speculations, that eternal punishment is justly due to us, and may be justly inflicted upon us, so far forth as we are considered to be or to have been sinful; but that so far forth as we are considered to be believers, this punishment cannot be inflicted upon us in consistency with what

---

[1] Bib. Sac., Vol. VIII, pp. 161—163.
[2] Bib. Rep., Vol. XXIII. p. 331. The Reviewer is speaking of retributive justice, as he regards it a serious heresy to resolve (with Pres. Edwards, Dr. Dwight, and others) real justice into benevolence.
[3] Bib. Rep., XXIII. p. 332.

is due to our Redeemer.[1] We certainly sympathize with the learned critic, when after twice qualifying an "unqualified" phrase, he comes over to the true faith; and even while he adheres to a false speculation, we cordially repeat the words with which himself is familiar, and which, considering their source, he will be slow to suspect of Schleiermacherism: "There *is* a region a little lower than the *head*, a little *deeper* than the reach of *speculation*, in which those who *think* they differ, or differ in *thinking*, may yet rejoice in Christian fellowship!"[2]

We now make a seventh and a general remark, that for various reasons, obvious and occult, theologians are often inconsistent with themselves; and while they would never come together if each were to follow out a few of his "radical principles," yet they are not always consecutive, and they often coincide by virtue of their inconsequent reasonings. Thus our Reviewer takes three "radical principles," viz. that "moral character is confined to acts, that liberty supposes power to the contrary [by which he means a natural, not a moral power, to choose right when one does choose wrong], and that ability limits responsibility,"[3] and from these principles he constructs, by a species of "comparative anatomy," a theological system, to which, as *he* says, the sermon under review belongs. In that system he declares that "the sovereignty of God in the salvation of men must of necessity be given up," and he contrasts with it his own system which "has for its object the vindication of the divine supremacy and sovereignty in the salvation of men."[4] But lo! a few minutes afterward he affirms, that in the system to which the sermon belongs, "the acceptance of the sinner is the act of a Sovereign, dispensing with the demands of the law!"[5] and herein it is said to be in *contrast* with his own system, which on a preceding page was said to exalt the divine sovereignty while the other excluded it! And this contrast he makes yet more pointed on p. 330, where he affirms that "according to the one system [*his* own, making *much* of sovereignty] the deliverance of a believer from condemnation is the act of a *judge*; according to the other [*our* own as *he* says, and one which makes *nothing* of sovereignty] it is the act of a Sovereign!" What will this gentleman say next? Those

---

[1] "The atonement has such a relation to the whole moral government of God, as to make it consistent with the honor of his legislative and retributive justice, to save all men, and to make it *essential* to the highest honor of his benevolence or general justice, to renew and save some." Convention Sermon, p. 562.
[2] Biblical Repertory and Princeton Review, Vol. XX. p. 140.
[3] Bib. Rep. Vol. XXIII. p. 323.   [4] Ib. pp. 308, 311.   [5] Ib. p. 312.

three "radical principles," that liberty supposes a natural not a moral power of choosing right when one does choose wrong, and that this natural power limits responsibility, and that moral character is confined to acts, are the principles of our old *Hopkinsian* divines; and did those sturdy men overlook the sovereignty of God? The stale objection to them was, that they thought and talked and preached of nothing else! And the historical fact is, that this precious doctrine was never insisted on with so much force and frequency and safety, as in the pulpits where it has been combined with those three "radical principles." It never was and never can be preached as it ought to be, where the New England doctrine of "natural ability" is not also preached. Ministers and people "shrink from" it, without its complement of human freedom. We thank our Reviewer for so frankly letting out the truth that the system which is not his own *does* exalt the divine sovereignty in the salvation of men; and if his own system does the same, then so far forth both systems agree; and when he denies that the system which is not his own exalts the divine sovereignty, then he contradicts himself, and of course in one of his statements he must agree with us.[1]

Again, the conductors of the Princeton Review, "or which is the same thing, our historian,"[2] assert: "Now we confess ourselves to

---

[1] The Reviewer represents the doctrines logically growing out of the three above-named "radical principles" as *Pelagianism*, and he repeatedly declares that the sermon under review advocates those Pelagian doctrines as literally correct and as essentially the same with the Augustinian! See Bib. Rep. XXIII. pp. 319, 320, 322, 326, 328, etc. Now the truth is, that a disbelief in those three "radical principles" as they are stated in the sermon, is far more logically connected with Baptismal Regeneration, Transubstantiation and other Romish absurdities, than a belief in them is with Pelagianism. We might far more honorably attempt to associate the Reviewer with Romanists, with infidel and Mohammedan fatalists, than he has attempted to associate us with Pelagians. It has long been an artifice of polemic divines to tie up the system of their adversaries with some unpopular scheme, as Mezentius bound his enemies face to face with the bodies of the dead. But it is too late. This whole style of disputing, or rather *nicknaming*, is what we may call, "for want of a better name," *Moral Pelagianism*. We make allowances, however, for our critic, as he evidently writes in a "language of feeling;" see, for example, his assertion on p. 326, that if the author of the Convention Sermon has not represented the Augustinian and Pelagian systems as both true and reconcilable, "he must be set down as either the most unfortunate or the most unintelligible writer of modern times." Hegel is one writer of modern times, and he said in his last days, that only one man in Europe understood him, and that one misunderstood him. To be more unintelligible than Hegel is "unfortunate."

[2] See Bib. Rep. Vol. VI. p. 431, and 92, 93.

be of the number of those who believe, whatever reproach it may bring upon us from a certain quarter, that if the doctrine of imputation be given up, the whole doctrine of original sin must be abandoned; and if this doctrine be relinquished, then the whole doctrine of Redemption must fall, and what may then be left of Christianity, they may contend for that will; but for ourselves we shall be of opinion that what remains will not be worth a serious struggle." On p. 455 of the same volume it is said of President Edwards: "As he had rejected all of imputation but the name, it is no matter of surprise that his followers soon discarded the term itself." And the same Review declares that Hopkins, as well as Dwight, "rejects the doctrine." And yet our Reviewer, doubtless considers that President Edwards, (who has been termed "the prince of American divines,") even at the time of abandoning this fundamental theory, was "in the main" correct, and preserved his essential orthodoxy by his logical inconsistency! And his followers, too, the Smalleys and the Robert Halls, did they make an utter shipwreck of the faith? Or if some of them did, can there be no hope that " the rest, some on boards and some on broken pieces of the ship escaped all safe to land?" Really, our critic must either save himself from pronouncing an absurd censure on those good men by a plea that he has exaggerated the importance of their deviations from his faith, or else he must allow that these mighty logicians were enabled to save their own orthodoxy by their logical blunders. To whichever horn of this dilemma our Reviewer may betake himself, he proves what we assert, that men may be so inconsistent with themselves as to agree on the substance of a creed, while they differ on important articles of it, and may preserve either their essential Calvinism, or their Christian charity by a self-contradiction.

Once more, our Reviewer says that in his own system, (irreconcilable with the sermon which he condemns,) Christ is not regarded " as simply rendering it consistent in God to bestow blessings upon sinners, so that we can come to the Father, of ourselves, with a mere obeisance to the Lord Jesus for having opened the door."! We read in Andrew Fuller's Gospel its own Witness, p. 194, Ed. 1801: "If we say, a way was opened by the death of Christ for the free and consistent exercise of mercy in all the methods which Sovereign wisdom saw fit to adopt, perhaps we shall include every material idea which the Scriptures give us of that important event." And did this meek divine, when he was received home to his Father's house, merely make his obeisance to his once suffering Friend " for having opened the door?" Has this been the superficial, not to say profane piety of the beloved missionaries of the cross who have received the teachings of Andrew Fuller? We see here this great man's view of the Atonement. We have already seen his view of our natural ability. He asserts again and again that we are never personally blamable without "the concurrence of our wills." Our critic confesses that Fuller was a disciple of Edwards, and that the disciples of Edwards renounced the *fundamental* doctrine of imputation. But has it come to this, that Andrew Fuller will be accused of "philosophizing away" the Gospel (if we may be indulged in one of our critic's chosen words)? "Although we judge him in the main to be truly orthodox," says the Princeton Review, Vol. XVIII. pp. 553, 554, "yet there are minor points on which we should take the liberty of differing from him." "We have made up our minds never to contend with any man for agreeing in doctrinal points with Andrew Fuller." The mind of that Review, then, is *made up.* So much is *fixed*. It will never contend with any man merely for his advocating the — "*radical principles of Pelagianism.*"! There is a certain "practical" sermon which has uttered a few words in favor of natural ability, and against an inevitable sin, but — "Nolo contendere, for Andrew Fuller said the same, and said it fifty times where the sermon has said it once." — Not sleep itself gives more occasional rest to a polemic divine, than do his own inconsistencies. "Blessed be the man that first invented sleep," and — contradictions.

Having now shown the particulars and the methods in which *some* men who dispute for opposing systems, may *sometimes* be more harmonious than their creeds, and some creeds may harmonize not in all respects but in "substance of doctrine," let us apply these familiar, not "German," principles, to the doctrines of imputed and of involuntary sin. These doctrines are singled out for various reasons. First, they have been imagined to be *the* fundamental doctrines of the Bible: see p. 606 above. Secondly, it is more difficult to reconcile the New England with the old Calvinism on these subjects than on any other. If we can succeed here, we can succeed everywhere; and above all, on the doctrines of imputed righteousness, atonement, inability. Thirdly, the style of the old Calvinistic writers is here eminently instructive, and the manner in which they often explained it may illustrate the meaning of the phrase "theology of feeling."

On the subject of Imputed Sin let us consider, first, what is the true doctrine in regard to the influence of Adam upon his descendants: Our benevolent Creator formed a constitution, according to which Adam was to be the head of our race, and the state of his posterity was so far suspended upon the conduct of their representative, that they were to be born like him in nature and condition. Because he sinned, they are subjected to manifold pains in this life, and are so constituted and circumstanced that, left to themselves, they will sin and only sin in all their moral acts. Even if they should not do wrong, they would suffer evil in consequence of his transgression; but as they do wrong uniformly, they not only endure pains in this world, but will, unless forgiven, be punished forever in the world to come. As they are condemned to eternal death, in consequence of their own sin, and as they are certain to sin in consequence of their corrupt nature, and as they receive this evil nature in consequence of Adam's disobedience, it may be said by an ellipsis only that they are condemned to eternal punishment as an ultimate result of the first disobedience. The Deity had benevolent reasons for making our character and condition thus dependent on him who was on probation for the race. We know not fully what these reasons are. We presume that they affect kindly the whole intelligent universe. We bow down before the Sovereign Author of this arrangement and say, "Even so, Father, for so it seemed good in thy sight." Here is one theory, and that critic must be in a peculiar state, who sees no essential difference between it and the Pelagian error that Adam's sin did not injure his descendants at all, or at most that it only presented an evil example for their imitation.

But in the second place, let us inquire what is the old theory, antagonistic to the preceding, in regard to Adam's influence upon his descendants. Its first and fundamental principle is, that God is influenced by retributive justice toward men in causing them to be born with an evil and suffering nature. The calamities which attend men at their very first formation are punishments, inflicted by God, acting not as a Sovereign but as a Judge; exercising justice not toward Adam alone, but toward the infants who have not yet seen the light. "For ourselves," says the Princeton Reviewer[1] (in language which when dying he will wish to blot), "we are free to confess that *we instinctively shrink from the idea*, that God in mere sovereignty inflicts the most tremendous evils upon his creatures, *while we bow submissively* at the thought of their being penal inflictions for a sin committed by our natural head and representative, and in violation of a covenant in which by a benevolent appointment of God we were included." In the immediate context he censures those New England divines who represent "*that* as a matter of sovereignty which *we*

---

[1] Bib. Rep. Vol. VI. p. 465.

regard as a matter of justice." And elsewhere he repeatedly condemns the theory which refers the calamities of our race to the "*arbitrary* appointment of God," by which phrase he means the sovereign appointment of Him who afflicts but does not punish us directly for Adam's sin.[1] Rivetus in his learned Treatise on the Protestant doctrine of Imputation, a Treatise which has been highly applauded by the most eminent theologians of modern times, by the Leyden Professors, by the great Turretin himself (Theol. Pars I. 691), has cited many authorities which ascribe the suffering of unborn infants to the exercise of retributive justice upon them.[2] On pp. 800, 807, 808, 809 of Riv. Opp., Tom. III. will be found the following and similar authorities:

Videlius affirms, that "the reason why God imputes the fall of Adam to his posterity, is the *justice* of God, but not his mere will, as the Arminians teach." Gomar says, that the fall of Adam "is ours by a *just* imputation." The synopsis of the four Leyden Professors, teaches, that Adam's "disobedience and fault with its consequent guilt, are *justly* imputed to all his descendants by God the Judge." "The proximate cause of original sin," says Wollebius, "is the guilt of Adam's first sin, in respect of which the punishment of God is most just." "The Catholic Church," says Vossius, "has always decided that the first offence [of our original ancestors] is imputed to all; that is, by the *just judgment* of God, it is *transmitted* to all the children of Adam, as to all its effects." Is this figurative justice, or literal and moral? What does the *argument*, as well as the phraseology, require?

This first and ground-principle being admitted, that Jehovah is influenced by punitive justice toward men, when he afflicts them before and independently of their own individual sin, it follows that they, without having ever acted in their own proper persons, *deserve* to be thus punished. God afflicts them justly; of course according to their proper merits. In Riv. Opp. III. pp. 802, 811, 812, 814, 817, will be found, unless otherwise specified, the following and other like authorities.

Aurelius teaches, that Adam's "first sin makes us *guilty* before God; *then*

---

[1] See, for one instance, Dr. Hodge's Commentary on Rom. 5: 12—21. How does the learned commentator justify himself in describing the divine sovereignty as *arbitrary* and in *shrinking* from it, when he avows that the distinctive aim of his theology is to exalt this doctrine, as we saw on p. 604 above?

[2] We prefer the citations from Rivetus to an equal number of British and American authorities, because the Princeton Review has often appealed to these citations as decisive. They are so. They are the true and the best representatives of the old theory of Imputation. The authors mentioned, were all eminently learned and useful men. The Treatise of Rivetus is entitled: Decretum Synodi Nationalis Ecclesiarum Reformaturum Galliae initio 1645 de imputatione primi peccati omnibus Adami Posteris, cum Ecclesiarum et doctorum pro-

it transfuses into us the corruption which has followed guilt in Adam; from which corruption now really inhering in us, we are *again* guilty by ourselves, and as infected with our own vitiosity, vile, spotted, and hateful to God, *not only* in Adam, or as we are regarded in him as the fountain and root of the human race, but as we are considered by ourselves and of ourselves, now so corrupted." — " The guilt *and* punishment of Adam's sin have passed over to all the posterity of Adam and Eve, Christ excepted." "For the opinion is false of those who teach that only the *punishment* of Adam's sin flowed into us, and not also the *guilt and fault* of that sin. For then we should be punished as undeserving. But the fault *first*, and *then* the punishment, passes over into us, and is cast upon us." Says Altingius, the sin of Adam " is imputed most deservedly, [*meritissime*, to his descendants] because all sinned in him as their stock and root." Crocius teaches, " that the disobedience of Adam is the *meritorious* cause of our condemnation; it is imputed to us, and on account of him, we are constituted sinners." Adam is called " the *meritorious* cause " of our ruin, by Fewbornius also. Speaking of the evils which we receive on account of our progenitor, Martin Bucer says, that these " evils are sent upon no man undeservedly." And even Calvin affirms that, " in his [Adam's] corruption, the entire human race was *deservedly* (merito) vitiated."[1] Was this *ill-desert*, which is the correlate of the Divine justice, a figurative ill-desert, or literal and moral? Reëxamine the phraseology, but mind well the demands of the argument.

This second principle being allowed, that men deserved to be formed with an evil and suffering nature, it follows that some moral offence must have been justly imputed to them before their own personal existence. They merited the evils which enter into their very *make ;* of course they cannot *deserve* such an afflicted nature, unless they be justly chargeable with a sin antecedent to their personal formation. A just God imputes the sin, and therefore he imputes justly. He commits no mistake; (see Haldane on Rom. 5: 12, 29.)

Calvin says often, that " there could have been no condemnation without guilt," and " it is contrary to the equity of the divine government to punish an innocent man for the fault of another;" and that " by Adam's sin we are not condemned by imputation *alone*, as if the punishment of another's fault were exacted of us, but we bear his punishment for this reason, that we are also guilty of fault ; for as our nature is vitiated in him, it is with God bound by the guilt of iniquity." Inst. Lib. II. Cap. VIII. § 19, Cap. I. § 8, and Com. on Rom. 5: 17, 18, 19. On the remark that " the imputation of Christ's righteousness is of grace, but the imputation of sin is of justice," Turretin says, " Grace can, but justice *cannot* ascribe to another that which does not belong to him ; because grace bestows favor upon the undeserving, justice does not inflict punishment except on the deserving. For in the imputation of Adam's sin, the justice of God does not inflict punishment on the undeserving but on the deserving, if not on account of the proper and personal, yet on account of the participated and common desert, which is founded on the natural and federal union existing between us and Adam." Turretin Theol. Elenct. Pars I. p. 587. Zanchius writes: " We therefore affirm that [Adam's] disobedience, although it could not pass over to us [as persons] in act [i. e. personal act], yet did pass over in fault and guilt by imputation, since

---

[1] Cal. Inst., Lib. II. cap. I. 86.

God (imputes) that sin of Adam as the head, to us as the members, and he imputes it most justly." Lubbertus teaches that "when Adam in a total apostasy revolted from God, he became guilty of death, and all his posterity are implicated in the *same* guilt, *no otherwise* than if they had all perpetrated the crime of treason against their Creator." Meisnerus says that "guilt could not be propagated to us [from Adam] unless the *imputation* of (his sinful) act had preceded, seeing that this imputation is the *ground* of that guilt. Wherefore St. Bernard writes that 'Adam's disobedience belonged to another, because we all sinned in *him*; but it also belonged to us, because *we* sinned although in another, and the disobedience was imputed to us by the just although hidden judgment of God.'" N. Hunnius, denying the *bare* imputation of Adam's sin to his descendants, affirms that " at the same time the fault *and* the guilt, together with the *resulting* punishment, are transfused (transfundi) into (his) posterity; nor by any means is the guilt separated from the punishment; therefore we judge it heterodox to believe that one can be a partaker of the punishment who was not also a partaker of the sin." Steegmannus writes that " no one can be exposed to a punishment unless he be guilty of a fault; and it is contrary to the justice of God that he should punish one for sins which another committed; wherefore the Scripture expressly asserts that punishment passed over from the first pair [to us, our ante-natal] guilt intervening." See Riveti Opp. Tom. III. pp. 809, 810, 816, 817, 818, for *most* of the preceding quotations.

Futile is the attempt to evade the preceding argument by the plea, that the word guilt, *reatus*, denotes a mere liableness or exposure to punishment. It has this meaning sometimes, but not in the statement of the Calvinistic *theory*. For, first, we are said to be guilty (*rei*) of Adam's crime *and also* exposed to his punishment; guilty of his fault *and likewise* of his death; exposed *and* obligated (obnoxii et obligati) to suffer his penalty. In the second place, the ambiguous word *reatus* is not the only word used in the argument. Turretin repeatedly affirms that the guilt of Adam's sin " passes over to all" his descendants, and "makes them *deserving* of his punishment" (dignos poena ea). Inst. Theol. Pars I. pp. 678, 690. Lubbertus and others write, "The same guilt [reatum with Adam's] or *which is the same thing*, the same crime [delictum] by which guilt is incurred, is imputed to all his posterity;" Riv. Opp. III. 809. Thirdly, the argument requires that the word guilt, as used in this theory, have its appropriate meaning of moral ill-desert. Substitute the phrase "exposure to punishment" for the word "guilt" in the preceding quotations, and they become mock-logic. " You cannot but perceive," says Augustine to Julian, "how *unjust* it would be to inflict punishment where there is no — [exposure to punishment? That will never do, but] *guilt*," i. e. ill-desert. Does the Westminster Confession speak of the exposure to punishment *whereby* we are exposed to punishment, when it speaks of the guilt *whereby* we are bound over to the wrath of God? If the word *guilt* be thus emptied of its moral import, the reasoning of the Calvinistic divines on this theme must go for little or nothing

This third principle being admitted, that a moral offence has been justly imputed to men before their own personal existence, it follows that they must have sinned before they began to exist personally. If it be punitive justice which sends upon us our first calamities, then we deserve those calamities, and if we deserve them, then we deserve to have a moral offence imputed to us, and if we merit this imputation, then we must have committed that offence. This is the logical sequence, whether it have or have not been adopted by those who admit the premise. Now has it been adopted? It was an old Jewish notion that all his descendants existed in the body of Adam. Tertullian, who believed in the propagation of the soul, asserted that all human beings formed a part of the first man, and sinned in him. Ambrose and some other fathers asserted the same; but Augustine, influenced in part by a Realistic philosophy, in part by the Rabbinical fancies, in part also by the Vulgate's mistranslation of Rom. 5: 12, "*in whom* all have sinned," reduced the theory of our oneness with Adam to a more definite form, and made it a standard doctrine of the church. He repeats in a hundred different ways, that Adam was all men, and all men were Adam; they and he forming one person, he being the entire human race, his act being theirs, and they sinning in him. Wiggers, in his Historical Presentation of Augustinism and Pelagianism, has clearly exhibited this predominating theory. In accordance with it, as it has been more or less modified, we find among the divines of and after the Reformation, unnumbered testimonies to the doctrine that, in the language of the learned Thomas Boston, "Adam's sin is imputed to us *because* it is ours; for God doth not reckon a thing ours which is not so."[1] Our sin precedes the imputation, and the imputation does not precede the sin. If we were regarded as guilty before we had sinned, we should be so regarded by a mistake, but Omniscience cannot err.

Chamierus teaches, that "all men are not only made sinners by Adam, but also are said to have sinned in him, *which is a very different thing*." "It is certain both that all men are constituted *really* unrighteous by Adam, and all the faithful are constituted *really* righteous by Christ." Bishop Davenant says, that "the sin of Adam is imputed to us for our condemnation, *no less* than if it were something formally inhering in us." But, on what principle can Adam's sin be rightly ascribed to us, just as if (aeque, pariter) we had actually committed it, unless we did really sin in him? In explaining Rom. 5: 12, W. Musculus says: "Some interpret the words, 'all have sinned,' to mean, 'all have been ruined, or virtually made sinners, on account of [Adam's] offence.' This is indeed true. But still nothing forbids our understanding by the words, the fact that all men existing in Adam's loins, did sin in his actual sin." Hundreds of times it is said by the standard Calvinistic writ-

---

[1] Boston's Body of Divinity, Vol. I. pp. 302, 303, 322, etc.

ers, "We were in Adam's loins when he sinned," "we sinned while we were in his loins," "we sinned with him and in him," "the whole race were deposited in him," "God placed us all in his body as a mass," "all his posterity sinned when he sinned, with him and by him, for all were comprehended in him." The following expression of John Junius has been generally credited, and is but one specimen of a large class: "In the sum of the matter, all the Reformed Churches agree, and teach with unanimous consent, agreeably to the sacred Scriptures and the general opinion of antiquity, that the sin of Adam was not a personal one, but was the sin of the whole human race, since this race was included in his loins, and it sinned in him the first parent of all, and the root of the entire human family." A volume might be filled with the repetitions of the following argument of Occitanus: "As the Levites who were to descend from Abraham, paid tithes in the person of their father, (as the Apostle teaches in Heb. 7: 9,) although they ought to receive tithes afterwards from their brethren; so likewise men who ought by natural generation to descend from Adam, were made guilty in the loins of their father, and were condemned to suffer the punishment of his disobedience; for his fall was the general fall of men who in the loss sustained by their ancestor, lost all the riches with which they ought (debuissent) to have been endowed." Meisnerus teaches, that "the sin of Adam was not personal, but universal, and was the act of the entire race, which existed in him as in a common stock, and therefore sinned at the same time with him, and died" (or was condemned). Martin Bucer teaches that infants are rightly represented as having sinned, and "since on account of that fault of disobedience which they all committed in Adam, they are born with such profound ignorance that they cannot understand the precepts of God their Maker, and with such rebellion of nature that they all resist these precepts; by the same law of obedience proposed not so much to Adam the father of the human race as to the whole race itself, they are justly condemned." Nothing can be plainer than the words of Turretin, (Inst. Theol. Pars I. p. 680), speaking of the common punishments which flow to us as well as to Adam from the first sin,—They "cannot justly be inflicted, unless there be supposed a common law and a common guilt; for if the punishment of the broken covenant be extended to all, the covenant also and the law ought to extend to all." The remark of Zanchius is often repeated, that "the command, together with its penalty, was not addressed to the person of Adam alone, but to the whole human family." "As God," says Francis Junius, "in the order of his creation placed the whole human race in Adam by nature, so in the order of his justice, he said to the whole human race in Adam, (in whom we sinned,) In the day thou eatest thereof, thou shalt surely die." And not only did all men transgress the law enforced upon them in our first parent, but also all men transgressed it voluntarily in him." This peculiar metaphysics was pushed along in a straight line; and it is often said that "all men lost their freedom by sinning, *of their own accord*, in Adam. (See the fifth subdivision of the following, the second head.) Some excellent divines have gone so far as to teach not only that we willed to eat the forbidden fruit, but even had natural power to avoid willing it! Our ante-natal sin is described in numerous other forms. It is affirmed in scores of instances, that all men must have participated in the first offence, because "a just participation in the punishment of that sin, presupposes a participation in the sin itself." Thus, the proof of the doctrine accompanies the statement of it. "Original sin, as well in Adam as in his posterity," we are told by Silesius, "includes these three deadly evils, the actual fault, legal guilt, or penalty of death, and the depravation or deformity of nature. For these meet together around the first sin in the parent and in his posterity; with this difference only, that

Adam sinning, was the *principal* agent committing the fault, deserving the penalty, casting off the image of God, and corrupting himself, [while] all these belong to his posterity, by *participation*,[1] *imputation*, and generation from a corrupted parent." " In the mass, they (his posterity) committed the same sin, and *therefore* it is imputed to all." For, says Fewbornius, " it is repugnant to the Divine *justice*, that any one should be a partaker in another's punishment, without a participation (κοινωνία) in that other's fault," and then he proceeds to show, that if Adam's posterity did not partake of his sin, they would not be ill-deserving, and if not ill-deserving, they could not be equitably punished. " *By what right*," says Scultetus, " are the descendants punished for the sin of their ancestors? Paul answers, ' Because all sinned in the first parents.'" (See Riveti Opp., Tom. III. pp. 799, 800, 804–8, 810–12, 814–17.) In like manner, the great Quenstedt (Theol. Didac., Pars II. p. 53) declares that " not only the first parents were the subjects of the first sin, but also all of their descendants," and he also says, that " not by a bare imputation, nor at all events by imitation, are we constituted sinners by Adam's crime, but also by the imputation of real guilt, and by propagation of natural depravity, and by participation in actual fault. And therefore the proximate cause why, the first man sinning, all his posterity have sinned, is the existence of the whole human species in the person of the first man." This is the reason why " God imputes the sin of Adam to them, most justly, for their condemnation." Our own President Edwards (Works II. p. 544, 546, 558, etc.) affirms, that Adam and all his posterity constituted " as it were, one complex person, or one moral whole." " And therefore the sin of the apostasy is not theirs, merely because God imputes it to them, but it is truly and properly theirs, and on that ground God imputes it to them." He appeals to Stapfer, who teaches that " the sin of the posterity, on account of their consent, and the moral view in which they are to be taken, is the same with the sin of Adam, not only in kind, but in number; therefore, the sin of Adam is rightly imputed to his posterity." Stapfer also affirms that the " chief divines " are of the same mind with him.

Let not the reader feel *bewildered* by this recital, for the theory which he is considering is often called " the *simplicity* of the faith," and all doubts concerning it are stigmatized as the results of " philosophizing," and as signs of a propensity " *obliquè pelagianizere*." Suffer then a word or two of further explanation.

We shall always misinterpret the old authors, unless we be mindful of the distinction between the personal existence of men as individuals, and their common existence in their progenitor. Thus many authors who contend for our real ill-desert on account of Adam's sin, do yet insist that we are thus ill-deserving not "personally," but only in our "common" union with him, not "*individually*" but "originally," not "formally" but by a "real imputation," not "separately" but "virtually," "potentially," "radically," "seminally," "hereditarily," etc. It is as *real* an ill-desert as if it were a separate one. In one respect the first sin is properly our own (cujusque est proprium); in a dif-

---

[1] The partaker, the accomplice, the accessory, is thought to be as really culpable as the primary offender.

ferent respect it is properly the sin of another person. In one view it is a foreign sin; in a different view it is ours. In one aspect it belongs to Adam alone; in another aspect it belongs to us as really as to him. It is not common to others in such a sense that it is not our own, nor is it our own in such a sense that it is not common to others. Therefore, says Lansbergius, "we are not guilty on account of a sin in which we have no participation (alienum), but on account of a sin which is our own (proprium) committed while we were in Adam's loins," etc. When some of the old Calvinists assert, therefore, that we could not have actually sinned thousands of years before our birth, they mean that we could not then have sinned in our distinct personality; but they do not mean that we were then free from fault; and the demerit which existed in us as parts of Adam, is now "communicated," "propagated," "transferred" to us as separate individuals. See Riveti, Opp. Tom. III. pp. 807, 808, 809, 815, etc. And Turretin says, in repeated instances, that the covenant in which we were involved with Adam, was a "moral" covenant, that Adam's sin was "morally" communicated to us, that his sinful choice although not ours personally, was ours "morally."[1] The whole dispensation with regard to the fall is a moral one. The judgment of God is a moral judgment. We *need* not suppose, then, that Turretin contradicts himself when he affirms, that our sin in Adam was not a moral one, i. e. in the sense of its being blameworthy in our own *persons*, just as it was not voluntary in the sense of its being our own individual, separate volition.[2]

Here, now, is the old theory of imputation; and in the third place let us inquire how it can be reconciled with the doctrine which we have previously (see pp. 607, 608, above) described as the true one. If we regard the old theory as expressed in literal terms, it cannot be harmonized with the truth. No one ever pretended that it could be. It is false, belonging neither to the theology of a sound intellect, nor to that of a right heart. But still, many who contend for this theoretic error have *substantially*, at least in their practical meditations, the same general faith with those who receive the pure truth, just as two men may have substantially the same nature, although one has, and the other has not, a horn growing out of his head.

But, this is not all; for, in the first place, the ground-principle which sustains this theory of our literal ill-desert for Adam's sin, is at times abandoned by the advocates of it, and the ground-principle

---

[1] Theol. Inst. Pars I. pp. 678, 679, 686, 689, 690.   [2] Ib. p. 716.

of the opposite doctrine is at times sanctioned by them. Their self-contradiction weakens the influence of their theory. In fact, their theory, *so far forth as it is contradicted*, is the same with its opposite. Its spirit is at last exchanged for that of its antagonist. Thus, when the question is put, how does God exercise retributive justice rather than sovereignty toward us, in causing us to suffer for a crime, long since consummated in Eden, we are often told that God imputed this crime to us *partly* because we are and were "of one blood" with Adam, i. e. we have and have had a "natural union" with him, but *principally* because God "willed" to form a covenant with Adam, according to which, the first man was to act for all his descendants, and his sin was to become theirs.[1] In part, and in *chief* part, then, his sin is imputed to us, because we were comprehended in the covenant which God made with Adam before the fall. Some divines go further still, and suppose this covenant to be the *whole* ground of the imputation. Adam represented us, and so we sinned in him, not naturally, but "representatively." Did we at that time deserve to be thus exposed to ruin? Did we really merit our subjection to the peril (how great, the Deity well knew) of that fall? Had we sinned in Adam *before* his sin? Surely this covenant was made not by retributive justice toward us, but by sovereign benevolence toward the universe. It constituted (according to the theory as now modified) a main reason for the justice of ascribing to us that ancient crime, and making us ill-deserving on account of it. Now, of course, the reason or ground for this justice, precedes and is distinct from the justice itself. It is a reason of sovereignty preparing the way for a strict retribution. That Turretin here supposed it to be a sovereign arrangement, is obvious from his pleading the authority of Calvin, who says, as often elsewhere: "Whence is it that the fall of Adam involves without remedy so many nations with their infant children in eternal death, unless because it so seemed good to Jehovah? Decretum quidem horribile fateor."[2] This general ruin occurred, says Calvin on Job xiv, "because we were all included in his [Adam's] person by the *will* of God." Even the same gentleman who 'shrinks from the idea that God in mere sovereignty inflicts the most tremendous evils upon us,' does yet in the same breath confess that God inflicts these evils by virtue of a "covenant in which by a benevolent appointment of God we were included."[3] This benevolent appointment is a sovereign appointment; for all our Father's sovereignty is

---

[1] Turretini Inst. Theol., Pars I. pp. 678, 679.
[2] Cal. Inst., Lib. II. Cap. XXIII. § 7.   [3] Bib. Repertory, Vol. VI. p. 465.

benevolence, and all his specific benevolence is sovereignty. And so the Reviewer comes at the end of a sentence, to the same principle from which he recoiled at the beginning. Our calamities hang suspended on the sovereign purpose of Heaven, we say, directly; he says, indirectly; we say, without any intervening links; he says, with the intermediate links of imputation, guilt, etc. We say that infants are exposed to their first calamities, by the sovereign constitution of their Maker. The Reviewer says, that this would be unjust, but infants must first be charged with a sin which they never personally committed! They cannot be treated justly unless accused of a crime which was perpetrated in a place which they never saw, and at a time which preceded the birth of their first-born ancestor! We then ask, why are they so accused? Because they were comprehended in the covenant with Adam, says the Reviewer. But we press the question, why were they thus comprehended? Because they deserved to be? Here the Reviewer is compelled to admit the distinctive principle of the New England theology, and to abandon the distinctive principle of his own; and the only dispute is, whether we shall come a few minutes sooner or a few minutes later to the same thing, i. e. to the Divine Sovereignty. So far forth, then, he has united the two schemes, by dismissing the genetic principle of his favorite one. Now, we might ask, what kind of ill-desert is that which is occasioned within us by a sovereign arrangement, irrespectively of our personal fault? We can understand how a wise parent may afflict us, without our antecedent misdemeanor; but to suppose that he subjects us to a demerit which precedes all personal disobedience, is one of the many contradictions involved in this theory, which, however, is saved by its contradictions.[1]

Nor is this all; for in the second place, the doctrine that we are literally and morally responsible for Adam's sin is sometimes altogether explained away by men who contend for it at other times. Not only practical Christians, but even polemic divines, who insist upon the justice of imputing to us the sin of Paradise, are often found to have forgotten their artificial theory, and to interpret its phrases as the mere language of emotion. It is natural for us, creatures of feeling, to use such language on so great a theme. Intent upon the

---

[1] It is an interesting fact that some European divines, staggering under their favorite doctrine of a literal imputation, have pronounced it utterly impossible to conjecture how or why the Deity has made such an imputation, and have *avowedly* resolved the whole into the mystery of a mere sovereign act, without any allusion to our sinning in Adam — naturally or representatively.

thought of our intimate connection with Adam, we are unsatisfied with calm words, and we exclaim "his blood flows in our veins and so our blood once formed a part of his body; his nature has been drawn forth into ours and so our nature was once involved in his; we were actually in his loins of old; what he did we did; we sinned in him, and fell with him in his first transgression." And what do we mean by these intense utterances? Nothing more than that Adam's offence was the reason why our Sovereign so made us and so placed us, as to cause the certainty of our suffering evil, and of our uniform sinful preferences. In order to express with emphasis the truth that we not only imitate our first progenitor in disobeying God, but likewise that on account of his apostasy, we are fashioned so that we sin and are circumstanced so that we suffer, we are sometimes incited to say, careless of the peril attending such words, "God imputes to us the transgression of Adam; his anger continues to burn against us for it." Feeling the dreadfulness of the woes to which it has exposed us, we confess that "we are guilty of the original crime." Sensitive to the fitness of the arrangement by which we are doomed to these evils as the insignia of the hatefulness of that crime, some men may venture in certain peculiar moods, upon the strong expressions, "We were ill-deserving in that first sin; we are justly afflicted for it." These afflictions illustrate so vividly the regard of Jehovah for his law that we call them by the forcible word, *punishment*. And thus we go on from strength to strength, until some scholastic philosopher becomes "*bewildered*," and mistakes these vehement expressions of feeling for the accurate statements of science. Metamorphosing these poetical and eloquent utterances into the literal language of the schools, he constructs his severe system: "We are justly punished for Adam's sin; therefore we were ill-deserving in it; therefore we committed it."

Now we maintain that while it is natural for a good man to use these bold metaphors sometimes in the *enforcement* of truth, he is unable to persevere in uniformly employing them as literal phrases. A theorist may urge himself onward to such a use, while fabricating or defending an artificial creed; but tired nature will give out, and in his unguarded moments he will drop his forced logic. His conscience may be overborne by the theory during his hours of systemmaking, but it will right itself in his hours of leisure and will reassert the truth. While, then, we concede that many theologians have believed that our moral guilt for the Paradisaical crime is a legitimate inference from our suffering on account of it, we still maintain that these theologians have often abandoned this belief in their hours of clearer vision, and of religious as distinct from controversial interest. Not seldom have they lost their hold of it in their controversies even. As a theory, it is too absurd to be retained in the mind without an unnatural effort, and such an effort must be intermittent. Accordingly, in all their theological treatises, we detect the frequent signs of a "falling away." Expelled nature forces herself back. While they framed a logical theory on the strict import of justice, ill-desert and punishment, they often exchanged this import during their practical reflections, for a looser meaning; justice being a sense of *fitness*, guilt and ill-desert being a *fit* exposure to evil;[1] and punishment being the fit evil, and thus they often rested in that wise and deep scheme of truth which, since thier time, has been defended by the ablest of our New England divines.

And now, in defiance of *Blair's Rhetoric*, or, as the Reviewer says (in the language of feeling), "the Scotch Principal's dull lectures," we forewarn our readers that we are going to be interesting. Our critic says that the author whom he condemns, "has undertaken a great work" in attempting to reconcile opposing sects and creeds, and' he adds: "when we reflect on what is necessarily even thqugh unconsciously [?] assumed in this attempt, when we raise our eyes to the height to which it is necessary the author should ascend before all these things could appear alike to him, we are bewildered."[2] But so far as this "fundamental" doctrine of imputation is concerned we see no valid reason why our critic should be thus *bewildered*. For he himself goes further than we go in *"explaining away"* the ancient creeds. While we affirm that *often* the standard Calvinistic divines disown the doctrine of our proper ill-desert for the first sin, he affirms that they never believed the doctrine; that in their writings the sin of Adam "is never said to be in us (truly sin) *verè peccatum;*" the guilt of it is not said to arise "out of the moral character" of men; it is not *moral* guilt; it is not even so much as a *fit* exposure to punishment, but a mere exposure to it; the phrases, "we sinned in Adam," "were sinners in him," were "ill-deserving," have "demerit,"[3] etc., do not imply our "moral pollution," express nothing with regard to

---

[1] Often, at least, the word guilt meant not a mere exposure to evil, but a *fit* exposure.

[2] Bib. Repertory, Vol. XXIII. p. 526.

[3] One of these phrases is "*ought*," "*ought* not," as we have seen above. Of course, if the Reviewer explains all these words as figurative, he will give the same explanations of imputed righteousness, etc.

our "moral turpitude." Notwithstanding all that we have heard about the sin of Adam being "transfused," "transferred," "passing over," being "communicated to us," he denies that Calvinists, as a class, have ever believed in "a transfer of moral character." And as to our oneness with Adam, which formerly was so "mystical" and "mysterious," the Reviewer sweeps away all the mystery of it, and says that it is and was all a figure of speech. "We were in Adam," he remarks, "as Levi was in Abraham. Was this literally?"—"We 'were in him as branches in a root,' 'as the members are in the head.' Well, what does this mean? Literal oneness? Surely not. Does every writer who speaks of a father as the root of his family, hold to the idea of a 'literal oneness' between them? You may make as little or as much as you please out of such figurative expressions taken by themselves."[1] Now Turretin, who according to our Reviewer, "is universally regarded as having adhered strictly to the common Calvinistic system," denies that the words in Heb. 7:9 "intimate a tropical and figurative thing, as if Levi were said to have been tithed only in a figure and not properly in Abraham."[2] Here then is a figurative ill-desert[3] and a figurative sin, which is in plain truth (verè) no sin at all, the punishment for it therefore cannot be a moral, but must be a figurative punishment; and the justice which inflicts it cannot be a moral, but must be a figurative justice; and that moral attribute of God which is justice only by a metaphor, must be his sovereign benevolence. So far as the "substance of doctrine" is concerned, the Reviewer admits all that we can ask of him. He denies all that we deny. He avows every article of the Pelagianism which he has discovered in the Convention sermon in regard to imputed guilt. If that sermon "eviscerates" the ancient standards, its Reviewer does so yet more fatally. Very true; he insists that Adam's sin is ours, but still not "personally or properly;" that it is imputed to us, but not so as to be a "ground of remorse."[4] In what way then is the first sin imputed to us? Only in this way; "we are regarded and treated as sinners" on account of it, while it never affects our "moral character."[5] But how are we, while not sinners, regarded as sinners by him who regards all men precisely as they

---

[1] Bib. Repertory, VII. p. 436, For the preceding references, see pages 413, 414, 415, 422, 424, 426, 434, 436—438, etc., and Dr. Hodge on Rom. 5: 12, sq.

[2] Turret. Theol. Pars I. p. 687.

[3] We are not responsible for the word *figurative*, in this connection. The Reviewer has forced it upon us. See Convention Sermon, pp. 8, 41, 2d Pamph. Ed.

[4] Dr. Hodge's Com. on Rom. p. 221, 1st Ed. [5] Ibid. p. 225.

are? The Reviewer modifies again, and says that "*nothing more* is meant by the imputation of sin than to cause one man to bear the iniquity [i. e. the punishment] of another.[1] But how are we punished for that primal transgression? In any way which implies that we are blamed for it by the Deity? No. Or condemned by our own conscience? No. Are we punished in the "most rigid and proper meaning" of the term? No. In what sense then? We are made to suffer evil "by a Judge, in execution of a sentence, and with a view to support the authority of the law."[2] But *was* He literally the moral judge of us, while we were only figuratively in existence? Was it literally a moral sentence, addressed to us centuries before we had any moral desert? Was it a moral law literally applied to us as moral beings, while we were moral beings only by a bold figure of speech? If the Reviewer regards all this as literal, he contradicts himself. Besides, *when* was this punishment inflicted upon us, irrespectively of our own sin? At a period preceding our personal life; for, says Dr. Hodge, " eternal misery is [not] inflicted on any man for the sin of Adam, irrespective of inherent depravity or actual transgression." That first "sin was the ground of the loss of the divine favor, the withholding of divine influence, and the *consequent* corruption of our nature."[3] And when does he suppose that this corruption of our nature begins? With the very beginning of that nature itself. The punishment therefore must be logically, if not chronologically, antecedent to this beginning, for our corruption is *consequent* to the punishment. But how can one be punished in the order of nature before one's existence? And what kind of a *sin* is

---

[1] Bib. Repertory, Vol. VI. pp. 459, 462, 472. Hodge's Com. on Rom., First Ed. p. 226, etc.

[2] Bib. Repertory, VII. p. 442. The dispute turns chiefly on this word, punishment, and is *merely* verbal. We suppose the punishment which God inflicts to be moral, and to imply the ill-desert of the person punished. The old writers often used the word loosely to denote any evil inflicted by God for the purpose of improving the character of his subjects, or of sustaining the honor of his law. Thus Calvin says that " creation bears part of the punishment deserved by man," Inst. Lib. II. Cap. I. § 5. And again, Com. on Rom. 8: 21, "All created things in themselves blameless, both on earth and in the visible heaven, undergo punishment for our sins; for it has not happened through their own fault that they are liable to corruption." Can we doubt that men are punished for Adam's crime, and that Christ was punished for ours, when the term is used with this loose signification? The Hopkinsians will agree with the Calvinists, except on the propriety of using an important word with so much looseness in a didactic treatise; for in this vague sense God punishes as a Sovereign.

[3] Hodge's Com. on Romans, First Ed. p. 229.

that which will not be followed by the second death, unless some *other* sin be added? It is a putative punishment, as the sin which occasions it is a putative sin. It is no proper punishment at all. The whole is a metaphorical, and in some states of mind an interesting mode of expressing the solemn truth, that God as a Sovereign has connected our destiny with Adam's character. We agree with our Reviewer, so far forth as he advocates the distinctive theology of New England. Nothing but a reverence for our mother tongue prevents us from saying with him, what we believe as "substantially" as he does: "That there is a very just and proper (?) sense in which we should *repent* of the sin of Adam we readily admit; and are perfectly aware that old writers insist much upon the duty. Not, however, on the principle that his sin is personally ours, or that its moral turpitude is transferred from him to us; but on the principle that a child is *humbled* and *grieved* at the misconduct of a father."[1] Now this use of humility for penitence, of grieving for repenting, is intensely figurative; it belongs to the theology of the heart, and in a didactic treatise would be condemned by Dr. Blair.

We do not mean to imply, that we always find our Reviewer in agreement with ourselves, or with himself. For, like other men, circumvented with technical, especially when figurative, terms, he often becomes entangled in them, so as to plunge into an error like that of our moral guilt for sinning before the flood. He has a sliding scale of definitions, down which he lapses from the high Calvinism of other times, into the biblical Calvinism of New England. At least five meanings of imputation are given by him. First, we find that manly one by which imputation is the antecedent ground of our being regarded and treated otherwise than we are in ourselves. This is Dr. Owen's view; and according to it, the imputation includes two things, the "grant or donation of a property," and then the consequent "dealing with us according unto that which is so made ours."[2] Thus, our Reviewer says, "His [Christ's] merit is so given, reckoned, or imputed to them, that they are regarded and treated as right-

---

[1] Bib. Repertory, Vol. VII. pp. 460, 461. This article is universally imputed to our Reviewer.

[2] Owen's Works. Vol. XI. p. 207, etc. It is a great mistake of modern writers to suppose that, according to the old standards, imputation of holiness or sin, is merely the regarding and treating of men as if they were holy or sinful. Imputation involves the *ground* of their being thus regarded and treated. See Rivet Opp., Tom. III. pp. 799, 806, 812-16, etc.; also Gill's Body of Divinity, Vol. I. p. 522, and Andrew Fuller's Works, Vol. III. p. 722. "To bear the punishment of sin, is not the same as to have sinned" in Adam, says Bucer.

eous."[1] To be so regarded and treated, *follows* the imputation. But, secondly, we find that this grant or donation is dropped, and imputation comes to mean merely the result, the regarding and treating us otherwise than we are in ourselves.[2] But, thirdly, even this is soon modified, and the imputation of the first sin means the regarding us sinful, *in such a way*, or *so far forth*, as to treat us like sinners.[3] Still, fourthly, we have a new amendment, and this imputation is "nothing more nor less" than for one man to bear the iniquity [i. e. the punishment] of another."[4] And then, fifthly, we learn that the word punishment is not used here in its "most strict and rigid" meaning, and does not imply any moral demerit in us.[5] Now, we avow before the wide world our hearty belief that our ancestor's crime is *so* communicated to us, that we are regarded and treated as sinners on account of it; by all which we mean simply that we are regarded and treated as sinners for it; by which we mean that we are regarded sinful only so far as to be treated like sinners; by which we mean no more than that we are punished for it; by which we mean, *at length*, that we are not punished in the most proper sense, but are merely afflicted with evils which are designed by our Judge to vindicate the sanctity of the law broken, not by ourselves, but by Adam. And thus, after so long a time, we come out of this forest of improper terms, venerable for its shade, and *bewildering* by its mazes, into the clear and open sunshine, where both the Reviewer and the author meet and walk in the same straight path of New England theology. When out of the underbrush of that forest, neither of them looks like a *Pelagian*. That word belongs to *a* "language of feeling." Both of them adopt "for substance" the teachings of Emmons and Dwight in regard to this theme. Soon after that amiable and excellent divine had gone home to his kindred in the skies, the Princeton Review contained an elaborate criticism upon "old Dr. Emmons," as it denominated the venerable saint, and while it charged him with "*confusion* of ideas," and of course with "Pelagianism," it was compelled to acknowledge for a time that his doctrine concerning our relation to Adam, contains "*the very thing* which the old Calvinists called the imputation of Adam's sin," and that "it is *really nothing*

---

[1] Bib. Repertory, Vol. XVII. p. 87. Dr. Hodge on Rom., p. 228, first ed

[2] Dr. Hodge on Rom., p. 221, etc..

[3] Dr. Hodge on Rom., p. 226. "For if the word [impute] means so to ascribe an action to a man as to treat him as the author of it."

[4] Bib. Repertory, Vol. VI. p. 459.   [5] Bib. Repertory, Vol. VI. p. 441.

short of the imputation of his first sin."[1] Now that doctrine of Emmons is in essence the same which we have advocated in this discussion, (Bib. Sac. VIII. pp. 174–5); but our doctrine is Pelagianism according to the Princeton Review, and therefore, according to the same authority, Pelagianism "*is nothing short of*" Augustinism on this "fundamental" doctrine, and contains "the *very thing* which the old Calvinists *meant;*" and hence our Reviewer lapses in one point when he says of our own assertions: "It is now asserted, for the *first* time, so far as we know, *since the world began*, that these two modes of representation [the Augustinian and Pelagian] mean the same thing."[2] When *did* the world begin? Eight years before the sermon was conceived to which that assertion has been falsely imputed, the Princeton Review asserted, (and *not* for the first time, *so far as we know*), that the doctrine which is now termed Pelagian means "nothing short" of the doctrine which is now termed Calvinistic. For ourselves we have uniformly believed that Pelagianism differs in essence from theories like those of Dwight and Spring, and that while the old Calvinists have, as practical Christians, been satisfied with such theories, they have as metaphysicians demanded a different scheme.

The learned Reviewer is in a trilemma. Either he believes that the old Calvinists, acting as logicians and as practical men, said what they meant in literal terms; in which case he contradicts himself; or, secondly, he believes, that as logicians, they said literally what they meant, and as practical men, they merged their language into bold figures; in which case he agrees with the proscribed sermon, and this will never do; or, thirdly, he believes, that both as logicians and as practical men, they used the language of their creeds as intensely figurative; in which case, he is as much more latitudinarian than the sermon, as he supposes the sermon to be more latitudinarian than the system of Dr. Gill. And he does in fact go beyond that discourse in thus "philosophizing away" the ancient standards. For, according to his theory, we must conceive of the giants of Calvinism as arguing, in their philosophical treatises, that we cannot be rightly punished unless we be previously exposed to punishment, that the liability to an infliction secures the justness of that infliction, that we

---

[1] See Bib. Repertory, XIV. pp. 543, 544. That Review also avers that Dr. Emmons and all the New Divinity men "not only reject the doctrine, but speak of it in the same contemptuous manner as did the Pelagians," p. 542. This is only one specimen of the self-contradictions into which a "figurative theology" winds its course. [2] Bib. Repertory, XXIII. 128.

should not have been thus "exposed to punishment," i. e. guilty, unless we had "sinned in Adam;" or, which is the same thing, unless we had been "treated as sinners;" or, which is the same thing, unless we had been punished! And did the sturdy Calvinism of the schools swing thus backward and forward in an incessant motion, without progress? Did those stern metaphysicians *think* that they were inferring man's exposure to punishment, i. e. his guilt, from the fact that man was punished, i. e. was treated as a sinner?[1] If so, then we have a new proof of the tendency of bold metaphors to "*bewilder*" a theorist? In his Commentary on Romans 5: 12, "Wherefore as by one man," etc., Dr. Hodge has exhibited what he regards as the metaphysical, as well as the practical, view of those dialectical writers. The word "sin," in the first phrase, "*by one man sin entered into the world,*" means imputed sin, and thus the entire phrase means, "On his [Adam's] account all men are regarded and treated as sinners!"[2] The word "death" in the phrase, "*and death by sin,*" means "the penalty of the law, or the evils threatened as the punishment of sin."[3] "Of course, as sin means imputed sin, this second phrase means: Because all men are regarded and treated as sinners, i. e. punished, therefore all men are exposed to "the penalty of the law, or the evils threatened as the punishment of sin." The third phrase, "*and so death passed upon all men,*" means, "All men became exposed to penal evils, or the penalty due to sin."[4] The fourth phrase, "*for that all have sinned,*" means, "All men are regarded and treated as sinners!"[5] Combining, then, the four phrases, we have the following argument: On account of one man, all men are regarded and punished as sinners; and because they are regarded and punished as sinners, they are subjected to punishment; and *so* all men become exposed to punishment, because all men are regarded and punished as sinners! Now, *if this be* the didactic Calvinism of the creeds, can we blame the New England writers for aiming to clear up the *phraseology* of those creeds? And can we avoid the necessity of admitting, that a calm intellect would never have devised such a metaphorical style for repeating over and over the same idea, and also that "the well schooled divine *may*, although he seldom *does*, escape the confusing ('bewildering') influence of this ambiguous nomenclature?" (Conv. Serm., p. 567.) *Is it not true* by our Reviewer's

---

[1] Even in their practical meditations, they did not always *thus* denude their argument of meaning, but used justice, etc., for fitness, etc. See pp. 618, 621, above.
[2] Com. on Rom, First ed. pp. 180, 190.   [3] Ib., pp. 180, 190.
[4] Ib., p. 181.   [5] Ib., p. 183.

own showing, that if men be over-charmed with favorite words, they will see Pelagianism where these words are missed, and if they only hear the grateful sounds they will care too little for the "*substance* of doctrine, and will be sometimes led to nullify the internal signs of inspiration, by emasculating the vigorous thought which it embodies? The plain fact is, that our Reviewer does not often venture to expose the old theory of imputation; nor even to state the biblical truth in the clear language of Mr. Stuart and Mr. Barnes, and he therefore hides the doctrine within a *nest* of technical terms. He uses the ancient phraseology, and denudes it of its theoretic meaning; he tacitly yields to the objections of New England divines, but like the ancient buyer, he cries, "it is naught, it is naught," and hurls at these divines the hard epithets of Neology, Rationalism, Röhr, and especially Pelagius; and all this, while he likens himself to "a man *behind* the walls of Gibraltar, or of Ehrenbreitstein." Bib. Repertory, XXIII. p. 319.

Having now seen that the old writers, in their better hours, have been wont to give up their doctrine of a literally imputed sin, let us pass to the doctrine of involuntary sin. This includes the second and third parts of original sin, as anciently defined. The three parts were, first, our participation in Adam's offence; secondly, our involuntary want of original righteousness, and thirdly, our involuntary depravation of nature, (see pp. 609—614 above). These last two divisions constitute original sin in its more recent and restricted meaning. They are sometimes called inherent and passive, in distinction from active and imputed transgression.

In the first place, let us inquire, What is the true doctrine with regard to the nature of sin? Both Inspiration and common sense reply: Sin is that which in and of itself, apart from its causes and results, deserves to be condemned by the conscience, to be repented of, to receive the eternal punishment inflicted by the Judge at the last day; and it consists in the choice or preference of that which the conscience requires us to refuse, or in the voluntary refusal of that which the conscience requires us to prefer.—When it is said that sin is the transgression of the law, the objector replies that sin lies deeper than in an outward, overt act. Very true, it involves the covert, deep preference for a wrong outward act. But the objector adds, it lies deeper still; not in the executive volition but in the inclination, disposition, propensity to choose wrong. Very true. It does not lie in the executive volition, but in the inclination, disposition, propensity to choose wrong, provided that these words be used, as they often are, to denote a generic choice or preference, lying deeper than the specific choices. The objector misrepresents this doctrine, when he supposes that it confines moral agency to the individual, subordinate preferences, or, still worse, to the imperative volitions. By no means. It asserts that sin consists in all preferences which the conscience condemns, and especially in those ultimate governing, predominating preferences which are often termed, loosely however, inclination, disposition, propensity. Every choice which the conscience disapproves, deserves eternal punishment, and it only is sin. But the objector replies, Sin goes deeper still; it belongs to the *man* who sins, and not to his acts alone. Just so; for acts *alone* cannot be conceived of. An act of a man is the man himself acting, just as "a form of theology is theology in a certain form." This is the distinctive New England divinity.

The fact that all men previously to Regeneration do sin and only sin in all their moral acts, implies, what our consciousness also teaches, that there is, lying back of our sinful choices and occasioning them, a disordered state of the sensibilities, or an involuntary corruption.[1] Part of this is called by Storr, Flatt, Reinhard and many others, "a preponderance of the propensities of our nature for the objects and pleasures of sense." The whole of it is called by Turretin, Calvin, and others, "vitiosity," "the depravation of nature formerly good and pure," "natural, native, hereditary depravity," the "disorder of nature," the insubordination of the lower to the higher nature, the disease, sickness of the soul, *lues, fomes, ἀταξία*, etc. A man is sinful in harboring, indulging, complying with his evil tendencies, but he is not sinful for the mere fact of their natural existence, of their existence antecedent to his choice. "Mankind are not themselves to be blamed for being born with a depraved nature."[2] Still this nature is so odious in itself and so pernicious in its influence, that our emotions often prompt us to stigmatize it as itself sin.[3] It is wholesome to form this con-

---

[1] Our critic has more than once confounded this truth with the Pelagian error, that all men have a nature precisely like that of Adam before he sinned! He also declares, p. 311, that in logical accordance with the sermon under review, Regeneration "cannot be the production of a new nature," but must "consist in some act of the soul." ! A moment's reflection will convince him, that according to that sermon, the nature inclining to more sin is changed in regeneration into a nature inclining to holiness, and that by the omnipotence of the regenerating Spirit.

[2] Storr and Flatt, B. III. § 57.

[3] "That inherent depravity is truly and properly sin, is a different intellectual

ception at certain times, even more so than to conceive of corporeal acts as themselves blamable, or of a cathedral or a chalice at the altar, or a baptismal font as themselves holy.—But these effusions of a pious heart are congealed by some into the stiff and literal expressions of a theory unlike the preceding. Therefore,

We will, in the second place, inquire, What is the theory of passive, inherent, involuntary sin. Our Reviewer frankly defines this doctrine, when he says, that we have "an innate, hereditary sinful corruption of nature;" that we have derived from Adam "a nature not merely diseased, weakened or predisposed to evil, but which is 'itself' as well as 'all the motions thereof truly and properly sin.'"[1] Having already admitted that many theologians have believed in our moral guilt for the crime of Adam, we also admit that some have believed in our moral guilt for the very *make* of our souls. The two themes have been by some indissolubly blended, and it has been, therefore, maintained that our inherent as well as our imputed sin is ill-deserving, and is justly punishable with the second death. Men have spoken of this inherent sin as propagated from parent to child, and have characterized it, in this relation, as the sin of nature distinct from the sin of person; "because the immediate subject of this [propagated] sin is not a person, but human nature vitiated by the actual transgression of a person; which nature being communicated to posterity, there is also communicated in it this inherent corruption. As therefore in Adam the *person* corrupts the nature, so in his posterity the *nature* corrupts the *person*."[2]

In the third place let us inquire, how can these two theories be harmonized? As two theories literally stated they cannot be; for the notion of a literally passive sin belongs to the theology neither of a right intellect nor of a right heart. Still the evangelical system which includes the one doctrine, may be essentially like that which includes

---

proposition from the statement that it is not properly sin." Bib. Rep. XXIII. 338. In this sentence, as also on p. 341, our Reviewer soberly represents us as endeavoring to show, that sinful and not sinful mean the same thing; and in the next sentence, that ability and inability mean the same thing! No wonder, that, having invented this design for us, he should find it necessary to say that we made use of some German theory to accomplish this design. The truth is, that we have represented the word "cannot" as often meaning the same with "*will not*," and the word "sinful" as often meaning the same with "odious and certainly inducing sin." Does not the Reviewer perceive his misstatements on this subject? They are but one specimen of the general style of his *critique*.

[1] Bib. Repertory, Vol. XXIII. pp. 310, 311, 314, 315.
[2] Turretin, Inst. Theol. Elenct. Pars I. p. 701.

the other, just as Homer and Milton were essentially like Virgil and Cowper, although the two former were blind, and the two latter could see the sunlight.

But this is not all. We rejoice in the assurance that multitudes who believe at times in the strict sinfulness of our involuntary and passive states, do still at other and better times contradict themselves, merge their proposition back into the mere language of feeling, whence it first came out, and then they agree with their adversaries. As architecture has been called "frozen music," so many a scholastic proposition may be called frozen eloquence, or poetry which often melts again into its primitive and impressive form. The following are some proofs of the substantial unity among disputants on this theme.

First, many who insist that our passive sin is the punishment for our imputed sin, do yet often betray a belief that it is not so in any proper sense of the terms, for they often affirm that one sin is never the punishment of another. What! does a pure Father inflict iniquity upon his children? The very phrase " God inflicts sin" is, as Sir James Mackintosh would say, one of those " uncouth and jarring forms of speech not unfitly representing a violent departure from the general judgment of mankind." Will a wise God punish sinners by sentencing them to sin, the very state which as sinners they love more than all things else! Yet if there is one expression of technical theologians, more common than another, it is, that God inflicts our inborn iniquity upon us as a punishment for our iniquity in Adam. Spiritual death is a punishment for our imputed sin; our native corruption is part of our spiritual death; this corruption is sin, therefore sin is the punishment of sin.

Dr. Twiss, the learned Prolocutor of the Westminster Assembly, justifies the declaration that " the original sin which the children of Adam contract is a punishment of the actual sin committed by the same man." Beza says, " There are three things which make man guilty before God; first, the fault flowing from the fact that we all sinned in the first man; secondly, the corruption which is a punishment of that fault, and was imposed upon Adam as well as upon his descendants," etc. The renowned Chamierus writes: " Whence also Augustine calls original sin *the punishment of the first sin*. But how can it be a punishment, unless that first sin itself be imputed to us." Strackius describes " the actual defection of all the descendants of Adam, who assuredly, in the loins of their progenitor, revolted from God to the devil; and on account of that revolt a corruption or vitiosity of nature has been *inflicted* on man by the Deity in just judgment; both of which make man miserable and obnoxious to the anger of God, and to eternal damnation," etc. etc. See Riveti Opp. Tom. III. pp. 802, 804, 806, 809. Turretin (Inst. Theol. Elenct. Pars I. p. 693) quotes with approbation the words of Peter Martyr, " when he teaches that our original corruption is a punishment for the sin of Adam:

'Truly there is no one who doubts,' says Martyr, 'that original sin is inflicted upon us for avenging and punishing the first offence.'" The learned Thomas Boston says (Body of Divinity, Vol. I. p. 308): " This want of original righteousness is a sin:—it is also a punishment of sin, and so is justly inflicted by God." See also Bp. Burgess on Original Sin, P. I. ch. 9. sec. 2.

Notwithstanding all the light reflected on this subject by New England divines, our Reviewer often adheres to the old representations. He says, "According to this view, hereditary depravity follows as a *penal* evil, from Adam's sin, and is not the ground of its imputation to men. This, according to our understanding of it, is essentially the old Calvinistic doctrine. *This is our doctrine*, and the doctrine of the standards of our church."[1] Again, after quoting with approbation the old Lutheran creeds, which declare that our defects and our concupiscence are punishments, the Reviewer sums up the whole by saying, "Hence, the loss of original righteousness, and corruption of nature, are *penal* evils. This, we are persuaded, is the common Calvinistic doctrine on this subject."[2] He often says, that our native corruption is the "effect," "result," consequence," of God's withdrawing His Spirit from our race; and all this is explained by the remark: "We think the position of Storr is *perfectly* correct, that the consequences of punishment are themselves punishment, in so far as they were taken into view by the Judge in passing sentence, and came within the scope of his design."[3] The Reviewer, then, is resolute at times in clinging to the old statement that original sin is the punishment of sin. But, are there not better hours in which his reverence for the moral government of God prevails over this artificial logic? He takes great pains to say in repeated instances, "*We do not teach, however, that sin is the punishment of sin.* The punishment we suffer for Adam's sin, is abandonment on the part of God, the withholding of Divine influences; corruption is consequent on this abandonment."[4] And what are we to believe? *Now*, original sin is a penal evil, but *then* "we do not teach that sin is penal? *Here* it is, as Melancthon says, a punishment, but *there* "we *hardly* teach" that it is a punishment. (Bib. Rep., Vol. VI. p. 456.) In

---

[1] Bib. Repertory, Vol. VII. p. 410.
[2] Bib. Repertory, Vol. VII. p. 430, 431.
[3] Bib. Repertory, Vol. VI. p. 464. This article is also unanimously ascribed to our Reviewer.
[4] Bib. Repertory, Vol. VI. p. 453. It is interesting to remember that Augustine abounds with repetitions of the remark, that *sin is the punishment of sin;* see Wiggers's Hist. Presentation, Ch. V. VI. *Pelagius denied it.* What does our Reviewer infer, whenever he detects a New England divine in any agreement with Pelagius?

conflict with one objection, original sin is "truly and properly sin," *deserving* the Divine wrath; in conflict with another, it is a consequence of a penal abandonment; and with still another, the foreseen intended consequence of a punishment is itself a punishment; but still, human nature at last breaks down this frail metaphysics, and the Reviewer has the manliness to avow that "sin is not the punishment of sin." We knew that he did not practically believe it to be a real punishment, when he asserted that it was so. A good man can never hold out in such a belief. He may adopt various modes of explaining his inconsistencies, but the true mode is to confess that a pious heart triumphs over erring syllogisms. If any pious divine should venture to say in his prayers,[1] "Thou hast inflicted sin upon me, as a punishment for my having a previous sin imputed to me," he would mean that the primal sin was imputed to him in a figure, and the inflicted sin is likewise metaphorical, and the punishment is equally a trope, and the solemn import of the whole is, that a holy Sovereign, in testimony of his opposition to Adam's crime, has entailed appropriate evils upon all Adam's descendants. And in this style often impressive, but alas! how far from the "simplicity of the Gospel," we believe with tears, that our Judge has inflicted a peculiar kind of sin (i. e. evil) upon us in a peculiar kind of punishment (i. e. appropriate suffering), for another kind of sin which was in a peculiar way chargeable upon us, before "the first man-child was born into the world."

Secondly, divines who contend that our passive nature is itself sin, often disown their doctrine by affirming that God is not the author of any sin. This argument is in a short compass. Our Reviewer says, "that we have derived from Adam a nature not merely diseased, weakened, or predisposed to evil, but which is '*itself*' as well as all the motions thereof 'truly and properly sin.'"[2] The first question is, Who made our nature? Did Adam create us? Did we create ourselves? The general belief of Calvinists is that God creates every human soul. Does not then the involuntary, inborn nature of the soul belong to the soul when made? It *is* the soul. The Maker of the spirit is the Maker of that nature. If that nature be sin itself, He is the author of sin. Does our Reviewer, in his calm hours, believe that? We presume not. Why not? Only because, in his calm hours, he does not believe that our nature as distinct from its

---

[1] Whatever is strictly true, may be expressed to the God of truth.
[2] Bib. Repertory, Vol. XXIII. pp. 314; 318.

"motions" is "truly and properly sin." Every body knows that when Calvinists are charged with making God the author of sin, they deny that our nature is sin, just as positively as our Reviewer has affirmed it. When Pelagius accused Augustine of believing in a "natural sin," the pious bishop resented the accusation, and would not even sanction the phrase "natural," but insisted on the phrase "original sin." Turretin is clear in avowing that "the Bible makes a distinction between *nature* and the *sin* adhering to it," that "human nature is termed lawless, *not because it is itself sin*, but because having sin in itself it is well denominated sinful," and that such phrases as imply that our nature itself is sin are used "for expressing the magnitude of our corruption the more *forcibly*,"[1] i. e. they belong to the theology of feeling. So the sharp-sighted Pictet denies, just as pointedly as our Reviewer affirms, that the nature of man is itself sin; for he says that if it be sin, the author of our nature must be the author of sin; see La Theologie Chretienne, Liv. VI. chap. VII., VIII. Will our Reviewer, in order to reconcile himself with these Genevan divines, admit that he spoke in the language of feeling?

Thirdly, many who dispute for the doctrine of passive transgression, expose their habitual want of faith in it, by denying that we can strictly feel either penitence or remorse for it, or deserve on account of it the condemnatory sentence of the last day. What kind of iniquity is that in view of which we are to have no repentance or compunction? This involuntary sin is said to be the "causal iniquity from which all other comes, and which is therefore more dreadful than any other." Bishop Burgess calls it "in some respects more grievous and heavy than actual sins," and yet he makes the following confession: "Now in this strict sense, though it be our duty with sorrow to be humbled for original sin, yet we cannot be properly said to repent of it, because it was not a sin ever committed by us *personally*, or through our own *actual* will. So that although we may not so properly (it may be) exhort men to repent of this original sin, yet we must press them to a deep and daily humiliation under it, and that not as a punishment or an affliction only, but as a true and proper sin."[2] Is not Pictet an authority on this subject? When an-

---

[1] See, among other passages, Turretin, Inst. Theol. Elenct. Pars I. p. 702. Still, Turretin admits occasionally into his dogmatic style the same improper use of terms which we find in our Reviewer. But what does he mean in his more considerate hours?—Augustine contradicted himself in the same way.

[2] Treatise on Original Sin, Part I. Ch. II. Sect. 8. "Men," says Bishop Burgess, "may use words as they please."

swering the objection that we have no compunction of conscience on account of Adam's or our own involuntary sin, he says, "that as we ordinarily feel remorse on account of that only which we have done ourselves, when we see that we could have abstained from it, we must not be surprised if we feel no remorse on account of this original corruption."[1] Hundreds of the like confessions are to be found among such polemic writers even. They agree in declaring that the evil which God himself has inflicted on our natures, and inserted within them, is to be mourned over, but not repented of; that it calls for humiliation, but not remorse. This evil is therefore a very peculiar kind of sin, if it be sin at all. And, we put it to the conscience of preachers, What must be the moral influence of saying, in didactic style, that there is a real and literal *wickedness* of which men both *cannot* and *need* not properly repent. Does Inspiration thus speak of any *iniquity* "which needeth not to be repented of?"

It follows, of course, that if our native and passive state deserve not to be viewed with remorse in this world, it will not be punished with remorse in the world to come. *The sure test of wickedness is,* its moral desert of the condemning sentence at the last day. If any condition do not merit the final sentence it is not criminal. A nature may be intimately associated with iniquity, and as such may, like an instrument of death, be viewed with dread. But if it be precisely such as God made it, and if it have never transgressed any rule of action, how will it be condemned to the punishment which the law threatens? Where is the verse of the chapter which specifies the legal penalty threatened for no act of disobedience? Imagine that a new-born or an unborn child has never indulged or felt one wrong emotion; — such a state can be imagined, whether it have or have not been ever real; — and *in that state* the infant is summoned before its Judge, to give an account of itself just as it was made. In what words would be pronounced its sentence to an eternity of strict punishment? Repeat the words of its moral condemnation to the remorse which is the worm that never dies. — "Because I was an hungered, and thou gavest me no meat!" — "Inasmuch as thou didst it not to one of the least of these my brethren, thou didst it not unto me!"

In order to maintain the *ill-desert* of infants as soon as born, some divines especially in New England have maintained, with Clement, Origen and other Greek Fathers, that an infant commences its actual transgression on the very day of its birth. Thus they renounce the theory of a passive sin. Others maintain that an infant will de-

---

[1] La Theologie Chretienne, Liv. VI. Chap. VII.

velop its evil nature as soon as it leaves the world, and will deserve to be punished for this development, and so *they* renounce the theory that the undeveloped nature deserves to be strictly punished. Others maintain that an infant merits the penalty of the law, because and only because it actively sinned in Adam, and thus *they* too renounce the theory of a passive sin, ill-deserving in itself. Some affirm with Augustine, who has been named *durus pater infantum*, " that infants dying without baptism will, on account of their imputed sin, be in the mildest punishment (in mitissima damnatione);" but the great majority of modern Calvinists are indignant at being accused of believing that infants *will* be punished at all. Whence come these doubts? If infants are guilty of real wickedness before their own personal choice, why will they not be punished for it? Are men who found their whole theology upon "justice," to be shocked at the idea that justice will be executed? Is not this attribute an amiable and a glorious one? Shall Calvinists recoil from it? And besides, men speak of original sin as the source, the fountain of all pollution, and therefore as in many respects the most flagitious of all. From it all our choices derive their vile character. They would be innocent, if it were not for this. Why is it, then, that this fontal sin deserves less punishment than do the outflowings of it? Why is the superlative transgression to be most mildly avenged? The plain truth is, that human nature and sanctified nature give out under the notion of a criminality in which the criminal has had no choice, and every sign of shrinking from the idea that infants will be punished for their passive wickedness, is a sign of a practical unbelief that such wickedness deserves punishment. The Hopkinsian theory that they choose wrong as soon as they are born, is indispensable to the fixed conviction that they are ill-deserving as soon as born. Without that theory their ill-desert is a mere fitness for receiving certain insignia of disgrace; their punishment is that disgrace; it is appropriate suffering inflicted, like the pains of this life, by a sovereign for the sake of manifesting abhorrence for all the occasions and concomitants of sin. *If* infants have *not* transgressed the law, they will certainly transgress it, unless saved by him who came to rescue the *lost*, and in this view they need the blood of the sacrifice. Now it is easy to see that such a loose idea of ill-desert and punishment is very common among those who deny the actual, and contend for the passive wickedness of infants. It is an idea which meets the moral taste. When Cranmer, exclaiming, " This right hand has offended," thrust it into the flames, he illustrated this vague and poetical notion of penalty. The fire consuming that hand first of all, emitted light on the odiousness of the wrong choice which had prompted the evil movement of that hand. It was *justice* as a sense of fitness, which inflicted this evil upon the erring member. The sin of the hand was figurative, the punishment figurative, the justice figurative; but it is this very kind of punishment, justice, and sin which Calvinists often mean when they speak of the just penalties of involuntary sin. Their theology on this theme is often the sound theology of the heart.[1]

Fourthly, many who contend, with our Reviewer, that our "nature itself" and "*all* the motions thereof," are "truly and properly sin," evince their practical disbelief of their doctrine, by confessing that we have by nature many amiable sentiments. Is there an amiable species of wickedness? They confess that Christ loved the unregenerate young man. Did he love sin? Is it to be said in a figure, that our great High Priest "was a sinner," and then literally that he loved a person whose "nature itself" and *all* whose motions, were "truly and properly sin"? The fearful question arises, *what* did Christ love in such a person? There is a limit, beyond which our Reviewer must not indulge in such extravagant language. When unguarded, it is full of danger. It drives men into Pelagianism. It has ruined thousands of souls. He must and will modify it into the assertion that Christ was pleased with a man whose nature was *on the whole* unlovely, and all whose VOLUNTARY "motions" were sin, but many of whose instinctive feelings were beautiful. What does the Princeton Review itself declare, when it approaches the truth "*at another angle*"? It says more than once, as in Vol. XI. p. 389, "*Every* one performs a multitude of acts, because they are right." But every one is not regenerate. Therefore, millions of unregenerate men, whose nature itself and "*all* whose motions are sin," perform right acts. Hence, as that Review divides original sin into imputed and inherent, and then subdivides inherent sin into negative and positive, it must complete its analysis by dividing our actual sin into right sin and wrong sin. That Review insists that its theology is not "philosophical." It is not; but it is far more philosophical than biblical, save when it turns back its theories into "intense expressions of the New England divinity."

Fifthly, many who contend for the doctrine of involuntary sin, virtually confess that they use the term, sin, in a metaphorical sense. Our Reviewer has abundantly shown that this word is often used as a figure of speech; for the whole doctrine of imputed sin is, accord-

---

[1] See pp. 618, 619 above.

ing to him, a doctrine of sin without any moral demerit. If, then, the first and fundamental part of original sin, be thus metaphorical, it is easy to show that the second and third parts of it have the same nature with their foundation.[1]

Many use the word, *sin*, to denote the occasion of a wicked choice. When asked whether the involuntary occasion, apart from the choice itself, deserves eternal punishment, they will often reply, or rather, He who made them, replies through them, No. We say the same. The natural tendency of an excited mind is, to indulge in the metaphor of "the cause for the effect." Thus we speak of a cannon as cruel, on account of the pain which results from it. Much more, then, may we speak of our disordered nature as sinful, because it so infallibly tempts us to transgression. But of such a style we say in our calmer hours, as Turretin says of Ezekiel 18: 20, "Non est absolute et simpliciter intelligendus prout sonat." Alcohol tempts men to iniquity, and is itself iniquity — in a figure of speech. Turretin, conceding that the law does not prohibit our being born with inherent corruption, yet affirms that this corruption is legally condemned, "because it opposes that righteousness and sanctity which the law does exact of all;[2] i. e. the law requires holiness, but not a *native* freedom from corruption, *in and of itself*. It is a sin, because it opposes holiness, i. e. because of its tendencies, not its nature. The renowned Pictet has the following note-worthy passage: "It is objected that God has not, in his law, forbidden original corruption, and therefore it is no sin. I reply, that *we must not be surprised if the law has not at all forbidden original corruption, because the law supposes*

---

[1] Here we may observe, in passing, that none are more inclined than our Reviewer to interpret certain phrases as figurative, and none are more inclined to complain of others for doing the same thing. He sometimes evades, for example, the biblical doctrine of General Atonement, by pleading the metaphorical character of the passages in which it is plainly taught. He opposes the commentators who do not infer from the Bible, that Christ was literally punished. But, why? Because the Bible plainly declares that he was punished. In what passages? "He bore our *sins*," etc. Are those passages literal? Then some venerable divines are right in affirming that Christ literally took upon him our *iniquities*; see p. 598 above. But, no, our Reviewer says, those passages are figurative; sin is used in a *metaphor*, for the punishment of sin. Indeed! Then the very phrases which affirm that Christ was literally punished, are, after all, metaphorical! Why was not this thought of before? So turns the kaleidoscope. Nothing, however, can be more natural than all this. It is a proverb, that we are willing to speak of our own favorite *words* or *friends*, as we are unwilling to hear others speak of them.

[2] Theol. Inst., Pars I. p. 699.

man innocent, and it forbids only actual sins, such as Adam could commit. Further, it cannot be denied that the law requires perfect holiness, to which this corruption is adverse."[1] What are we to infer? Plainly that our passive sin becomes a transgression of the law, merely as it induces that which *only* is a transgression of the law, and which *only* is sin in the biblical sense. This is the theology of the Convention Sermon.

But, again; these divines often confess that they use the term passive sin, to denote a mere result of wrong preference. When asked whether the result, apart from that choice, merits everlasting punishment, they will often give way to the inspirations of Heaven, and answer, just as we answer. No. Nothing is more natural than for a man, grieving over the dire effects of his perverse will, to exclaim, they are sinful effects, just as he speaks of the peace flowing from a good life, as a holy peace, just as he uses, in any other instance, the metaphor of the "effect for the cause." In this manner our involuntary evil propensities are termed sinful, because we have voluntarily indulged, and thereby strengthened them. If we had uniformly resisted them from the earliest period of our moral agency, we should have secured that aid by which we should have subdued these inward foes. Our sin lies in not choosing to resist, in preferring to gratify, in harboring them, in adopting them as our own, and this sin is metaphorically extended to the objects which it cherishes.[2]

It is psychologically interesting to see how often our native corruption is termed sin because, according to the ancient Calvinistic theory, it is the result of our own ante-natal offence. It is so termed, not because apart from its occasion it deserves the penalty of the moral law, but because it presupposes that ourselves have in some way performed an act which deserves the penalty of that law. The judgment of man will at last wind itself through all sorts of theories into the belief that nothing can be blamable, save as it stands related to a choice. It is because original sin involves our choice in Adam, that many Calvinists have supposed it to be our real sin. It is not our inherent, as separate from our justly imputed wickedness that condemns us; but it is original sin in the large sense, including our primitive volition to incur all our present evils.[3] In Riv. Opp. Tom.

---

[1] La Theologie Chretienne, Liv. VI. Chap. VII.

[2] So likewise it has been pretended, that we are morally guilty of Adam's sin, because we acknowledge that sin as our own, by every act of voluntary transgression. We adopt it, and so far forth are voluntary in it.

[3] No source of mistake is more copious than this. We are apt to suppose that

III. pp. 801, 803, 813, 815, 817, 820 will be found nearly all the following citations, which are no less important for the mere psychologist than for the theologian.

It is not only said by Cardinal Toletus that "all in Adam were forbidden to eat of the tree," but Protestant Molinaeus declares that "we sinned in Adam and therefore in him we *willed* this depravation." N. Hunnius teaches, that as the first sin "was committed voluntarily by Adam, so likewise it was committed *voluntarily* by all individuals, and as all were voluntarily made sinners in Adam, so all coming from him are born voluntary sinners." "They who pronounce that sin (of all men in one) simply involuntary," says Francis Junius, "are very much deceived, since the same thing may be said to be voluntary and involuntary in various respects, whether you regard its generation or its constitution. For, on account of our common origin, it was the voluntary offence of all men in Adam sinning (although it was not voluntary in respect of our individual origin); and it is voluntary in respect of ourselves as individuals on account of what we are, (although it arose from a corrupt nature brought upon us and not from our own will); that is, from the origin of our individual nature and not from our volition." Grossius, speaking of the sin which *all human nature* committed in and with the first pair, says "For the will of the progenitors was the will of their descendants, and the descendants *willed* in their progenitors, in whom as in the root of the entire human race, the descendants sinned and transgressed the law." Pfeilen says, that the sin of the first man, which may be regarded as a sin of nature rather than of a person, "cannot be termed involuntary in respect of infants, because it took its origin from a vicious will, and the first will of sinning man was, as it were, the will of the entire human race." The phrase "as it were" means that the will was that of the race virtually, though not in their separate individuality; see pp. 614–15 above. The noted Transylvanian

---

when the old writers ascribe a bad moral quality to our passive nature, they always do it without regard to our having willed that nature. Sometimes they do so; but the *theory* is, that original sin as a whole is blameworthy, because it involves our Paradisiacal choice.

There is another theory which may here be mentioned as illustrating the fundamental law of human belief, by which men are *compelled* to admit the indispensable connection between all blameworthiness and choice. It is the theory of the *scientia Dei media*, according to which God foresaw how all men would have acted, if they had been in Adam's place, and he therefore holds them ill-deserving for what they would have done if they had existed then, there, and in those circumstances. He *interpreted* Adam's act as if it had been theirs, because it would have been theirs if they had been in the condition to perform it, and thus they did perform it "*interpretatively*," and are punished justly! This theory is often resorted to as a temporary refuge from the absurdities of our really sinning in Adam. But why flee to these fictions of a *presumed* or a real choice? Why not say, that we are guilty without any choice, real or presumed? It is because every body knows, maugre all his theories, that our choice is *essential* to our guilt. Suppose it be said that we cannot be blameworthy, unless we be poets. Would our divines endeavor to prove that all men are poets in Adam, or were *presumed* to be poets? Why not? Because there is no law of the mind *demanding* such a belief. All these fictions of our Paradisiacal sin are the signs of our constitutional tendency to believe in the voluntariness of all sin.

Catechism expresses the doctrine with singular clearness. The question stands: "Is original sin a punishment or a sin?" The answer follows: "*It is a sin* (culpa), *if you consider the whole human race to have been in Adam as the root*, (Rom. 5: 12); *but it is a punishment if you regard the corruption which inheres in each individual.*" That is; it is a sin so far forth as, and in the sense in which we existed in Adam, but as our individual attribute it is not a sin but a punishment. As a *mere* passive state it is not blamable, but as involving our original choice it is so. That stout English champion for inherent sin, Bishop Burgess, frequently contradicts himself by admitting that it " doth *necessarily* imply," has " an *inseparable* connection" with, and " is *always* to be looked upon as a relative to" imputed voluntary sin. Bishop Burgess on Original Sin, Part I. Chap 9. Sect. III.; also Chap. 2. Sect. X.

Did such great men practically believe, that we had put forth a moral choice before the birth of Cain? Believe it? They believed it, just as they believed that an equitable ruler requires us to accomplish literal impossibilities, and will punish us eternally for not doing what no being in the universe can do; for not even an omnipotent Being can accomplish impossibilities. Believe it? They founded a theory upon it. They reasoned at times as if it were true; and their theory was, that "our voluntary participation in the crime of our first parents" is the cause of our inborn corruption, and therefore we are blamable for that corruption, and that corruption is our sin, so far forth as it is the result of our own voluntary sin, for all our sin is voluntary in its origin, voluntary on our part, and all our corruption is sin only as it was thus originally willed by us. That original will being given up, the corruption ceases to be our sin. The wickedness of the cause was thus metaphorically extended to and over the result. Even the diluted Calvinism with which our Reviewer contents himself, recognizes the principle that our evil nature is the effect of our antecedent sin, of a voluntary sin *imputed* to us. So far forth as it is imputed, it is our own voluntary transgression, and the cause of our corruption. Therefore he says, "if the doctrine of imputation be given up, the whole doctrine of original sin must fall."[1] Why so? No other reason can be divined, than that our disordered nature is not sin except as related to our causal imputed crime; i. e. it is not sin in and of itself. We are born with this disordered nature. This is a fact. No metaphysics can explain the fact away. Is this nature sin? '*It is sin, if the doctrine of imputation be true; it is not sin, unless that doctrine be true.*' Exactly right. The passive sin depends on the imputed sin, and our Reviewer confesses *at times* that the sin, as imputed, is not a moral, ill-deserving one; and therefore, if he be self-consistent, he must confess that the passive sin has the same figu-

---

[1] Bib. Repertory, Vol. VI. p. 93. See also Dr. Hodge on Rom. 5: 12—21.

rative character. It is reprehensible, just as our sinning in Adam was reprehensible, and our critic, in certain states of mind, abandons the doctrine that our Paradisiacal crime was a reprehensible one. By a single application of his match, he has exploded that ingeniously articulated system of imputation which ancient theorists imagined would be more durable than the Kremlin itself; and now he must not attempt to hold firm the superstructure of an edifice which he has shattered to its foundations. It is a plain case. There is no help for our Reviewer. He must agree with us so long as he does not retract his reiterated concessions. Here it stands. Is sin a transgression of the law? Yes. What law was addressed to our nature before our birth? No law except that addressed to our nature in Adam. Then there was no real sin, except as we were once in Adam. But our Adamic life was figurative, as our critic admits; then the resultant sin is figurative; and this is our passive sin. How can there be a literal transgression of a figurative law? How can the embryo child be ill-deserving for its nature, viewed as opposed to a command addressed to it impersonally, i. e. metaphorically? We by no means imply, that the masters of Calvinism have never represented a passive state to be blamable, apart from its voluntary origin. They have done so. Often, too often. But they have not seldom detected the absurdity of the representation, and have then allied the passive with the first voluntary sin, and have derived from the latter all the guilt of the former. They have conceded, that the nature was culpable because the result of a blameworthy cause; and if the voluntariness of the cause be denied, the criminality of the effect ceases. If a corporeal movement is wicked, merely as the result of an antecedent will, then it is not wicked in itself; and if our senses and intellect and entire nature are wicked, merely as related to the crime which we virtually committed in Eden, then they are not wicked in themselves. Here again Calvinism and Hopkinsianism coalesce in denying the criminality of any state which does not involve our own choice. Here, too, we see the inconsistency of those who believe in a passive, inborn wickedness apart from our own fault in the first man. They sever the branch from its root. They cherish the result of a principle while they discard the principle from which alone that result can rightly spring.

But again, and more in general, the believers in a passive sin often virtually confess, that they use the term *sin* to denote all the concomitants of transgression; not only the cause and the result, but also the other adjuncts of it. Deep emotion prompts us to call a plat of ground holy, when it is connected with holiness, and to call a nature sinful, when it is connected with sin. Unregenerate children are termed "holy," in 1 Cor. 7: 14, by the metaphor of an adjunct for the main subject; much more, then, may an uninspired man venture on the same metaphor, and term such children criminal, when in point of fact, "they have done neither good nor evil," Rom. 9: 11. Now, that standard writers have often employed the phrase, inherent sin, in this tropical sense, is obvious from the fact, that they represent this sin as existing in the reason, the judgment, the appetites, indeed in all the powers and states of the intellect and body. Sin is in our blood. Augustine often describes our wickedness, as belonging not merely to the soul, but to the "whole man," soul and body.[1] Calvin speaks of the intellect, will, and *flesh*, the entire person, as being "nothing else than concupiscence," which is sin;[2] and he speaks of sin as "spread over our *senses* and affections," and "all parts of our nature," "every part, without exception,"[3] of course physical and intellectual. Turretin often calls the body corrupt, and calls corruption sin; he denies that sin is propagated either into the body or the soul, as separate from each other; he denies that the body, apart from the soul, is the subject of sin formally and completely, but he affirms that it is so, initiatively and radically.[4] The Symbols of the Reformers describe original sin as "a corruption of the whole nature, and of all the powers, but *especially* of the higher and principal faculties of the soul, in mind, intellect, heart, and will;" "the mass out of which men are now made by God, has been corrupted and perverted in Adam;" the elements of our bodies are "contaminated by sin;" "concupiscence is not only a corruption of the corporeal qualities, but also," etc.[5] Bishop Burgess not only "anatomizes the sinfulness of the memory, and other intellectual powers," but he also admits the sinfulness of "the whole body." Sometimes, however, he explains himself to mean that "sin is not properly, till the soul be united to the body, yet because that (the body) is part of man, sin is there inchoatively and imperfectly, because it is in tendency to make up man," etc.[6]

Our respect for the good sense of these writers, forbids us to be-

---

[1] Wiggers's Hist. Pres., Ch. V.   [2] Inst. L. II. C. 1, § 8, 9.
[3] Com. on Rom., 7: 24.
[4] See among other places, Tur. Inst. Theol., Pars I. pp. 706–710.
[5] Form. Con., pp. 640, 647. Con. Aug., 55, [25.]
[6] Treatise on Original Sin, Part I. Ch. I. § 1. See also Boston's Body of Divinity, Vol. I. pp. 309–321. Gill's Body of Divinity, Vol. I. pp. 523, 529, 530.

lieve that they fell into the habitual absurdity of supposing the intellect or the body to be sinful in the literal sense. In fact, they *could* not have forced their minds up to such an anomalous conviction, without long intervals of rest. Nature will not bear it. For a man to act on the principle that his nerves and bones are in themselves criminal, is no more consistent with mental sanity, than for him to act on the principle that they are intelligent; and, out of Laputa, a man can no more persevere in practically believing his mere intellect to be criminal, than in believing a rock or a clod to be so. And yet, a thorough Calvinist can no more believe in the passive sin of the heart, than he can believe in the sin of the muscles and veins. It must habitually be regarded as a figurative sin.[1]

Sixthly, the advocates of the doctrine that our nature is itself sin, often virtually confess that they use the word *nature* in a figurative sense. Properly it denotes that which is distinct from action and, above all, from voluntary action. It denotes either our faculties and sensibilities themselves, or the mutual relation between them, or both. But when divines affirm that this nature is criminal, they often tacitly conjoin with it a state of action, and especially of voluntary action. Thus they all appeal to "the flesh" and to the "law of the members," in Gal. 5: 17 and Rom. 7: 23, as illustrations of the corrupt nature; but this "flesh" and this "law in the members" are not generally conceived of as a dormant state or condition, but rather as an energetic principle, not indeed identical with a wicked choice, but yet intimately allied with it, and often comprehending it. At times we distinguish the tendency from the preference. In general we confound them. It is very difficult, especially for untrained minds, to imagine the youngest infant as altogether inactive and involuntary. Andrew Fuller goes farther than this, too far, and substitutes *impossible* for *difficult*. "To talk of an involuntary propensity in the mind of a rational being," he says,[2] "is to talk without meaning, and in direct contradiction to the plainest dictates of common sense. If, then, the concurrence of the will denominates a thing blameworthy, we need have no more dispute whether an evil disposition in a rational being be in itself blameworthy; seeing the concurrence of the will is included in the very nature of a propensity." This, although an extreme statement, is yet sufficient to show the tendency of men to

---

[1] Pres. Appleton says, "Intellects, simply considered, are not the seat of moral disorder, [i. e. sin.] The understanding, if we speak with precision, cannot be depraved, [i. e. sinful.] Lectures, Vol. I. pp. 443, 444, 447, etc.

[2] Fuller's Works, Vol. II. p. 527.

include a choice in a propension, and to ascribe the sin of the propension to the choice which it includes, rather than to an involuntary state.

Seventhly, many who dispute for a sin of nature as distinct from one of choice, expressly declare, that they do not mean by sin a moral quality. What was the opinion of that authoritative bishop from whom, more than from any other man, the doctrine of original sin has been derived? Augustine, especially during his later years, taught, with as much emphasis as our Hopkinsian divines, that all moral character consists in preferences; that all iniquity has and must have its origin in the will;[1] also, that the "sin in the members" of the baptized "is not called sin in the sense of making us guilty, but because it was produced by the guilt of the first man; and because, by rebelling, it strives to draw us into guilt," etc. etc. "As far as respects us, we should always be without sin, until the evil (our concupiscence) were cured, if we were never to consent to evil."[2] He often denominates this evil an infirmity, but not of itself our fault; and says of concupiscence that "though called sin, it *is not so called because it is itself sin, but because it is produced by sin, just as writing is called the* HAND *of some one, because the* hand *produced it. But sins are what are unlawfully done, said, or thought, according to carnal concupiscence or ignorance, and when committed they, unless forgiven, hold the persons guilty."*[3]

Our Reviewer represents us as attempting to accomplish a "feat" in reconciling Augustinism with the "radical principles" of the sermon which he has assailed. Did he not know that Augustinism has been repeatedly explained by its great author, as in essential harmony with those radical principles? Did he not know that Augustine often wrote in the language of feeling, and that after all his eloquent expressions in regard to passive sin, he declared them to be only figurative expressions? Does our Reviewer agree with Augustine? If not, is he ready for his favorite inference, that whoever differs from the African bishop is a Pelagian? Does our critic now see any need of his stating or rather mis-stating a German theory, as one by which we might be suspected of harmonizing Augustine's reïterated assertions that all sin is voluntary, with the same assertions in a New England discourse?

A volume might be filled with similar testimonies from ancient

---

[1] See his Unfinished Work, IV. 103   [2] C. Jul. II. 9, 10.
[3] C. Duas Epp. Pel. I. 13, a work written only ten years before Augustine's death, and eight years after he commenced his controversy on original sin.

worthies. Notwithstanding all that our critic has imagined (p. 819) about "the names of all generations of saints inscribed on" the walls of his own Gibraltar, yet even he must confess that the Alexandrine and Greek Fathers stood upon no such fortress of strife and tumult, but occupied the same broad and peaceful ground which the Dwights and Appletons of New England have enlarged and enriched as the garden of the Lord, and on which the sword will soon be beaten into the ploughshare.— But leaving the fathers, let us listen to the voice of the clearest thinker among the Reformers. Zuingli, in his De Peccato Originali Declaratio, says, that he will not contend about a word, that he will permit men to call our native tendency to self-love by the name of sin, and, if this be not sufficient, by the name of wickedness also, crime and profligacy; but he insists that so far forth as it is passive and inborn, it is "not a sin but a disease."[1] "Original sin I have called a disease and not a sin, because sin is conjoined with fault, but fault arises from the transgression of one who has chosen wickedness."[2] "Our original fault is not called a fault truly, but metaphorically on account of the offence of our first parent."[3] "Therefore that propension to sin through self-love is original sin, which propension indeed is not properly a sin, but is a source [of it] and natural bent [to it]. We will give an example from the young wolf. It is in all respects a wolf as to its natural bent, and by its ferocity would be led to commit all depredations. But as yet, it has borne away no plunder, because it could not on account of its age. In consequence of its nature, however, the hunters no more spare it than they would spare a wolf from whose jaws they seize the prey; for although young, yet even now its nature is so thoroughly understood by them that they know it will, when grown up, follow the ways of its species. This native bent, then, is original sin or vitiosity, but the act of plunder is sin, which comes from this native bent; this itself is sin in the act, which more recent authors call actual sin, and which properly is sin."[4] So in his celebrated Confession of Faith, Zuingli says: "Whether we will or not, we must admit, that original sin, as it exists in Adam's descendants, is not properly a sin, as has now been shown; for it is no wicked act

---

[1] Huldrici Zuinglii Opera, Vol. III. p. 628.   [2] Ib. 629.   [3] Ib. 629.

[4] Zuingli believed, as we do, that our native disease would expose us to future suffering, unless it were removed by Him who came to heal our sicknesses. This suffering is not a punishment, in the sense of implying any real sin. It is a punishment in a loose sense.

[5] Huldrici Zuinglii Opera, Vol. III. pp. 631, 632. The same also is frequently repeated in this Treatise.

against the law. It is therefore properly a disease and a condition: It is a disease, because as he fell through self-love we also fall in the same way; it is a condition, because as he became a servant and guilty of death, so we are born servants and children of wrath, and consequently are subjected to death."[1] That our original sin is improperly so termed, and is merely a "disease," a "rupture," is often reiterated by this excellent reformer, in his Treatise on Baptism, his Commentary on Romans, and his Letters to Oecolampadius. And so, on this doctrine, and if on this, then on many other doctrines, Zuingli has bound together multitudes of verbal polemics; for various parties are willing to confess, that our nature is itself sin, *provided that* it be such a kind of sin as is produced by God who never produces any real iniquity; such a kind of sin as is viewed, in and of itself, with regret instead of remorse, humiliation instead of penitence, and is followed with suffering instead of *that* punishment which the law threatens against all transgressors; such a kind of sin as derives all its wickedness from its being a cause or effect or concomitant of what is truly iniquitous; such a kind of sin as, according to Augustine, the chief author of the doctrine, is properly called a disease rather than a transgression of the law. And we ask as a favor from our assailants, if they persevere in asserting that "our nature itself, as well as all the motions thereof, is truly and properly sin," to give a definition of the conscience which condemns this passive nature; and also, that they point out the inspired passage in which this inborn nature is prohibited by the law, and that they rehearse the words in which it will be sentenced to the legal penalty at the last day. *When* and *where*, (and if nowhere, why so) are we exhorted to "*resist the beginnings*" of this germinal iniquity? not to *enter* upon that state which to its own wickedness superadds the shame of originating all other abominations? Commit a passive iniquity? Exhort men against being born with evil tendencies? What is the passive voice of the verb, *sin?* What is the inactive form of the word, *evil-doers?* Why is language made without any such phrases as to endure or suffer a criminality without any criminal volition? The language of every man whispers the truth, that in practical life, whatever he may do among his books, he no more believes in this peculiar metaphysics of involuntary sin, than Bishop Berkeley believed in the non-existence of the material world.[2]

---

[1] Martin Luther's Sämtlichen Schriften, Band XX. ss. 1942—1943, and Huld. Zuing. Opp. Tom. IV. p. 6.

[2] We request an answer to these and similar questions *as a favor*. We are entitled to demand such an answer *as a right*. It may do for once, but it will not do

"'Truly,' says John Calvin, "I abominate mere verbal disputes, by which the church is harassed to no purpose; but I think that those terms ought to be religiously avoided, which sound as if they had an absurd meaning, especially where error is of pernicious consequence."[1] Now, it has been a great aim of New England writers, to dispense with such terms in doctrinal discussion, and confine them to their appropriate sphere. They have watched the theology of good men in its alternating forms of beauty and of power, and have tried to seize and portray, and even *daguerreotype*, those features into which it has been wont to settle down as its natural expression, after all the changes of its emotive style. Thus have they held up the enduring substance of doctrine, to be looked at not only through the stained glass of the old artists, but also in the pure light of heaven. It was natural that men who criticised the endeared phrases of other times, and condemned the errors into which those powerful phrases had often beguiled their adherents, should be repaid by volleys of intemperate words, even from those who at times make the same criticisms, and renounce the same errors. If rivers have been stained with blood by means of the verbal controversies on Nominalism, still more in theology, where the feelings of men are swift to rise, must we expect that "Gibraltar or Ehrenbreitstein" will bristle with armor, whenever the gentlest query is whispered about the safety of some figurative expressions. But, our consolation is this, that the distinctive theology of New England is not opposed at the present day, unless it be first misrepresented; and when its arguments press hard, we are often told that we say "*the very thing* which the old Calvinists" meant; and when we name the great and good men who have stood forth as champions of our "three radical principles," we are assured that "Nolo contendere" is inscribed on every gun which was once pointed against the theology of Andrew Fuller; and when we assail the old doctrine "Lumborum Adae," we are gracefully reminded that the doctrine is covered all over with fig-leaves and flowers of rhetoric, and it now lies snugly hidden "*behind* the walls of Gibraltar or Ehrenbreitstein." Very well, if our opponents will be so kind as to qualify all the terms which we criticise, why may we not

---

twice, for our Reviewer to escape from all objections by the plea: "*Having failed so entirely to understand the Sermon, we shall not be presumptuous enough to pretend to understand the Reply*," Bib. Repertory, XXIII. p. 307, and by then proceeding to discuss a theory of Schleiermacher, which has no more connection with the Sermon or Reply, than it has with an acute-angled triangle.

[1] Inst., Lib. II. Cap. II, § 7.

cultivate the pacific arts and virtues? This is our aim. With this design was an humble sermon preached on "the one theology in two forms." It was intended not to shield such men as Pelagius from the charge of heresy, but such men as our Reviewer, from the charge of remaining *steadfast* and *uniform* in an absurdity. It was meant to be an olive branch of peace. But it is now found out to be first a '*weapon*, striking a blow upon *sturdy* trees;'[1] secondly, "the last *arrow* in the *quiver;*"[2] and thirdly, if it be what its author avows it to be, then it is a "penny whistle."[3] We shall not dispute about a name. We only reässure our excellent Reviewer, that the Sermon was intended to call forth no such "*sort* of a model of candor and charity,"[4] but to accelerate the coming of the day when every "weapon" of war shall be turned into a pruning hook, and when "the leopard shall lie down with the kid."

ARTICLE VIII.

NOTICES OF NEW PUBLICATIONS.

I. Andrews's Edition of Freund's Lexicon.[5]

It is a little remarkable, that the people that are most fond of theorizing, and of daring speculation, furnish the most patient lexicographers. Holland has lost her old reputation for plodding scholarship. The mantle has fallen on the cousins beyond the Rhine. Men are found, who will devote themselves, year after year, with uncomplaining and iron diligence, to all the researches, comparisons, discriminations, reëxaminations, protracted and almost endless studies, which are needed, in order to complete their great vocabularies. Scarcely had Pape come to the end of his Greek Lexicon of more than 3100 octavo pages, and while the new edition of Passow was lingering in mid course, when Drs. Jacobwitz and Seiler, moved by the want of a good Greek lexicon, brought out the "greater Manual" containing 208 *Bogen*.

---

[1] Bib. Repertory, XXII. p. 674.   [2] Ib., XXIII. p. 320.   [3] Ib., XXIII. p. 341.

[4] "We wrote a Review which we intended to make a *sort* of a model of candor (?) and charity," (!) etc. Princeton Review, XXIII. p. 307.

[5] A Copious and Critical Latin-English Lexicon, founded on the Larger Latin-German Lexicon of Dr. William Freund; with Additions and Corrections from the Lexicons of Gesner, Facciolati, Scheller, Georges, etc. By E. A. Andrews, LL. D. New York: Harper and Brothers. 1851. pp. 1663.

ARTICLE VII.

NEW ENGLAND THEOLOGY;

WITH COMMENTS ON A THIRD ARTICLE IN THE BIBLICAL REPERTORY AND PRINCETON REVIEW, RELATING TO A CONVENTION SERMON.

By Edwards A. Park, Abbot Professor in Andover Theol. Seminary.

WHEN Napoleon had made his majestic march to the Kremlin, and while he was retreating on a peasant's sled in a storm, he uttered the maxim that "there is but one step between the sublime and the ridiculous." We have been reminded of this incident by the late incursion of Dr. Hodge into our northern country, and his later precipitate egress. He advanced with the brave announcement that, "a man behind the walls of Gibraltar or of Ehrenbreitstein, cannot, if he would, tremble at the sight of a single knight, *however* gallant or well-appointed;"[1] but he has now hurried back with the excuse, "There is another feature of Professor Park's mode of conducting this discussion, which is very little to our *taste*."[2] He smiled up along our rock-bound coast and cried aloud, "A man at sea with a stout ship under him, has a sense of security in no measure founded upon himself."[3] After *doubling* and *redoubling* his course, and *doubling* it over again, he has sped homeward with the apology, "When we ran out of the harbor in our yacht, to see what 'long, low, black schooner' was making such a smoke in the offing, we had no expectation to be called upon to *double* Cape Horn."[4] We had said, in a plain way, that the same *truths* may be expressed in diversified forms, all reconcilable with each other. Our assailant rushed forward, with a seeming readiness to meet any foeman, anywhere, and proposed some of his own theories which he defied us to reconcile with our doctrines. We proved to him that his theories were not true, and that he himself did not believe them in his better moods. He now exclaims, "Where is this matter to end? — This is a great deal more than we bargained for."[5] And there is something rather ominous in the excuses which our antagonist has left behind him, for his very unexpected departure. After having publicly accused

---

[1] Bib. Repertory, Vol. XXIII. p. 319.
[2] Ib. p. 693. The italics throughout the present article are *our own*.
[3] Ib. p. 319.   [4] Ib. p. 676.   [5] Ib. p. 676.

us of Rationalism, Schleiermacherism, Infidelity, profaneness, and, worse than all, "Pelagianism," he has retired because the discussion has assumed a "*personal* character!"¹ After having introduced various doctrines, to which we had not even alluded, and having attempted to prove some of his theories, he listens to certain New England objections, and then retreats with the words, "We regard it, therefore, as a matter of *great* importance, that such questions should not be open, at least within the church (i. e. among Christians), to perpetually renewed agitation!"² This is significant. But the most instructive sign is, that our critic has declined an answer to our first Reply, because he did *not* understand it;³ and has declined an answer to our second Reply, because he *did* understand it, and its contents were quite familiar to him.⁴ It is a singular fact, that he has written an Essay twenty-one pages long, for the sake of excusing himself from answering our last argument, which might have been refuted in a single page, if it could have been refuted at all.

And among the apologies assigned by him for abandoning his position, there is one which deserves a formal statement. Our Reviewer drew out a creed⁵ which would have answered well enough as an amusing caricature of our faith, but which he dignified with the name "anti-Augustinian;" and he represented us as actually believing that strange creed to be true. He contrasted it with another system which he called the "Augustinian," and which likewise he represented us as believing to be true. He even ventured so far as to introduce a quotation, with the regular quotation marks, and to charge it upon ourselves, in which pretended quotation we are made to say of the Augustinian creed, "Let us admit its *truth*, but maintain that it does not differ from the other system" [the anti-Augustinian]. "Both [creeds] are *true*, for at bottom they are the same."⁶ He has ventured to accuse us repeatedly of having "*declared*," yea, of having "*proposed* to show" that those two creeds are "*identical;*" and only "different modes of stating the same general *truths*."⁷ Now we affirm, that neither we nor any body else ever heard of that anti-Augustinian creed, until Dr. Hodge collected its discordant parts into one mass. No man, woman or child, not even "Pelagius" himself, ever believed it as a whole. It is no *system* at all, but a conglomerate of different schemes that contradict each other. Dr. Hodge himself has not dared to accuse any individual of believing it, except

---

¹ Bib. Repertory, Vol. XXIII. p. 688.   ² Ib. p. 678.   ³ Ib. p. 307.
⁴ Ib. p. 678, etc.   ⁵ Ib. pp. 308—312.   ⁶ Ib. p. 319.
⁷ Ib. pp. 319, 320, 322, 326, 328, 692, 694, etc.

the author of a late Convention sermon. And his courage failed even here; for he once confessed that, "so far as the present discussion is concerned, he [Prof. Park] may hold neither of these systems in its integrity, or he may hold the one which we believe to be true, or he may hold the opposite one;"[1] that is, he may attempt, "*ex professo*," to prove that *both* are true, and still not acknowledge that either is true! We have once and again disclaimed a belief in that heterogeneous compound of errors mingled up for us by Dr. Hodge. We have pointed out some of its contradictions and eccentricities.[2] Had we deemed it worth our while, we might have resented the imputation of it to us, as at least an indecorum. But after all, — and will the reader believe it? — Dr. Hodge retires from his self-sought discussion, partly because we do not confine our Reply to the incoherent creed which was originated by himself, and then injuriously imputed to us.[3] First, he requires us to *prove* a negative, viz. that his anti-Augustianian creed is not fairly stated: very well; we have shown that we favor no such compound of errors; that, *as our creed*, it is not fairly stated, and has no more to do with our faith than Mohammedanism has to do with our Reviewer's.[4] Or, secondly, he requires us to *prove* another negative, viz. that the *nondescript* creed imputed to us is not allowable: very well; we have shown that we do not allow it, and we challenge any man to name the individual who ever did allow it as a whole. Or, thirdly, he requires us to *prove* still another negative, viz. that he has not understood our theory: well, we have shown that we have harbored no theory like that which he has invented for us,[5] and he himself is sometimes compelled to admit, that he imputes it to us merely by his own inference, which we will not sanction. Or, fourthly, he requires us to prove that our theory is philosophical: well, we have abundantly shown that it is demanded by the philosophy of common sense, and that he himself is necessitated to believe it in his better hours. But what if we had shown none of these things? What if we had not even denied that we believe that creed, which was never made to be *believed*, but to be *imputed*? If the anomalous medley of errors which our

---

[1] Bib. Repertory, Vol. XXIII. p. 320.
[2] Bib. Sacra, Vol. VIII. pp. 604, 605, 624, 627, etc.
[3] Bib. Repertory, Vol. XXIII. p. 694.
[4] Bib. Sacra, Vol. VIII. pp. 604, 605, 627, 628, etc. Also Ib. pp. 104—174.
[5] Ib. pp. 594, 596, 627, 628, 640, etc. The first fourteen pages of our second Reply, detail the only theory on which we have attempted to reconcile opponents, and this is a sufficient proof that we have never made use of the scheme which Dr. Hodge, by mistake, ascribes to Schleiermacher.

critic has been so kind as to devise for us be a logical result of our principles, he ought to have *proved* that it is so, instead of summoning us to prove that it is not. He ought to have produced at least one argument, to show that those errors grow up from our "three radical principles." But when or where has he even hinted at so much as a single proof, that our principles lead into that medley? He has done nothing but *assert* that it is so; and now he has hastened out of the contest in which he promised to be so victorious, and can plead no better apology than that we pay very little respect to his mere, sheer assertions. And is it enjoined in the ninth commandment, that anonymous Reviewers load an author with conjectural and false accusations of heresy, and then make a bold request that he spend all his time in proving a negative, and none of his time in showing that his principles have been once and again avowed by his accuser,— avowed in words which have suddenly become '*very little to the taste*' of the man who first uttered them?[1]

---

[1] One chief benefit of theological controversy is, that it manifests the comparative *necessity* which the disputants feel for misrepresenting each other. He who has the greater need of this malpractice, has the weaker cause. We have long thought that our Reviewer impairs the public confidence in his theological system, by the *extreme* to which he carries his misstatements of other systems. Thus, because we have said that some men, speculatively believing different creeds, do yet in practical life disown their differences and heartily agree, Dr. Hodge goes so far as to ask: "Has any one, before our author, ever inferred from these facts, that idealism and materialism are different modes of one and the same philosophy, or that Arminianism and Calvinism, Moravianism and Pantheism, are but different forms of one and the same theology?" (Bib. Repertory, Vol. XXIII. p. 692.) He thus implies that we have a more absurd theory than any body else, and yet his great object has been to stigmatize us as adopting nothing new, but rather an old Schleiermacherian theory! He overleaps himself; for a candid reader, instead of believing that we have ever represented Materialism, Arminianism and Pantheism as, in any sense, allowable, will believe that our critic was compelled to make such a misstatement, because he was unable to oppose us in a more honorable way. We have said far less to authorize this caricature of our views, than our critic has said to justify us in publishing him as a worshipper of the Virgin Mary. For, notwithstanding all his protests against our effort to show the practical agreement of good men, he goes so far as to declare his speculative agreement not only with New England divines, but also with Romanists; see Bib. Repertory, Vol. XXIII. pp. 324, 677, 686. etc. If, then, we should portray our Reviewer as sanctioning all the puerilities of Rome, we should have a better pretence for caricaturing him than he has for having caricatured us; but we should dishonor our dogmatic faith, by betraying a consciousness that we cannot defend it, except by misrepresenting its assailants.

But let us leave our author's ingenious reasons for not holding out in the contest which he began. In his last Reply, he has made some remarks on New England Theology, which have induced us to discourse on the same theme, with an occasional reference to that Reply.

In the preface to the first printed sermon ever preached in America, is the following sentence: " So far as we can yet find, it [New England] is an island, and near about the quantity of England; being cut out from the main land in America, as England is from the main of Europe, by a great arm of the sea, which entereth in forty degrees, and runneth up north-west and by west, and goeth out either into the South Sea, or else into the Bay of Canada."[1] This "great arm of the sea" means the Hudson river; the "South Sea" means the Pacific ocean, and the "Bay of Canada" means the river St. Lawrence. Now it were about as easy to learn the shape of New England from the preceding account, as to learn the type of New England Theology from the statements which some of its recent opposers have deemed it wise to make.

We beg leave, therefore, first of all, to explain the term, New England Theology. It signifies the formal creed which a majority of the most eminent theologians in New England have explicitly or implicitly sanctioned, during and since the time of Edwards. It denotes the spirit and genius of the system openly avowed or logically involved, in their writings. It includes not the peculiarities in which Edwards differed, as he is known to have differed, from the larger part of his most eminent followers; nor the peculiarities in which any one of his followers differed, as some of them did, from the larger part of the others; but it comprehends the principles, with their logical sequences, which the greater number of our most celebrated divines have approved expressly or by implication. As German philosophy is not adopted by all Germans, and is adopted by some foreigners, so New England Theology is not embraced by all New Englanders, and is embraced by multitudes in other parts of the world. Its more prominent standards, however, are from these north-eastern States. It was first called New-light Divinity; then New Divinity; afterward, Edwardean; more recently, Hopkintonian or Hopkinsian. From the fact that Edwards, Hopkins, West and Catlin resided in Berkshire County, it was once called Berkshire Divinity. When it was embraced by Andrew Fuller, Dr. Ryland, Robert Hall, Sutcliffe, Carey, Jay and Erskine, it was called American Theology by the English, in order to dis-

---

[1] The Sin and Danger of Self-Love Described, in a Sermon preached at Plymouth, in New England, 1621, p. iii.

criminate it from the European systems. It has been denominated New England Theology by Americans, in order to distinguish it from the systems that have prevailed in other parts of the land. In 1756, two years before the death of Edwards, there were, according to Dr. Hopkins, not more than four or five clergymen who espoused this new theology. In 1773, according to Dr. Stiles, it was advocated by about forty-five ministers; and Dr. Hopkins says that, in 1796, it was favored by somewhat more than a hundred. Still, even while it was thus restricted in its influence, it was distinguished as a system peculiar to New England. In 1787, Dr. Stiles mentioned as among its champions, the two Edwardses, Bellamy, Hopkins, Trumbull, Smalley, Judson, Spring, Robinson (father of Dr. Robinson of New York), Strong, Dwight, Emmons. In 1799, Hopkins appended the names of West, Levi Hart, Backus, Presidents Balch and Fitch. We may now add such honored men as Dr. Catlin, President Appleton, Dr. Austin. Divines of this class were foremost in the Missionary enterprises of the day. They were conspicuous in the establishment of our oldest Theological Seminaries, as Andover and Bangor. They gave its form and pressure to our theological system. They were imperfect men. They did not harmonize on every theme, but a decided majority of them stood firm for the "three radical principles," that sin consists in choice, that our natural power equals, and that it also limits, our duty. Idle, idle is the late attempt to draw a line of demarcation between the elder Edwards, Bellamy, on the one side, and the younger Edwards, Emmons, West, on the other, with regard to these three principles. Hopkins was the beloved pupil of the first President Edwards, and through life, was the most confidential of his friends; was with him in sickness and in health, in the house and on journeys, by day and often by night. He was also an adviser and more than a brother to Bellamy. He was the teacher and a spiritual father of the younger Edwards, West, Spring, and he was an intimate friend of Emmons. He serves, therefore, as a *commune vinculum* between the elder Edwards and Bellamy on the one hand, and the "choir leaders" of the "Exercise Scheme" on the other. But in more than two hundred of his free, private letters, and in all his published works, we have sought in vain for the slightest hint that, on these radical principles, there was even an approach to a disagreement between the two classes. He reached out his fraternal arms to Edwards and to Emmons, and gave them both his approval and his blessing in their maintenance of these three doctrines, and he often expressed, as clearly as words can express, his hearty union with the forerunner and the follower. And all the theories which the original Edwardeans and the later Coryphaei of the Exercise Scheme were harmonious in espousing, are parts of the New England system.

What worthy end, now, could our Reviewer aim to accomplish, by insinuating that we "regard the little coterie to which" we belong, "as all New England?"[1] We belong to no party which has not been honored throughout the Christian world; but does our assailant dream that "*all* New England" must unite in the New England Theology? What! a single speculative creed for the Churchmen and Come-outers, the Presbyterians and the Quakers, the Baptists and the Swedenborgians, the Sub-lapsarians and the Supra-lapsarians, the Owenites and the Baxterians, the Burtonites and the Emmonites, of a community whose fathers were John Robinson and Roger Williams! We have never pretended that New England Theology is the dogmatic faith of every man, woman and child, or of a majority of the laymen, or even clergymen, of these free States. It has, however, been the faith of certain elect minds, whom New England has loved and will ever love to venerate.

We now proceed to say, in the second place, that the Theology of New England is marked by certain new features. We have seen that for a hundred years it has been called "new;" it has been opposed as new, it has been admired as new. All its designations which we have just repeated show it to have been new. The younger Edwards wrote an essay on the "Improvements made in Theology by his father, President Edwards."[2] We do not mean to say, that the Edwardean school discovered principles which were never thought of before. They claim to have brought out into bold relief the obscurer faith of good men in all ages. They gave a new distinctness, a new prominence, to doctrines which had been more vaguely believed by the church. They produced new arguments for a faith which had been speculatively opposed by men who had practically sanctioned it. We say that Aristotle first discovered the syllogistic art, although Adam reasoned in syllogisms, whenever he reasoned at all. We say that Bacon first detected the law of induction, although Eve made obeisance to that law before she decided to eat the apple. We say that Longinus and Tully were among the first to find out the principles of rhetoric, and yet we are aware that all men, in all times, have known enough of those principles to comply with them in their

---
[1] Bib. Repertory, Vol. XXIII. p. 694.
[2] See Dr. Jonathan Edwards's Works, Vol. I. pp. 481—492.

speech. He is called a discoverer who makes that palpable which had been dim, and shows that to be reasonable which had formerly been held by an instinct.

We might illustrate these remarks by referring to several doctrines, but we will confine our illustration to the single truth, that an entirely depraved man has a natural power to do all which is required of him; a truth which has been so clearly unfolded by the New England divines, that it properly belongs to their distinctive system.[1] All unsophisticated thinkers, we are aware, have practically believed that a just God will not command men to do what they have no power to do; that he will not punish them with unending pain for doing as well as they can; that, in every case, physical ability is commensurate with obligation. In what sense, then, may so old a doctrine be called new? In this sense: the Edwardean school have made it more prominent and more effective than it has been made by some; have shown more fully than others have done its agreement with the truths of man's entire sinfulness and of God's decrees; have defended it against those metaphysical Calvinists who speculatively deny their own practical faith; have been the first to make obvious, prominent and impressive, the consistency of those two truths, which all good men have more or less secretly believed, — that a sinner can perform what a reasonable law requires of him, and that he certainly will never do as well as he can, unless by a special interposition of Heaven. They deserve far more gratitude for their originality in developing these truths, than Hume deserves for his originality in unfolding the laws of mental suggestion.

---

[1] Dr. Hodge errs in supposing that our natural power to repent must be the same as a power to regenerate ourselves. (Bib. Repertory, Vol. XXIII. pp. 682, 683.) The very term, regenerate, implies that there is a parent, and also a child distinct from the parent. It has a different relation from the term repentance. It refers to the renewing Father, as well as to the renewed offspring. To say that a man can repent, is as different from affirming that he can regenerate his soul, as to say that he can learn is different from affirming that he can impart knowledge to his soul; or as to say that he can go from one place to another is different from affirming that he can carry himself in his arms from one place to another. Dr. Hodge asks, "Where is the man who has ever regenerated himself?" We answer by asking, first, Where is the commandment which requires a sinner to regenerate himself? and secondly, Is there no difference between a man's actually doing what the law does require of him, and his being able to do it? There is a requisition that we make ourselves new hearts; but no requisition that we be born again, by a special divine influence; and it is one thing to have a power of obeying, and another thing to obey actually. Our Reviewer is not alone in overlooking these distinctions.

It has been lately maintained, however, that on this topic Edwards and his followers taught nothing which the Calvinistic standards had not taught with equal uniformity and consistency; that New England Divinity does not recognize a sinner's power to use his faculties aright, but simply recognizes the fact of his possessing a reason, a conscience and a will. When the word *able* is used in its literal and proper sense; a sense too simple to be made clearer by a definition; then, we are told, the Edwardean school believe, not that a sinner is able to use his capacities aright, but only that he is endued with the above named capacities, distinguishing him from brutes. After all his past opposition to Edwards on the Will, Dr. Hodge now seems to believe that Edwards, "Bellamy, Dwight, and the other great men of New England," *denied* that "ability limits responsibility," and meant no more than that "since the fall man retains all his faculties of soul and body, and is therefore a free, moral agent.[1]

Are our opponents right, then, in affirming that the far-famed "natural ability" of the Edwardean school means nothing more than the natural capacities of soul and body, and does not include an adequate power to use those capacities as they should be used?

1. This explanation is utterly inconsistent with the language of that school. It may agree with some of their expressions, but not with the rich variety of them. Our standards teach that, in the "proper sense of the terms," man *can* now repent, has now power to love. Do they say that a child, while it remains an *infant*, has power to speak, because it has the natural faculties of a speaker; that it can walk in its earliest days, because it has the natural faculties of a walker? Of what use is it to prove that man has the capacities of a moral agent, if he cannot use them in the right way? How can they be called power, in its only "proper" signification?

---

[1] This novel mode of explaining the Edwardean system has been advocated by several recent authors, and is here ascribed to Dr. Hodge on the ground of his assertions in Bib. Repertory, Vol. XXIII. pp. 681—683, 685, 686, 693, 694. On those pages he gives in his adhesion to the great New England standards concerning the will and sin, and alludes to our own "*hallucination*." In the same paragraph which refers to *our* hallucination, he says, that the advocates of the "Exercise Scheme" were led to a "*denial*" of the doctrine that sin consists in sinning, and that the three radical principles which he has imputed to a Convention Sermon, were never "*rejected*" by any class of New England divines reputed orthodox, except the Emmons and the New Haven schools (p. 694). We presume that he meant here, as we hope that he has meant elsewhere, exactly the opposite of what he said; but it was not very *opportune* for him to speak of our own hallucination, in the very paragraph which combines so singular a want of carefulness, with so singular a kind of charity.

and yet in this signification Edwards often affirms that we have power commensurate with duty. He refers not only to the existence, but also to the degree and extent of our faculties. Thus he writes: "We can give God no more than we have. Therefore if we give him so much, if we love him to the utmost *extent* of the faculties of our nature, we are excused. But when what is proposed, is only that we should love him as much as our capacity will allow, this excuse of want of capacity ceases, and obligation takes hold of us, and we are doubtless obliged to love God to the *utmost* of what is *possible* for us, with such faculties *and* opportunities *and* advantages to know God *as we have*."[1] The *faculties* must have *opportunities* enabling them to act.

Dr. Bellamy teaches, in a volume which Edwards recommended, that the heathen are without excuse because they enjoy "sufficient means of knowledge;" that God's law is on "a perfect level" with man's "natural powers *and* natural advantages;" "that if God looks upon the advantages of the heathen sufficient, no wonder that he so often speaks of the advantages of his own professing people as being *much more than* barely sufficient, even although they enjoy only the outward means of grace, without the inward influences of the Spirit;" "and thus we see how all mankind have *not only* sufficient natural powers, but *also* sufficient outward advantages to know God, and perfectly conform to his law, even the heathen themselves."[2] By sufficient outward advantages, Bellamy means all advantages except the special interposition of God's Spirit.

What says Dr. Smalley? "It must, I think, be granted that we do generally suppose a man's present duty cannot exceed his present *strength*, suppose it to have been *impaired* by what means it will."[3] If, then, the strength of the faculty be lessened, the duty is lessened. This strength of the faculty, and not the mere faculty itself, is power "in the proper sense of that term." The faculty must be strong enough to overcome all natural hindrances to right choice. Hence Dr. Smalley often speaks of a "want of opportunity" as excusing the sinner from blame.[4] Dr. Jonathan Edwards expressly declares that, on his father's theory, men have physical power to remove their moral inability; that is, they are able to do what they are unwilling to do."[5]

---

[1] Edwards on Original Sin, Part I. Ch. I. Sect. V.
[2] See Bellamy's Works, Vol. I. pp. 107, 109, 112, 115, 116, 117, 118, etc.
[3] Smalley's Sermon on Moral Inability, p. 5. Ed. 1811.
[4] Smalley's Sermon on Natural Ability, p. 38. Ed. 1811.
[5] Edwards's Works, Vol. I. p. 309. Dr. Edwards here, as elsewhere, affirms directly what Dr. Hodge implicitly denies, in Bib. Repertory, Vol. XXIII. p 6 &2

Dr. Hodge has seen fit to inform us, that "the aberration of the advocates of the Exercise Scheme" on this topic "was in the direction of ultra-Calvinism."[1] Let us then go a little way in this ultra-Calvinism. The greatest of those advocates addresses the unregenerate thus: "You are as able to love God, as to hate him. You are as able to turn from sin as to continue sinning. You are as able to love God before you do love him as afterwards." He often says that unrenewed men are "as able to do right as to do wrong, and to do their duty as to neglect their duty; to love God as to hate God, to choose life as to choose death; to walk in the narrow way to heaven as in the broad way to hell;" "as able to embrace the Gospel as a thirsty man is to drink water, or a hungry man to eat the most delicious food;" "they can love God, repent of sin, believe in Christ and perform every religious duty, as well as they can think, or speak, or walk."[2] And this is the common representation of the "Exercise" school, and this, according to Dr. Hodge, is "in the direction of ultra-Calvinism." It certainly is an avowal of something more than a mere impracticable faculty.

Again, if natural ability be nothing more than the capacities of reason, conscience and disabled will, what then is natural inability? Is it the want of reason, conscience and disabled will? When New England writers affirm that man has not natural power and is therefore not required to become as holy as his Maker, do they mean that he has not the faculties of a moral agent? Dr. Smalley answers the question by saying, "Natural inability consists in, *or arises from,* want of understanding, bodily strength, *opportunity,* or *whatever* may prevent our doing a thing when we are willing, and strongly enough disposed to do it;" and also, "Persons who have ordinary intellectual powers, and bodily senses, *and are arrived to years of discretion,* and *live under the light of the Gospel,* labor under no natural inability to obtain salvation" [by faith in Christ].[3] It is the common remark of

---

[1] Bib. Repertory, Vol. XXIII. p. 694.

[2] Emmons's Sermons, Vol. V. pp. 154, 175. Vol. IV. pp. 352, 357—359, 361, 514. Vol. VI. p. 92. The authority of Dr. Emmons on this subject is very important. He was the brother-in-law of Dr. Samuel Spring, and agreed with that divine more nearly, perhaps, than with any other. "When Dr. Spring died, I lost my right arm," was a remark which he often repeated. The most munificent founders of Andover Theological Seminary were the devoted adherents of Dr. Spring, and admirers of his theology, and this was Emmonism.

[3] Smalley's Sermons on Moral Inability and Natural Ability, pp. 9, 37, Ed. 1811. See also Catlin's Compendium, Essay XV. Griffin's Park Street Lectures, Lect. I. West on Moral Agency, Part I. Sect. 2. Dwight's Theology, Sermon 133.

the Edwardean school, that men have no inability to repent except their unwillingness, and this unwillingness is a sin, and sin is a voluntary act.

Our opponents are misled by confining their attention to one class of words, and using that class in its narrowest sense. When they read in Bellamy, for example, that the natural power to do right means "the capacities of a moral agent," they overlook his frequent explanations that "men's natural powers are *adequate* with the law of God, and so they, as to their natural capacities, are *capable* of a perfect conformity to the law."[1] We allow that, speaking in a general way, New England divines do often affirm, that our natural power is our natural capacity; but they do not mean to trifle; they employ the word *capacity* in its widest sense; they refer to a capacity which is *capable* of doing what is justly demanded of it; and not to an incapable capacity, which is nothing better than a natural incapacity, the very thing which they always deny. So when they speak of our natural powers and natural abilities, they mean abilities which are able, and powers which are sufficient to bear what is rightly laid upon them.[2] "Nothing can be plainer," says Emmons,[3] "than that those who have a natural power to act, have the same natural power to refrain from acting;" hence it is obvious that he uses the terms will, choice, moral agent, in their fullest sense, and, so used, they imply not a mere faculty of will, but a faculty able to choose or to refuse the same thing. What if a man have powers utterly incapable of performing the part assigned them? Merely because he has ears, can he be required to hear the conversation of the antipodes? Merely because he has eyes, can he be bidden, on penalty of eternal death, to see the remotest star of the universe? And on the same principle, what if he have a power of will? Can he be justly required to put forth a choice equal to that put forth by an archangel, or to perform any kind of act to which his powers are naturally inadequate?[4]

---

[1] Bellamy's Works, Vol. I. pp. 105, 106, 109, 115, etc. etc. Dr. Bellamy here uses the word "adequate;" Dr. Hodge objects to this word above all others relating to the subject, and yet claims to agree with Bellamy. See Bib. Report. Vol. XXIII. pp. 681—683, 693, 694.

[2] Smalley's Sermon on Natural Ability, pp. 38, 39. Ed. 1811. Bellamy's Works, Vol. I. p. 93. Ed. 1850.

[3] Emmons's Works, Vol. IV. pp. 304, 305.

[4] We had hoped that our Reviewer would attempt to explain the difference between the morality of requiring a man to love God when man has no real strength to do so, and the morality of requiring a man to love God with a greater degree of strength than belongs to man's constitution. See Bib. Sac. Vol. VIII. pp. 600,

The doctrine of New England is, that any powerlessness, in the original, literal and proper meaning of the word, is incompatible with obligation.

2. The new explanation which our opponents give of natural power, is inconsistent with the history of the disputes on the subject. President Edwards often says, that "no Arminian, Pelagian or Epicurean," can even conceive of any freedom greater than he ascribes to man; "and I scruple not to say, it is beyond all their wits to invent a higher notion, or form a higher imagination of liberty."[1] He has always been opposed by the assertion that, before the fall, men had more freedom than they have now; and that although in paradise they lost their liberty and power to obey, yet God has not lost his right to command. Here has been and is now, a dispute. Edwards affirms, that for men to have more than their present freedom is inconceivable. His opponents object, that they once had more and lost it. He says, that for men to have a power of freer choice than they now have, is as impossible, as for an animal in Terra Del Fuego to take a step always before the first step. His Calvinistic opponents reply, that this power which he ridicules was once possessed by Adam. What do they mean? That Adam had once a moral power to do right? But Edwards never disputed this fact, for this moral power is holiness itself. Do they mean that Adam lost the natural capacities of a moral agent? They disclaim such an idea. They must mean, therefore, that Adam had and lost the power of using his capacities aright; he lost his natural ability. But Edwards affirms, that the race have as real a natural ability as they ever had.

Again, the Edwardean affirms, that holy beings in heaven possess a natural but not a moral power to do wrong. Does he mean that they have the natural capacities of a moral agent? Then there would be no dispute. But there is a dispute. The Edwardean is reproved, and told that the blessed in heaven have *no* power to do wrong. Now does the objector mean that they will not (i. e. they have a moral impotence to) do wrong? The Edwardean agrees with

---

601. But our assailant has chosen an easier part, and has merely reaffirmed some irrelevant distinctions. See Bib. Report. Vol. XXIII. p. 681, 682. Does he really believe that the "civil good" of the old divines has any reference to the supposed holiness which exceeds our constitutional powers? If not, why did he flee to the misapplied distinction between "civil" and "spiritual obedience?" Our question still remains unanswered: What is the moral difference between punishing a man for not being virtuous when he is literally unable to be so, and punishing him for not being more virtuous than he is literally able to be?

[1] Letter to a Minister of the Church of Scotland.

him. Still, the objector perseveres in impugning the Edwardean, and denying just what the Edwardean affirms, that the spirits in heaven have a power to make a wrong use of their capacities, and this disputed power is natural ability. It is a singular phenomenon that our opposers ascribe to Adam in paradise, more liberty than to any other being in the universe. "The inhabitants of heaven," they say, "have no power to sin. Men and fallen spirits have, in themselves, no power to be holy. But Adam, being left to the freedom of his own will, had a power to do right and also to do wrong, and used his power in doing both"!

3. This new explanation of physical ability is disrespectful to the memory of our fathers. Many of them have supposed, that our national literature is honored by the Edwardean discriminations between physical and moral ability. And when the younger Edwards declared that before these distinctions were made, "the Calvinists were nearly driven out of the field by the Arminians, Pelagians and Socinians,"[1] did he mean that the tide of war was turned by his father's discovering man to be endued with reason, conscience, and disabled will? And when Dr. Dwight was borne so high as to sing,[2]

> "From scenes obscure did Heaven his Edwards call,
> That moral Newton and that second Paul,"—
> [Who,] "in one little life, the Gospel more
> Disclosed than all earth's millions kenned before,"—

did the bard thus exult because this "moral Newton" had found out that man, who was always known to be *wilful*, really had the capacity of will? And was it because this "second Paul" had detected a difference between the natural faculties of a moral agent, and the agent's inclination to use those faculties in a holy way, that another poet exclaimed on hearing of Edwards's death,

> "Nor can the muse in deepest numbers tell,
> How Zion trembled when this Pillar fell?"[3]

Did several of our strong-minded fathers publish volumes of long-drawn, wire-drawn arguments, to prove that the possession of a will was not the same thing with true virtue, which is moral power to do right? Did they expose themselves to cavil and obloquy, and the charge of "Pelagianism," merely for the sake of proclaiming the discovery that impenitent man was not a stone nor a brute, but was

---

[1] Dr. Jonathan Edwards's Works, Vol. I. p. 481.   [2] Triumph of Infidelity.
[3] See first edition of Edwards on Original Sin, p. x.

elevated above both by rational and moral faculties? Robert Hall teaches us, that the "important distinction" between physical and moral impotence "was not *wholly* unknown to our earlier divines;" and adds "The earliest regular treatise on this subject it has been my lot to meet with, was the production of Mr. Truman;" and yet the learned minister of Cambridge questions even Mr. Truman's "claim to *perfect* originality."[1] Did the profound genius, then, of Robert Hall, pay homage to Mr. Truman for anticipating our own Edwards, in the discovery that man, since the fall, retains his human nature and that this is not real holiness?[2] And have our fathers not only been cheating themselves with this "hallucination," but have their opponents been gravely disputing what few skeptics on earth ever called in question before? No. The New England theory of the will is a distinct and philosophical, and therefore uncommon, exposition of the very common faith, that a sinner can do without help what he is justly required to do without help, and can do with aid what he is justly bidden to do with aid. The theory may well be called original, for its faithfulness to human nature and the divine government; a faithfulness, alas! how unusual in scholastic treatises. So far forth as the theory unfolds the before hidden teachings of conscience, it is a specimen of the New England system; the substance of which is old, like all truth, but the form is novel, because it is a luminous and harmonious development of ideas which *had* been confused.

In the third place, New England Theology is Calvinism in an improved form. It does not pretend to be a perfect system. Both Edwards and Hopkins reiterated the wish and hope, that their successors would add to the improvements which the Genevan faith had already received. Neither does our system profess to be original in its cardinal truths. It has ever claimed that these great truths are the common faith of the church; that they are recognized in many evangelical creeds; that Calvinism contains the substance of New England Theology, not always well proportioned, not seldom intermingled

---

[1] Hall's Works, Vol. II. pp. 450, 451. American edition.

[2] Although Dr. Hodge claims to agree with Edwards on the Will, he fails to remember that, according to Edwards, a moral power to do right is a disposition to do right, and the want of this power is a disposition to do wrong. With much emphasis, Dr. Hodge insists that, "since the fall, men are *both* 'indisposed and disabled' to all spiritual good." (Bib. Repertory, Vol. XXIII. p. 681.) This expression means, on the theory of Edwards, that men are *both* indisposed *and* indisposed to all spiritual good. To be morally disabled is, with Edwards, only to be disinclined.

with the remnants of an erring scholasticism, and sometimes enveloped in inconsistences and expressed in a nervous style. "The voice is Jacob's voice, but the hands are the hands of Esau." The substance of our theology is Calvinistic; here it is old. Much of its self-consistency is Edwardean and Hopkinsian; here it is new. It is not mere Calvinism, but it is consistent Calvinism. Instead of pretending to be an entirely new revelation, it has always professed to be a revised and corrected edition of the Genevan creed. As such, it was extolled by its early friends, and ridiculed by its early foes. That Hopkins was far from having an ambition to shine as the originator of an altogether novel creed, is apparent from the following modest words which he wrote in his eightieth year: "I believe that most of the doctrines, if not all, I have published, are to be found in the writings of former divines; viz. Calvin, Van Mastricht, Saurin, Boston, Manton, Goodwin, Owen, Bates, Baxter, Charnock, the Assembly of Divines at Westminster, Willard, Ridgley, Shepard, Hooker, etc. These, indeed, did not fully explain some of those doctrines which are asserted or implied in their writings; and many, if not most of them, are, in some instances, inconsistent with themselves, by advancing contrary doctrines."[1] It was in reference to his labor in fitting together the heterogeneous parts of the Genevan creed, that Emmons said, "I have spent half my life in making joints." Both he and Hopkins defended the substance of Calvinism earnestly and reverently; and the Genevan divine who now assails their memory, must be ignorant of their controversial successes, or careless of that grace which is called "the memory of the heart."

Let us now allude to a few particulars, in which the New England divines have been employed in straightening the crooked parts of Calvinism, and have loved to retain all its theories which could be made to hold together. A favorite New England idea has been, that the certainty of human action is distinct from its necessity. But this is Calvinistic; for the great Genevan himself has said: "By impossible I mean that which never was, and which is prevented from being in future by the ordination and decree of God." "There is no reason for cavilling at the remark, that a thing cannot be done, which the Scriptures declare will not be done."[2] "I will not hesitate, therefore, simply to confess with Augustine, that the will of God is the necessity of things, and that everything is necessary which he has willed, just as those things will certainly happen which he has fore-

---

[1] Hopkins's Ms. Letter in possession of the author.
[2] Institut. Lib. II. Cap. VII. § 5. See also § 21.

seen."[1] An Edwardean never complains of such definitions, but only regrets that they are so often forgotten by the Genevan school, and that a necessity is merged into a fate.

So are New England writers satisfied with many definitions which Calvinists give of human freedom. In describing the liberty which is "inseparable from the will," that learned old Puritan, W. Perkins, says: "Liberty of will consists in a double faculty; the first is, that when of itself it chooses anything, it can also on the other hand refuse the same; in the schools, this is called the liberty of contradiction. The second is, that when it chooses anything, it can choose another or the contrary; and this is called the liberty of contrariety."[2] We are often told by the Genevan divines, that the will is not determined to its volitions by a *natural* or instinctive necessity, as the sun is necessitated to shine, and the fire to burn, and the horse to eat grass or hay;[3] but that our freedom involves the intellectual faculty or power to discern good or evil, the power of will to choose or refuse either, and also the strength to execute the choice.[4]

What more can a New England theologian desire? Only one thing; that the Calvinists would not here, as elsewhere, disown their faith. But this they do; for they no sooner ascribe to us free agency, than they take it all back, and affirm that man is free only to evil, and has not the slightest degree of power to choose good. This free will, "inseparable from man," is yet said to be "injured and destroyed;" we have an "utter and absolute impotence to do right;" and, in the words of Boston, "our father Adam, falling from God, did by his fall so dash him and us all in pieces, that there was no whole part left, either in him or us," etc. etc.[5] Now we affirm, that if it be possible for human language to express a contradiction (like iron-wood, σιδηρόξυλον), it does express one in the Calvinistic sentence, that (properly speaking) man *must* have the ability to choose between right and wrong, and yet has not "the least particle of ability" to choose right.[6]

---

[1] Instit. Lib. III. Cap. XXIII. § 8.

[2] "The Free Grace of God and the Free Will of Man," translated in the Southern Pres. Review, Vol. IV. pp. 527—540.

[3] See Turretin, Inst. Theol. Pars I. p. 729. Van Mastricht, Lib. IV. Cap. 4. § xxx.

[4] See, for example, Bucan. Inst. Theol. Loc. XVIII. § 1. Thomas Boston gives a definition equally unlimited.

[5] Boston's Works, Fol. Ed. p. 815.

[6] Dr. Hodge is indignant at us for quoting sentences in a Princeton Review, which are understood to declare that man has an adequate power of choosing

It is to relieve evangelical doctrine from this strife with itself, that our divines have explained the sinner's power of choosing right, to be consonant with the certainty of his choosing wrong; and the certainty of his choosing wrong, to be no literal necessity; and thus they have united the opposite poles of science into one attractive system. The process is a simple one, but nearly all discoveries appear easy to him who has once made them.

In their dogmatic theories, rather than in their practical faith, Calvinists have contradicted themselves with regard to the divine agency in producing sin. Inspiration declares, that God 'hardens the heart of men,' and 'moves them to do wrong,' and 'puts a lying spirit within them,' and 'deceives them,' and 'creates evil.' These intense expressions of a profound truth have been transferred into the reasonings of the Genevan school; and even the learned founder of that school, who was far milder on this topic than many of his successors have been, has yet sometimes written as if the fervid words of inspired prophets were to be used like the exact phrases of a metaphysical creed. In reply to men of "delicate ears," who choose to say that God permitted, rather than caused, the obduracy of Pharaoh, Calvin remarks, that "there is a difference between suffering a thing to be done, and actually doing it; and God sets forth in this passage not his endurance, but his power. It troubles me not to say, and confidently to believe, what is so often said in the Bible, that God brings the wicked into a reprobate mind, delivers them over to shameful vices, blinds their intellect and hardens their heart. It may be said that God is thus made the author of sin, and this is detestable impiety; but I answer, that he is not blamed in the least, when he is said to exercise judgment; therefore if the blinding of the mind be his judicial act, he cannot be charged with crime for inflicting this penalty."[1] "What says the Spirit? Hardening is from God, that he may urge them on (praecipitet) whom he designs to destroy."[2] In his Commentary on Rom. 9: 18, Calvin censures those men as *diluti moderatores*, who say that the hardening of the heart is a mere permission of wickedness. But the ablest men of his school often deny

---

between good and evil; and for not quoting other sentences in the same Review which are understood to deny that man has such a power. But this indignation is unwarranted; for we expressly said, and our aim was to show, that the Review contradicts itself; and need we particularize *all* the instances in which its pendulum swings from one to the other extreme? Comp. Bib. Sac. Vol. VIII. pp. 600—602, with Bib. Repert. Vol. XXIII. pp. 688, 689.

[1] Calvini Opp. Om. Tom. I. p. 269, in Exodum 4: 21.
[2] Op. Om. Tom. I. p. 35, in Josue 11: 19.

that God exerts any positive agency in the production of sin, and then contradict themselves, by saying that our passive nature is itself sin. Must not this nature have a creating and sustaining cause? Adam does not create it, nor Satan. It is created, then, by God. Calvinists believe that preservation is a continued creation, and they are driven to admit that our nature is constantly re-created by Jehovah, and yet the nature is sin. In this dilemma, they rush to a scholastic distinction which, even if it mean anything, avails nothing; and they affirm that God is the author of our nature as an essence, but is not the author of it as sin! Who then is the author of it as sin, or as *a* sin?[1] It must have an author. Is man himself the personal cause of his passive iniquity, which exists before his own personal action?[2] Nothing is gained by saying, that nature often means disposition.[3] For, we ask, who is the author of this passive disposition? There is no way of covering up or retreating from the inference, that if our passive disposition, which we cannot separate from our infantile nature, be iniquity, or *an* iniquity, then the author of that disposition is the author of iniquity. And yet men who hold the premise, reject the conclusion, and deny, with emphasis, that He who made us, made also the nature, i. e. the disposition with which we were made! Seeing these theorists in trouble with their own hopeless incongruity, the New England divine went to their help, more than a half century ago. He taught that men must be the agents of all their own sin, and at the same time that God has made and placed them so that they will certainly and freely do wrong; that God never causes wickedness, in such a sense as renders it literally impossible for the sinner to avoid it, and yet that he never leaves the impenitent man in a state in which his wicked choices are uncertain. Thus is preserved the profound meaning of the declarations, that men harden their own hearts, and that God hardens them; and thus it is perfectly consistent to deny that Jehovah is the author of sin, and at the same time to affirm, that he so constitutes and circumstances men, that they will certainly do evil. The New England theory has been well expressed by the two Edwardses, thus: "The divine disposal, by which sin certainly comes into existence, is only establishing the certainty

---

[1] Each created human nature is itself sin. Then it is *a* sin. There are as many passive sins, therefore, as there are infants. Truly, we need a new *language*, or else New England Divinity.

[2] Some reply, that we were the causes of our own passive sin, when we were in Adam. But there is yet wanting a *personal* cause of this sin, existing in ourselves as distinct persons.

[3] Bib. Repertory, Vol. XXIII. pp. 624, 685.

of its future existence. If that *certainty*, which is no other than moral necessity, be not inconsistent with human liberty, then surely the cause of that certainty, which is no other than the *divine disposal*, cannot be inconsistent with such liberty."[1] Hopkins expresses this truth, when he says: "Something must have taken place previous to his sin, and in which the sinner had no hand, with which his sin was so connected as to render it certain that sin would take place just as it does."[2] Here is the substance of Calvinism, in the self-congruous form of New England Theology.

Were it seemly to smile, while writing on so grave a theme, we should be tempted to do so by the lame English on which our Reviewer essays to get away from the logical results of his creed. He is so fond of using fervid expressions in his argumentative paragraphs, that he is often misled by them into errors from which he can extricate himself only by an unwholesome strain upon his mother tongue. At first he said with much apparent emotion, that our nature is "truly and properly sin."[3] We replied, that if our nature be sin, the sin must have been committed by the author of our nature, just as the author of any actual sin committed that sin.[4] Now what does our Reviewer rejoin? He gravely attempts to defend himself by the plea, which at the best would be unavailing, that the word nature, when it is called sin, means not essence, but disposition.[5] Now sub-

---

[1] Dr. Jonathan Edwards's Works, Vol. I. pp. 485, 486. See the same idea in the President's Inquiry on the Freedom of the Will, Part IV. Sections 9 and 10.

[2] Hopkins's Works, Vol. I. p. 106, new Edition. It is readily admitted, that this writer and a few others in New England, have sanctioned the phraseology that God is the author of our wickedness. But, first, this is not the common phraseology of our best divines; and secondly, it does not express, without much qualification, the real philosophy of our writers who employ it. They never mean that Jehovah is the author of moral evil, in any such sense as takes from man the full natural power to avoid every kind and degree of sin. They teach that our iniquity is as really our own, and as really our free act, as if God had never made it certain. They affirm that he never produces any sin which precedes or overpowers, or in any way opposes, our own choice, and that our choice remains as free as the choice of any one can be, on earth or in heaven. Such a phrase as 'God is the author of iniquity,' has recommended itself to them by its *strength*, and not by its philosophical exactness. It is unfaithful to their precise meaning, and belongs to the style of excitement and impression, rather than to that of calm discussion. It was Hopkins's reverence for Calvin, and his fondness for expressing his creed in the powerful language of inspired men, which led him to say that our sins are *caused*, when he meant that they are *made certain*, by the positive efficiency of our Sovereign. His phraseology on this topic has been improved by more recent divines.

[3] Bib. Repertory, Vol. XXIII. pp. 314, 315. [4] Bib. Sac. Vol. VIII. pp. 631, 632.

[5] Bib. Repertory, Vol. XXIII. pp. 684, 685, 690.

stitute the word "disposition" for its synonym "nature," in our Reviewer's creed as first written, and see if it be, in his own language, "designed to state with all possible *precision* the intellectual propositions to be received as true." Here is the sentence: "It [Dr. Hodge's creed] acknowledges Adam as the head and representative of his posterity, in whom we had our probation, in whom we sinned and fell; so that we come into the world under condemnation, being born children of wrath, and deriving from him a nature [i. e. a *disposition*] not merely diseased, weakened, or predisposed to evil, but which is 'itself,' as well as 'all the motions thereof,' 'truly and properly sin!'"[1] Then our disposition, so strong to sin, is *weakened*, and even our *disposition* is *predisposed* to evil, and this predisposed disposition is, in itself, as well as its motions, sin. Who committed *this* sin? Did any divine ever use such language before? Can a parallel to it be found, except in our Commentator's exegesis of Rom. 5:12; which amounts to the doctrine that by one man all are punished, and because they are punished, they are punished, and so all men are exposed to punishment, because they are punished.[2] Is it wise for our friend to cherish so weakened and predisposed a disposition for technical terms, that he cannot tear himself from their net-work without maiming the idiom of our fathers? Would it not have been more consonant with the genius of an "easy English," for him to take up with what he calls "the last arrow in the quiver," i. e. the theory of a Convention sermon, and to confess outright, that his first affirmation was not what John Foster calls "the simple, general language of intellect,"[3] but was too intense for the Reviewer's own "sober second thought."[4]

---

[1] Bib. Repertory, Vol. XXIII. pp. 314, 315.   [2] Bib. Sac. Vol. VIII. p. 625.
[3] Foster's Essays, Andover edition, p. 192.
[4] We are happy to confess that although Dr. Hodge has not recalled his assertion, Our passive nature is sin; yet in the creed which he gives in his last Review, p. 677, he has amended it; and he now says, that we are "*by* nature the children of wrath, infected with a sinful depravity *of* nature." The *depravity* is the *disposition* belonging to the nature. In *some* connections the word nature means disposition; but never in such connections as those in which our Reviewer used it. As Dr. Hodge has avowed his deference to the great Edwardeans of New England, we commend to his notice a remark of the younger Edwards (Works, Vol. I. p. 483), that it is hard to conceive of a distinction between the authorship of an act and of the sinfulness of that act. How can Dr. Hodge conceive of God as the author of a disposition and not as the author of the sinfulness of it? Does not our Reviewer rush into two difficulties in order to avoid one? See Bib. Repertory, Vol. XXIIL pp. 684, 685.

In the fourth place, New England divinity has been marked by strong, practical common sense. Its framers were remarkable men, invigorated by the scenes of an eventful era, and claiming our deference for their love of plain, wholesome truth. We might extol them as diligent readers. It is supposed that, on an average, Hopkins studied twelve hours a day, for more than half a century. He read in the original Latin the whole of Poole's five folios, nearly the whole of Calvin's nine folios, Turretin, Van Mastricht, and the standard treatises of English divines. For seventy years, Emmons remained like a fixture in his parsonage study, and like his brethren read "books which are books." Dr. West sat near his library so long, that his feet wore away the wood-work in one part of his room, and left this enduring memorial of his sedentary habit. We care not, however, to extol our divines as readers. Many of them had been disciplined for practical life. The younger Edwards, who perused Van Mastricht seven times, was noted for his wisdom in his intercourse with men. It was a blessing not to be despised, that some of our standard-bearers had been early trained to rural labors in a new country, and by this discipline they gained a healthy and practical judgment. Nearly all of them had been teachers of the common school, and Luther has well said, that "no man is fit to be a theologian, who has not been a school-master." They were married men, and thus were saved from writing like the exsiccated monks of the Middle Ages. That melancholy phrase, "He hath no children," could not be applied to our divines, as to many who have speculated in favor of infant damnation. Our later theologians, as Dwight and Appleton, were adepts in the philosophy of Reid, Oswald, Campbell, Beattie, Stewart; and this has been termed *the philosophy of common sense*. The tendency of literature, during the last hundred years, has been to develop "the fundamental laws of human belief," and has aided our writers in shaping their faith according to those ethical axioms, which so many fathers in the church have undervalued. A modern reviewer has termed these axioms the germs of infidelity; but without them skepticism is our only refuge. There has never been a more independent class of thinkers than our Edwardean theologians. They lived under a free government in church and state. Nor council nor university could awe them down. Hence they did not copy after other men, so much as exercise, and thereby strengthen, their own judgment. They were peculiar, also, in being called to write a theology for the pulpit. In general, divines have written for the schools; but our fathers wrote for men, women and children.

The Germans have wondered that several of our theological systems are in the form of sermons. It is a practical form, and it was designed to exhibit a practical theology. We can say of it, as of few other systems, it is *fit* to be preached. It has been accused of metaphysics, by men who distinguish between the sin belonging to us as natures, and the sin belonging to us inchoatively as bodies, and the sin belonging to us as persons. But the metaphysics of New England Theology is such as the yeomen of our fields drank down for the sincere milk of the word. It is the metaphysics of common sense. There are pious men, trained under other systems, who say in their creeds, that let man do whatever he can possibly do, there is no atonement available for him, if he be of the non-elect. But when these pious men are preaching to the non-elect, they hide this notion, "like virtue." We can hardly repress a smile, when we hear good old Thomas Boston at one time exhort his impenitent hearers never to commit a sin, at another time assure them of their utter impotence to do anything which is not sin, and after all say to them, " Do what you *can;* and, it may be, while ye are doing what ye *can* for yourselves, God will do for you what ye *cannot*."[1] It is because our theology has been practical in its aims, that it has been, more than any other system, devoted to the ethical character of the acts preceding conversion, to the wisdom of demanding an immediate compliance with the law, and to the scientific refutation of all excuses for prolonged impenitence. Dr. Hopkins valued none of his speculations so highly as those in which he proved the duty of a sinner's instant surrender to God.[2]

But let us illustrate the practical nature of New England divinity, and its agreement with the intuitions of a sound judgment, by a reference to its theory concerning the nature of moral evil. This theory is just what Dr. Hodge affirms it not to be, "that all sin consists in sinning; that there can be no moral character but in moral acts."[3] We regard it as a dishonor cast upon the faith of our greatest divines, to deny that it has been and now is characterized by the adoption of this simple truth.

1. The mode in which our Edwardean authors have reasoned on

---

[1] Boston's Works, Fol. Ed. p. 52.
[2] It were easy to trace the influence of this doctrine upon the missionary spirit which distinguished the early advocates of the New England creed, and also upon the revivals of religion in the midst of which that creed was developed, and to the furtherance of which it has conduced more than any other system.
[3] Bib. Repertory, Vol. XXIII. pp. 693, 694.

the doctrine of ability, proves that they must have had the good sense to resolve all sin into moral acts. Even our Reviewer will allow that they believed sin to consist in some kind of violated obligation. They are understood, by nearly all their friends and foes, to have believed that ability is commensurate with obligation. And if any man admit that he is able and obligated to avoid all sin, he must either contradict himself, or else admit that he has no sin antecedent to his choice. For if the doctrine of power commensurate with duty be true, and if we be literally unable to do or to have a thing, we are not obligated to do or to have it. Now we are literally unable to have a well-balanced nature preceding our first choice. We are, therefore, not obligated to have it, and are not sinful for not having it. We are equally unable to avoid an ill-balanced nature preceding our first choice. We are, therefore, not obligated to unmake ourselves before birth and before our first act, and are not sinful in being born just as we were made by the Power which we could not resist. And not only is it true that our nature, antecedent to our first choice and beyond the reach of our faculties, is free from moral blame, but also if we cannot afterwards change it, and can only resist it, we are not blamable for not changing it, and are only blamable for not resisting it. And this is the consecutive theology of New England.[1]

2. That our Edwardean divines were practical enough to regard all sin as a moral act, is evident from their mode of reasoning on the doctrine of our Paradisiacal offence. According to their creed, we are never obligated to perform an act which we cannot perform, and therefore are never obligated to perform an act *where* and *when* we cannot perform it. Now we never could have obeyed a law in Eden, for we were never there. Of course we were never obligated to obey a law of that place, and therefore we never sinned in not obeying it. Again, we never could have obeyed a law at the time of Adam's dwelling in Eden, and of course were never bound to obey it, and thus were never sinful in not obeying it. Now we can no more prevent an evil *make* of our souls before choice, than we could have prevented an occurrence in Paradise. We might as justly be commanded to go back six thousand years and refuse to eat the apple, as we can be commanded to go back one week before birth, and unmake our natures. And if we are not sinful for Adam's offence because it eludes all our natural power, then, by parity of reasoning, we are not

---

[1] President Edwards often declares, that the kind of necessity which "the will has nothing to *do* in," "does excuse persons, and free them from all fault or blame." Inquiry on the Will, Part IV. Sect. iii.

sinful for our bad moral structure before birth, because that eludes all our natural power. And so far forth as it is literally impossible for us in one instant to renovate our natural sensibilities, just so far forth are we free from sin in not renovating them, and are bound only to refuse the wrong indulgence of them. This is the *consistent* theology of New England.

3. The speculations of our Edwardean divines on moral agency, are a proof of their having adopted the maxim of common sense, that all sin consists in sinning. And here the great fact is, that they looked upon moral *agency* as essential to good or ill desert, and upon a moral *agent* as the only responsible being, and they frequently describe men as becoming sinners "as soon as they become moral *agents*," and not before. Whenever they speak of the brutes, who "do not act from choice, guided by understanding," or of anything "that is purely passive and moved by natural necessity," they deny that such existences are sinful.[1] According to Dr. Hodge, there is sin in a nature which is incapable of any action; but according to the Edwardeans, men "are subjects of command or moral government in nothing at all, and all their moral agency is entirely excluded, and no room is left for virtue or vice in the world,"[2] so far forth as there is no possibility of virtuous or vicious acts. In whatever degree men deny the existence of virtuous action, they "do evidently shut all virtue out of the world, and make it impossible that there should ever be any such thing in any case, or that any such thing should ever be conceived of."[3] Both Edwards and his disciples often assert, that if there be an act which precedes every act of will, it cannot be subject to any command or precept, directly or indirectly, and therefore cannot be either obedience or disobedience: "if the soul either obeys or disobeys in this act, it is wholly involuntarily; there is no willing obedience or rebellion, no compliance or opposition of will in the affair, and what sort of obedience or rebellion is this?"[4] Now, *a fortiori*, if there can be no involuntary sinful *act*, there can be no involuntary sinful *nature*. Volumes might be filled with the repetitions which these men make of the assertion, that all sin is perverted free-*agency*, and that free-agency "consists in choosing, and in nothing else."[5] What says Dr. Dwight, with whom our Reviewer professes to agree on this subject? "*Man is the actor of his own sin*. His sin is *therefore* wholly his own; chargeable only to

---
[1] Edwards on the Will, Part I. Sect. V. and Part III. Sect. II.
[2] Ib. Part III. Sect. IV.   [3] Ib. Sect. VII.   [4] Ib. Sect. IV.
[5] Dr. William R. Weeks's Nine Sermons, p. 72.

himself; chosen by him unnecessarily, while possessed of a power to choose otherwise; *avoidable* by him; and *of course* guilty and righteously punishable. *Exactly* the same natural power is in this case possessed by him, while a sinner, which is afterwards possessed by him when a saint; which Adam possessed before he fell, and which the holy angels now possess in the heavens. This power is also, in my view, perfect freedom; a power of agency, as absolute as can be possessed by an intelligent creature."[1] "The advocates of the Exercise Scheme," whose aberration, according to Dr. Hodge, "was in the direction of ultra-Calvinism,"[2] uniformly say, "When we talk of moral agency, we talk of some kind of *action* or *exertion*, and not merely of something which may be a foundation for action, and is yet perfectly and entirely distinct from it. When we speak of a person, or moral being, as the subject of punishment or reward, or as having in him desert of praise or blame, it is agreeable to the common sense and understanding of men, to consider him *as in exercise*, at least as *having put forth* some motion or exertion."[3]

The standard Edwardean definition of law is, a rule of moral conduct. What other law is there to be transgressed? The standard definition of conscience is, the faculty to regulate moral conduct. What faculty is there to regulate a condition preceding choice? And where has obligation been described as anything more than a force binding to obedience? And what is obedience but activity? Here are facts, and they are more decisive than particular words and phrases, in favor of the proposition, that the New England Theology defines sin as the chosen rebellion against law, conscience and duty.

4. The speculations of our Edwardean divines on the nature of virtue, give evidence of their having adopted the sensible theory, that all sin consists in moral acts. Everybody knows their doctrine to have been, that the whole of virtue is comprehended in love to the Creator and his creatures; in "love to being in general;" and is not this love a voluntary act? Virtue is said to imply "consent and union with being in general;"[4] and what is consent but an act of will? It is said to consist in principle; but, says Edwards, "a principle of virtue, I think, is owned by the most considerable of late writers on

---

[1] Dwight's Works, Sermon 27.   [2] Bib. Repertory, Vol. XXIII. p. 694.
[3] West on Moral Agency, Part I. Sect. 1. In the very first sentence of his Treatise, this "patriarch of Berkshire" says, that moral agency "consisteth in spontaneous, voluntary exertion." See also Prof. Wines's Inquiry, *passim*.
[4] Edwards on the Nature of True Virtue, Chap. I. See also Hopkins on Holiness. Dwight's Sermons, 97, 98, 99.

morality to be general benevolence or public affection;"[1] and is not bene-*volence* a voluntary feeling? And does not Edwards often say, that affections "are only certain modes of the exercise of the will?"[2] His whole doctrine of the affections is, that they "are no other than the more *vigorous* and *sensible* exercises of the inclination and will of the soul;" and that "true religion in great part consists in holy affections;"[3] that is, in the more vigorous and sensible holy exercises.

But the objectors say, Virtue, according to Edwards, lies in "a good will." True, but what is a good will? It is, he adds, "the most proper, direct and immediate subject of command," "for other things can be required no otherwise than as they depend upon, and are the fruits of a good will." Now what is the immediate subject of command? He says: "The first and determining act" of the will is that which "more especially" "command or precept has a proper respect to," and "this determining, governing act must be the proper object of precept, or none."[4] This determining, governing *act* of the will, is, then, the "good will" in which moral excellence resides.

The objectors reply, that virtue, according to Edwards, lies "in the tendency and inclination of the heart to virtuous action;" but when he speaks thus, he means a voluntary tendency, and inclination, for he says that "one, even the least, degree of preponderation (all things considered), is *choice*;"[5] and also that the virtuous "habits or qualities, as humility, meekness, patience, mercy, gratitude, generosity, heavenly-mindedness," — "all these things are dispositions and inclinations of the heart."[6] Now what are these dispositions and inclinations? In one of the most emphatic passages of his best treatise, Edwards remarks: "Whatever names we call the *act* of the will by, choosing, refusing, *approving, disapproving, liking, disliking*, embracing, rejecting, determining, directing, commanding, forbidding, *inclining*, or *being averse*, a *being pleased or displeased, all* may be reduced to this of *choosing*. For the soul to act *voluntarily* is, evermore, to act *electively*."[7]

---

[1] Edwards on the Nature of True Virtue, Chap. VI.
[2] Edwards on the Will, Part III. Sect. IV.
[3] Edwards on the Religious Affections, Part I. Sect. I.
[4] Edwards on the Will, Part III. Sect. IV. and Part IV. Sect. I.
[5] Edwards on the Will, Part III. Sect. VI.   [6] Ibid.
[7] Edwards on the Will, Part I. Sect. I. When our theologians say, "Virtue is voluntary," it is idle for Dr. Hodge to interpret them as meaning, virtue "inheres in the will," but is not an exercise of it. He might as well represent them as thinking that the finiteness of the will is voluntary, for finiteness inheres in the will, or as saying that the existence of the will is voluntary, for existence belongs to the will.

It is, then, a settled principle, that in the Edwardean theology all virtue consists in the love of beings according to their value; that is, in the love of the greater more than of the less; and this love is an act. It is an act of the will, for, according to Edwards, the will is "that by which the mind chooses anything," and to love the greater more than the less is to choose the greater. Now the Edwardean theology has been shown to be self-consistent; and as virtue consists in action, so does sin. "It must be also observed and kept in mind, that sin, as does holiness, consists in the motions or exercises of the heart or will, and in nothing else. Where there is no exercise of heart, nothing of the nature of moral inclination, will, or choice, there can be neither sin nor holiness." "Sin consists in that affection and those exercises which are directly opposed to disinterested benevolence to being in general."[1] Our Reviewer has suddenly announced his agreement with Dr. Dwight on the nature of sin. Now every one knows, that Dwight resolved all virtue into benevolence, and he therefore says, in consonance with himself: "Sin, universally, is no other than selfishness or a *preference* of one's self to all other beings, and of one's private interests and gratifications to the well-being of the universe, of God and the intelligent creation."[2] "Selfishness consists in a *preference* of ourselves to others and to all others; to the universe and to God. This is sin, and *all that in the Scriptures is meant by sin*."[3] Now if the word "preference" do not express an intelligent act, involving comparison and volition, no word can express it.

Need we say more? Is it not notorious that certain Princeton divines have long been fearful of Edwards's theory of virtue, and have dreaded to admit it within their walls, lest, like the Trojan horse, it let out an army of Hopkinsian heresies, which they have loved to call "Pelagian"?[4] They have known perfectly well, that

---

[1] Hopkins's System of Divinity, Chap. VIII. See also his Treatise on Holiness, *passim*. See also Bellamy's Works, Vol. I. pp. 130 seq.

[2] Dwight's Works, Sermon 80.   [3] Ibid.

[4] Dr. Miller, in his Memoir of Pres. Edwards, treats "the father of Hopkinsianism" with great urbanity, but expresses the opinion that if Edwards "had foreseen the use which has since been made of the doctrine of this Dissertation [on Virtue], he would either have shrunk from its publication, or have guarded its various aspects with additional care," p. 244. But Edwards adopted his theory of virtue while he was a member of Yale College; he wrote his Dissertation upon it three years before his death. It therefore contains his matured views. It is written with far more care than his Treatise on Original Sin. It was probably the theme of frequent conferences with Hopkins, who drew from it the conclusions so much regretted by Dr. Miller. Edwards was accustomed to subject all his works to the criticism of Hopkins, his nearest clerical neighbor

if holiness be reduced to a disinterested love, sin will be reduced to a partial love, and if a consecutive logic has once resolved moral character into these voluntary acts, it will next infer an ability to perform or omit them, and this ability cannot exist, for it was believed in by "Pelagius."

5. That our Edwardean divines were practical enough to resolve all sin into wicked practice, is evident from their sharp discriminations between sin and the occasions of sin. Two of their most prominent doctrines have been, that the moral character of an act lies in the act itself rather than in its cause, and that the first occasion of wicked acts cannot be itself wicked. "If all sin," say they, "be caused by that which is sin, then sin exists as a cause, before it exists at all." If an active choice cannot be well or ill deserving, unless it proceed from a passive nature that is well or ill deserving, then its character lies not in itself, but in something antecedent to itself, and this is the error which the New England divines have regarded as subversive of their entire system.[1]

They often speak of sin as literally belonging to "the native bent," the "dispositions," "inclinations," "propensities," "tendencies," "habits," "relish," "taste," "temper," of the heart. But these terms, when thus used by our most eminent authors, are designed to signify the acts which involve choice. Dr. Bellamy, whom our Reviewer describes as strenuous in his opposition to the doctrine that all sin consists in act, says "that sinners are *free* and voluntary in their bad temper," "hearty in it;" that "this evil bent of our hearts is not of his [God's] making, but is the spontaneous propensity of our own wills; for, we being born devoid of the divine image, ignorant of God, and insensible of his glory, do, of our own accord, turn to ourselves, etc.—from whence we natively *become* averse to God," etc.

---

for seven years, and to follow that great man's advice. It is on record that, in 1755, Hopkins and Bellamy spent two nights and a day with Edwards, in examining his kindred Dissertation on the End for which God created the World. Both this and the Dissertation on True Virtue were first published by Hopkins, seven years after Edwards's death. Is it at all probable, that so inquisitive a man as the original editor of these two works, had never conversed with Edwards on the consequences logically resulting from them? Can we believe, that so plain-spoken a divine as Hopkins would have built his system upon them, and not apprized his readers that his familiar friend, who drew out the premises, would not accept the conclusion?

[1] See, for example, Edwards on the Will, Part IV. Sect. I. Dr. Jonathan Edwards's Works, Vol. I. pp. 429—432, etc. Hopkins's System of Divinity, Chap. IV. West on Moral Agency, Part I. Sect. IV.

He approves of Mr. Stoddard's remark, that "self-love is the very root of original sin."[1] He has left the following memorable words:

"These [sinful tendencies] are the earliest dispositions that are discovered in our nature; and although I do not think that they are concreated by God, together with the essence of our souls, yet they seem to be the very first propensities of the new-made soul. So that they are, in a sense, connatural; our whole hearts are perfectly and entirely bent this way, from their very first *motion*. These propensities, perhaps, in some sense, may be said to be contracted, in opposition to their being strictly and philosophically natural, because they are not created by God with the essence of the soul, but *result from its native choice*, or rather, more strictly, *are themselves its native choice*. But most certainly these propensities are not contracted in the sense that many vicious habits are, namely, by long use and custom. In opposition to such vicious habits, they may be called connatural. Little children do very early bad things, and contract bad dispositions; but these propensities are evidently antecedent to every bad thing infused or instilled by evil examples, or gotten by practice, or occasioned by temptations. And hence it is become customary to call them natural, and to say that it is our very nature to be so inclined; and to say that these propensities are natural, would to common people be the most apt way of expressing the thing; but it ought to be remembered that they are not natural in the same sense as the faculties of our souls are; for they are not the workmanship of God, but *are our native choice, and the voluntary, free, spontaneous bent of their hearts*. And to keep up this distinction, I frequently choose to use the word *native*, instead of *natural*."[2]

President Edwards and Dr. Hopkins often speak of holiness as literally existing in our spiritual discernment, and of sin as literally existing in our spiritual blindness; but they mean a discernment

---

[1] For these and similar testimonies, see Bellamy's Works, Vol. I. pp. 97, 98, 153, 154. Vol. II. pp. 554, 555, 581. Dr. Smalley differed from Bellamy (as well as from himself), on this topic, at least in words. He says that there is a sin of nature, "so entirely independent of the will as to be prerequisite to" every wrong volition. He does not allow, however, that the sinful principle is dormant, but styles it an active principle.

[2] Bellamy's Works, Vol I. pp. 138, 139. The treatise from which this passage is taken, is the one which President Edwards endorsed publicly. Dr. Nathan Strong says: "What we call a new moral principle, may also be called a new taste, relish, temper, disposition, or *habit of feeling* respecting moral objects and truth." "A temper, disposition, inclination, taste or relish, which are right or wrong, mean the same as a heart or will that is right or wrong." "The will, the heart, and the affections may in most moral and evangelical discourses, be used as words of the same meaning." Now what are the affections? "The sensible *exercises* of the heart and will are what we call the affections, such as love, delight, rejoicing, hatred, enmity, mourning, and all these are *exercises* of the heart." Sermons, Vol. I. pp. 103, 104, 105, 167, 168.

which involves a right choice, and a blindness which involves a wrong choice, and in the choice alone lies the holiness and sin. "It will be found on examination," says Dr. Hopkins, "that if *practical judgment* has any meaning, it intends something which implies a sense of heart or a degree of inclination or will." "Everything practical or that relates to practice, belongs to the heart or will." "Whenever, therefore, there is a practical judgment concerning anything that is presented to the mind, as the object of choice, that it is good, eligible and excellent, there is taste and *choice actually begun*." "By understanding, knowledge and wisdom, in Scripture, is commonly meant true holiness, which consists not at all in mere speculation, but in the *exercise* of a right taste and inclination of heart, in a view and sense of divine truth."[1] On the same principle, these divines often speak of our ignorance, stupidity, etc. as sinful, because these states involve a wrong "taste," "inclination," "tendency," etc., all of which terms are here used to denote exercises of will.[2]

There is, however, another sense in which our divines occasionally use the words, "taste," "propensity," "disposition," etc. They intend to denote by them not a choice, but a foundation for choice, and therefore not a sin, but an occasion of sin; an evil, not a wickedness. Thus Dr. Hopkins says, that in regeneration the Holy Spirit "begets a *right* and *good* taste, temper, or disposition, and so lays a foundation for holy exercises of heart." He then adds:

"It is difficult and perhaps impossible to form any distinct and clear idea of that in the mind or heart, which is antecedent to all thought and exercise of the will, or action, which we call principle, taste, temper, disposition, habit, etc.; by which we mean nothing properly active, but that from which right exercise of the will or action springs, as the reason and foundation of it, and without which there could have been no such exercise. Perhaps the real

---

[1] Hopkins's Two Discourses on Law and Regeneration, pp. 46, 50. Ed. 1768. This distinction between the neutral principles and the moral exercises of the soul, is the basis of Hopkins's distinction between regeneration and conversion.

[2] That Edwards generally uses the word inclination as synonymous with choice, or else as implying choice, and as distinguishable not from acts but from *external* acts, is evident from Part III. Sect. IV. and Part IV. Sect. I. of his Inquiry. That he generally uses "habits" and "dispositions" as synonymous with *accustomed* acts of choice, is plain from Part III. Sect. VI. of his Inquiry. When, therefore, he says in the Preface to his Inquiry, that "all virtue and religion have their seat more immediately in the will, consisting more especially in right acts and habits of this faculty," his meaning must be that holiness belongs primarily to the occasional and habitual acts of the will, and not to any nature distinct from those acts.

truth of the matter, when examined with true philosophic, metaphysical strictness, will appear to be this: that what we call principle, disposition or frame of mind, which is antecedent to all right exercise of the heart, and is the foundation and reason of it, is wholly to be resolved into divine constitution or law of nature. But this I leave to the inquiry and decision of those who are inclined to examine this matter to the bottom, seeing I have not room here to go into a more particular consideration of it; and, whatever is at bottom the truth of the case, nothing will be said on this subject that immediately depends upon it."[1]

Does any one suppose that Dr. Hopkins would call this evil bias a real, or even original, sin? Hear him: "Original *sin* is that total moral depravity which takes place in the hearts of all the children of Adam, in consequence of his apostasy, which consists in exercise or act, as really as any sin can do, and therefore cannot be distinguished from *actual* sin." "This *sin* which takes place in the posterity of Adam, is not properly distinguished into original and actual sin, because it is all really actual, and there is, strictly speaking, no other sin but actual sin."[2] Besides, the wrong bias which leads to wrong choice, is resolved by Hopkins into a "divine constitution or law of nature;" and did he believe that this is a real sin? Then

---

[1] Hopkins's Two Discourses on Law and Regeneration, p. 38. Ed. 1768. Here is seen the *substantial* agreement of Hopkins with "the Exercise Scheme." The earlier advocates of that scheme believed that all our sin is occasioned by a law of nature; and gave as a definition of nature's law just what Newton and other philosophers have given; viz. "the established mode of divine operation." Edwards on Original Sin, especially Part IV. Chapters II. and III., gives the same idea of a law of nature.

[2] Hopkins's System of Divinity, Chap. VIII. Here is but a single specimen of this author's mode of regarding Original Sin. Only a very small proportion of the best New England divines have dissented from it. After Hopkins's System was published, Dr. Jonathan Edwards wrote his freest criticisms upon it, and did not intimate the slightest dissatisfaction of himself or his brethren with the above named theory of Original Sin. It has had great influence on the New England clergy, as it pervades all the works of this good man. As early as 1787, Dr. Stiles writes: "It has been the *ton* to direct students in divinity, these thirty years past, to read the Bible, President Edwards, Dr. Bellamy, and Mr. Hopkins's writings; and this was a pretty good sufficiency of reading." He adds that the younger theologians were inclined to differ from Hopkins, in some particulars, but he does not specify the nature of moral evil as one of them. He says that none of the younger divines will "be equal to those strong reasoners, President Edwards and Mr. Hopkins." When, therefore, Dr. Hodge says, that " Bellamy, Dwight, and *the* other great men of New England, were no less strenuous than Edwards" in opposing the theory that all sin is actual and avoidable, he must have included Hopkins among these opposers, or else have used language inaccurately. Bib. Repertory, Vol. XXIII. p. 694.

he must have believed God to be not only the author but also the actor of moral evil. Still further, he supposed that in regeneration this bad relish is removed, and a good relish substituted for it; and in conversion this good relish is exercised. But this good relish is, of itself, no real holiness. According to him, it does not commend the subject of it to the divine approbation. Unless it be *exercised*, the man who has it as a passive quality, will not be saved. Hopkins quotes an objector as saying: "If persons are regenerated before they are enlightened and believe on Christ, what will become of them? Where will they go, to heaven or to hell, if they die after they are regenerated, and before they believe? It seems they are fit for neither; their hearts are renewed, so [they] cannot go to hell; but they are in an unpardoned, unjustified state, therefore cannot go to heaven!" Now what answer does Hopkins make? Does he say that this good, passive disposition will be accepted as a compliance with the conditions of life? No. He only affirms, that the disposition will be exercised before death, and the *acting* of it will, through grace, entitle the agent to the promises. "And," he replies, "what if a person who is elected to salvation dies in an unconverted state; will he be saved or not? Let the objector answer this question, and he will drop his objections, having fully answered it himself. His answer must be, there never was, and never will be such an instance. All that are elected shall be converted before they die."[1]

Dr. Bellamy expresses the same idea thus: "The promises of the gospel are not made to the holy principle, *passively considered*, but to its acts and exercises, even as the blessings of the first covenant were not promised to that image of God in which Adam began to exist, but to his *active* compliance with that covenant." Bellamy then states the objection, that on his theory "a regenerated [but unconverted] soul may be in a state of condemnation for a time, and consequently perish, if death should befal him in that juncture." And he answers the objection in the words of Flavel, by remarking that the regenerated soul *will* be converted, i. e. the soul having the holy principle *will exercise* it before death, and by this action will secure an entrance into heaven. Death will not intervene between regeneration and conversion.[2] Bellamy does indeed call this principle "true holiness;" but he calls it so only as it implies the certainty of its being exercised. *In itself*, apart from its exercise, it is not a true holiness which God will accept as a condition of salvation;

---

[1] Hopkins's Two Discourses on Law and Regeneration, p. 50. Ed. 1768.
[2] Bellamy's Works, Vol. II. p. 634.

nothing which he has ever promised to reward. But has he not promised to reward all that which is true holiness in itself? And, on the same principle, what kind of sin is that which in its own nature deserves no punishment?

But does the choicest friend of Hopkins and Bellamy sanction their theory of an inward, neutral occasion of holiness and sin? They derived their theory from him more than from any other divine. President Edwards often speaks of "kind affections" which "are implanted by the Author of nature" within all men, and which are "the fruit of God's mercy," and, of course, are not sin.[1] He speaks of "the common, natural principles of self-love, natural appetite, etc., which were in man in innocence."[2] He then says, that these principles being left "to themselves, without the government of superior divine principles, will certainly be *followed* with the corruption, yea, the total corruption of the heart."[2] "When God made man at first, he implanted in him *two kinds* of principles. There was an *inferior* kind, which may be called *natural*, being the principles of *mere* human nature, such as self-love, with those natural appetites and passions which belong to the *nature of man*, in which his love to his own liberty, honor and pleasure were exercised."[2] These inferior "principles, that are essentially implied in, or *necessarily* resulting from, and *inseparably* connected with, *mere* human nature," were designed "to be wholly subordinate and subservient." But when the Divine Spirit left the soul, "the inferior principles of self-love and natural appetite, which were given only to serve, being alone and left to themselves, of course became reigning principles." "The immediate *consequence* of which was a fatal catastrophe, a turning of all things upside down, and the *succession* of a state of the most odious and dreadful confusion. Man did immediately set up himself, and the objects of his private affections and appetites as supreme, and so they took the place of God."[2] Edwards needed not to state more clearly that man's voluntary wrong action, which was his first sin, resulted from a previous disorder in his involuntary principles. He adds: "these inferior principles are like fire in a house, which we say is a good servant, but a bad master; very useful while kept in its place, but if left to take possession of the whole house, soon brings all to destruction."[2] Now is sin a good and very useful servant? If not, these principles are not sin; but Edwards adds, that "*in consequence*" of them, "arises enmity in the heart" against God. "And therefore as God withdrew spiritual communion and his vital, gracious influence

---

[1] Nature of True Virtue, Ch. VI.   [2] Original Sin, Part IV. Ch. II.

from the common head, so he withholds the same from all the members, as they come into existence; whereby they come into the world mere flesh, and entirely under the government of natural and inferior principles, and so *become* wholly corrupt, as Adam did."[1] Can language express more decisively the truth that our lower principles, which left to themselves become the infallible occasions of sin, are yet in and of themselves *not* sin? This great father of New England Theology asks: "Is there anything in nature to make it impossible but that the superior principles of man's nature should be so *proportioned* to the inferior, as to prevent such a dreadful consequence as the moral and natural ruin and eternal perdition of the far greater part of mankind?" And he answers his own question in this emphatic style: "If we are Christians, we must be forced to allow it to be possible in the nature of things, that the principles of human nature should be so *balanced*, that the *consequence* should be no propensity to sin in the first beginning of a capacity of moral agency."[2] Here he not only asserts that our inferior principles of action might exist in a perfectly sinless being, but he sanctions the phrase that our sin results from a disorder, a wrong *balance*, a bad proportion of our sensibilities. These are Edwardean phrases, and yet men who never read him with care, if at all, denounce them as "German" and "Pelagian."

We are now prepared to notice a singular fact. The very reasons adduced for proving that our New England writers do not believe sin to consist in act, prove that they do thus believe. For example, the Treatise of Edwards on Original Sin has induced our Reviewer to say, that "the world-wide fame of President Edwards, as a theologian, rests mainly on his thorough refutation of"[3] the doctrine that all sin consists in sinning, and that power equals and limits duty. It is true that, in some particulars, this treatise of Edwards is alien from the spirit of New England divinity, and contains a number of phrases incongruous with the prevailing style of Edwards himself. Still, it is the leading doctrine of that treatise, that all sin is an act, committed in our own persons, or else in the person of him who infolded us within himself. Why does the prince of metaphysicians make such gigantic efforts to prove that our sin is the same with Adam's, not only "in kind" but also "in number," if he deemed it right that we should be punished for anything other than our own action? He says that infants, as "all know, never committed any sin in their own

---

[1] Edwards on Original Sin, Part IV. Ch. II.   [2] Ib. Part I. Ch. I. Sect. IX.
[3] Bib. Repertory, Vol. XXIII. p. 694.

persons."[1] Are they, then, guilty for 'a nature which, apart from its motions, is truly and properly sin'? No; for he declares that they "could be sinners *no other way* than by virtue of Adam's transgression,"[2] and he expressly denies that the children of Adam "come into the world with a *double* guilt; *one* the guilt of Adam's sin, *another* the guilt arising from their having a corrupt heart."[3] — "The guilt a man has upon his soul at his first existence is *one and simple*; viz. the guilt of the original apostasy, the guilt of the sin by which the species first rebelled against God. This, and the guilt arising from the first corruption or depraved disposition of the heart, are not to be looked upon as *two* things, distinctly imputed and charged upon men in the sight of God."[3] He repeatedly affirms, that "the *first existing* of a corrupt disposition" in the hearts of men, is the same *identical* thing with Adam's first corrupt disposition; is the "extended pollution of that sin;" is "the consent and concurrence with it," is a "participation" in it.[3] Now what was Adam's first sin but an act? Edwards says, that "the first evil disposition or inclination of the heart of Adam to sin, was not properly distinct from his first *act* of sin, but was included in it;" and as we are identically the same with Adam, so is our first evil disposition identically the same with his, and is not distinct from our first moral act. As Adam's "guilt was *all* truly from the act of his inward man," so is our guilt all truly from the act of our inward man; for our act is the same with his, just as the sap in a branch of the tree is the same identical sap which was once in the root.[3] The idea of our literal oneness with Adam, is indeed a strange phenomenon in mental history, but so great a man as Edwards must commit great errors, if he commit any at all. For the sake of retaining the doctrine, that all our sin consists in our own active "*consent* of heart," and also the doctrine that the sin of Adam is imputed to us, he seized on the astonishing theory, that as Adam's rebellion was not imputed to him, until he had actively engaged in it,

---

[1] Edwards on Original Sin, Part II. Chap. IV. Sect. II. and Part IV. Chap. IV.
[2] Ib. Part II. Chap. IV. Sect. II.
[3] These and many similar quotations, are from Part IV. Chap. III. of the Treatise on Original Sin. If their author had been asked, whether we had the natural power of avoiding Adam's sin, he would have said, that in the sense in which we committed it, we had the natural power to avoid it. Thus Andrew Fuller (Works, Vol. II. p. 472. Ed. 1845), cites the following objection to Edwards's theory: "We could not be to blame, for what we could not avoid;" and replies, "Very *true*; but if the notion of a union between Adam and his posterity be admitted, then it cannot properly be said, we could not avoid it." i. e. the sin in Adam.

so our rebellion is not imputed to us until we have actively engaged in it; and as we are one moral person with Adam, so our rebellion is one moral act with his; and, therefore, his act being ours is of right imputed to us as our act; and "the first existing of a depraved disposition in Adam's posterity, I apprehend, is not distinct from their guilt of Adam's first sin."[1] But, the objectors reply, Edwards does speak of a confirmed evil principle as imparting a distinct additional guilt to the soul. True, but he adds, "this confirmed corruption, by its remaining and continued *operation*, brought additional guilt on his [Adam's] soul,"[2] and does the same on the souls of his posterity. But our opponents inquire, Does not Edwards speak of an evil disposition, propensity, tendency, which precedes our own personal action and is *itself* not only sin but also a *consequence* of the imputation of Adam's sin? No, we reply. Our opponents have mistaken a theory of Dr. Hodge, for the exactly opposite theory of our New England divine. Edwards reiterates his belief: "The first being of an evil disposition in the heart of a child of Adam, whereby he is disposed to approve of the sin of his first father, as fully as he himself approved of it when he committed it, or so far as to imply a full and perfect *consent* of heart to it, I think is not to be looked upon as a *consequence* of the imputation of that first sin, any more than the full consent of Adam's own heart in the act of sinning; which was not consequent on the imputation of his sin to himself, but rather *prior* to it in the order of nature. Indeed, the derivation of the evil disposition to the hearts of Adam's posterity, or rather the coexistence of the evil disposition, implied in Adam's first rebellion, in the root and branches, is a consequence of the union, that the wise Author of the world has established between Adam and his posterity; but not properly a *consequence* of the *imputation* of his sin; nay, rather, *antecedent* to it, as it was in Adam himself. The first depravity of the heart, and the imputation of that sin, are both consequences of that established union; but yet in such order, that the evil disposition is *first*, and the charge of guilt *consequent;* as it was in the case of Adam himself."

Such remarks give a key to Edwards's otherwise enigmatical

---

[1] All the quotations in the text of this page are from Edwards on Original Sin, Part IV. Ch. III.

[2] It is useless to pretend that Edwards uses guilt in these passages as denoting a legal exposedness, and not a moral stain; for he expressly declares that "men are really, in themselves, what they are in the eye of the law, and by the voice of strict equity and justice." Part I. Ch. I. Sect. III.

Treatise on Original Sin. When we read in it of our evil propensities, we are either to understand, first, that they are real *choices*, and thus real sins; or, secondly, that they are the *effects* of our having transgressed the law in Adam, and are thus metaphorically sins, just as our wrong outward actions implying a wicked motive are sins by a figure of speech; or, thirdly, that they are sinful by a like metaphor, as they are *occasions* of our personal disobedience to law; or, fourthly, that they are sinful by a double metonymy of cause for effect and effect for cause. How else can we explain many expressions like the following: "Man's nature or state is attended with a pernicious or destructive tendency in a moral sense, when it *tends* to *that* which *deserves* misery and destruction." This evil propensity is odious and detestable, "as, by the supposition, it *tends* to that moral evil *by* which the subject *becomes* odious in the sight of God, and liable as such to be condemned." It is "a tendency *to guilt and ill-desert* in a vast overbalance to virtue and merit." Part I. Ch. I. Whether our personal sins be induced by an inward propensity to them, or by animal appetites, etc., the occasion of those sins is pronounced to be equally "evil, corrupt and dreadful." Part I. Ch. I. Sect. IX. But are our animal appetites literally disapproved by conscience? Is it not plain that Edwards discriminates between real guilt and the guiltless occasion of it?[1]

---

[1] Against all such modes of interpreting Edwards, our Reviewer and others are fond of quoting his remark: "It is not necessary that there should *first* be thought, reflection and choice, *before* there can be any virtuous disposition." Bib. Repertory, Vol. XXIII. p. 685. But why does Edwards make this obviously true remark? He is opposing a theory that our choices must be self-determined; that before a preference can be right or wrong, we must think of it, of its good and evil influences, and then must choose to exercise it, and must thus make the preference an effect of a foregoing choice. He denies, as we all deny, that we must choose to choose, that "thought, reflection, *and* choice must go *before* virtue, and that all virtue and righteousness must be the fruit of *preceding* choice." Treatise on Original Sin, Part II. Ch. I. Sect. I. He teaches, that virtue need not be *preceded* by a distinct choice, but that virtue *is* the "leading choice." Again, Edwards is opposing a theory that virtue and vice consist, primarily, in subordinate and imperative volitions, which do not involve the "leading choice." In his intense aversion to this theory, he says: "The act of choosing that which is good, is no further virtuous than it proceeds from a good principle or virtuous disposition of mind." Treatise on Original Sin, Part II. Ch. I. Sect. I. But he here means by "good principle or virtuous disposition," precisely what he elsewhere means by the "original," "determining," "leading," "governing," "regulating act," or "choice." Inquiry on the Will, Part II. Sect. X. and Part III. Sect. IV. It is this regulating choice in which, primarily, virtue consists, and not in any choice preceding it, nor in any subsequent choice not including it.

It has been already stated, that Edwards's work on Original Sin is not a perfect exponent of what is now termed the Edwardean faith. Perhaps no two of our eminent theologians have adopted its theory of our sameness with Adam. Very few of them have imitated all of its intense expressions. It was written amid the constant alarms of an Indian war, under many embarrassing influences of its author's frontier parish, and with a constitution shattered by the fever and ague. Ill health prevented his revising it as faithfully as he had revised his other works, and when he had published only a few sheets of it, death ended his labors. Accordingly, it bears more signs of hurried composition than are to be found in some of his writings, which had lain by him for years. The principal regret which he is said to have felt in prospect of his untimely death, arose from his inability to modify some things which he had written; and there are several reasons to believe, that he meant to remove some verbal incongruities from the work which he had not finished with his wonted care, and which he had deemed it needful to publish with more than his usual haste. Were it not for his sudden decease, he might have explained a few remarks, which in the fervor of composition he had left unqualified, and thus he would have saved a class of men from wrongly imputing to him the error, that sin lies in something beside moral agency—an error hostile to the whole spirit of his creed.

In the fifth place, New England Theology is a comprehensive system of Biblical science. Hopkins says of President Edwards: "He studied the Bible more than all other books, and more than most other divines do." "He took his religious principles from the Bible, and not from any human system or body of divinity. Though his principles were Calvinistic, yet he called no man father. He thought and judged for himself, and was truly very much of an original."[1] What had an Indian missionary, on the very bounds of civilized life, to fear from church authorities? The distance of our fathers from the old world, made them cleave to the Word of God as their dearest standard. Who was ever more inwardly and thoroughly Protestant in

---

This "governing," "habitual" choice is the "virtuous disposition or principle." It is love of being in general. It implies "thought and reflection" on being in general, but not thought and reflection on itself before it is exercised. Still less does it imply a distinct choice of itself, before it is exercised. This is Edwards's theory of virtue, and the same, *mutatis mutandis*, is his theory of sin.

[1] Hopkins's Life and Character of the late Reverend, Learned and Pious Mr. Jonathan Edwards. Ed. 1799. p. 47. It was Edwards's own opinion, that he had developed some new truths from the inspired volume.

his rule of faith, than Samuel Hopkins? He expounded the entire Scriptures three several times to his congregation at Newport. Altogether too sternly would he have frowned upon the remark of Dr. Hodge: "If the point assailed can be shown to be a part of *the common faith of the church*, then we think the necessity for further debate is, in all ordinary cases, at an end."[1] Altogether too severely would he have reprimanded the spirit of this remark, as leading its author into the unreasoning dogmatism of Rome. The more recent divines of New England have felt a similar preference for the Bible above creeds. They have, accordingly, given such an impulse to Scriptural investigation as was previously unknown to the English world. Their mode of interpreting the sacred volume, is the only mode which will save consistent thinkers from Romanism. The principles of exegesis on which our Reviewer proceeds in defending a limited atonement, inability, etc., are the very same on which the Romanists proceed in defending the Real Presence and the Supremacy of Saint Peter. If he stands, they stand. Indeed, the hypothesis that all men sinned in Adam, had never found currency in the church, if the Vulgate had not mistranslated the $\dot{\epsilon}\varphi'\ \dot{\psi}$ of Rom. 5: 12. The Calvinistic theories which oppose the New England Calvinism, are founded either on the scholastic metaphysics, or on a literal interpretation of oriental metaphors; and these are the fruitful sources of Papal error. Painful, indeed, is the violence which those theories have done to such clear sayings as, "the son shall not bear the iniquity of the father;" and Christ is the propitiation, "not for ours only,

---

[1] Bib. Repertory, Vol. XXIII. p. 677. There is a truth in this canon of our Reviewer. Yet he is wont to carry his reliance on church authority too far. In the present controversy, for example, his principal argument against us has been derived, not from the Word of God. but from the opinions of men. In citing these opinions, however, he has been unfortunate. He appeals to the Romish standards on the nature of sin, etc. But the Council of Trent, at their fifth session, decided that our inborn proclivity to sin is called sin, only because it arises from and tends to moral evil, and "cannot hurt but him that consenteth to it." See Paul Sarpi's Historie of the Councel of Trent, p. 184. See also Möhler's Symbolik, Theil I. Kap. III. § XIII. and Theil II. Kap. VI. § XCIII. Our assailant has labored with rare assiduity, to prove that we agree with Schleiermacher. Suppose that success had crowned his toils. What then? Has he shown that the great German is in error? He has merely appealed to authority, and said that "such men as Hengstenberg regard [Schleiermacher's system] as subverting some of the essential doctrines of the Gospel." Bib. Repertory, Vol. XXIII. p. 692. But Hengstenberg also says, that Dr. Dwight is a Rationalist, on the very topics now controverted; and our Reviewer avows that he agrees with Dwight on these topics.

but also for the sins of the whole world." Those artificial theories are useful, so far forth as they are symbols of great truths. Viewed as poetry and eloquence, they pertain to the form of presentation suited to earnest feeling; but viewed as doctrines literally expressed, they pertain to *a* theology of a "bewildered" reason, and not to *the* theology of a sound head or heart.[1] They may be regarded not as true theories, but as the poetry and eloquence which give to accurate statements a readier power over the feelings. The Princeton Review has spoken, once at least, of "a true thought in a false expression."[2] A rare merit of the New England system is, that it has looked through the metonymy and the hyperbole of the oriental expression, and seized the "true thought" intended by it; while many of its opposers have clung to the false theories which that expression literally denotes. These theories have often repelled the inquirer, into infidelity. He has mistaken figures of rhetoric for a literal creed, and has therefore revolted from that creed. The first sentence of Dr. Smalley's sermon on Original Sin, betokens one grand aim of the New England system, to preclude all occasion for infidel schemes, by so interpreting the Bible as to make sensible men confide in it.

The New England system is not only scriptural, but is scriptural *science*. Are its advocates condemned as too inquisitive? they *do* search for the truth; as too metaphysical? they do reason against a philosophy falsely so called; as too fond of novelties in speculation? they do love to "grow in knowledge;" as too ready to examine the

---

[1] See Convention Sermon, Bib. Sacra, Vol. VII. p. 563. This sermon has been represented as implying that certain doctrines literally expressed by words like "Imputed and Passive sin," belong to the theology of feeling, and that the New England faith is suited to the intellect only. One aim of that sermon is, to show that these doctrines belong to the theology of feeling, when they are viewed as *symbols, illustrations*, of the real truth; and that the New England system will adopt all truth, be it expressed in the prosaic style fitted for speculation, or the poetic style fitted for emotion. It will allow the theology of the intellect and also the theology of the heart, which are the same substance in two forms. The doctrines *literally* denoted by words like Passive Sin, Guilt of Adam's Offence, and regarded as truths plainly expressed, do not belong to the right theology in either form. But the mass of Christians who contend for them, have not practically viewed them as credible in a literal interpretation. One of the best preachers in this or any age, has styled those doctrines, as they are treated by the multitude, "the theology of the tympanum; for if the words which express them tinkle well in the ear, they are loved, let them mean anything or nothing." We have chosen to call them by a more reverential name, and partly because the phrases suggesting them are associated with the venerable piety of ancient days, and thus have a goodly sound.

[2] Vol. XIII. p. 81.

foundations of their faith? they are not afraid of "open questions," nor of exposing their creed, in all its parts, to a rigid scrutiny. They know themselves to be imperfect. Free inquiry has made them humble; and can an arrogant temper, disdainful of all improvement, be either the seed or the fruit of science? They have borne much of abusive criticism. Two of their most eminent champions had not lain long in their graves, before they were publicly declared, even in the city of Brotherly Love, to have made their bed in hell. One of the men, thus humanly condemned, was the sainted Hopkins himself. But have our divines retaliated such calumnies? In reading the seven or eight volumes of Emmons, would any one suspect that he had ever been defamed? Would not the immortal ancestors of Dwight have frowned upon him, if, in one of his eleven volumes, he had returned railing for railing? The New England divinity can defend itself without personal vituperation, and in the purity of its argument it breathes the spirit of a divine philosophy. It has developed its scientific temper in systematizing those old truths on which, as a broad, deep basis, many varying superstructures have been reared. By its accordance with the sensibilities of our race, it authorizes an intelligent use of the tropes which those sensibilities demand; demand not as faded, but as rhetorical figures; suggesting their original images, but understood in their rational import. It unfolds the meaning and the fitness and the power of that style, in which we summon the blind, deaf, dead, and twice dead, to see, hear, rise, walk, and take heaven by violence; in which we assert that God sits, and rests, stands up, and returns to his place, rises betimes, and plucks his hand out of his bosom; is wounded and is comforted, grieved, afflicted, and eased; considers and wonders; turns violently and tosses his foe like a ball; is quiet, or jealous, or angry, or froward; punishes the innocent, and beholds no sin in the vile; exacts impossibilities from the weak, condemns them for a misdeed of their ancestor, and smites his hands together and causes his fury to rest; and whets his glittering sword, and yet is love without change and without end. All these expressions are found in the hymns of our worship or in the tracts which are welcomed to our houses, and they are all admired as symbols of the truth explained in our dogmatic treatises.[1] In uncovering the profoundest philosophy that lies under the richest of the inspired poetry, and in illustrating the self-consist-

---

[1] "A slavish adherence to systematic divinity has much injured some of the finest passages of Revelation; and which were intended to be *felt*, rather than *criticised*." Jay's Exercises for the Closet, Oct. 21.

ent character of the inspired volume, our theological system claims to be a true science.

Because it is a science, it is comprehensive. A Unitarian opposer shrinks "with a feeling approaching horror," from the "stern and appalling theology" associated with the name of Hopkins.[1] A Calvinistic opposer, as early as 1817, mourns over the Hopkinsian Seminary at Andover, because the doctrines taught there "do, in their nature and necessary consequences, lead to the Socinian ground."[2] The vane of the Princeton Review points to Emmonism on one day as Pelagian, and on another day as ultra-Calvinistic. What is the source of these charges, that nullify each other? It is the comprehensiveness of the Edwardean scheme. This scheme unites a high, but not an ultra Calvinism, on the decrees and agency of God, with a philosophical, but not an Arminian theory, on the freedom and worth of the human soul. Its new element is seen in its harmonizing two great classes of truths; one relating to the untrammelled will of man, another relating to the supremacy of God. Because it has secured human liberty, it exalts the divine sovereignty; and its advocates have preached more than others on predestination, because they have prepared the way for it by showing that man's freedom has been predestined. They have insisted on an eternally decreed liberty, and on a free submission to the eternal decrees. Their faith ascribes to man a noble structure of mind, and sinks him the lower for abusing it. In reprobating his wickedness, it exceeds all other systems; because it exceeds them all in unfolding the equity of the Sovereign against whom the subject, so richly endowed, has so needlessly rebelled. When its opposers think of its efforts to justify the ways of our Heavenly Father, they hastily accuse it of Arminianism; and when they turn their minds to its description of the Supreme, Universal Governor, they hastily accuse it of hyper-Calvinism. In these alternations between conflicting charges, they copy old replies to old theories, and misdirect them to a new doctrine. They overlook the element which Edwards disclosed to the church, the union between certainty and spontaneous choice. They forget the very genius of his system. This genius is, to blend the loftiest truths concerning the Creator, with the most equitable truths concerning the creature; to heighten our reverence for God, by disclosing his generosity to man, and to deepen our penitence for sin, by showing the ease with which it might have been avoided. A pious heart longs to glorify God;

---

[1] Channing's Memoir, Vol. I. p. 142; and Works, Vol. IV. pp. 342 seq.
[2] Willson's Historical Sketch, p. 184.

a sympathizing heart would arouse men to free action; a comprehensive theology teaches in order to exhort freely, and exhorts freely in order to teach. If Cecil had been familiar with the New England scheme, he never would have felt the necessity of oscillating between his own speculative creed, and the speculative creed of his opposers. He betrays the disproportions of mere Calvinism, and its consequent failure to satisfy a practical Christian, in the following apothegms:

"The right way of interpreting Scripture is, to take it as we find it, without any attempt to force it into any particular system. Whatever may be fairly inferred from Scripture, we need not fear to insist on. Many passages speak the language of what is called Calvinism, and that in almost the strongest terms. I would not have a man clip and curtail these passages, to bring them down to some system: let him go with them in their free and full sense; for, otherwise, if he do not absolutely pervert them, he will attenuate their energy. But, let him look at as many more, which speak the language of Arminianism, and let him go all the way with these, also. God has been pleased thus to state and to leave the thing; and all our attempts to distort it, one way or the other, are puny and contemptible."

"No man will preach the Gospel so *freely* as the Scriptures preach it, unless he will submit to talk like an Antinomian, in the estimation of a great body of Christians; nor will any man preach it so *practically* as the Scriptures, unless he will submit to be called, by as large a body, an Arminian. Many think that they find a middle path: which is, in fact, neither one thing nor another; since it is not the incomprehensible, but grand plan of the Bible. It is somewhat of human contrivance. It savors of human poverty and littleness."[1]

Mr. Simeon, also, whom the Princeton Review so justly extols, would have found the Edwardean scheme sufficiently copious and liberal to satisfy his many-sided heart, and to save him from adopting one speculative creed for one purpose, and an opposite speculative creed for another purpose. He says:

"Here are two other extremes, Calvinism and Arminianism (for you need not be told how long Calvin and Arminius lived before St. Paul). 'How do you move in reference to these, Paul? In a golden mean?' 'No.'— 'To one extreme?' 'No.'— 'How then?' 'To both extremes: to-day I am a strong Calvinist; to-morrow a strong Arminian.'—'Well, well, Paul, I see thou art beside thyself: go to Aristotle, and learn the golden mean.'"[2]

---

[1] Cecil's Remains, pp. 162, 163. Boston edition. There is nothing in a late Convention sermon that approximates to the license of these remarks; yet the Princeton Review says, "Cecil is one of our classics," and it recommends him as tending "to cure young men of the hum-drum or *Blair* method." (Bib. Repertory, Vol. XVII. p. 639.)

[2] Memoirs of the Life of the Rev. Charles Simeon, M. A. By the Rev. William Carus, M. A. London Ed. 1847. p. 600.

Is it possible to conceive, that either of the Edwardses, or Hopkins, or Emmons, would indite such an apology for Antinomianism or Arminianism? They dreaded each of these creeds, as an angel of death. Yet they have been condemned for sanctioning both; condemned, because they have been misunderstood; misunderstood, because their system is original and novel; original and novel, because it combines the one-sided truth which the Antinomian had distorted, with the one-sided truth which the Arminian had distorted; separates the two truths from the errors with which the Antinomian and the Arminian had intertwined them, and harmonizes the two into one capacious system; a system rigidly accurate in form, and still indulgent enough to allow many bold, hearty expressions of its own truth; a system the *minutiae* of which Calvin and Augustine would have consistently defended, if they had lived when the laws of interpretation and the philosophy of common sense had been as clear and prominent, as they have been during and since the time of the Edwardses.

In the last place, the Theology of New England is the only system of speculative orthodoxy which will endure examination; and it is, therefore, destined to prevail. It is impugned by men who are often forced to own its "radical principles." They are driven to it, and soon they disavow it, and then come to it, and leave it once more, and afterwards flee back to it, and as soon abandon it, only to return another time, and so forsake it yet again. Dr. Hodge often appears upon its ground, either as a friend or foe; and our only complaint is, that, in either capacity, he stays too short a time. In his onsets and retreats, he represents the character of all opposition to the truth. He writes condemnatory words upon our creed, and then we quote from him other words, in which he has uttered the identical sentiments which he now controverts. We produce against him the very Essays, from which he has mainly derived his fame, as an "accomplished Reviewer." He replies, that we impute to him Essays, "some of which [he] probably never even read."[1] This is to be re-

---

[1] Bib. Repertory, Vol. XXIII. p. 688. We have ascribed to Dr. Hodge's authorship, not more than four Articles in the Bib. Repertory, and those are the Articles which have been long admitted to be his, by "common fame;" an authority which ought not, since 1837, to have been "excinded" from his remembrance. We have quoted other Essays, indeed, as expressing opinions, which he is known, from other sources, to entertain; but we have been careful to mention him as the author of not more than four, and those, the very Essays, which have been most unanimously imputed to him. Their spirit and style bear a marked resemblance to the spirit and style of his assault upon a harmless Con-

gretted. He has enjoyed, for many years, the ovations of a party for those bold Reviews; and now, when their self-nullifying character is exposed, he never read them, "probably." For twenty years, has he been shining in borrowed plumage? The Conductors of the Biblical Repertory have virtually avowed themselves responsible for two of the four Essays which we referred to our assailant; and is he prepared to assert, that he was not then a Conductor of the work, which one of his admirers has denominated " Professor Hodge's Biblical Repertory?"[1] He says, that we have "gone back twenty years," for the self-contradictions which we have collated from his reputed writings.[2] What! Does "Gibraltar" crumble into the Mediterranean, within a span of twenty years? Has it come to this, "that those old walls, which have stood for ages, even from the beginning,"[3] turn out to be made of a substance, which will not keep so long as a third part of a man's life? This is a frail plea, since all the more important Essays, which we cited, have been republished within five years, and are even yet applauded, as the very Ehrenbreitstein of our Reviewer's theology; a brittle theology, indeed, when the stoutest defences of it are not to be touched, because they were put up "twenty years" ago! Our critic has condemned us for having opposed the Augustinian doctrine of Imputation. We have adduced the most decisive words of renowned Augustinians, to prove

---

vention sermon, and are the legitimate results of a faith which shrinks from being investigated. Thus, in one of these Articles, he accuses Dr. Beman of reviving the "often refuted slander of Socinians and Papists;" of having made a "wicked misrepresentation;" of writing a book, according to which "the atonement must be rejected, as either incredible or worthless;" of leaving out "the very soul of the doctrine," etc. The Reviewer adds: "That Dr. Cox, in his Introduction, should applaud such a book, neither surprises nor pains us. We are all aware, that he knows no better." Bib. Repert. Vol. XVII. pp. 117, 137, 138. Was it not natural for us to infer, that the author of such phrases is the same gentleman, by whom we are accused of having an alembic for evaporating the doctrines of the Bible, and by whom we are likened to a Frenchman trying to teach English, and our words are said to be "kept going up and down, like a juggler's balls," etc.? Bib. Repert. Vol. XXIII. pp. 675, 687, 695, etc. We shall be happy to hear an unequivocal statement, that not one of these sentences came from the writer on the "Way of Life." We are sorry to say, however, that the four Essays which we have ascribed to him, are marked with his well-known facility of controverting himself, and with his tendency to pervert the quotations which he ascribes to his antagonist, and with what we may call, "for want of a better name," his *striking* style.

[1] See Dr. Brown's Law of Christ respecting Civil Obedience, Supplementary Notes, p. 17. See also Bib. Repert. Vol. II. p. 431.

[2] Bib. Repert. Vol. XXIII. p. 688.   [3] Ibid. p. 319.

that our critic himself has often opposed it. He replies, first, that we are ignorant; and, secondly, that we quote authors of whom he has never heard.[1] Yet these very authors are cited by Rivetus, as the standard-bearers of orthodoxy, and the Princeton Review has translated one part of their testimony, and expressed a desire to see the remainder "translated and published in a volume;"[2] and just so soon as we have begun to comply with the wishes of that Review, it turns round, and protests that it never heard of the authorities, which it has recommended once and again. And in the same breath, it accuses us of turning a "corner," and performing a "pirouette."[3] Rivetus "was the greatest theologian of the age," says that same Review, and the Treatise from which we have quoted our authorities, is the most celebrated of his works, and Turretin (Pars I. p. 691) has recommended it as containing the standards of orthodoxy; and still the Review has never heard of some of those standards, and advises us to read Turretin, and condemns us for having "read up," *already*,[4] and pretends, withal, that its course is self-consistent. In our critic's endeavor to evade the responsibility of Essays, which have been so long regarded as the exponents of his dogmatic system, in his not having heard of the authors who have been so celebrated for avowing the old Calvinism in the plainest words, he has betrayed the vacillating character of the faith which he would set up against our own. We asked him for the bread of instruction; and he has given us back the stone of reproof, charging us with having misunderstood the Augustinian doctrine of Imputed Sin. But this very charge is a sign of his precarious position; for we have represented the Augustinian doctrine, just as it has been portrayed by Dr. Jonathan Edwards, Smalley, Dwight; by Neander, Brettschneider, Marheinecke, Hahn, Hase, Knapp, Reinhard, Doederlein, Meier, Schott, and, indeed, all the more eminent theologians of Germany.[5] But while Dr. Hodge avows his agreement with the old Augustinians, and denies that their doctrine involves an identity between ourselves and Adam, what is his reason for passing over, in ominous silence, their argu-

---

[1] Comp. Bib. Repert., Vol. XXIII. pp. 678, 679, 682, 695.
[2] Bib. Repertory, Vol. XI. p. 579.   [3] Ib. Vol. XXIII. p. 687.
[4] Comp. Bib. Repertory, Vol. XXIII. pp. 678, 695.
[5] We have repeatedly asserted, that the doctrine of our having literally sinned in Adam, was the *prevailing* doctrine of the Augustinians, and that there were subordinate parties, who held other theories. See various theories stated in Hahn's Lehrbuch des christl. Glaubens. Theil II. § 81, Brettschneider's Entwickelung, § 89, vierte Auflage. Knapp's Theology, Art. VI. § 57 and Art. IX. § 76. Hase's Hutterus Redivivus, §§ 82—87.

ment, that we are doomed not unjustly, but justly, to our earliest spiritual death; and therefore we deserve that death, and hence must have deserved it before we were visited with it, that is, before we were conceived in sin; and, accordingly, we must, ere we were shapen in our penal iniquity, have participated in Adam's offence? This is a standard argument. Our critic is logically bound to explain its origin and meaning. Instead of doing so, he busies himself in discoursing about Schleiermacher. The notable argument which he thus neglects, is useful in illustrating the old phrases, which pervade the Augustinian metaphysics. And why has not our Reviewer accounted for those phrases, if they do not, when used in philosophical prose, imply that we are morally blamable for Adam's transgression? Why do we read, in the most unimpassioned metaphysics of Calvinism, that "the sin of Adam is ours by propagation, by imputation, and *also by participation;*" that "as children are a part of their parents, so children are, in a manner, partakers of their parents' sin" (Pareus); that Adam's offence was "transferred," "brought over," "transmitted" to us as *persons*, because we had, as *natures*, previously existed and sinned in him."[1] The mental state which led philosophers to the use of these as logical phrases, is a marked phenomenon; it demands an explanation from our Reviewer. No wonder, then, that he threatens to retire from the controversy, unless we confine ourselves to his freshly compiled "anti-Augustinian" creed. Why has he forborne, in all his hundred pages against us, to write one paragraph on the astounding theories which have been formed, for explaining the mode of our participation in the sin of Eden? He avers, that the old Calvinists were guiltless of believing in our moral demerit for that offence. What, then, was the need of their herculean efforts to prove that we were voluntary in the primal transgression? What necessity was there for the doctrine of "spermatic animalcules," by and in which we, who have grown up from them, were contaminated in the person of our ancestors? What induced men to invent their phenomenal explanations of personal identity, if they did not regard the entire race as morally identical with the first ancestor? And why has our Reviewer, seeing these old doctrines rise before him in such a questionable shape, refused to look at them, and turned

---

[1] Bib. Sac. Vol. VIII. pp. 609—614. That many of these phrases were originally poetical, and are often now dissolved into the same, we have stated. But what is their meaning in logical formulas? How will our Reviewer interpret Gerhard, Loci Theol. Tom. IV. § 52, p. 316, and Marckius, Theol. Cap. XV. §§ 31, 32? He has quoted these authors, and therefore heard of them.

away his eyes to what he calls the "Paine light" in a Convention sermon, and imitated Tully in the "public-place," who "spoke Greek," while "those that understood him smiled at one another, and shook their heads."[1] And why has the learned Reviewer been so unwilling to explain the difference between the Calvinistic doctrine of Imputed Sin, and that of Imputed Righteousness? There has been a difference. The tomes of Calvin and his disciples are pervaded by the sentiment, that the sin of Adam is imputed to us "deservedly," but the righteousness of Christ " undeservedly ;" the former, "justly ;" the latter, "gratuitously ;" the one, "*after* and *because* we had sinned ;" the other, *before* we had been holy. What does this difference mean? And over and above his eloquent silence on these grave questions, why does our critic shrink from confessing, that the old Calvinists believed in our moral identity with Adam? Why does he not believe in it himself? What if we could not have been present in that garden? "Power does not limit responsibility." What if we could not have known the law of Paradise? "We may sin without any knowledge of law." What if we did not act, in eating the apple? "All sin does not consist in acting." If we may be blamable for events which preceded our choice by one hour, we may be blamable for events which preceded our choice by six thousand years. And the only reason why our worthy critic recoils from the hypothesis of "ante-natal" sin, is, that he practically believes in the three radical principles, which he intermittently disapproves. Once overlook the axioms, that power must equal duty, that knowledge is essential to holiness or sin ; — then, we have nothing to hold us back from the faith that we ought to have obeyed the law in Eden, and to have performed a thousand unknown and impossible deeds. Our assailant cannot write a page on this theme, without betraying his regard for those principles of common sense, which undermine his theories.

Take an example. He describes us as saying, that "a man is put to death by a sovereign act ;" and he describes himself as gainsaying us by the assertion, that a man is put to death " with the trifling, intermediate links of guilt and just condemnation."[2] But hold him close to this word "guilt ;" he will at once try to escape, with the plea that he does not mean *moral* guilt : fasten him to the word "just condemnation ;" he will struggle to get free, with the apology that he does not mean " morally just." What, then, does he mean? Nothing more than this : men, without any sin of their own, are subjected

---

[1] Shakspeare's Julius Caesar, Act. 1. Sc. II.
[2] Biblical Repertory, Vol. XXIII. p. 680.

to evil, because they are "exposed" to it, by Him who designs, in this exposure, to express his abhorrence of sin in Adam. This is the New England representation, in all things except its verbiage. The Reviewer does, indeed, call our first suffering "penal," and "judicial;" but he has divested these words of their moral import, and thus given up the theoretical life, while he retains the dead letter of the ancient system.[1] He has reduced the words to *trifling* ambiguities. Pregnant with meaning is his assertion, that he connects the first suffering of men with their previous state, by "the *trifling*, intermediate links of guilt and just condemnation."[2] They are trifling links, when he has burned out their pristine temper. On many other doctrines, as well as on this, he is led astray by his favorite words; and he alternately disclaims and acknowledges their ancient meaning. He builds up a platform of metaphorical terminology; but no sooner does an examiner step on it, than it caves in. It is out of joint, and will not bear the weight of a lexicon. It cannot stand. In the hour of trouble, its advocates always flee to the New England system. This system is sustained by argument, and not by suspicious intimations about Schleiermacher. It is a system which will bear to be looked at, and is not a theology of mere "Dissolving Views." The science of the world is in favor of it. The spirit and plain import of the Bible, are in favor of it. The moral instincts of the race are in favor of it. The common sense of common men, is in favor of it. They can be kept back from it, only by the incessant roll of a polemic drum, which alarms them by its discordant sounds.

More than thirty years ago, an eager antagonist announced, that "the grand enemy of truth, the most to be dreaded, because the most insinuating and the most to be opposed, is Hopkinsianism;" and that "a very large majority of the professors of religion in the United States, are either Hopkinsians or entire Arminians;"[3] and he invoked the genius of Princeton against the creed which drew its life from

---

[1] In his last Review (p. 679), he represents us as saying, that the difference between the ancient theory of Imputation and our own, is merely verbal. He mistakes. We said the very opposite. We represented as merely verbal the difference between our theory and that which our Reviewer adopts in those better hours, when he abandons the old Augustinism.

[2] Bib. Repertory, Vol. XXIII. p. 680.

[3] Willson's Historical Sketch, pp. 210, 215, 191 seq. On pp. 184, 185, this writer quotes the Pastoral Letter of the Synod of Philadelphia, dated Sept. 20, 1816, and warning the churches against "Arian, Socinian, Arminian and Hopkinsian heresies." According to Hopkins, he says (p. 158), "the atonement really amounted to *nothing*."

Edwards, Bellamy and Hopkins. Nor was his invocation idle; for, many a time, has Princeton declared, that the evils of Hopkinsianism may be traced to Edwards, who is said to have rejected the fundamental doctrine of the Gospel. Only six years ago, it spoke of "that pitchy cloud of religious and philosophical heresies, that *covers* the land of the Puritans;" and, after proclaiming that "the New England Theology has stood now almost a hundred years," characterizes it as "a system that had its origin in opinions, too much like 'another gospel;' although its teachers seemed, indeed, scarcely less than angels of God."[1] But, "*laborant, cum ventum ad verum est.*" The "northern heresies" are suddenly shut up to a "small coterie." "That pitchy cloud" has become no bigger than a man's hand. The stars that rose in the eastern sky, to shed disastrous light on half the church, have now only one "aberration," and that "in the direction of ultra-Calvinism." "The father of Hopkinsianism" now lies entombed in the confidence of theologians who once viewed him with dread. They have garnished the sepulchre of Bellamy, and embalmed "the other great men of New England." Through much tribulation, did those great men enter into the kingdom of truth. Their royal genius is now honored by their foes. Well, then, may we do homage to our fathers' memory. How can we be recreant to their faith, when its past successes are but an earnest of its future triumph?

ARTICLE VIII.

NOTICES OF NEW PUBLICATIONS.

I. PATMOS, AND THE SEVEN CHURCHES.[2]

THIS work is intended as a contribution to the Sacred Geography of the New Testament.

The modern name of Patmos is *Patino* or *Patmosa* (not *Palimo* or *Palmosa*, as in some of our helps); the ruins of Ephesus are near the Turkish village of *Aja-soluk*, thought to be a corruption of *hagios theologos*, 'Holy

---

[1] Bib. Repertory, Vol. XVIII pp. 25, 26.

[2] Patmos, and the Seven Churches of Asia; published by Rev. Josiah Brewer of Middletown, Ct. and John W. Barber of New Haven, 1851.

ARTICLE VIII.

THE RELATION OF DIVINE PROVIDENCE TO PHYSICAL LAWS.

"A few years ago, a rudely formed boat pushed out from one of the wharfs of Calcutta, and, after some days' sail on the broad bosom of the Ganges and the Bay of Bengal, entered the waters of the Brahmaputra. It was bound for Sadaiya, one of the principal towns of Assam, far up the river, near the foot of the Himmalah mountains. In it were two missionaries of the cross, who counted not their lives dear unto themselves, that they might win souls to Christ. They had come from a far distant country, and were bearing the light and knowledge and blessings of the Gospel to that still remote and benighted land. For many weeks their voyage was prosperous, and their hearts beat high with hope and Christian zeal. At length, when they had well-nigh accomplished it, when they were already near the scene of their expected labors, one of these devoted servants of Christ was stricken down by sore illness. The other hastened forward in a smaller boat to procure, if possible, medical assistance. Urged on by every motive which humanity, friendship, and piety could offer, he was within sight of the mission premises at the town whither they were going, when suddenly two trees, whose connection with the adjacent bank the winds and the stream had loosened, falling upon the boat and crushing it to pieces, he sank beneath the waters, and that heart, so true to all its obligations, was stilled forever. To the friends of the missionary and of the mission the event was a dark and mysterious providence. To the devotees of Budh, it was a manifest interposition of their deity, in protection of the faith which the infidel stranger had come to subvert and destroy.

"On the 16th of August, 1688, there lay in the harbor of Helvoetsluys more than six hundred vessels — transports and ships of war — waiting for an easterly wind to bear them to the neighboring coast of England. One of these vessels bore a flag on whose ample folds was embroidered the motto, 'I will maintain the liberties of England and the Protestant religion.' In it was William, Prince of Orange. On the evening of the 19th the entire armament weighed anchor and spread its sails to a favoring breeze. Before, however, half the distance between the two coasts had been traversed, a violent storm arose, which broke up and scattered the fleet.

"When tidings of the disaster reached the ears of King James, whose religion and crown the expedition threatened, he recognized in it a Divine interposition, in answer to the prayers of his Catholic subjects. 'What wonder,' he said devoutly, 'since the Host has been exposed for several days.' To many of the Protestants, who were looking to William and his noble armament for the protection of their liberties and their faith, its dispersion by the tempest, when approaching their inscrutable providence. William himself, however, interpreted the disaster differently. He saw in it only the work of adverse elements. Collecting the scattered vessels and repairing the injuries which they had received, he prepared for renewing the expedition. With undaunted courage, a second time he committed his fortune to the waves; and now, after a four days' sail under a smiling sky and with favoring breezes, the whole armament rode safe in the harbor of Tor Bay. During the disembarkation, the water of the Bay was as smooth as glass. But no sooner had the landing been effected, than the wind rose from the west, and swelling into a fierce gale, drove back King James's fleet, already in close pursuit. It was now the Protestants' turn to claim the favor of Heaven. Many of them, 'men of more piety than judgment,' says Macaulay, 'fully believed that the ordinary laws of nature had been suspended for the liberties and religion of England. Exactly a hundred years before, they said, the Armada, invincible by man, had been scattered by the wrath of God. Civil freedom and divine truth were again in jeopardy; and again the obedient elements had fought for the good cause. The wind had blown strong from the east while the Prince wished to sail down the channel, had turned to the south when he wished to enter Tor Bay, had sunk to a calm during the disembarkation, and as soon as the disembarkation was completed, had risen to a storm and met the pursuers in the face.' In all this King James saw only the hostility of the elements."

These historical facts are cited by Professor Chace,[1] as illustrations of the mode in which men are inclined to infer the moral purposes of God from the events occurring under his government. The designs of God as a *natural* Governor we always know from *natural* phenomena, for all these phenomena are the results and indices of his individual purposes; for "he worketh all things after the counsel of his own will." But as a *moral* Governor, what does he intend in the events which he causes to take place? From the historical occurrence we learn what he intended as a mere Sovereign; but how can we know what appeal he designed to make to the will of voluntary agents; what lessons he designed to teach; what spiritual impression to produce; in fine, what he aimed to effect as a Director of the choice, judgment, or conscience of sentient beings? There are some rules by which we may determine some things with regard to his moral intention in the phenomena of the universe.

---

[1] They are found on pp. 15—17 of "A Discourse delivered before the Porter Rhetorical Society of Andover Theological Seminary, August 1, 1854, by George I. Chace, LL. D., Professor in Brown University. Boston: Ticknor and Fields, 1854."

In the first place, we may ascribe an event to a moral purpose of the Deity, just so far as the Bible connects that event with that purpose. In the inspired record of his transactions we may learn somewhat with regard to the motives which prompt them. And we learn that his comprehensive design is to encourage holiness, and to discourage sin. "For we know that all things work together for good to them that love God," and that as a moral Governor, the Most High intends to persuade men to do right, dissuade them from doing wrong, and express his kindly interest in his friends by leading them into the wilderness in order 'to humble them and to prove them, by giving them manna, 'that he might make them know' their dependance upon him, by showing them many a 'manifest token of the righteous judgment of God, that they may be counted worthy of the kingdom of God, for which they also suffer.' We know that "whom the Lord loveth he chasteneth," and that 'all things are for their sakes,' and that ' whatsoever they ask, they (substantially) receive, because they keep his commandments, and do those things that are pleasing in his sight.' See Gen. 50: 20. Deut. 8: 1—3: 16. Jer. 24: 5—10. Zech. 13: 9. Rom. 8: 28. 2 Cor. 4: 15—17. Phil. 1: 19, 20. 2 Thess. 1: 5. Heb. 12: 6—12. 1 John 3: 22. Rev. 3: 19, et al. We are not arrogant, then, for we have inspired authority, in saying that, in some mode or other, the dispensations of God toward his children are designed for his children's spiritual welfare. There are minute specifications which the Bible does not expressly and distinctively authorize us to make; but it allows us to believe that the general spirit of the Christian disciple will be favored by the particular and special Providence of God. From the Bible we derive no right to affirm that the missionary on the Brahmaputra was subjected to the afflictive dispensation of Heaven, for the purpose of accelerating or retarding the progress of his individual opinions on the subject of baptism, or the parity of the clergy; but we have a Biblical warrant for affirming that the event which befel him was designed to promote in some way or other the spirit of evangelical benevolence. As believers in the Gospel, we are logically bound to infer that the event was divinely intended to cherish a Christian fidelity, rather than a devotion to Budh. In like manner, we have no particular inspired authority for affirming that the dispensations of Providence toward the fleet of the Prince of Orange were morally designed for an endorsement of his individual theories on the Episcopate, or of the tendencies of his army to favor the Zuinglian rather than the Lutheran view of the sacraments; but we have inspired authority for regarding these dispensations as designed, in some method, to purify the true friends of Christ, to cultivate a piety which consists in hearty obedience, rather than to encourage an empty and haughty formalism. Just in proportion to the evidence which the inspired word gives us in favor of the correctness and the importance of any doctrine, we have reason to expect that the humble, honest, cordial and consistent believer in that doctrine will receive benefit from the providences of God. On the great whole, he will present his word and his works in admirable harmony. The moral intent, then, of many divine dispensations is learned from the Bible.

In the second place, we may ascribe an event to a moral purpose of the Deity, just so far forth as that purpose is normally connected with that event by the established and appropriate tendencies of things. Thus, that God intends to dissuade men from intemperance by the accidents, and ill-health, which are consequent upon that vice, we believe, because these evils result normally from the vice, and by the laws which He has established they tend to deter men from falling into it. So the calamities which follow the gamester's arts, were designed to prevent men from the practice of those arts; as we learn from the two-fold fact, that the arts have obviously appropriate tendencies to induce these disasters, and the disasters tend normally to dissuade men from such ruinous arts. In fact, there is a tendency in every sin to work some evil, and there is a tendency in every evil to suggest motives against the sin from which the evil results; and these tendencies, being established by the Deity, indicate that he designs by them to cultivate our virtuous, and to discountenance our vicious, feelings. Just so far as we can trace these tendencies, we have a philosophical rule for ascertaining the moral intent of the phenomena resulting from them.

An event has recently occurred which affords an apt illustration of this rule. On the 17th of September, 1854, one of the strongest ships which ever sailed over the Atlantic, a ship which would have been uninjured by a collision with any ordinary vessel, was struck by a propeller of far inferior strength, and sunk. Perhaps that propeller was the only craft then on the ocean, which could have injured the thick-ribbed Arctic by a collision. The propeller was long, and unusually low, and her bow was of iron and shaped like a wedge, just fitted to perforate the steamer which she struck. The Arctic, at the moment of the collision, was on the top of a wave, and her bows lifted above the water line. Therefore the Vesta drove her iron wedge into the Arctic *below* the water line, and perforated the Arctic's plank where it was impossible to repair it. A common steamer would have struck the Arctic at a higher point, where the "thick work" of the Arctic would have resisted the most terrific shock, and where any injury might have been more easily repaired. The firemen, engineers, and "underdeck-hands" of the Arctic, were the first to detect the disaster which had befallen their ship, and, availing themselves of their *private* knowledge, contrived means to escape, taking with them nearly all the apparatus which could have secured the safety of the passengers. The captain of the Arctic, apprehending no danger to his "irresistible" steamer, despatched for the relief of the Vesta, his best life-boat, and his first officer, the very officer who had the immediate command of the crew, and without whose vigilance the men would be unmanageable. Suddenly it was announced to all who were left on board the Arctic, that the vessel hitherto deemed impervious to assault, was penetrated in its most dangerous part; the passengers became frantic, the sailors ungovernable, and, in the midst of a long-continued, dense fog, the noble ship, and more than three hundred of her company, went down to the bottom of the sea. The attention of the civilized world has been directed to the fact, that on the wide ocean the paths of two such peculiar steamers should have intersected each other at just that point; that the vessels should have approached one another at the very angle where the collision would be most perilous, and at the moment when the impenetrable fog rendered it impossible to foresee the coming danger, and that the firmest as well as the most richly freighted of the two ships should have received the most fatal injury, and her captain, while ignorant of his peril, should have so singularly deprived himself of his most efficient helpers. What means this intervolved Providence by which so many hopes and plans of thousands have been disappointed forever! Did God intend to chastise for their peculiar sinfulness the three hundred who found a watery grave; to rebuke our nation for any of its political delinquencies, for its infliction of wrong upon the Indian or the slave? How *do* we, how *can* we, be assured that such was his intention? We only *know* in the general, that He designed this dispensation, as every other, for the furtherance of good principles in some way, for the check of evil principles in some way; for the rebuke of those faults which have an appropriate tendency to occasion such a disaster. That carelessness of human life resulting from that haste to be rich, which allows the unwarrantable rapidity of the ship's movement, and the neglect of a hundred prudent maxims, of an alert watch, of the alarm bell, of the precautionary whistle, has received here a reprimand which is well fitted to deter men from a fault legitimately resulting in such a catastrophe. That selfishness which indisposes navigators and merchants to provide for the moral culture of seamen; and that habitual worldliness which leaves travellers unprepared for sudden emergencies, takes away their presence of mind, their energy, their practical tact whenever an imminent danger stares them in the face; in fine, all such iniquities as are in their own nature adapted to occasion so complex a disaster, are philosophically reproved, and therefore were divinely intended to be reproved by this variously instructive Providence. That many other intentions animated the divine Mind, we are unable to deny; what they were we are equally unable to affirm.

"I do not believe," says Professor Chace, "that a careful collection of statistics on this subject would show, or render probable even, that the agencies of the natural world are directly employed by God in the administration of His moral government. I do not believe it would be found that as the inhabitants of any district or province have become more virtuous and more Christian, the elements of nature have shown themselves more kindly and beneficent — that the sun has shed his rays more genially — the clouds poured out their waters more abundantly or more uniformly — and the earth yielded its fruits in greater profusion, and with less labor from the husbandman. I do not believe it would be found, that as this same people have declined in virtue and piety, the heats have become more parching, the droughts more withering, the frosts more blighting, and the tempests more devastating. And yet it is in cases like this, if in any, that we should look for an interposition of the Divine power in bringing the natural world into relation with the moral. Occasionally, in the course of physical events, there are marked occurrences, which might seem to be specially ordered. But in by far the greater number of instances, there is nothing observable to indicate moral design or purpose."[1]

---

[1] Discourse, etc., pp. 13, 14.

We suppose that Prof. Chace means to deny, here, the *supernatural* interpositions of God in the physical world, but has no intention of disputing the natural, but the no less divinely intended, adaptedness of a virtuous life to promote peace of mind, and a consequent soundness of intellect, and innumerable blessings legitimately resulting therefrom. We do not understand him as disbelieving that a spirit of comprehensive obedience to the will of God has a normal fitness to promote health and vigor of body, as well as of mind, and thus tends, by philosophical law, to secure the numberless advantages that flow from the *mens sana in corpore sano*. The experience of individuals and of nations proves that the observance of moral rules, the fear of the Lord, the keeping of his Sabbaths, the reverence for his word, have an appropriate tendency to gain the countless benefits which result from industry, frugality, temperance and fortitude. The history of the race evolves no one truth more distinctly than, that, according to the established tendency of things as well as the special provisions of grace, "godliness with contentment is great gain," and " is profitable unto all things, having promise of the life that now is, and of that which is to come." The prevalence of Christianity has, in some respects, changed the face of nature even.

Although the two rules now laid down, are, as far as they extend, more decisive than any other, yet they do not extend far enough to remove all indeterminateness from our judgments concerning the particular moral intentions of the Deity. We still remain doubtful, not with regard to the general, yet with regard to the specific, design of God in many of his minuter dispensations. Hence we add an auxiliary remark:

In the third place, when any event strikingly coincides with any well-known plan of God, we may, in a modest spirit, ascribe that event to his intention to fulfil that plan. There must be a *striking* coincidence between the particular phenomenon and the general scheme of the divine government; and, just in proportion as the coincidence fails of being definite and marked, must the confidence which we build upon it with regard to the specific divine purpose be the less firm and strong. The plan of God with which the event coincides must be *well known*, and just in proportion as it fails of being clearly disclosed to us, must we be cautious and diffident in the inferences which we draw from an agreement of certain phenomena with it. If an event have a questionable symmetry with a divine plan, and if the plan be conjectured or but dimly proved, we must reason far less confidently than if the event have an obvious agreement with the divine economy, and this economy be clearly unveiled before us.

It is, for example, a well-known plan of Jehovah to answer the prayers of his children. The Scriptures reveal this plan. The normal tendencies of things likewise prove that our requests for *spiritual* blessings will be answered, *always* answered. Perhaps no part of the divine economy is plainer than that our Heavenly Father will comply with the devout solicitations of his children. Still, his children supplicate for many temporal favors which are not granted. Prayers are offered for the recovery of the sick, and the sick remain unhealed; for the life of men in danger, and their life is lost. Two disciples entreat the Lord with equal intensity of love, the one for rain, the other for sunshine at the same place and at the same time. One or the other of the suppliants must be disappointed. When, therefore, and how, can we determine that a specific temporal favor which we receive comes from a divine purpose to answer a supplication which has been offered for that favor? Our faith that this blessing results from this intention, may be just as strong as our knowledge of God's plan to comply with the requests of his children is clear, and as the coincidence between the reception of this favor, on the one hand, and this well-known plan on the other, is exact and striking. So far forth as we doubt whether the supplication were humble and sincere, or whether the economy of God's government allow him to notice *such* cries as were addressed to Him for *such* favors, or whether the favor received correspond with the prayer offered, just so far forth must we hesitate to ascribe the event in question to his regard for the entreaty addressed to him. Sometimes the hesitation is greater, sometimes less; but there are such striking coincidences as will not fail to remove all practical distrust from the hearty suppliant. The churches of New England had a right to feel that their entreaties *for their own safety* were answered, when such decisive incidents occurred as are alluded to in the following quotation from Dr. Dwight and Dr. Wisner: "I am bound," says President Dwight, "as an inhabitant of New England, to declare, that, were there no other instances to to be found in any other country, the blessings communicated to this would furnish ample satisfaction concerning this subject, to every sober, much more to every pious, man. Among these, the destruction of the French armament, under the Duke D'Anville, in the year 1746, ought to be remembered with gratitude and admiration by every inhabitant of this country. This fleet consisted of forty ships of war; was destined for the destruction of New England; was of sufficient force to render that destruction, in the ordinary progress of things, certain; and sailed from Chebucto in Nova Scotia for this purpose."[1] " In the mean time," adds Dr. Wisner, " our pious fathers, apprized of their danger, and feeling that their only safety was in God, had appointed a season of fasting and prayer to be observed in all their churches. ' While Mr. Prince was officiating [in the Old South Church of Boston, says a writer in the Columbian Sentinel, of 1821] on this fast day, and praying most fervently to God to avert the dreaded calamity, a sudden gust of wind arose (the day had till now been perfectly clear and calm), so violent as to cause a loud clattering of the windows. The reverend pastor paused in his prayer; and, looking round upon the congregation with a countenance of hope, he again commenced, and with great devotional ardor supplicated the Almighty to cause *that wind* to frustrate the object of our enemies, and save the country from conquest and popery. A tempest ensued, in which the greater part of the French fleet was wrecked on the coast of Nova Scotia. The Duke D'Anville, the principal general, and the second in command, both committed suicide. Many died with disease, and thousands were consigned to a watery grave. The small number who remained alive, returned to France without health, and without spirits.' And the enterprise was abandoned, and never again resumed."[2] *Ne resecandum ad vivum.* That the destruction of property and life was an answer to prayer, that the rising of any particular wave of of the sea, or particular "gust of wind" was the result of a particular supplication therefor, we need not be confident; but that the *safety* of the Lord's heritage in New England, which was the supplicated favor, was vouchsafed in compliance with

---

[1] Theology, Vol. V. pp. 40, 41.
[2] See the History of the Old South Church in Boston, by Benjamin B. Wisner, D. D., pp. 29, 30, and ' Recollections of a Bostonian," No. 8, in the Columbian Sentinel, Boston, 1821. Dr. Wisner adds some corroborative testimony from members of the Old South Church.

the supplication, we may rationally believe. The analogies of divine Providence warrant the belief. The peculiarity of the coincidence between the phenomenon and the whole scheme of divine government brings with it a self-evidencing light. The healthy feelings of the renewed soul prompt to such a faith. In his Eulogy on Adams and Jefferson, the late Mr. Webster has intimated the influence which our well-ordered emotions have on our interpretation of providential events. When noticing the fact that these two men were called from life on the same day, and that the natal day of our liberties, he says: " Both had been presidents, both had lived to a great age, both were early patriots, and both were distinguished and ever honored by their immediate agency in the act of independence. It cannot but seem striking, and extraordinary, that these two should live to see the fiftieth year from the date of that act; that they should complete that year; and that then, on the day which had first linked forever their own fame with their country's glory, the heavens should open to receive them both at once. As their lives themselves were the gifts of Providence, who is not willing to recognize in their happy termination, as well as in their long continuance, proofs that our country and its benefactors are the objects of His care?"[1]

We may or may not sympathize with Mr. Webster in his interpretation of this individual phenomenon. Men will differ, as their varying tendencies of mind, habits of association, experiences of life prompt them to differ in regard to some departments of the divine administration. We have disclaimed the pretension that all events can be traced definitely and precisely to the individual aims which prompted them. But while we must give a certain degree of latitude to the action of diversified temperaments, we are still persuaded that some events are so *peculiarly* harmonious with the known scheme of the divine government, as to authorize us in referring them to the same divine motive which prompted that scheme.

Let us now conclude this branch of our discussion with the remark, that we may ascribe many events, in part, to the divine intention of humbling men and making them submissive to the mysteries of God's will. It is his known plan to cultivate these lowly graces in the hearts of his children. There are many events

---

[1] Discourse in Commemoration of the Lives and Services of John Adams and Thomas Jefferson, 1826, pp. 7, 8.

fitted to nurture the spirit of modest acquiescence in his sovereign pleasure. He causes these events, and, as we are authorized to believe, he causes them in subservience to the plan which they are adapted to fill out. For many phenomena we should be sinfully arrogant were we to assign a particular motive in the divine mind. They may have been devised with this motive, or with that. We have no right to *deny*, more than we have a right to affirm, that they were prompted by the first or the second motive. But we have a right to believe, that they resulted from *some* intent, and from the comprehensive design to make the inquirer lowly and deferential. " It is the glory of God to conceal a thing." And his design in " hiding himself in thick darkness" is to prompt the cry: " O the depth of the riches both of the wisdom and knowledge of God! how unsearchable are his judgments and his ways past finding out! For who hath known the mind of the Lord [where the Lord hath not chosen to reveal it] or who hath been his counsellor?" We have no logical right to deny that the afflictions of Job may have been sent with either of several imagined purposes; but the history of Job authorizes us to believe that they were designed to humble men in view of men's inability to comprehend all the purposes of God. We have no logical right to deny that the slaughter of the Galileans by the Roman governor, was the consequence of one or another conceivable design of Heaven; but our Saviour's comment on that Providence justifies us in thinking that the event resulted from the general purpose to nurture a humble spirit in men who contemplate this sign of their Ruler's supremacy. The tower of Siloam did not fall upon the eighteen men for the purpose of designating them as peculiarly flagitious; still we cannot disprove that it fell for some particular moral end hidden from all survivors; and we may affirm that it fell for the general intent of cultivating in men that lowliness which leads to 'the fear of the Lord which is the beginning of wisdom." We are expressly assured that the divine intention in afflicting a certain man with blindness, was not to designate either him or his parents as sinners; still there may have been various divine intentions in the Providence, and we are carefully informed that one of them was to reveal the ways of God in bringing good out of evil. If any man should assert that events do occur, affecting our condition in life, yet without any particular moral design on the part of the Deity, the assertion should be proved. But it were difficult to prove such a negative. For even if there were no other conceivable intention for those events, they may have been in part designed to cherish our humble deference toward the mysteries of the divine government.

The Discourse of Professor Chace, to which we have already alluded, has been understood as denying that God has any moral intention in some of the phenomena which exert an influence over sentient beings. It is not our purpose now to inquire, whether he has been correctly interpreted in this respect, or whether his peculiar use of certain technical terms has exposed him to be misinterpreted. He has certainly used some expressions which involve the theory, that all the events affecting our interest proceed from a definite moral purpose of the Deity. He says:

"The Scriptures undoubtedly teach — and the doctrine is consonant with both reason and experience — that under God's government no real harm can befall those who love and keep His commandments; that every condition in which they may be placed, every event and circumstance of their lives, rightly improved, becomes a means of grace and blessing."[1]

Now if *every* circumstance in our life, even the most minute, may become the *means* of good to us, it was intended by God to be such a possible means. Again, he says:

"In the case of every dispensation of God's Providence, whether joyous or afflictive, it is right and proper, and our duty, to inquire, what use we should make of it? how He would have us behave under it? what lessons derive from it? And if the inquiry be reverently and humbly made, we may hope to be guided to a right answer. But beyond this we may not go. Why the event was ordered, what ends it was intended to accomplish, whether it respects chiefly ourselves, or has other and higher relations which determined its form and occurrence — are questions pertaining to the secret things of God — to the immediate purposes of Him who giveth not account of any of His matters. It is vain and useless to ask them."[2]

But if "every dispensation of God's Providence" deserves this inquiry into its usefulness, it must have a divinely intended usefulness. If the intentions of God be hidden from us, the very concealment implies that there are intentions. If the event be mysterious, the very mystery implies that there are purposes of God wrapped up in it. Providences do not amaze a considerate Christian, except as they suggest a query with regard to the

[1] Discourse, pp. 38, 39.   [2] Ib. pp. 39, 40.

divine intention which prompted them. Prof. Chace distinctly affirms that "*any* future event in which we are interested and concerning which the will of God is unknown to us, is a legitimate subject of petition."[1] But how can we rightly pray for "any" favors, if they be not within the sphere of God's intentional providence? The doctrine of prayer involves the doctrine of a providential government, extending to every phenomenon in regard to which we may supplicate Heaven. Again, Prof. Chace inculcates the duty of "submission to the will of God, because it is His will; because such submission is right, and proper, and becoming us, as His creatures; because His will itself is perfect goodness, and because its appointments, although including much partial and incidental evil, all look ultimately to the securing of the best interests of His universe."[2] But how can we morally submit to the will of God, unless we believe that he has a moral intent with regard to the evils which call for our submission?

The fact that God designs to humble men by the inscrutableness of many of his dispensations, is sufficient to rescue the doctrine of his universal government from the abuses into which it sometimes falls. Prof. Chace thus describes the selfishness and "egoism" which induce a class of Christians to make exorbitant demands upon God's administration, and to be dissatisfied unless His Providence appear to culminate on themselves.

"Everything in nature as well as in human society, must minister to the safety and welfare of the favorite of Heaven. The winds are commanded to blow gently upon him. The lightnings and the tempests are charged to do him no harm. The sun is withheld from smiting him by day, and the moon by night. Disease and misfortune and calamity are turned from his dwelling, or if permitted to enter, they come not as ministers of wrath, but as angels of mercy, bearing with them hidden blessings. Every event is ordered with reference to his interests, and made tributary to his good. His conception of the Creator and Governor of the Universe, would seem to include little beyond the idea of an All-powerful Being, constantly attendant upon his steps, defending him on every side from accident and harm, holding over him continually the shield of his protecting power, and personally ministering to all — even the most minute and trivial of his wants. The same care is supposed to be extended — in a less degree, indeed, to all the objects in which self is interested — over which by a ready and natural expansion it spreads itself. Family, friends, brethren of the same faith, kindred and country, severally come in for their due share of the

---

[1] Discourse, p. 64.

Divine favor. That many of the ordinarily supposed providences, are mere reflections of this lively interest which every man feels in his own personal welfare, I think no reflective mind can doubt. Indeed, such would seem but a natural inference, from the almost universal observation that these providences are seen only in events favoring the hopes, wishes or interests of the persons immediately affected, and are seen by them alone."[1]

But there is no inconsistency between a belief that all things shall work together for good to the individual who loves his Maker, and a belief that they shall also work out innumerable other benefits to innumerable other beings. Because a providence of our Father *extends* to the least of his children, that lowly child need not imagine that the Providence is *confined* to him. In the chariot of the Most High the prophet saw a wheel within a wheel. A single event may reach a variety of ends. It is not, then, a *use* of the doctrine of particular Providence, it is a *misuse* which results in the fancy that the individual thus provided for is "in the centre of the universe," and all other existences must revolve around him. In blessing one disciple God blesses all, and in blessing all, he blesses that one. Besides, the fact that multitudes of the divine dispensations are, and appear so, inexplicable, tends to convince every Christian that the divine government takes a broad range, is concerned with a large variety of interests, and therefore every individual, rejoicing in the minute care of that government over himself, ought to feel his own comparative insignificance, his short-sightedness, his liabilities to err in judging of a scheme so vast as the Divine. From the very fact that God is "ever attent unto the cry" of an individual so ignorant and so erring, flows a new motive for not only a humble, submissive temper, but also for admiration of the Ruler's condescending love, and for gratitude in view of every good and perfect gift which cometh down from Him.

It were vain, however, to conceal the truth that men do often pervert the doctrine of Providence, by fancying themselves to understand the secret counsels of Omnipotence, and especially by imagining that their own whimsical theories, or partisan schemes are the central objects of the divine care. A few weeks before his death, Gen. Jackson is said to have explained the reasons which actuated the divine Mind in permitting Gen. Harrison to be elected President of the United States, and then

---

[1] Discourse, pp. 23, 24.

the reasons for calling the President from office and life. Mr. Harrison died so that Mr. Tyler might be enabled to save the country by his vetoes! When the last comet appeared in Russia, a Greek priest in the vicinity of Warsaw " summoned his congregation together, although it was neither Sunday nor festival, and, having shown them the comet, informed them that this was the same star which had appeared to the Magi at the birth of our Saviour, and that it was only visible now in the Russian empire. Its appearance on this occasion was to intimate to the Russian eagle, that the time was now come for it to spread out its wings and embrace all mankind in one orthodox soul-sanctifying church. He showed them that the star was now standing immediately over Constantinople, and explained that the dull light of the nucleus indicated its sorrow at the delays of the Russian army in proceeding to its destination." Says Professor Chace:

"The blood of the martyred saint, sacredly treasured through centuries, annually liquefies, betokening, by the readiness with which it flows, the smiles or the wrath of heaven. The silken veil of a Christian maiden, who had preferred the fagot to denying her Lord, turns aside the burning stream of lava, and saves from destruction the town which it threatened. The plague is miraculously cured at the tomb of a saint, and a whole city even is saved from its ravages by his effigy borne through the streets. The fires of the stake are quenched at the touch of the holy martyr; lions crouch as meek as lambs at his feet; and even the wounds which the unrelenting sword, or still more cruel instruments of torture, have inflicted, angels are sent with celestial medicines to assuage and heal."[1]

In many of these instances, we must presume, the spirit of imposture is mingled with superstition; but scores of instances might be adduced in which there is no chicanery, but an honest, though audacious, attempt to particularize the exact motives which prompted certain divine arrangements mysterious probably to the angels. Sectarian warfare, and even family discipline have been embittered by the arrogant claims of men to understand what "the Father hath kept in his own power." The objections of several writers which seem to be aimed against the *reality* of special providences, are strictly applicable to nothing more than *our ability to understand* these providences. We apprehend that some remarks of Prof. Chace which have

---

[1] Discourse, p. 18.

been understood as gainsaying the doctrine that God accommodates certain events of his administration to our moral wants, were simply intended to teach that we cannot modestly presume to know the particular design of those events,—that they have no aim which we are authorized to interpret minutely.

As, then, we must admit the existence of God's particular designs, obvious or mysterious, in all the phenomena of the universe, the question arises: how are these designs executed? In what mode does the Universal Sovereign accomplish "his will in the army of heaven and among the inhabitants of the earth?"

There are various theories relating to the manner in which the providential scheme is conducted. Some of these let us now state.

First, we will allude to some of the theories which pertain to the Divine government over *material* phenomena. One of these theories is, that God has so arranged and does now so preserve the forces and tendencies of matter, as to secure all the events which take place, he having originally foreordained these events, and adapted his material universe to their occurrence. On this theory every event is the result of a *particular* providential act of God. Every event occurs in consequence of an arrangement made by the Creator, an arrangement which, as he foresaw, would lead to that event; an arrangement which in determining to adopt, he determined to secure that event. According to this theory he chose the occurrence of every phenomenon which does take place. He chose it either on account of its own nature or tendencies, as a good, or a means of good; or else he chose it on account of its dependence on some other phenomenon which was valuable in its nature or tendencies. He chose to cause or to permit everything which exists, rather than to give up his present system. He did not prefer evil to good, but he preferred to admit the evil rather than to abandon the system with which evil is connected. In consonance with this theory, there is no event so minute, none so evil in itself, as to be unworthy of God's providential care. His providence is not only general, extending to the main current of phenomena, but is universal and therefore particular, extending to every individual phenomenon, just as really as if every phenomenon were the result of a supernatural interposition of his power. I may move the index of a watch just as really by touching the interior wheels, as by touching the index itself. If I impregnate the fountain lake, I may as effectually corrupt or purify the waters flowing from the pipes, in the mansions of the city, as I could do if I should impregnate the city reservoir, or the street aqueduct. In order to transmit intelligence from Boston to Washington, it is not necessary for me to begin my telegraphic communication at Baltimore. I may start the intelligence from Boston itself.

In a recent Essay by Prof. Hitchcock, of Amherst College, he speaks, as follows, of a theory in some respects like that now under consideration: "What possible difference can it make, whether we suppose God to have arranged the agencies of nature at the beginning, so as to meet every exigency, or to interpose, whenever necessary, to accomplish specific purposes by some new force or law? Why is not the one as special as the other? If he did in eternity arrange and balance the forces of nature in a particular manner, with the express design of meeting a particular exigency, what matter how many ages intervene between the arrangement and the event?"[1] We do not understand Professor Chace as opposing the main principles of this first theory of a Providence extending to every event. His remarks, which have been understood as impugning the doctrine that a divine provision has included all the phenomena of history, were not intended to impugn the doctrine that such a provision was made *at the commencement* of the created system. He disclaims any such application of his words. He says distinctly:

"It will be observed that the question here, is not whether the course of events in the natural world was pre-arranged in view of the requirements of man's moral probation, but whether the Divine power is continually interposed in altering that arrangement to meet emergencies not provided for in it."[2] He says again: "In its wider and more general signification, the whole course of human actions and events — everything which has transpired in our world — may be said to be included in God's Providence; inasmuch as all has proceeded from the constitution of things which He established, and must from the beginning have been foreseen by Him. In this sense every occurrence in life may, with propriety, be spoken of as providential. Accidents originating in the grossest carelessness, death, although by the hand of the assassin, may still be regarded as providential."[3]

---

[1] Bibliotheca Sacra, Vol. XI. p. 781.   [2] Discourse, p. 13.   [3] Ib. p. 28.

In a published explanation of his Discourse, its learned author remarks that he "takes for granted a general, all-embracing providence, including the little as well as the great, the most minute as well as the most stupendous, the falling of a pebble, as well as the rolling of the spheres. The distinction which is made between this and God's particular[1] or special Providence, is, that, while the latter includes only such actions and events as *are specially provided for*,—as hold the place of *ends* in the economy of the divine government,—the former embraces also all the incidental or collateral results developed by the means employed for their attainment."

A second theory with regard to the mode in which God's providential government over the material universe is conducted, differs from the preceding only in this respect: it teaches that, in particular instances, God interposes his supernatural influence, and changes the regular operation of the forces of nature. He preserves in existence all the powers of matter, with all their tendencies, and, if he should not interpose to prevent, they would ensure a certain phenomenon; but he does interpose, he does deflect them from their regular operation and thus, by his immediate volition, he ensures an entirely different phenomenon. On this theory, a special providence is an interposition of God to secure an event which would not have resulted from the appropriate working of nature's laws; and a common providence is His preserving of nature's forces so that they will normally produce a certain event. The definition of special providence, then, is different, on this theory, from the definition on the first theory. On the first theory, the providence is *special* in its direct intention to produce particular phenomena on account of their own intrinsic or relative value; and a

---

[1] We have no disposition to condemn an author so select in his style as Professor Chace, for using the word "particular," as synonymous with "special," Providence. We have been accustomed, however, to speak of a *particular* Providence as referring to a care extending to every event, however minute; and of a *special* Providence as referring to that peculiar care which secures the occurrence of events fitted to arrest attention by their striking adaptedness to a moral design. On the theory that the Providence of God consists in the preservation of all the arrangements, forces, tendencies and activities of matter, in such a state that they will produce the phenomena which do occur, his Providence must be universal and particular. It must be particular in being universal. But it is not special, unless it be fitted to arouse attention by its peculiar and striking adaptedness to a moral design. Special is opposed to common, and particular is opposed to that which is merely general.

common providence is his incidental intention to produce or permit the phenomena which are not chosen on account of their own worth or usefulness, but which necessarily result from the phenomena specially provided for. Thus, on the first theory, the structure of a man's eye is a result of God's special providence; but the fact that his eye is one shade lighter or one shade darker, results from God's universal or particular providence indeed, but from his common or incidental, and not from his special providence. But, on the second theory, God has a special providence over the eye, only when he directly interposes and changes the action of its laws; and his other providences are particular and universal, but common. In this view, a special providence is of comparatively rare occurrence. Sometimes it is miraculous, when certain laws of nature are *manifestly* violated, and sometimes it is supernatural, when the action of these laws is changed by an immediate interposition, but still there is no *obvious* counteraction of them.

The main intent of Professor Chace's Discourse is to gainsay this *second* theory of Providence. He opposes, not the doctrine that all phenomena are made certain, *at the beginning*, by the structure of nature's laws, but the doctrine that "material agencies are *diverted* from their obvious *design* "by *interpositions* which *disturb* the order and harmony of nature;" that there is a "*modification* of natural phenomena, by a power acting *behind* the laws that govern them;" that there is "a *suspension* or modification of natural laws," a substitution of "the immediate and special exertion of the Divine power *in place of* a government carried on by general agencies, under general laws." Sometimes he makes remarks apparently hostile to the universality of Providence, but they are elsewhere explained as applicable to the doctrine of a Providence still interposing *supernaturally* or *miraculously* in the material world. His arguments against a special Providence are applicable to those interpositions merely which *alter* the arrangements of the physical universe "in order to meet emergencies *not provided for in it*." That he does not intend to deny the doctrine of special providence as defined in the first theory, may be learned from his own published comment on his Discourse. "In indicating," he says, "what part of the Divine government we may suppose to be administered by special Providences, the Discourse proceeds by exclusion. It first places without the pale of such providences, all moral evil and also natural evil, so far as it is not dependent upon moral causes. 'To suppose either suffering or sin the object of design on the part of the Creator, or in itself pleasing to Him, is not more repugnant to every right sentiment, than it is inconsistent with the remedial provisions so generally introduced for their alleviation or cure. Only good and worthy ends can, therefore, be embraced in the Divine Providence.' It next removes from the domain of special Providences the unimportant as connected incidentally with the important, and also the little as subordinate to, or involved in, the great. 'While the great, the true, the real, the essential, are secured by agencies and laws pressing on to their accomplishment with the resistlessness of fate, tho little, the apparent, the formal, the unessential, are left to follow, in subordination to them, from the general provisions of the system.' After these two exclusions, the whole field of nature and human society is left to be occupied by special Providences, conceived each in infinite wisdom as well as goodness, and together so arranged and combined as to secure the best interests of God's moral universe. Even the events which are not included in these special Providences, furnish, nevertheless, means of human probation, and thus become indirectly subservient to his moral purposes."

A third theory pertaining to the method of God's physical Providence is, that He immediately and directly causes all phenomena which occur, and makes no use of material forces. Indeed, matter has no power, but all its apparent action is a reception of an influence from the great and only efficient cause in the heavens. On this theory, all common events take place by as real and direct an intervention of God, as do the so-called miraculous or supernatural events; and the special Providence of the Deity is simply his production of certain *peculiar* phenomena, such as are called wonders, miracles, etc.

A fourth theory is, that the powers of nature exert an energy, and God at the same time acts on, in, and with them, starting them, immediately directing and controlling them, sometimes counteracting them. This includes the various forms of the *Concursus*.

But, without lingering on other theories, we will simply allude to one (which has been sometimes termed the want of a theory), which is, that God controls the material universe so as to secure all the phenomena which ever occur, but he adopts, at different times, different methods of control, and some of these methods, if not all, are entirely unknown to us and were designed to be kept mysterious.

We will allude, in the second place, to some of the theories relating to the method of God's Providence in the spiritual system.

The first is, that all the powers and tendencies of the mind are so made and adjusted and preserved in their activity, as to secure all the mental acts and states which are ever experienced. The second theory is, that, while many spiritual notions and conditions may be referred to the Providence of God, acting in the powers and tendencies of the created spirit, many other actions and conditions must be referred to the immediate and supernatural interpositions of God. Some who believe in his supernatural interpositions for altering the activity of material laws, believe that he thus interposes *far more frequently* in directing the agency of mind. Some who deny that he interposes in the physical system, cordially affirm that he interposes in the spiritual. They do not allow that he supernaturally changes the direction of the wind in order to direct a ship toward the endangered raft of the Arctic, but he supernaturally inclines the steersmen of several merchant-ships to sail near the frail raft. They do not admit any supernatural interposition in modifying the tempest which withheld its force until the Prince of Orange had reached his haven, and which then arose as a shield against his pursuers, but they will admit a supernatural interposition in persuading the Prince to sail at just the right hour and in just the right course to obtain all the advantages of the fluctuating winds and waves. The theory of Prof. Chace is, that God conducts his moral government, not by disturbing the course of nature, but in part by so interposing as to incline the soul to receive benefit from the *fixed* course of nature. He says:

"Having formed men, He immediately operates upon their hearts, by the influence of His Holy Spirit. He has only to touch, here, the springs of feeling, and desire and action, and these flow out in accordance with His most perfect will."[1] "By the union of these several modes in its administration, there is secured to the Divine government, at the same time, firmness and flexibility. While neither moral nor physical law bends to circumstances, the government, through the third and variable element embodied

---

[1] Discourse, p. 7.

in it, adapts itself to all the requirements of our moral and religious probation. Whatever ends, necessary to such probation, are not attained by constitutional provisions, are secured by the direct interpositions of His Spirit."[1]

The Scriptures definitely assure us, that God operates on the soul of man by direct and supernatural interpositions of his power. This fact seems, of itself, to be a sufficient answer to *some* of the *à priori* arguments adduced to disprove his supernatural interpositions in the sphere of matter. If the welfare of men is sufficiently important to justify his direct mental influence, why is not the same welfare important enough to justify his direct physical influence?[2] "Although the avalanche pause not," says Professor Chace, "in its precipitous descent, the traveller may be removed from the place overwhelmed by it."[3] But so far as the worth of that traveller's life is concerned, why may it not be just as seemly for Providence to interfere and stay the avalanche, as to interfere and delay the traveller? Again, if there may be interpositions of Providence in the realm of spirit without injuriously affecting the stability of mental laws, why may there not be equal interpositions of Providence in the realm of matter, without injuriously affecting the perpetuity of material laws? Professor Chace remarks:

"That which creates the difficulty in the one case, is wanting in the other; viz. invariability of manifestation. Did the same mind always act, under the same circumstances, in precisely the same manner — did the same truths presented to it at different times, produce invariably the same effects, then there would be no room for the supposition of Divine interpositions, modifying the mental phenomena. Or were matter like mind, subject to moods," . . . "there would be no difficulty in the supposition of Divine interpositions in material phenomena. On the contrary, the idea of such interpositions would naturally be suggested."[4]

---

[1] Discourse, p. 27.

[2] With regard to events which are deemed too unimportant for a divine superintendence, Turretin aptly asks: Quid pediculis, ranis, locustis, vermiculis, caeterisque insectis abjectius? Haec tamen Deus excitare dicitur ad executionem judiciorum suorum, Exodus 8: 16, 17 and 10: 12; imo vocantur exercitus ejus robustus, faciens verbum ejus, Joel 2: 11. On the contrary, Thomas Aquinas says, as if the Deity would be wearied by a universal care over the *minutiae* of the world: "Licet Deus sciat numerum individuorum, numerus tamen boum et culicum et aliorum hujusmodi non sit praeordinatus a Deo."

[3] Discourse, p. 27.

[4] Ib. pp. 64, 65.

But are not the operations of mind as regular as those of matter? May we not as easily explain the laws which lead to every particular volition, as the laws which lead to every particular rising of a wave, or every particular gust of wind?

The question appears to be one of pure revelation. Unless it had been revealed that God interposes in the sphere of mind, we should have been obliged to trust in the entire uniformity of all mental laws, and to withhold our faith from the theory of his spiritual interpositions. So unless it be revealed that God interposes in supernaturally counteracting some laws of matter, we must confide in the uniform operation of all material laws, and must withhold our assent from the theory of his physical interpositions. We doubt whether any *à priori* objection ought to influence us in the one case more than in the other, provided that the Biblical argument be as strong in the one case as it is overwhelming in the other. The details of the Biblical evidence on this topic we have not space now to examine, nor can we more than allude to the remaining theories which respect the method of God's spiritual administration; the third theory, which is that he causes our mental and moral acts without any concurrence with our own powers; the fourth (of which there are various modifications), that he uniformly concurs with our own powers and incites them to some kind and degree of activity; and the fifth, that his methods of controlling the mind are (far more than his methods of controlling matter) diversified, and some of them are entirely beyond our comprehension.

The requisites for every true theory of Divine Providence are, that it represent God as ever active in conducting the minutest as well as the greatest affairs of his universe, and the universe as always and in every part dependent upon him for its own activity and its very being; that God be represented as ever able and ready to interpose his supernatural influence, and as actually interposing it when and where the exigencies of his kingdom render such an interposition desirable; that he has interposed in the miracles recorded by inspired men and in every instance of regeneration and sanctification which has occurred, and doubtless in unnumbered other instances which have not been fully disclosed to us; and that all this constant agency of God was designed by him at the beginning. That these elements are involved in the doctrine, is evident from such Scriptures as Acts 14: 17. 17: 25—28. Eph. 1: 11. Heb. 1: 3. Col. 1: 17.

Prov. 16: 33. Matt. 4: 4. Luke 4: 4. Deut. 8: 3. Matt. 5: 45. 6: 26 —30. 10: 29—31, etc.

Several passages teaching the doctrine of Providence, directly imply that of the eternal purposes of God. The truth of his eternal purposes makes the truth of his Providence the more emphatic and prominent. We are well aware that, when we speak of all providential events as having been "designed from the beginning," we use words which are often misunderstood by philosophers. There are scientific men who uniformly speak of God's design or plan, as implying that the purposed event is chosen as an end, as a good. Therefore they say that, in the structure of the human body, pain is not an object of contrivance; it is not the end for which the body was planned, it was not specially *designed* in the formation of the system; but all the *purposed* arrangements of the system are for happiness. So they affirm that the evils and the *minutiae* of the world were not foreordained by God as *ends*, and therefore were not objects of his eternal decree. But the doctrine of divine purposes is not defined by technical theologians, as implying that the sin and evil of the universe are chosen for *their own sake*; that God made the wicked *on purpose* to destroy them, and predestinated their iniquity and their ruin *as a good in itself*. The doctrine of the divine decrees is technically explained as teaching, that all things are made certain by the purpose of God, some things as *ends*, good in themselves; some things as *means*, conducive to these ends; and some things as results incidental to these ends; that all things are predetermined either primarily, on account of their own intrinsic or relative worth; or secondarily, on account of their dependence upon the events which have an intrinsic or relative worth; that the phenomena which are good were chosen for their goodness, and the phenomena which are evil were chosen, not on account of their evil, but on account of their certain connection with good; that the evil was chosen not *in preference* to a good which was consistent for the Deity to substitute for the evil, but it was chosen *rather* than a greater evil, the abandonment of the very good with which this evil is certainly intervolved. We suppose that this use of the terms design, purpose, decree, etc., is conformed to reputable English usage. We have high literary as well as theological authority for saying that a patient chooses the pain of amputation *rather than* the continuance of a diseased limb; a traveller designs to endure the inconveniences of a voyage *rather than* relinquish his plan of a transatlantic tour; a monarch purposes the exposure of his army to death *rather than* sacrifice the freedom of his country; and every man predetermines that which he foresees must attend any operation which he insists on performing.

Adopting the phraseology to which his favorite sciences have inclined him, the accomplished naturalist whose Discourse on Providence we have already noticed, makes repeated objections to the doctrine " that everything which occurs in our world is in accordance with [God's] will," and " is immediately ordered by God;" that " evil is as really provided for, as much the object of Divine contrivance and design as good; that suffering and sin spring as directly from the constitution of things and must have been as truly intended as happiness and virtue."[1] These and similar assertions will be understood as involving a direct denial of the Divine purposes. Are the assertions qualified or explained? They must be compared with the author's favorite phraseology with regard to the term Providence. As he uses the word in a restricted sense to denote " a system of *special* provisions for securing certain definite and specific *ends*," which are to be distinguished from " the actual and foreseen, but not desired or necessary *consequences*" of the plan adopted for the attainment of those ends; so he uses the words design, decree, etc., in a restricted sense, to denote a *special* purpose of securing an event as an *end*, and as a *good*. In agreement with this confined use of the term, he supposes that nothing is strictly " the subject of a divine purpose," unless it have an intrinsic excellence, or utility and importance. Still he admits that " there is a certain generalized and technical sense in which *everything* that actually happens, may be said to be embraced in the divine decrees or purposes,"[2] that " all the events of which the earth has been the theatre, moral as well as physical, have proceeded from God. They were all foreknown to Him at the time of its creation, as *destined* to follow from the laws under which He placed it."[3] " I do not suppose," says Professor Chace, " that any one will seriously contend for an interpretation that shall make the number of hairs on the head of a disciple of Christ, the subject of a divine decree or purpose."[4] Why not? 'Because' (would be the answer given by some philosophers), ' although the fact that hair covers the crown of the head results,

---

[1] Discourse, pp. 54, 55.   [2] Ib. n. 38.   [3] Ib. n. 39.   [4]

as a special benefit, from a special Providence, and therefore from a special decree, yet the fact that the number of hairs on the head is precisely so great, and not one hair greater, is no special benefit, is of no consequence, and therefore has not been specially *provided for*, and hence not specially decreed; the body was not made on a plan different from what would have been otherwise adopted, merely for the sake of one additional appendage so minute, so unimportant. Still, the number of hairs on the head of a disciple is foreknown as a result of his physical structure, therefore was predetermined as incident to that predetermined structure, and in the general, technical sense was as really foreordained as was the existence of the body itself.'[1]

When we compare our own insignificance with the great scheme of Jehovah, and our own ignorance with the objects of scientific interest in the finest filament of the minutest leaf, we find ourselves incompetent to decide that any phenomenon is too unimportant for the Deity to foreordain or to provide for, and we learn to appreciate the celebrated Section of Bucan on the query: "Annon dedecet summam illam Dei Majestatem usque ad curanda etiam, haec infima, sese demittere?" The entire section consists of these terse words: "Non, quia sicut non dedecuit ea creare, sic non dedecet creata curare." Inst. Theol. Soc. XIV. § 21. How the whole can be planned without the particulars of which it is essentially composed, and how we can decide that any one of the particulars is unimportant, we are

---

[1] We are not confident that this answer, given by many philosophers, would be given, in this sense, by the eminent Professor whose Discourse we have repeatedly alluded to in this Article. Some of his expressions (as that on p. 55, in which he opposes the view of election and reprobation "not as determined by character, but as determining character"), we cannot easily reconcile with any Calvinistic theory of the Divine decrees. It is the more difficult to interpret them, because he says, p. 38: "I have avoided, as far as possible, the use of technical expressions, whether derived from physical or theological science," and also because he disclaims the intention, which would otherwise be imputed to him, of controverting some doctrines which seem to be impugned. "There are a large number," he says, p. 66, "of theological questions clustering about the two main points of this inquiry — many of them presenting great difficulties — concerning which I wish it to be distinctly understood, that I say, and have intended to say, nothing. And I ask that any terms or expressions looking in these directions — if I have chanced to employ such — may be interpreted in accordance with the declared aim and purpose of the discussion." Every author has of course the right to shun the technical phraseology of theologians, if he will so apprise his readers.

unable to say. "Nothing great," says Count de Maistre, on the Generative Principle of Political Constitutions, p. 73, "has great beginnings. There will not be found in the history of all ages a single exception to this law. Crescit occulto velut arbor aevo, is the immortal device of every great institution."

ARTICLE IX.

NOTICES OF NEW PUBLICATIONS.

I. Herodoti Orientalia Antiquiora.[1]

We are here presented with selections from the first book of Herodotus, designed for the use of students in the earlier part of their classical course. "The plan of the present selection," says the editor, "has been, to take such parts as would give a connected history of the Asiatic countries and of Egypt. To this I was determined by two considerations: first, the growing interest in the history and antiquities of those regions at the present time; and, secondly, that the other Greek and the Roman authors, commonly put into the hands of students, do not cover this ground at all." "The present volume brings down the history of the East to the death of Cyrus the Great. The Aegyptiaca and the subsequent portions of the Orientalia will be completed at as early a day as practicable."

The text is preceded by an Introduction, which sketches briefly the life and times of Herodotus, and the character of his history, including his "reliableness," his plan, his political sentiments, and his style. A summary of the entire first book is also prefixed. Following the text is an account of the Ionic dialect, with "synoptical tables" of its euphonic changes and its forms. We have then a somewhat minute commentary, interspersed with fuller summaries of passages not contained in the selections, and occasional critical and historical remarks, "for the most part reserved to the end of the chapter, where they are placed in a separate paragraph, generally brief and calculated to awaken reflection and incite to further inquiry."

We think the plan and the general execution of the work will commend themselves strongly to teachers and students. The oriental history thus

---

[1] *Herodoti Orientalia Antiquiora;* comprising mainly such portions of Herodotus as give a connected History of the East. By Herman M. Johnson, D. D., Prof. of Philos. and Eng. Lit. in Dickinson College.

to tickle by means of them, and thus to glorify one's self rather than to serve God and one's fellow-men; or the words, being through frequent use deprived of their soul, become at last 'as sounding brass.' To this danger is the clergyman more than others exposed. Since he is required by his vocation so often to hold up the word of God to others, and to have always at hand, and to give expression to, those truths and ideas which are most of all suited to move, startle, and penetrate men's hearts, it is only too apt to be the case that these truths lose for him their terribleness, so that their force and effect on his own heart is neutralized or weakened, and the constant direction of his attention to others keeps him from watching himself, so that while he works on the hearts of others he neglects his own, and lets the weeds in it grow up unheeded. ..... My later observations and experiences have only too much confirmed my opinion of the greatness of the danger, and taught me how many of the most gifted clergymen fall a prey to it, and how prevalent has become in our time the plague of using set phrases without thought, which serves more than everything else to make men insensible to the power of the truth, and disinclined to struggle after an earnest and more profound conviction, and which explains the readiness with which now, at a given signal, 'testimonies' and 'confessions' are made at wholesale, often in rapid succession and in contradictory directions. Hence so little deed Christianity, and so much mouth Christianity."

Hupfeld died an easy death at noon of the twenty-fourth of April, after fully completing his seventieth year, in consequence of a stroke of apoplexy supervening on an inflammation of the diaphragm.

ARTICLE IX.

THEORIES IN REGARD TO THE NATURE OF THE WILL.

We propose to state in the present and in subsequent Book Notices, various theories entertained by various writers more or less recent in regard to the will. The present notice is confined to two works, which differ widely from each other in various particulars, but agree with each other in the theory that *choice is not an act of the will.* The first of these books is entitled:

ESSAY ON CATHOLICISM, LIBERALISM AND SOCIALISM, considered in their Fundamental Principles. By Don Juan Donoso Cortès, Marquis of Valdegamas; from the original Spanish. To which is prefixed a Sketch of the life and works of the author. From the Italian of G. E. De Castro. Translated by Madeleine Vinton Goddard. 12mo. pp. 295.

The introductory sketch states that the author of this work was born at Valdegamas, May 6, 1809; pursued the study of the law at the University of Salamania; received a high political office in 1832; was active as a political journalist and author at Madrid; was the Spanish minister Plenipotentiary at the Court of Prussia in 1848; became a religious man at the age of forty; and the present work is the result of his religious meditations. He commences the work with the words of M. Proudhon: "It is surprising to observe how constantly we find all our political questions complicated with theological questions" (p. 17). "Sophisms," he says, "produce revolutions, and sophists are succeeded by hangmen" (p. 20). He divides his volume into three books. In the first and second chapters of the second book he discusses the subject of the will. He says: "The opinion generally entertained respecting free-will is in every respect false. The will does not consist, as is commonly supposed, in the power of choice between good and evil, which importune man with contrary solicitations. If free-will consisted in this faculty, the following consequences would necessarily result, the one relative to man and the other relative to God, and both evidently absurd. The consequence respecting man would be, that the higher the degree of excellence he attained the less free he would become, as he could not advance toward perfection without becoming subjected to the influence of good, and he could not yield to the sway of truth without removing himself from the rule of evil." "Man being free, and at the same time aiming at perfection, he cannot preserve his freedom without renouncing perfection, neither can he become perfect without losing his liberty." "As relates to God, the consequence of this hypothesis would be this, that God, not being subject in his nature to contradictory solicitations, would not be free, if freedom consisted in the full power to choose between opposing solicitations; and if, according to this supposition, he must have the power to choose between good and evil, between sanctity and sin, in order to be free, then there exists between the nature of God and liberty, thus defined, a radical contradiction and an absolute incompatibility. And, as it would be an absurdity to suppose, on the one side, that God cannot be free if he is God, and that he cannot be God if he is free; and on the other that man cannot attain perfection without losing his liberty, nor be free without renouncing perfection, it follows that the idea of liberty that we have just examined [of liberty as consisting in choice] is altogether false, contradictory, and absurd" (pp. 94–96).

Choice, then, according to this theory, is not an act of the will; and if so, the soul must be divided into the intellect, sensibilities, the power of choice, and the will, four departments instead of three. The formal freedom of the will does not consist in choice; still less does the material freedom. Where is liberty then? The author proceeds: "The error that we have just exposed consists in placing freedom in the faculty of choice, when it really rests in the faculty of will, which supposes the faculty of understanding. Every being endowed with understanding and will is free, and his liberty is not a distinct thing from his will and his understanding, but the two united. When we affirm of a being that he has will and understanding, and of another being that he is free, we assert with regard to both the same thing, expressed in two different ways.

"If liberty consists in the faculties of will and understanding, then perfect liberty consists in a perfect will and understanding. These are the attributes of God alone, from which it follows, as a necessary inference, that God alone is perfectly free.

"Again, if liberty consists in the faculties of understanding and will then man is free, because he is endowed with will and intelligence; but he is not perfectly free, as he is not endowed with an understanding and will infinite and perfect. The imperfection of his understanding is, that it is limited on the one hand, and on the other subject to error. The imperfection of his will is, that he does not desire all that he ought to wish for, and that he may be importuned and conquered by evil. From whence it follows that the imperfection of his liberty consists in his power of choosing evil and embracing error; that is to say, the imperfection of human liberty lies in precisely that faculty of choice which, according to the vulgar opinion, constitutes its absolute perfection" (pp. 96, 97).

"If the above is true, it is certain that the faculty of choice bestowed upon man, far from constituting a necessary condition of freedom, endangers liberty, since through it arises the possibility of a renunciation of good, and of falling into error; of a denial of God, and of a subjection to tyranny. All the efforts of man, with the assistance of grace, should be directed to the keeping of this faculty under, so that he may even lose it, if possible, by inaction. He alone who loses it understands good, desires it, and performs it; and he alone who does this is perfectly free; and he alone who is free is perfect; and only he who is perfect is happy. None of the blessed have this faculty of choosing between good and evil, neither God, nor his saints, nor the choirs of angels" (p. 99).

Throughout this volume are found frequent contradictions of the statement that liberty does not consist in choosing, as on pp. 150, 273. The volume abounds with acute remarks, rich apothegms, but is on the whole declamatory, rather than scientific. It is an earnest defence of the Roman Catholic dogmas, and a spirited attack upon the theories of Socialism. In its tone and style it is signally unlike the second work which we here notice, and which is entitled:

FREEDOM OF THE MIND IN WILLING; or, every Being that wills, a Creative First Cause. By Rowland G. Hazard. 12mo. pp. 455. New York: D. Appleton and Co.; London, 16 Little Britain. 1864.

The author of this work is an enterprising manufacturer in the State of Rhode Island. He certainly merits our respect for his interest in moral, as well as in physical science. He has evinced in the present volume a sharp and vigorous mind. His style is not always clear, and is too redundant. He does not always conform to the established usage of words, but is satisfied with his own nomenclature. His speculations are the more interesting as they are pursued from a point of departure not commonly taken. He has divided his work into two books. The first book he devotes to an explanation and proof of the "Freedom of the Mind in Willing." He is a stout advocate of human liberty. Hence it is the more singular that he should exclude the act of choice from the sphere of will. He considers choice as "the perception, the knowledge, that one thing is superior to another," and is, therefore, antecedent to the act of willing; and he regards all liberty as consisting in the mind's willing, and not at all in the mind's choosing. He strenuously and persistently objects to "the confounding of choice and will" (p. 440). "Will is the power or faculty of the mind for effort" (p. 24), and in this effort consists the mind's freedom. Freedom is "that condition in which the mind directs its own action or movement." He considers the moral character also as residing, not in the choice, but in the effort, the willing. If a man wills to do an act which is good and noble, it matters not concerning his virtue whether his effort be successful or otherwise; the effort is, itself, the triumph in him of the good and noble over the bad and base" (p. 152). "As in the *moral nature* the willing, the persevering effort is itself the consummation, there can in it be no such failure [as there may be in his external relations]; and the mind in it is therefore not only a creative, but a supreme creative first cause" (p. 152). "As the moral quality of the action lies wholly in the will, and no other being can will for him [man], to be morally good without his own efforts is an impossibility; all that any other being can do for him in this respect is to use means to excite his wants and increase his knowledge; and thus induce him to put forth his own efforts. Even omnipotence can do no more than this; for doing more, the making man virtuous without voluntary effort of his own, involves a contradiction" (pp. 153, 154). "A man habitually holy, who has eradicated the conflicting wants, loses the power to will what is unholy; and as he cannot be unholy except by his own voluntary act, he has then no power to be unholy" (p. 158). Mr. Hazard still maintains that the mind is free in willing to be holy, even when it has no power to will otherwise.

Mr. Hazard devotes his second book to a review of Edwards on the Will. Of course he differs radically from this divine; for Edwards considers free-agency as consisting, not in imperative volitions, but in choice; whereas Mr. Hazard considers free-agency as consisting, not in choice, but in imperative volitions. We do not think that the interpretation which the author of this volume puts upon Edwards is correct; still it is similar to that which is sanctioned by many other critics. Quite a remarkable passage in the second book is found on pp. 393–395. We subjoin a few passages illustrating Mr. Hazard's independence in thought and in style.

The Faculties of the Mind. "The mind has but one real faculty or power to do anything, and this faculty is designated by the term *will*" (p. 15). Thus memory "is but a condition, and a necessary condition, of knowledge of the past. Without it such knowledge could not exist. In this sense it is only an expression of one form of our knowledge. To say *I remember an event*, is to say *I know an event in the past*. If from any cause an event of the past comes before the mind, it is then a simple mental perception. When we make an effort to bring an event of the past into the mind's view, we call it an exercise or *effort* of *memory*, and this of course is an act of will, a *trying to do this thing*" (pp. 11, 12). It is the will only which makes an effort. An effort of the mind in forming a judgment is an act of the will. "The same may be said of reasoning, imagining, conceiving, etc. In the sense in which these are spoken of as faculties or powers, they are but names of varied modes of effort, or of efforts for *different objects*, made by the same unit — mind, manifesting its power to produce change by its efforts or acts of will " (p. 12). "As the mind cannot act except by exercising some of its powers, every act of the mind is an effort or act of will, and the phrases, 'acts of will,' 'acts of mind,' and 'mental action,' are really synonymes" (p. 424). According to Mr. Hazard, then, there is no *involuntary* effort. But do we not necessarily ascribe every act to a power of acting — an act of remembering to a *power* of memory, for instance; and is not the strenuous acting of any power rightly called an *effort* of that power?

"*We may know what is not true.*" (?) "In strict propriety " the term *knowledge* is " applicable only to those ideas or perceptions of the mind of which we entertain no doubt, and it is applicable to such even though they are not conformable to truth" (p. 18). Like most other words in frequent use the word *knowledge* has a variety of significations. It is often used to express a mere undoubting assurance. But, *distinctively*, it expresses the undoubting assurance of a fact, of a truth. Distinctively, it implies that the reality is as it is believed to be. When we have believed a proposition to be true, and afterwards discovered that it is false, we are apt to say, " We thought we knew it to be true, but we did not know so much as we thought we did." The omniscience of God is not his mere assurance of *propositions*, but his assurance of *truths*.

The human mind is a creator. "The finite mind of man, made in the image of God, has finite powers corresponding to omnipotence, omniscience, omnipresence, and other creative attributes of the Infinite; and, so far as we know, exerts these powers in the same mode and under the same conditions" (p. 49). "This creative power is exerted by the finite in the only way in which we can conceive of its exercise by the Infinite Intelligence, and under the same conditions " (p. 45). It is true, that we often speak of mental creations, the creations of genius, etc., but in the proper sense we mean by creation, the bringing of some material or mental *substance* into existence. Some of the most eminent artists have recoiled from the use of this term in application to their works, and have insisted on limiting the word *creator* to Him who causes the beginning of substances.

We need not add, that while we cannot adopt the theories of the will which are contained in the two works here noticed, we still must regard them, and other theories hereafter to be noticed, as suggestive of many important truths.

ARTICLE X

THE TOPOGRAPHY OF JERUSALEM.

BY REV. SAMUEL WOLCOTT, D.D., CLEVELAND, OHIO.

The Dictionary of the Bible edited by Dr. William Smith, and published in England in three large octavo volumes, is about to be republished entire in this country, under the editorial supervision of Professor Hackett of Newton, whose special qualifications for this service will be recognized by all. It is but fair to add that the paper here offered has grown out of an Article prepared by the writer, at his request, for the Dictionary — it being his purpose to render the American edition even more complete than the English. More than sixty of the eminent scholars in Great Britian, and a few in our own country, have contributed to its pages, and it embraces the fruit of more learned research than any other work of the kind which has been issued. It is, consequently, a necessity to every thorough student of the Bible, and an invaluable auxiliary to all who seek a fuller acquaintance with the word of God.

In most of the Articles we are presented with the latest *results* of Biblical science — ascertained facts, and not mere speculations and theories. On controverted or unsettled questions we are, in most instances, furnished with the facts or reasonings on each side, from a fair statement of which the reader is left to draw his own conclusion.

A portion of the Article on "Jerusalem" is an exception to this rule. More than forty pages with double columns are given to the general topic, and its importance justifies this extended treatment. It is mainly divided between two writers, one of whom presents *The Annals of the City*, from its foundation to its destruction by Titus (with a brief sketch of its later history by another pen), and the other devotes seventeen pages to *The Topography of the City*, of this portion the whole warp and

Dr. W. Wright, now Professor of Arabic in the University of Cambridge, England.

They certainly must feel, in looking upon the completed work, that it is well adapted to the end which the author declares will be, by the favor of God, the coveted reward of his labor — the real aiding of the student to gain a good knowledge of the Old Testament scriptures in the original tongues.

ARTICLE X.

DR. HODGE'S SYSTEMATIC THEOLOGY.[1]

An orator recently addressing the Massachusetts Medical Society remarked that "progress is the pride of the day; and the charm of antiquity is broken. In the early history of the country, medicine and theology were allied together, each having firm faith in the infinite and none in the infinitesimal; but now sugar is the staple article both in theological and medical dispensaries." In the system of theology which Dr. Hodge is giving to the public, there are signs of progress. It contains more of the saccharine element than is found in the older treatises emanating from his school. Still, it is in the main, allopathic rather than homoeopathic in its treatment of its patients. It is in this respect as it should be. It gives evidence of its author's sound mind and extensive learning. It is written in a vigorous and flexile style. It presents theology in a compact form. The spirit of it is candid and fair. It propounds various theories which we regard as untenable, and defends the real truth by some arguments which we regard as inconclusive. The excellences and the faults of the system — the excellences being greater than the faults — appear in almost every chapter. Let us look, for example, at volume one, part one, chapter one, entitled " Origin of the Idea of God."

Dr. Hodge supposes that the existence of God can be proved, and also that it is self-evident. We have an "innate knowledge" of his being. Dr. Hodge defines innate knowledge to be "that which is due to our constitution as sentient, rational, and moral beings." "The soul is so constituted that it sees certain things to be true immediately in their own light. They need no proof. Men need not be told or taught that the things thus perceived are true." These immediate perceptions are called "intuitions," "primary truths," "laws of belief," "innate knowledge or ideas"

---

[1] Systematic Theology. By Charles Hodge, D.D., Professor in the Theological Seminary, Princeton, New Jersey. Two Vols. pp. 648 and 732. New York: Charles Scribner and Company; London and Edinburgh: T. Nelson and Sons. 1872.

(I. 195). "All that is meant is that the mind is so constituted that it perceives certain things to be true without proof and without instruction" (I. 192). "What is seen immediately without the intervention of proof to be true, is, according to the common mode of expression, said to be seen intuitively" (I. 193).

Among the truths of which we have an innate knowledge, Dr. Hodge specifies the following: "The part of a thing is less than the whole;" "A straight line is the shortest distance between two points;" "Nothing cannot be a cause;" "Every effect must have a cause;" "Sin deserves punishment," etc.

Dr. Hodge places the truth of God's existence in the same category with the axioms which we have now specified, and affirms that it is a "primary truth," one of which we have an "immediate perception," "intuition," "innate knowledge," "innate idea."

I. Let us inquire whether Dr. Hodge has shown that the perception of God's existence is so *immediate* as to prove the perception to be innate. Has he shown that we believe in God's existence as soon as the truth is presented to us, and without the intervention of any other truth? If there be the intervention of *another* truth, then *this* truth is perceived through a medium; and not being perceived immediately, it is *not* perceived intuitively. Dr. Hodge says: "All the faculties and feelings of our minds and bodies have their appropriate objects; and the possession of the faculties supposes the existence of those objects. The senses suppose the existence and reality of the objects of sense. The eye, in its very structure, supposes that there is such an element as light; the sense of hearing would be unaccountable and inconceivable without sound; and the sense of touch would be inconceivable were there no tangible objects. The same is true of our social affections; they necessitate the assumption that there are relations suited to their exercises. Our moral nature supposes that the distinction between right and wrong is not chimerical or imaginary. In like manner, our religious feelings, our sense of dependence, our consciousness of responsibility, our aspirations after fellowship with some Being higher than ourselves, and higher than anything which the world or nature contains, necessitates [necessitate] the belief in the existence of God" (I. 200). From the fact that a fish has an instinct for the water we may draw the inference that there is water in which the fish has the power to swim. Dr. Hodge will not doubt that this is an *inference*, and is not an independent belief. From the fact that a bird has an instinct for flying we may come to the conclusion that there is an atmosphere in which the bird has the power to fly; but Dr. Hodge will not say that this *conclusion* is a "primary perception." He may, indeed, say that we have a primary perception of an atmosphere, but not on the ground that there exists an instinct to fly in it, or an apparatus for breathing it. From the thirst of a young animal for milk we may derive an inference that milk is somewhere provided for it, and is good for it; but this inference is not innate knowledge. "From the very structure of the eye" we may draw the conclusion that there is such an element as light; but will Dr. Hodge affirm that this conclusion is "a law of belief?" He may say that light is seen "in its own light," but is it not a self-contradiction to say that it is seen "intuitively," "primarily," in "the very structure of the eye?" If we learn that there is a being endued with a sense of hearing we infer that there will be sound which he can hear, but *this* belief in sound is not derived from sound itself, but from another object; it comes through a medium, and is not immediate. If we are informed of a being who has the sense of touch, we conclude that there will be objects which he can touch; but this conclusion is not "innate knowledge." Dr. Hodge says that the sense of hearing and of touch would be inconceivable without audible and tangible objects. (I. 200). He might as well say that audible and tangible objects would be inconceivable without the sense of hearing and touch. We cannot form an apprehension of the sense without forming an apprehension of its objects; nor can we form an apprehension of its objects without forming an apprehension of the sense; but a mind may think of visible, audible, and tangible objects, before it believes in the *existence of* any sense to recognize them, and it may think of a sense of sight, sound, and touch, before it believes in the *existence* of any visible, audible, or tangible objects to be recognized. If we are told of beings who have a constitutional love for parents and children, we reason in favor of the proposition that parents and children do or will exist. The idea of a parent involves the idea of a child, and *vice versa;* but the idea of a parent does not imply the actual existence of a child, and the idea of a child does not imply the actual existence of a parent. Our reasoning in favor of their actual existence is the opposite of an "innate knowledge" of it. "In like manner our religious feelings" constitute a premise from which we reason in favor of the existence of an object on which these feelings may rest; but the belief that there actually exists such an object forms the conclusion, and this conclusion is, of course, not a "fundamental law of belief." Dr. Hodge says that our sense of dependence "necessitates" our belief in the divine existence; so does our perception of the adaptation of means to ends throughout the material universe. First, we are conscious of a sense of dependence; secondly, we recognize the truth taught by observation that all our constitutional feelings have their appropriate objects; thirdly, we apply this truth in our argument proving that our constitutional sense of dependence has its appropriate object—God. Dr. Hodge says that our "consciousness of responsibility" necessitates our belief in the being of God. What is our consciousness of responsibility? It is a consciousness of accepting as true the statement that we are responsible. What is the accepting of *this* statement as true? It is the acceptance of the statement as true that we shall receive a reward for doing well, and a punishment for doing ill. So far we have intuition. But so far we have no intuition of God's existence. Our accepting of the statement as true that we shall be rewarded for doing well or punished for doing ill may be a mere imagining, or apprehending, or surmising, or thinking, or supposing, or presuming, or hoping, or fearing, or expecting, or it may be a *believing*, that we shall be thus recompensed; but even this *belief* is not the "innate knowledge" of a God. It involves the premise of an argument. The argument is this: We shall be rewarded; therefore there will be a rewarder; we shall be punished; therefore there will be a punisher; *moral agents* have been and now are rewarded and punished; therefore there has been and is now a rewarder and punisher; there has occurred the event, the happiness, or the misery of a moral agent; this event has a cause, a moral governor; this moral governor is God.

Again, if it be true that our sense of accountability involves an "innate knowledge" of God, then it involves an "innate knowledge" of our future existence. The dying man has a hope of reward, or fear of punishment; this reward or punishment cannot be experienced in this life; therefore it will be experienced in a life to come. This is reasoning; but it is analogous to our reasoning in favor of the divine existence; if the latter reasoning be resolved into an innate belief, so may the former.

II. Let us inquire whether Dr. Hodge has shown that the knowledge of God is so universal as to prove it to be innate. He admits that when he affirms this knowledge to be inborn he uses the word God "in a very wide sense"; only "in the general sense of a being on whom we are dependent and to whom we are responsible" (I. 194, 195). But if our constitutional feeling of responsibility involves an innate belief in God, then it involves an innate belief in a *holy* God; also in a holy God who knows every secret act of virtue or sin which our own consciences approve or condemn. Can Dr. Hodge maintain that *all* men have this innate knowledge of a God who thus "searches the heart," and who will reward our most secret holiness, and punish our most hidden sin? He says that our belief in God's existence is necessitated by our "aspirations after fellowship with some being higher than ourselves and higher than any thing which the world or nature contains" (I. 200). Is this *merely* a being on whom we are dependent and to whom we are responsible? Will Dr. Hodge maintain that the fetich-worshippers have those lofty aspirations? Do the worshippers of an insect, who crush it when they are vexed with it, feel such a responsibility as involves a knowledge of "an invisible being, higher than self, and higher than man" (I. 197)? Is Dr. Hodge consistent with himself when at one time he represents this intuitively known being as so spiritual, so far exalted above nature; and at another time affirms that the being is merely one to whom we are accountable and on whom we are dependent? He teaches: "As we are born with the sense of touch and sight, and take cognizance of their appropriate objects as soon as they are presented; so we are born with the intellectual faculty of perceiving these primary truths as soon as they are presented" (I. 193). Therefore, do all the heathen perceive the truth of God's existence as soon as it is presented to their minds? Dr. Hodge affirms not only that they do, but that the Bible teaches that they do. He writes: "The apostle tells us that those who have a written revelation shall be judged by that revelation; that those who have no externally revealed law, shall be judged by the law written on the heart. That the heathen have such a law he [Paul] proves first from the fact that 'they do by nature the things contained in the law,' i.e. they do under the control of their nature the things which the law prescribes, and, secondly, from the operations of conscience. When it condemns, it pronounces something done to be contrary to the moral law; and when it approves, it pronounces something to be conformed to that law (Rom. ii. 12–16). The recognition of God, therefore, that is, of a being to whom we are responsible, is involved in the very idea of accountability" (I. 196). On examining *one* written law we reason in favor of the fact that Solon existed; on examining *another*, we reason in favor of the fact that Draco existed; on examining a *third*, we reason in favor of the fact that Justinian existed. On examining a *fourth*, i.e. the law which is written on the heart of man, we reason in favor of the fact that God exists. Our belief that this fourth law has a cause is no more intuitive than is our belief that the three other laws have a cause. Dr. Hodge proceeds: "Hence every man carries in the very constitution of his being as a moral agent, the evidence of the existence of God" (I. 196). This is true. Every man has in his constitution a *proof* that there is a God. The evidence of God's existence is not in the statement of it, but in the constitution of the soul; the truth is not self-evident, but is learned from something lying under it. Dr. Hodge continues: "And as this sense of sin and responsibility is absolutely universal, so must also, according to the Bible, be the knowledge of God" (I. 196). On the same principle if, during the reign of king David or Solomon, a Jewish peasant had a knowledge that he had violated a Jewish law and had made himself liable to a civil punishment, he must have had an innate knowledge of the existence of David or Solomon. "The simple fact of scripture and experience is, that the moral law as written upon the heart is indelible; and the moral law in its nature implies a lawgiver, one from whom that law emanates, and by whom it will be enforced" (I. 198). The moral law implies a lawgiver, in the same sense in which a law in a certain French code implies a lawgiver; but the mind has not an "innate knowledge" that Napoleon was the author of that code. The thought of a substance is not separate from the thought of its qualities; and the thought of qualities is not separate from the thought of their substance; but the thought of a particular event is separate from the thought of its cause, and the thought of a cause is separate from the thought of a particular event. The thought of a particular event leads to a thought of its cause; but we must not mistake the fact of its *suggesting* a cause for the fact of its *involving* one.

Dr. Hodge regards not only the scriptures, but also history, as showing that the knowledge of God is so universal as to prove it innate. That the divine existence is perceived intuitively he attempts to prove by alleging the fact that it "is one of those truths which reveal themselves to every human mind;" that it belongs to "a class of truths so plain that they never fail to reveal themselves to the human mind." He remarks: "Hence the criteria of those truths which are accepted as axioms, and which are assumed in all reasoning, and the denial of which renders all faith and all knowledge impossible, are universality and necessity. What all [men] believe, and what all men must believe, is to be assumed as undeniably true. These criteria, indeed, include each other. If a truth be universally admitted, it must be because no man can rationally call it in question. And if it be a matter of necessary belief, it must be accepted by all who possess the nature out of the constitution of which the necessity arises" (I.193,194). Dr. Hodge, then, is discussing the question, not whether the belief in God is intuitive to *some* men, but whether it is intuitive to *all* men (I. 193). In answering the objection "that travellers and missionaries report the existence of some tribes so degraded that they could discover in them no traces of this knowledge" of God, Dr. Hodge says: "Even if the fact be admitted that such tribes have no idea of God, it would not be conclusive. Should a tribe of idiots be discovered, it would not prove that reason is not an attribute of our nature. If any community should come to light in which infanticide was universal, it would not prove that parental love was not one of the instincts of humanity" (I. 196, 197). Here we remark, first, that Dr. Hodge is inconsistent with himself. He is attempting to show that the knowledge of God is intuitive, in *the sense that* it never fails to reveal itself to the human mind (I. 193). Can it be intuitive in *this* sense, if it does fail to reveal itself to whole tribes of men? He says: "When it is asked whether the existence of God is an intuitive truth, the question is equivalent to asking whether the belief in his existence is universal and necessary" (I. 194). On this principle, if we answer the second question by asserting that the belief in God's existence is not universal, our assertion is *equivalent* to answering the first question by asserting that the belief is not intuitive.

We remark, secondly, that Dr. Hodge confounds one statement with another. He confounds the question whether all men *do* believe immediately in the Divine existence, with the question whether they have the faculty for thus believing. The inquiry whether all men do *exercise* the faculty of reason is entirely distinct from the inquiry whether they *have* the faculty. The question whether all men actually exercise the parental sensibility is different from the question whether all men *possess* the sensibility. If he attempts to prove that all men possess this sensibility by asserting that all men exercise it, this last assertion would not be valid, provided that whole tribes of men do not exercise it. If he attempts to prove that all men possess the faculty of reason by asserting that all men exercise it, this last assertion would not be justifiable, provided that whole tribes of men do not exercise it. On the same principle, if he attempts to prove that all men have the faculty for an immediate perception of God, and to prove this by asserting that all men *do* perceive God immediately, this assertion would not be allowable, provided that whole tribes of men have no idea of God at all. Dr. Hodge is professedly discussing the question, whether all men have the innate idea of a deity; but he sometimes wanders into the other question, whether all men have the faculty for gaining this idea. He ought to be engaged in proving that the knowledge of God is universal, and *therefore* results from the very constitution of our nature; but sometimes he inverts the proposition, and asserts "that the knowledge of God results from the very constitution of our nature, and is therefore universal." (I. 196). The universality of the belief he makes an *inference from* the fact that it is intuitive; but he professes to be proving that the universality of the belief is an *argument for* the fact that the belief is intuitive. We remark, thirdly, that Dr. Hodge seems to be reasoning on the principle that the universality of a belief is not only a sign but a *sure* sign that the belief is intuitive. There are various beliefs, however, which are universal, and yet founded solely on argument. The mere universality of a belief is *one* sign, but is not an *infallible* sign that the belief is a fundamental law of the mind. In order to be an infallible sign, the belief must be shown to arise in all men before or without their perception of an argument for it; therefore, to arise as early and as uniformly as the nature of the mind at different periods allows.

III. Let us next inquire whether Dr. Hodge has shown that the belief in the divine existence is so necessary as to prove it to be innate. To the question whether the existence of God is a truth "to which the mind *cannot refuse* its assent," is "*forced* to assent"; a truth in which "no man *can possibly* disbelieve," which exists "*of necessity*" in every human mind, he gives an affirmative answer. Still he admits it to be "possible that the moral nature of a man may be so disorganized by vice, or by a false philosophy, as to have its testimony for the existence of God effectually silenced." He adds: "This, however, would prove nothing as to what that testimony really is" (I. 198). But if it be *possible* for a man to withold all testimony in favor of this truth, how can it be *necessary* for him to give the testimony? Dr. Hodge may reply: "The denial is forced, and can only be temporary." But how long may it continue? Why not during a man's entire life? If one man can thus remain through life without a knowledge of God, why cannot a whole tribe of men? Dr.

Hodge says that, "the *probability is*" in favor of a *universal* belief in God (I. 197). Therefore he can only say that the *probability* is in favor of a *necessary* universal belief in God. He derives this probability from an inadequate premise. Speaking of tribes who are reported to have no idea of a Deity, he says: "Unless such people show that they have no sense of right and wrong, no consciousness of responsibility for character and conduct, there is no evidence that they have no knowledge of such a being as God" (I. 197). He has failed to show that this "sense of right," and this "consciousness of responsibility" *involve* the knowledge of God; and if they do *result* in it, he has failed to show that they result in it necessarily; and if they result in it necessarily he has failed to show that this necessity is a *sure* sign of the knowledge being innate; for he says or implies: It "may be very true" that "there are many things which children and illiterate persons learn and can hardly avoid learning, which need not be referred to the constitution of their nature" (I. 199).

We agree with Dr. Hodge in thinking that the belief in some kind of a deity is universal, but we do not regard it as uniform in all men so as to prove the belief to be intuitive. We agree with him in thinking that the belief is necessary in certain conditions of the mind, but we do not regard it as unconditionally necessary so as to prove it to be intuitive. We differ from him in his main position that we are conscious of believing without proving that there is a God; and we think that in the general course of his discussion he first assumes that we do believe this truth without reasoning in favor of it; secondly, he infers that such an unreasoning belief is universal and necessary; thirdly, he uses his own inference as an argument to prove that we believe the truth without reasoning in favor of it.

It is, of course, unfair to pronounce any unfavorable opinion of a work until that work is finished. The parts which are to appear may modify those which have appeared already. The two volumes of Dr. Hodge's Theology which have been thus far published contain the Introduction, in six chapters; Part I., Theology proper, in thirteen chapters; Part II., Anthropology, in nine chapters; Part III. Soteriology in fourteen chapters. We look for the third volume with much interest, and have no doubt that it will be well stored with sterling thought. It is certainly an encouraging sign that a work involving so much thorough discussion is so well patronized by the public. If a larger number of such volumes emanated from the American press we should hear no more of our age as a superficial one, and of our country as one abandoned to material interests.

For Product Safety Concerns and Information please contact our EU
representative GPSR@taylorandfrancis.com
Taylor & Francis Verlag GmbH, Kaufingerstraße 24, 80331 München, Germany

www.ingramcontent.com/pod-product-compliance
Lightning Source LLC
Chambersburg PA
CBHW052140300426
44115CB00011B/1456